History of Australian Bushrangers
&
The Jerilderie Letter

More Skomlin Books

Royal Highness by Thomas Mann

Rosinante to the Road Again by John Dos Passos

One Man's Initiation: 1917 by John Dos Passos

The Comedienne by Wladyslav Reymont

Pierre and Luce by Romain Rolland

Oriental Encounters by Marmaduke Pickthall

The Journal of Countess Francoise Krasinska by Klementyna Tanska-Hoffman

Hell by Henri Barbusse

The Artist as Mystic by by Alex Stein and Yahia Lababidi

The Reign of the Evil One by Charles Ferdinand Ramuz

Beauty on Earth by Charles Ferdinand Ramuz

Riversong of the Rhone by Charles Ferdinand Ramuz

What if the Sun... by Charles Ferdinand Ramuz

Count Brühl by József Ignacy Kraszewski

Countess Cosel by József Ignacy Kraszewski

The Secret Child by Jean-Michel Olivier

History of Australian Bushrangers
By George E. Boxall

&

The Jerilderie Letter
By Ned Kelly

Skomlin
House of Memory and Imagination

Skomlin publishes memory and imagination and enriches lives by reclaiming the forgotten past; publishing the lesser known works of great writers and the great works of forgotten ones. For more information visit *www.skomlin.com*

A SKOMLIN BOOK
Published by Skomlin
PO Box 303BK, Black Hill 3350 Australia

History of Australian Bushrangers first published in London 1908
The Jerilderie Letter first published in Adelaide 1930
© Skomlin, 2017

All rights reserved. No part of this book may be used or reproduced in any manner whatsoever without written permission from the publisher, except in the case of brief quotations embodied in critical articles and reviews. Published in the United States, Great Britain, Europe and Australia by Skomlin.

ISBN: 978-0-6481826-2-7 *(paperback)*

A catalogue record for this book is available from the National Library of Australia

The paper used in this publication meets the minimum requirements of ANSI/NISO Z39.48-1992 (R1997) (Permanence of Paper). The paper used in this book is from responsibly managed forests. Printed in the United States of America, the United Kingdom and Australia by Lightning Source, Inc.

Contents

Chapter I   1

Introductory; Characteristics of the Convicts Sent to Australia; Bushranging: Origin and Meaning of the Term; The Cat and the Double Cat; Condition of the Prisoners: Some Terrible Revelations; The Desperation of Despair; Some Flogging Stories; The Bushranging Act and Its Abuses; Opinions of the Magistrates; Savage Treatment of Criminals Continued to the Present Time; Brutality not Cured by Brutal Punishment; Where Bushranging First Began.

Chapter II   16

Van Diemen's Land; The First Bushranger; Mike Howe, the King of the Ranges; The Raid on the Blacks; The Black War; Musquito; Outrages by the Blacks; Brutal Treatment of Blacks by Bushrangers; A War of Reprisals; Gigantic Scheme to Capture the Blacks; A Cordon Drawn Round the Disaffected District; Details of the Scheme; Its Failure; Only Two Blacks Captured; Estimated Cost; Fate of the Blacks.

Chapter III   31

Pierce the Cannibal; A Terrible Journey; A Shocking Confession; Escapes from "the Western Hell"; The Ruffian Jefferies; Brady the Bushranger; Escapes from Macquarie Harbour; Sticks up the Town of Sorell; The Governor's Proclamation; Brady Laughs at it; The Fight with Colonel Balfour; Betrayed by a Comrade; Captured by John Batman; Sympathy at his Trial; End of the Epoch.

Chapter IV   45

Bushranging in New South Wales; Manufacturing Bushrangers; Employing Bushrangers; The First Bank Robbery in Australia; Major Mudie and his Assigned Servants; Terrible Hollow; Murder of Dr. Wardell; The Story of Jack the Rammer; Hall Mayne and Others.

Chapter V   56

John Lynch; Murder of Kearns Landregan; Lynch's Trial and Sentence; His Terrible Confession; Murder of the Frazers, Father and Son; Murder and Cremation of the Mulligans; His Appeals to Almighty God.

Chapter VI   66

Jackey Jackey, the Gentleman Bushranger; His Dispute with Paddy Curran; Some Legends About Him; Jackey Jackey Always Well-dressed and Mounted; His Capture at Bungendore; His Escape at Bargo Brush; Jackey Jackey Visits Sydney; His Capture by Miss Gray; Paddy Curran's Fight with the Police; Re-captured and Hung; John Wright Threatens to Make a Clean Sweep.

Chapter VII   76

The Jewboy Gang; "Come and Shoot the Bushrangers;" Constable Refuses to Leave His Work to Hunt Bushrangers; Saved by his Wife; Robberies in Maitland; Bushrangers in High Hats; The Bullock-driver Captures the Bushrangers; An Attempt to Reach the Dutch Settlements; Mr. E. D. Day Captures the Gang; Assigned Servants' Attempt at Bushranging; Some other Gangs.

Chapter VIII   88

Bushranging in South Australia; The Robbers Captured in Melbourne; A Remarkable Raid in Port Phillip; Going Out for a Fight with Bushrangers; A Bloody Battle; Cashan and McIntyre; The Fight with the Mail Passengers; Cashan Escapes from the Lock-up; Is Re-captured; McIntyre Caught at Gammon Plains.

Chapter IX   95

Bushrangers and Pirates; Capture of H.M. Brig Cyprus by Bushrangers; A Piratical Voyage; Stealing the Schooners Edward and Waterwitch; Mutiny of Prisoners on H.M. Brig Governor Phillip at Norfolk Island; The Trial of the Mutineers at Sydney; How Captain Boyle Recaptured the Vessel.

CONTENTS

CHAPTER X   102

Van Diemen's Land Again; A Hunt for Bushrangers in the Mountains; Some Brutal Attacks; "Stand!" "No, thanks, I'm very Comfortable Sitting;" A Degrading Exhibition; A Determined Judge; Cash, Kavanagh, and Jones, an Enterprising Firm; The Art of Politeness as Exhibited by Bushrangers; A Bushranger Hunt in the Streets of Hobart Town; The Capture of Cash; Break Up of the Gang; A Doubtful Mercy.

CHAPTER XI   114

Norfolk Island: Its Founding as a Penal Station; The Terrible Discipline, in Norfolk Island; An Attempt to Ameliorate it; Its Failure; The Rigorous Treatment Restored; The Consequent Riot; Jackey Jackey's Revenge; An Unparalleled Tale of Ferocity; The Soldiers Overawe the Rioters; Thirteen Condemned to the Gallows; Jackey Jackey's Remarkable Letter; The End of Several Notorious Bushrangers.

CHAPTER XII   124

The Third Epoch of Bushranging; the Gold Digging Era; Influx of Convicts from Van Diemen's Land; Passing of the Criminals' Influx Prevention Act; Attitude of the Diggers Towards the Bushrangers, and Other Thieves; The Nelson Gold Robbery; Some Pitiful Stories; A Rapid Raid; Insecurity of the Melbourne Streets.

CHAPTER XIII   136

Captain Melville Takes to the Road; He Ties and Robs Eighteen Men; He Goes to Geelong for a Spree, and Boasts of His Exploits; His Sensational Capture; Sent to the Hulks; Murder of Corporal Owens; Melville Removed from the Hulk Success to the Gaol; Murder of Mr. John Price and Mutiny of the Convicts; Melville Attacks Mr. Wintle; Death of the Noted Bushranger.

CHAPTER XIV   146

Murder of a Bullock-driver; Sticking Up in the Melbourne Streets; Stealing £100,000 in Bank Notes; Want of Efficient Police Protection; Murders and Robberies at Ballarat, Bendigo, Mount Alexander, and other Diggings; The Robbery of the McIvor Gold Escort; A Bushranger Intimidated by a Bottle of Brandy; Robbery of the Bank of Victoria at Ballarat; Capture of Garrett in London; Prevalence of Horse-stealing; The Doctor's Creamy.

CHAPTER XV   160

An Escape from Norfolk Island; Stealing a Government Boat; The Convicts of New South Wales; A Terrible Indictment; Thomas Willmore; Murder of Philip Alger; Murder of Malachi Daly; Fight between two Bushrangers; Hunting down Willmore; His Capture while Asleep; The Last of the Van Diemen's Land Bushrangers; Wilson and Dido; Some Minor Offenders; An Unfounded Charge; Change of Name to Rid the Island of Evil Associations.

CHAPTER XVI   174

The New Bushranging Era; Fallacy of the Belief that Highwaymen Rob the Rich to Enrich the Poor; The Cattle Duffers and Horse Planters; The Riot at the Lambing Flat; Frank Gardiner, the Butcher; Charged with Obtaining Beasts "on the cross," he Abandons his Butcher's Shop; Efforts to Establish a Reign of Terror in the District; A Letter from Gardiner; The Great Escort Robbery.

CHAPTER XVII   190

Johnny Gilbert; His First Appearance in Australia; Miscellaneous Bushranging Exploits; Mr. Robert Lowe Makes a Stand; Mr. Inspector Norton Captured by the Bushrangers; A Plucky Black Boy; "Mine know it, Patsy Daly like it, Brudder;" A Brave Boy; O'Meally Shoots Mr. Barnes; A Bootless Bushranger; Capture of John Foley; Something about the Foley Family; Ben Hall.

Contents

Chapter XVIII   202

Racers as Mounts for the Bushrangers; The Shooting of Lowry; The Bushrangers visit Bathurst; They hold the Town of Canowindra for Three Days; Burke Shot by Mr. Keightley; Female Bushrangers; Death of O'Meally at Goimbla; A Newspaper Man and his Wife Stuck Up; Lively Times During the Christmas Holidays.

Chapter XIX   215

A Heavy Sessions at Goulburn; Ben Hall Hard Pushed; An Amateur Mail Robber; Discovery of Frank Gardiner; His Trial and Sentence; The Old Man; A Brush with the Police; The Chinkies show Fight; Messrs. Hall & Co. Take a Lease of the Main Southern Road; Capture of Mount and Dunleavy; Johnny Dunn; A Desperate Duel and Death of Sergeant Parry; A Country Ball and its Sequel.

Chapter XX   228

Meeting the Gold Escort; Murder of Constable Nelson; A Brush with the Police; Attempt to Stick Up the Araluen Gold Escort; Death of Constable Kelly and Pluck of Constable Burns; Sir Frederick Pottinger Resigns; Death of Ben Hall; Sketch of his Life; Death of Johnny Gilbert; Record of John Dunn and the Gang; Capture and Trial of Johnny Dunn; His Execution; Fate of the Chief Members of the Gardiner Gang.

Chapter XXI   239

Bloodthirsty Morgan; Morgan's Opinion of the Police; Murder of Sergeant McGinnerty; Murder at the Round Hill Station; A Pseudo Morgan; Morgan Threatens to Brand all Hands; He Shoots Sergeant Smyth; Challenged to Visit Victoria; He Accepts the Challenge; His Death at Peechelba.

Chapter XXII   249

The Brothers Clarke; The Raid at Nerigundah; Deaths of William Fletcher and Constable O'Grady; Murder of Four Special Constables at Jinden; Annie Clarke at Goulburn; Capture of Thomas and John Clarke; A Terrible Record; A Plucky Woman; An Attempt to Escape Custody; "Shoot Away, I Can't Stop You"; Some Daring Robberies; Murder and Cremation of the Brothers Pohlmann; Blue Cap.

Chapter XXIII   266

Bushranging in the Northern District of New South Wales; Captain Thunderbolt Robs the Toll Bar; A Chinaman Bushranger; A Long Chase; A Fight with the Police; "Next, Please"; The Bushranger Rutherford; Captain Thunderbolt and the German Band; Desperate Duel between Captain Thunderbolt and Constable Walker; Thunderbolt's Death.

Chapter XXIV   281

Bushranging in the Wild Paroo; A Raid into South Australia; A Relic of the Bushranging Era; Agitation for the Release of Gardiner; Official Reports as to Twenty-four Bushrangers Still in Gaol; The Cases of Gardiner and William Brookman; Gardiner and the Other Bushrangers Released; Gardiner Leaves the Country.

Chapter XXV   292

Bushranging in Victoria; Robert Bourke; Harry Power: He Escapes from Pentridge Gaol and Sticks Up the Mail; An Amateur Bushranger; The Police Hunt Power Down and Capture him Asleep; A Peacock as "Watch Dog"; The Power Procession at Beechworth; The Trial of Power; His Sentence; Engaged to Lecture on Board the Success; His Death.

Contents

Chapter XXVI — 302
Bushranging in New Zealand; Alleged fears of the Escort being robbed; The First Bushranger, Henry Beresford Garrett; The Maungapatau Murders; Arrest of Sullivan, Kelly, Burgess, and Levy in Nelson; Sullivan's Confession; The Discovery of the Bodies; Sullivan's Release.

Chapter XXVII — 310
Bushranging in Queensland; Some Bushrangers from Over the Southern Border; A Bogus Ben Halt; The Wild Scotchman: Queensland's Only Bushranger; A Man of Many Aliases; He goes to Fight a Duel with Sir Frederick Pottinger; He Escapes from the Steamer; Recaptured and Tried.

Chapter XXVIII — 316
Captain Moonlite; The "Reverend Gentleman" Robs the Bank, and Nearly Makes his Escape; He Breaks out of Ballarat Gaol; He Becomes a Reformed Character; He Sticks Up Wantabadgery Station; A Desperate Battle with the Police; Moonlite is Captured; His Young Companions in Crime; Sentenced to Death; The Wild Horse Hunters Turn Bushrangers; An Abortive Attempt to Rob a Bank.

Chapter XXIX — 327
The Kelly Gang; Horse-stealing, a Great Industry of the District; Faking the Brands; Assault on Constable Fitzpatrick; The Bush Telegraphs; Murder of Sergeant Kennedy and Constables Scanlan and Lonergan; Sticking up of the Faithfull Creek Statior Robbery of the National Bank at Euroa; A Big Haul.

Chapter XXX — 338
The Kellys Stick up the Town of Jerilderie; Robbery of the Bank of New South Wales; A Symposium in the Royal Hotel; A Three-days' Spree; "Hurrah for the Good Old Times of Morgan and Ben Hall"; the Robbers Take a Rest for a Year; The Kelly Sympathisers Again; The Kellys Reappear; Murder of Aaron Sherritt.

Chapter XXXI — 349
Fight Between the Police and the Bushrangers at Glenrowan; The Railway Torn Up; Attempt to Wreck the Police Train; The Glenrowan Inn Besieged; Ned Kelly in Armour; His Capture; The Burning of the Inn; Deaths of Dan Kelly, Steve Hart, and Joe Byrnes; Trial and Conviction of Ned Kelly; His Death; The Kelly Show; Decrease of Crime in the Colonies. 349

Chapter XXXII — 358
The Jerilderie Letter, dictated by bushranger Ned Kelly to fellow Kelly Gang member Joe Byrne in February 1879 during an armed robbery in the town of Jerilderie, New South Wales.

Index — 389

One

Introductory; Characteristics of the Convicts Sent to Australia; Bushranging: Origin and Meaning of the Term; The Cat and the Double Cat; Condition of the Prisoners: Some Terrible Revelations; The Desperation of Despair; Some Flogging Stories; The Bushranging Act and Its Abuses; Opinions of the Magistrates; Savage Treatment of Criminals Continued to the Present Time; Brutality not Cured by Brutal Punishment; Where Bushranging First Began.

The species of brigandage known in Australia as bushranging was, without doubt, evolved, more or less directly, from the convict system established as the basis of the earlier settlements in the island continent. The first bushrangers were simply men who took to the bush to escape work and enjoy freedom of action. Under the harsh laws of the Georgian era the greater criminals were hung, and not transported, and the convicts sent to "Botany Bay," in the eighteenth and the earlier years of the nineteenth centuries, were generally men to whom the trammels of the civilisation of their day were irksome. Many of them were political agitators, industrial rioters, and machine-breakers. The others were poachers and similarly comparatively mild offenders against the laws, who, under the present laws of Great Britain, would be sufficiently punished with a few months' imprisonment. Many of these men, when they were removed to a new land where the social conditions did not press so heavily on them, became honest and reputable citizens, and, perhaps, but for the harsh treatment they were subjected to, numbers of others who were driven to continue their fight against authority, might also have lived quiet and useful lives. This subject is a very delicate one, and it is not my intention to pursue it further here; but if it could be fully treated without giving offence to numbers of worthy and, in some cases, justly honoured residents of Australia, some very valuable lessons might be learned from the histories of some of those families whose founders could not live in England without offending against the laws, but who could and did earn the respect of their fellow colonists in Australia who were not "sent out."

The student of history in Australia is reminded, perhaps more forcibly than his fellow in England, that the humanitarian spirit, now so distinguishing a trait in the Anglo-Saxon character, is of very recent growth. Under the operation of this new force the criminal law of England was rapidly softened and ameliorated, and with every advance in this direction the character of the convicts sent out to Australia steadily deteriorated, if I may so describe the process. With every alteration in the law a fresh class of criminal was transported, and these with few exceptions would, a few months before, have been hung. At first, pickpockets, then sheep and horse-stealers, forgers and others, who had previously only escaped the gallows in rare instances, when they could find some influential friend to take sufficient interest in them to plead their cause, were now transported as a matter of course. This process continued until transportation ceased, and as the last batch of prisoners sent out was presumably the worst, having been guilty of more heinous crimes than their predecessors, we are too apt to judge the earlier convicts harshly from our knowledge of the later ones. The general effect was that while, with the amelioration of the laws, crime steadily decreased in England, it just as steadily increased in Australia, and no doubt the worst criminals were transported to Van Diemen's Land after transportation had ceased to New South Wales in 1842. The laws of England previously to the great changes made during the past sixty years seem to me to have operated, whether designedly or not, to clear the country of the disaffected and the discontented, rather than the criminal. How far the introduction of large numbers of this class into the country may have paved the way for modern advances in liberal government in Australia, is a question which it might be profitable to study; but it only relates to the bushrangers so far as it enables us to account for the large number of men who "took to the bush."

The earlier bushrangers seem to have been idle and dissolute, rather than criminal, characters. They watched for an opportunity to escape into a patch of scrub whenever the eye of the sentry in charge of them was turned away, and the nature of the country was so favourable to this method of evasion that it constituted a continuous challenge to them to

CHAPTER I

run away, and, almost incredible as it may appear now, numbers of men started northward or westward in hopes of reaching the Dutch or English settlements at Batavia, Singapore, Hong Kong, or some other place in that direction. It must be remembered that the majority of the working classes at the beginning of the century could not read and had no knowledge of geography. They had heard sailors speak of these settlements and had no idea that hundreds of miles of sea flowed between them and Australia. How many of these poor ignorant men lost their lives in the attempt to achieve the impossible cannot be said, but some terrible stories of cannibalism have been related in connection with this phase of bushranging. The majority of the "runaways," however, had no such definite ideas as these, erroneous as they may have been. They hoped to be able to live in freedom in the bush and to subsist on fruits, roots, or other native growths. Some few joined a tribe of blacks and stayed longer or shorter times with them; others simply wandered about until hunger drove them back; while very many remained at large until they were captured, and these lived by stealing from farmers and other settlers any articles which could be eaten or sold. When one of these early bushrangers grew tired of his freedom he gave himself up at the nearest police station and received fifty lashes. The penalty for a second offence was twelve months in a chain gang.

There was no adequate system of classifying the convicts. It was the custom in advertising runaways to give the name of the man and that of the ship in which he was transported. Then followed the personal description, and that was all. It was admitted to be inconvenient, but no attempt appears to have been made to improve it. Besides this, for administration purposes, convicts were divided into three classes according to their sentences. Thus there were men who had been transported for "seven" years, for "fourteen" years, or for "life." They were also classified as "young," "middle-aged," and "old," and usually the crime for which they had been transported was specified, but such a description gave no indication of the character of the man. Finally they were divided into "town thieves," "rural labourers," and "gentlemen." This was a step in the right direction, but it was too vague to be of much use. The educated convicts were all classified as "gentlemen" whether they came from the towns or the rural districts.[1] It

---

[1] *Evidence of Sir Francis Forbes, Chief Justice of New South Wales. Report of the Select Committee of the House of Commons, July, 1899.*

is worthy of note that the proportion of skilled labourers, or tradesmen as they are called, was very small. Very few men who had been apprenticed to a trade were among the convicts sent to Australia at any time.

There were no regulations as to hours of work, and the severe taskmaster might work his assigned servants as many hours as he pleased. It was generally understood that Sunday was to be a holiday, or day of rest, but excuses were readily found for making the convicts work on this day, and this was a fruitful source of discontent. Very frequently men absconded on Saturday night, remained in the bush on Sunday, and returned on Monday to take the customary fifty lashes and resume work.

If flogging is efficacious in preventing crime, it should have made the convict colonies the most virtuous places on earth, for the "cat" was in almost continuous use in New South Wales and in Van Diemen's Land. The "cat" generally used was the ordinary military or naval cat; but "the cat used at Macquarie Harbour was a larger and heavier instrument than that used generally for the punishment of soldiers or sailors. It was called the thief's cat, or double cat-o'-nine-tails. It had only the usual number of tails, but each of these was a double twist of whipcord, and each tail had nine knots. It was a very formidable instrument indeed."[2] How far the influence of this barbarous instrument of torture tended to make the prisoners at Macquarie Harbour the most reckless and ferocious of the convicts of Australia it is unnecessary to enquire, but there can be no doubt that its influence was for evil and not for good. It is with the ordinary "cat," with which England in these barbarous times flogged her defenders as ferociously as she did her prisoners, that we have to deal; and, frightful as the tortures were which were inflicted on the convicts, we have positive evidence that their lot was looked upon with envy by the soldiers who guarded them. Several soldiers in New South Wales deliberately committed crime so that they might be convicted, in the hope that, by good conduct, they might earn some of the indulgences open to convicts. The fact is that any prisoner who contrived, by obsequiousness or in any other way, to make friends with an official, had his way made easy for him, while the independent, whether industrious or not, were ruthlessly persecuted until, in many cases, they were finally forced to the gallows.

[2] *Despatch from Governor Macquarie to Earl Bathurst, June 28, 1813.*

Chapter I

"The prisoners of all classes in Government are fed with the coarsest food; governed with the most rigid discipline; subjected to the stern, and frequently capricious and tyrannical will of an overseer; for the slightest offence (sometimes for none at all—the victim of false accusation) brought before a magistrate, whom the Government has armed with the tremendous powers of a summary jurisdiction, and either flogged, or sentenced to solitary confinement, or retransported to an iron gang, where he must work in heavy irons, or to a penal settlement, where he will be ruled with a rod of iron. If assigned to a private individual he becomes a creature of chance. He may fall into the hands of a kind indulgent master, who will reward his fidelity with suitable acknowledgments; but, in ninety-nine cases out of a hundred, he will find his employer suspicious, or whimsical, or a blockhead, not knowing good conduct from bad, or a despot, who treats him like a slave, cursing and abusing, and getting him flogged for no reasonable cause. He may be harassed to the very death—he may be worked like a horse, and fed like a chameleon. The master, though not invested by law with uncontrolled power, has yet great authority, which may be abused in a thousand ways precluding redress. Even his legal power is sufficiently formidable. A single act of disobedience is a sufficient ground of complaint before the magistrate, and is always severely dealt with. But, besides the master's power, the prisoners are in some measure under a dominion to the free population at large; any man can give him in charge without ceremony. If seen drunk, if seen tippling in the public-house, if met after hours in the street, if unable to pay his trifling debt, if impertinent—the free man has nothing more to do than to send him to the watch-house, and get him punished. The poor prisoner is at the mercy of all men."[3] This appears to be a fair and unexaggerated statement of the conditions, and therefore it is little cause for wonder that the general tone of morality in the colony was low. Mr. J. T. Bigge says that "every opportunity was seized for cheating. When the convicts attended at the store to draw their weekly rations, supplies were frequently drawn for men not at work there. False lists of men employed in the various gangs were made out."[4] In fact, the Government of the Colony was a military despotism under which corruption was

---

[3] *Sydney Gazette*, November 40, 1830.]
[4] *Commission of Enquiry into the state of the colony of New South Wales, 1822.*

rampant, so that the authorities themselves set an example of immorality which the convicts were not slow to follow. "The police made a considerable revenue by blackmailing convicts who were in business."[5] Those who could pay were allowed to continue to enjoy a freedom to which they were not legally entitled, while those who would not, or could not, be blackmailed, to satisfy the exorbitant demands of the so-called custodians of the peace, speedily "got into trouble," and were prosecuted. It was said that if a man could escape from a country district and go to Sydney he might, if he could afford to dress well, pass as a free man without attracting attention. A blacksmith named Brady, assigned to Major James Mudie, of Castle Forbes, eluded the police in this way for nearly two years. He was recognised by a fellow convict, some time before he was captured, but this man "let him go for £5." Such cases, however, were exceptions to the general rule. The majority of runaways went into the bush and not into the town, and the Sydney and Hobart Town Gazettes in early times contain numerous proclamations by the various governors calling upon all well disposed persons to assist the military in capturing runaways. Some of the issues of these Gazettes contain columns of the names and descriptions of persons variously styled "absconders," "absentees," "bolters," or "bushrangers." In these the term "bushranger" appears most frequently in New South Wales, while "bolter" was the more popular in Van Diemen's Land. The first bushrangers, therefore, were men who "took to the bush" to escape work, and therefore it was quite possible for a man to be a bushranger without committing any depredations on his more prosperous fellows.

But laziness was not the sole cause of bushranging in early times. A more powerful impulse perhaps was discontent, love of change. "One of the most common indications of the misery of convicts under existing circumstances is a passionate desire for change of place; and when serving considerate masters they are sometimes indulged in this by being transferred (though always as a sort of punishment) to their disadvantage. In other cases, however, the desire becomes so strong that they will steal, or commit some equal offence, expressly to be condemned to a road gang or penal settlement."[6] In fact the monotony of their lives became insupportable, even

---

[5] *Report of the Select Committee of the House of Commons on Transportation, July, 1839.*
[6] *Report by Captain Maconochie, forwarded to the Colonial Office by Sir John Franklin, October 7th, 1837.*

in those cases where they were not cruelly treated. Captain Maconochie cites cases of men who have so acted within a few months of their being entitled to a ticket-of-leave, and who have thus forfeited their chances of freedom in the near future. In some cases this was due to the "inhuman treatment" of the master. In one case a valuable servant—a blacksmith—whose time had nearly expired, was goaded into running away so that he might be condemned to a further term of service before obtaining his ticket-of-leave, and this was not an isolated case.

"Generally," said Dr. J. D. Lang, "the condition of the assigned servant in New South Wales is superior to that of the farm labourer of England. He is better clothed, better fed, and as comfortably lodged. He is under personal restraint, not being allowed to leave his master's property without a pass, but he has many comforts and means of amusement which render his situation by no means irksome or severe."[7] But it was just this restraint which the persons with whom we are now dealing found intolerable. They had not the patience, the long-suffering resignation of the English farm labourer. Many of them had been English farm labourers and had found the conditions in which they lived intolerable, and when they realised that they had not very much improved these conditions by being sent to Australia, they rebelled again. "The experience furnished by the penal settlements," said Judge Forbes, "has proved that transportation is capable of being carried to an extreme of suffering such as to render death desirable, and to induce many prisoners to seek it under its most appalling aspects...I have known cases in which it appeared that men had committed crimes at Norfolk Island, for the mere purpose of being sent to Sydney to be tried, and the cause of their desiring to be so sent was to avoid the state of endurance in which they were placed in Norfolk Island."...Several cases occurred in which "men at Norfolk Island cut the heads of their fellow-prisoners with the hoe while at work, with the certainty of being detected, and the certainty of being executed. They did this without malice, and when charged said it was better to be hung than to live in such a hell."[8] Sir Richard Bourke said: "Capital crimes have been committed in that penal settlement from a desperate determination to stake the chance of capital

---

[7] *Select Committee of the House of Commons on Transportation, August, 1838.*
[8] *Ibid.*

conviction and punishment in Sydney against the chances of escape which the passage might afford to the accused and to the witnesses summoned to attend the trial."[9] The early bushrangers of Australia ranged therefore from the comparatively innocent wanderer in the bush, to such desperadoes as these, while the crimes they committed varied from petty theft to burglary, bank robbery, robbery on the high road, and murder. The modern idea of a bushranger is a bold highwayman, and no doubt many of the bushrangers come up to this ideal, but the story of the bushrangers would not be complete if it took no note of the others.

The settlement on Norfolk Island was established with the view of sending all the reconvicted prisoners there. It was the penal settlement of a penal settlement. It was abandoned for a time, after the founding of a similar settlement on the banks of the Derwent river in Van Diemen's Land, but was re-established as a place of punishment in connection with that colony, and many of the most notorious of the bushrangers ended their days there, as we shall see later. It was in the convict settlements in those islands that the greatest brutalities were perpetrated on the prisoners, and Norfolk Island, Macquarie Harbour, and Port Arthur were each known as "The Hell" among the "old hands," as the convicts were called after transportation had been abolished. It was in these settlements that the more violent and refractory of the convicts were gradually collected, and the history of these places tends to prove that brutality cannot be cured by brutal means. Flogging which was an every-day occurrence had no reformatory effect. The early bushrangers thought nothing of it. It certainly did not deter them from absconding whenever they thought fit. When an absconder tired of wadering about the bush, he returned to the settlement to take his flogging "like a man." In the stories told by the old hands, the absconder or offender in some other way was represented as walking jauntily up to the triangles, throwing off his jumper, placing himself in position for tying, and then, when he had been secured, telling the flagellator to do his "d——est," and, if the descriptions of the manner in which the floggers performed their task which have come down to us are true, the punishment was a terrible one. It is said that there were two floggers in Sydney who were regarded as artists in their profession. These men

[9] *Despatch to Colonial Office, entitled "Administration of Justice at Norfolk Island, November, 1838."*

performed together, the one being right-handed and the other left. They prided themselves on being able to flog a man without breaking the skin, and consequently there was no blood spilled. But the back of the flogged man is described as having been puffed up like "blown veal." The swelling "shook like jelly," and the effects were felt for a much longer period than when the back was cut and scored as it generally was, for we are told that the ground, in the Barrack Square in Sydney, all round where the triangles stood, was saturated with human blood, and the flogging places elsewhere must have been in the same condition. But to return. When the man had received his dose and was cast loose, he would throw his jumper across his shoulders and walk away with a grin—or with some such remarks as "Well, is that all you can do? —— you!" and afterwards boast that "the —— couldn't get a whimper" out of him. I have heard a story of a man who was flogged. The flagellator kept hitting him low down across the loins. The prisoner turned his head round once and said fiercely: "Hit higher, blast you!" The flogger took no notice, and the prisoner made no other sign until he was untied. Then he knocked the flogger down with his fist, and was immediately seized up for another "dose."

"I can assure you, from personal observation, that it is not uncommon to see a poor wretch working on the roads, or labouring in the fields, with his coarse shirt sticking to the green and tainted flesh of his lacerated back, and that, too, for the most venial offence...I have it from unquestionable authority, that it frequently occurs in the summer season that the eggs of the blue-fly become inserted and hatched in the wounds of the punished offender, from which they are occasionally extracted by some humane companion."[10]

The blow-fly in Australia, although frequently called "blue-bottle," is not blue. It deposits its young alive in the form of maggots, and great care has always to be taken to prevent sores on man or beast from being "blown." It is very common for flannel shirts, which have become greasy from perspiration, to be blown on the backs of workmen, and the maggots thus deposited will attack and irritate any scratch or sore they can find if not removed quickly.

[10] *Secondary punishment discussed by an Emigrant of 1821.—Launceston Advertiser.*

The convict, so far from having been ashamed of being flogged, boasted of it. But nothing pleased them better than the relations of stories about the flogging of "freemen," as those settlers who had gone to the colonies neither as convicts nor officials were called. One story, which may or may not be true, has been told as having occurred in every convict district in Australia. It was to the effect that a master one day gave a letter to an assigned servant and told him to take it to the nearest gaol. The servant, surmising that the letter was somewhat to the following effect:—"Dear Sir,—Please give the bearer fifty for absconding (or what not), and oblige, yours truly, &c.," told a plausible tale to the first freeman he met and induced him to deliver the letter. The point of the story generally lay in the ingenuity with which the convict induced the freeman to deliver the letter for him, but the astonishment of the freeman when he was seized up to the triangles in spite of his struggles and protestations, and given the "fifty," was a perpetual source of joy and hilarity to the convicts who heard the story. There is nothing inherently improbable in this story. It is quite probable that the incident may have occurred more than once. Although freemen were legally exempt from flogging, unless under sentence of a qualified Court, many authentic instances of freemen having been flogged have been told. Here is one. "A store-keeper in Hobart Town had offended his neighbours, and one of them, in revenge, posted a written placard libelling the offender. The placard was affixed to a big gum stump at the corner of Collins and Elizabeth Streets. just as the complainant was putting this bill on the stump the man libelled in it passed and called the attention of the Military Commandant, who was near at hand at the time, to it. A sort of informal drum-head Court Martial was held on the spot, and the libeller was found guilty and sentenced to receive three hundred lashes, which were administered at once, in spite of the protests of the victim that he was a freeman and was therefore entitled to a judicial trial. When two hundred lashes had been administered, a cry of 'Ship ho' was raised, and the last hundred was got rid of as quickly as possible, the Commandant, the flagellator, the spectators, and others all rushing away to the wharf to hear the news from Europe."[11] If the law could be thus set at defiance by a military official in the case of a free immigrant holding a

[11] *History of Van Diemen's Land from 1820 to 1835.*

CHAPTER I

good position, what chance of justice could there be for a convict? A story illustrating the reckless manner in which prisoners were flogged is told by the "Launceston Advertiser." A prisoner was found guilty of absconding, and sentenced to receive fifty lashes, when some circumstances were disclosed which proved that the prisoner was innocent, but had lost his pass. "Never mind," said the Launceston magistrate, "the warrant is signed, let him be punished now; I will forgive him the next time he's brought up." The tyranny-of the officials was boundless. One Government rule was that all convicts should take off their hats to officers and officials whenever they passed. In January, 1839, a party of convicts was building some steps at Woolloomooloo Bay, on Sir Maurice O'Connell's estate. Several of them were rolling a heavy stone down to be placed in position when an officer passed along and the convicts immediately rose up and took their hats off. The stone rolled quickly down the steep embankment, struck the overseer and knocked him down, almost breaking his leg. Captain O'Connell gave orders that the men should not salute anybody in future while at work. A few days later Colonel Wilson, Chief Police Magistrate of Sydney, passed, accompanied by his daughter. The convicts continued at work without noticing him. "Take off your hats," cried the Colonel. Several of the men did so, but Joseph Todd, who was carrying a heavy load, took no notice. "Take off your hat, you scoundrel," said the Colonel. Todd said he had been ordered not to. The Colonel shouted "I'll have your back skinned for you, you rascal," called the sergeant of police who acted as guard, and gave Todd in charge. Captain O'Connell appeared to defend his man and said Colonel Wilson was trespassing and had no right to interfere with assigned servants on their master's estate. Sergeant Goodwin deposed that the path was a common one and people frequented it to get to the bathing place. Sergeant Mather said that Todd had struggled when arrested. The Bench held that Todd being an assigned servant had been guilty of disorderly conduct in resisting the police. Had he been a freeman he would have been justified in resisting arrest without a warrant; but, being a prisoner, his conduct had been highly disorderly, and he was, therefore, sentenced to receive fifty lashes. A week later Todd was again arrested for being out after hours, and was sentenced to receive thirty lashes. The paper in reporting this charged Colonel Wilson with tyrannical conduct, and says that he went to see Todd flogged.[12]

I am not relating the worst cases in order to "make out a case" for the bushrangers, but simply facts to illustrate the life in the colonies at the time, and thus account for the large number of men who "took to the bush," and the special Acts passed to prevent this breach of the law were as tyrannical as the acts of the officials or the masters which went so far to create it. The "Bushranging Act" (II George IV., No. 10) authorised the military or civil police to arrest any person on the mere suspicion that he or she was illegally at large, and the onus of proof was thrown on the suspected party. This Act was a fruitful source of complaint. No one was safe except well known officials, and it is said that the Act was extensively used for purposes of extortion and black mail. A young woman was arrested by an ex-constable and charged with being illegally at large. It was in vain that she protested that she was "free" and did not require a pass. He insisted on taking her to the lock-up. Fortunately, while walking along the street she met some one who knew her and who threatened the ex-policeman with prosecution if he did not release her. The fellow did so and was not prosecuted. Probably had an enquiry been held it would have been found that he was acting in collusion with the police. Even the officials were not always safe. Mr. Jacques, the Government auctioneer, had been to a dinner party. Being near the Custom House he decided to walk to the wharf from whence the steamer, which ran to Balmain, started and go home in her. Not having walked to the wharf from that point before, he found it necessary to apply to a constable for information as to which turning he should take, and was immediately arrested as a convict illegally at large. Id spite of his protests he was conveyed to the nearest police station. The sergeant in charge refused to believe his story, and thought that the presence of a well-dressed man in that quarter was suspicious. Mr. Jacques was therefore detained till morning, when he was recognised by the magistrate and discharged. In 1834 a circular letter was addressed by the Governor to the various police-magistrates in New South Wales, enquiring whether, in their opinion, the Act should be reaffirmed or not, and the replies were by a large majority in favour of its being continued,

[12] *Sydney Gazette*

while others merely suggested that it might be amended in various ways to prevent the abuses which had grown up under its operation. Judge Burton was almost alone in his condemnation of the Bushranging Act, which, he said, was repugnant to the laws of England. "England and the United States of America," he said, "are the only two countries in the world where passports are not compulsory," and he deprecated the introduction of the passport system into Australia. It was held that the conditions existing in the colony made such an act necessary, and it was therefore re-enacted without amendment.[13] It is worthy of note, as illustrating Colonial Office procedure of that day, that it was the paid officials, and not the public, who were consulted in this matter.

The facts being as I have stated, the wonder is not that large numbers of prisoners "took to the bush" but that all did not do so, and the more we study the early history of the convict settlements the less we feel inclined to blame the early bushrangers, however savage or atrocious their actions were. But we have not yet quite escaped from barbarism. In spite of the positive evidence that flogging brutalises and does not reform it is still continued. We also continue to hang criminals, although there is no proof that it deters crime or effects any good whatever. I do not belong to any society for the abolition of capital punishment. I may admit that perhaps there may be men whose death is desirable or expedient; but, if it is so, if there are men unfit to live or whose death might add to the happiness or security of the majority, then I think that we might extend to our fellow creatures, however ferocious or abandoned they may be, the mercy which we show to savage or superfluous dogs and cease from torturing them in their last moments. Hanging has had a sufficiently lengthy trial in Australia if it has not in England. Old residents in Sydney or in Hobart Town or in any other locality where penal settlements have existed can point out numbers of places where the gallows has been erected, and in some cases trees are still standing where numbers of men have struggled away their last few moments of life. This, however, is not the place to enlarge upon this subject, but the story I have to tell shows a lamentable waste of life, and many even of the more notorious of the bushrangers have exhibited qualities which might under happier conditions have fitted them for useful

[13] *Dispatch of Governor Bourke to the Colonial Office, 1835*

work. This is specially true of the earlier bushrangers who were the victims generally of unjust laws. Of the later ones, the native-born bushrangers, it is impossible to speak in the same terms. They were not driven to crime by want or oppression, but they were the vicious products of a vicious past. Their crimes were due to vicious environment and education, but they are gone now and, if we may draw some lessons of utility for the future, even their lives may not have been altogether wasted.

From the evidence I have adduced it will be seen that the early bushrangers were very numerous. "In one case it became known," said Mr. James Macarthur, "that a gang of about sixty convicts, employed in the Government gangs in Liverpool, intended to break out on a certain night and take to the bush. It was considered advisable to allow them to break out, proper precautions having been made to capture them. It was the intention to attack our farming stations at Camden. We armed twelve of the best-conducted of our convict servants, but the absconders found that their design had been discovered and did not attempt to put it in force."[13] Thus the bushrangers did not always go out singly, or in twos or threes. Mr. J. T. Bigge says: "At Windsor, and in the adjoining districts, the offence termed bushranging, or absconding in the woods, and living upon plunder and the robbing of orchards, are most prevalent...At Emu Plains, or the district of Evan, gambling, absence from work, insolence to overseers, neglect of work, and stealing, are the most common offences...As the population of New South Wales has, until lately, been virtually limited to the occupation of a small tract of land that lies between the Blue Mountains and the sea, and as few temptations to plunder existed in the tracts contiguous to these boundaries, excepting those that are afforded by the wild cattle in the cow-pastures, the offence of bushranging, or continued absence in the woods, has not of late been common. Instances have occurred of the departure of convicts for the purpose of traversing the country with a view to escape, of the escape of some from Newcastle, sent thither for punishment, and their wandering and temporary existence in the vicinity of Windsor; and latterly, a few instances of escape from the road parties in the districts of Liverpool and Bathurst; but there has been no systematic or continued

---

[13] *Select Committee of the House of Commons on Transportation, July, 18, 1837.*

CHAPTER I

efforts of desperate convicts to defy the attempts of the local Government in New South Wales, or to subsist by plunder, such as have existed until a very late period in Van Diemen's Land."[14]

It is in Van Diemen's Land, therefore, that our story of the more serious phases of bushranging first begins.

---

[14] *Commission of Enquiry into the state of the colony of New South Wales, 1822.*

Two

Van Diemen's Land; The First Bushranger; Mike Howe, the King of the Ranges; The Raid on the Blacks; The Black War; Musquito; Outrages by the Blacks; Brutal Treatment of Blacks by Bushrangers; A War of Reprisals; Gigantic Scheme to Capture the Blacks; A Cordon Drawn Round the Disaffected District; Details of the Scheme; Its Failure; Only Two Blacks Captured; Estimated Cost; Fate of the Blacks.

The first settlement in Van Diemen's Land was founded in 1803, when a penal establishment, to which the more refractory of the prisoners in Sydney might be despatched, was founded on the banks of the River Derwent. Subsequently other penal stations were opened, and of these we shall hear later. The island continued to be the chief penal establishment of New South Wales until 1825, when it was erected into an independent colony. The first shipment of convicts, direct from England to Van Diemen's Land, took place in 1823, and from that date, until transportation to the island finally ceased, in 1853, 64,306 convicts were sent to that colony from the British Isles. The number sent previously from New South Wales was not large, nevertheless it included the majority of the most turbulent of the convicts and relieved the mother colony of their charge and control. The island was in fact "nothing but a jail on a large scale." The early conditions in the colony appear to have been favourable to bushranging. In 1805 there was such a dearth of food stuffs, owing to the non-arrival of store ships from Sydney, that a famine appeared to be imminent and, to relieve the store, the Lieutenant Governor ordered the liberation of the convicts and sent them into the woods to catch kangaroo and other wild animals for food. When the stores arrived and food became plentiful, the attempts to recall the convicts were only partially successful. Many had learned how to subsist in the bush and disregarded the proclamations issued by the Lieutenant Governor ordering them to return to work. At first the bushrangers or bolters were similar to those of New South Wales and contented themselves with petty thefts. The first proclamation in which reference is made to "a gang of bushrangers" was published in the Hobart Town Gazette by Lieutenant Governor Davey and dated September 10th, 1810. It offered rewards and indulgences to convicts for the capture of any members of a gang which, under the leadership of a convict named Whitehead, had been committing depredations on the property of settlers and farmers in the vicinity of Hobart Town.[1]

Whitehead, therefore, was the first to organise a gang which combined highway robbery with burglary and petty larceny. Bushrangers were not at that time specialists. From time to time other proclamations were issued in which this gang was mentioned, but it was not until May 14th, 1813, that a special proclamation was published, calling upon the "bolters" to surrender. Those who neglected to obey this order were to be proclaimed "outlaws" on December 1st.

Very few particulars are published about this gang in the newspapers, and the proclamations rarely specify the facts in connection with the robberies committed. The newspapers of the time seldom mention the names of the bushrangers, and appear to have been quite as averse to mentioning the Christian names as the modern English papers are those of professional cricketers. Thus Whitehead is referred to as "the convict Whitehead," or the "notorious bushranger Whitehead," and so on. He is debited, however, with one horrible crime. The gang captured a half-crazy fellow named John Hopkins, and accused him of trying to betray them. As a punishment for this offence a pair of moccassins, roughly made of bullock hide, was fitted on to his feet, and in these were placed a number of the great red ants, commonly known in Australia as "bull-dog" or "soldier" ants (myrmccia gulosa).

These ants are an inch and a quarter long, and of most ferocious appearance. They are the dread of the colonists. They sting quite as severely as a bee or a hornet. But a bee stings only once, while a soldier ant will continue to sting until removed. It is always ready to fight, and never lets go when it has taken hold; hence its popular names. The horrible barbarity of such a punishment can be best appreciated, perhaps, by those who have inadvertently stood on a "soldier's" bed or nest. The victim is said to have died in agony.

---

[1] *History of Van Diemen's Land from 1820 to 1835.*

Whitehead was shot by a party of soldiers in October, 1814, and Michael Howe, commonly called the "First of the Australian Bushrangers," was elected captain of the gang in his stead. Mike Howe, as he was usually called, was transported from England for highway robbery, and soon after his arrival at Sydney "got into trouble," and was again transported to Van Diemen's Land, where his violence caused him to be repeatedly flogged and otherwise punished. He made his escape and joined Whitehead's gang, and soon, by his superior education, gained an ascendency over his comrades. His previous experiences as a footpad in England no doubt tended to fit him for the leadership of the gang, and he is still regarded as one of the most notable of the revolters against law and order in the colonies. One of his earlier achievements was to organise a raid on a tribe of blacks for the purpose of providing himself and his comrades with wives. This is said to have been the first act in the tragedy which closed with the complete annihilation of the blacks of the island. The savages, of course, resisted, and many of them were shot, and the women were forced away to the bushrangers' camp. In revenge, the blacks attacked, not the bushrangers' camp, but the houses of settlers who had no connection with the bushrangers, and fights between the settlers and the blacks became frequent. Some of the black women seem to have become reconciled to the change, and Howe's "wife," Black Mary, is associated with him in most of the stories told of him. It is said that it was her knowledge of the bush which enabled him to escape so frequently from the military bands sent out to capture him.

Howe addressed a letter "From the Bushrangers to the Hon. T. Davey, Lieutenant Governor of Van Diemen's Land," in which he protested against the charge, made against himself and his mates in the proclamations, of having been guilty of "horrid and detestable crimes." He asserted that he had never committed murder and had only used violence when it was necessary to avoid capture. The letter was conveyed to Hobart Town by an American whaler named Richard Westlick, who had an interview with his Excellency, and was sent back with a verbal message that the Governor "did not wish to take the life of any man," but merely to preserve order. If, therefore, Howe, or any of his comrades, would surrender no charges should be made against them for their acts while "in the bush." No

Chapter II

notice was taken of this generous offer, and the depredations continued. Later on Mike Howe addressed a letter "From the Governor of the Ranges to the Governor of the Town," and sent it to Lieutenant Governor Sorell, who had succeeded Colonel Davey. In this the bushranger offered to give himself up on condition that he received a free pardon. He demanded that some recognised official should be sent to meet him at an appointed spot, so that they might "confer as gentleman to gentleman." The fact that this insolent offer was accepted affords incontrovertible evidence of the power of the bushrangers, and shows the anxiety of the Governor to put a stop to the robberies which harassed the industrious settlers and made the roads of the colony unsafe. Captain Naime, of the 46th Regiment, was sent out to meet the bushranger, and the result of their conference "as gentlemen" was that Howe accompanied the Captain back to Hobart Town. On his arrival there he was informed that the Lieutenant Governor had no power to grant pardons, but that he would write to Governor Macquarie in Sydney and urge him to grant a pardon without delay. Howe agreed to wait in Hobart Town. He was liberated on parole, and soon became very popular in the city. Then a rumour began to spread to the effect that Howe had committed no less than four murders, not reckoning the blacks he had killed, and that, therefore, the Governor declined to grant him a pardon. As soon as Howe heard this rumour he, without waiting for its confirmation, broke his parole and returned to the bush. A Proclamation was immediately issued declaring him an outlaw, and offering one hundred pounds reward for his capture, dead or alive. Smaller rewards were offered for other members of his gang, whose names were known.

The estimates of the strength of his gang vary extremely from time to time. Sometimes he is said to have a hundred or more followers, while frequently he is represented as acting alone or in company with only one or two others. The facts appear to be that many men, who merely "bolted" into the bush as a relief to the monotony of their lives, became bushrangers; and, when hard pressed, or when they tired of that pursuit, returned to the town, gave themselves up, and were punished as ordinary bolters. One day, not very long after his escape from Hobart Town, Howe was surprised while asleep by two ticket-of-leave men named Watts and Drew. They captured and tied him. Howe fought like a lion and contrived to break the rope with which he was tied. He snatched a knife and stabbed Watts. He then seized Watts' gun and shot Drew dead. Watts ran away, while Howe was employed in re-loading the gun, and managed to secrete himself in the scrub for a time. When the way was clear he crawled to a farm and gave information. He was cared for as well as circumstances permitted, but he died from loss of blood before a doctor could be brought to him. Howe was followed by the military, but escaped.

Several skirmishes took place between Howe and his gang and the soldiers, and more than one of his accomplices were shot, but the chief always contrived to get away. At length a kangaroo hunter named Warburton led William Pugh, a soldier commonly known as "Big Bill," and a seaman named John Worrall, to where Howe was camped under a gum tree. A terrific fight took place, Howe's brains being beaten out before it was over.

In his review of this period, Mr. J. T. Bigge said: "The excesses of the bushrangers in the neighbourhood of Port Dalrymple, and likewise near Hobart Town, had attained their utmost height and most sanguinary character at the latter end of the year 1813. They had been joined by two persons who had held subordinate stations in the commisariat department, named Peter Mills and George Williams, and continued a system of violent depredations upon the homes and property of individuals of every description. So great was the intimidation produced by their combined efforts, that the inhabitants of several districts abandoned their dwellings and removed for safety to the towns...Colonel Davey issued a proclamation offering rewards for the apprehension of a party of nine, and with the advice of Mr. Ellis Bent another proclamation calling upon them to surrender before December 1st...The effect of this was the reverse of what was intended. It increased the crimes and audacity of the bushrangers during the six months that it allowed for their return; they profited by the pardon by making a temporary surrender, and then resumed their habits of plunder...Hector McDonald, the leader, was shot by two convicts sent in pursuit of a gang of four. Another was shot by a soldier of the 48th regiment, and the other three were captured and on conviction flogged and transported."[2]

[2] *Commission of Enquiry into the state of the Colony of New South Wales, 2-23.*

CHAPTER II

For the time, bushranging in Van Diemen's Land was said to have been put down, but "the Guerilla War" between the whites and the blacks, inaugurated by the bushrangers, continued. Mr. Gilbert Robertson was appointed conciliator, with a view to arranging terms of peace, but he was not very successful. Several proclamations were issued assuring the blacks that if they would come in and make peace the Government would endeavour to protect them against their enemies the bushrangers; but, as was pointed out at the time, issuing proclamations to savages who could not read was absurd. Then a pictorial proclamation was issued. In one portion the governor was shown shaking hands with a blackfellow; in others blacks and whites were exhibited mingling together in friendship. In the two bottom compartments a white man was shown being hung for having shot a black, while a blackfellow was being hung for having speared a white man. Copies of this pictorial proclamation were posted on trees and other places where the blacks might see it. Lieutenant Governor Arthur in fact, on his arrival in the colony, tried by every means in his power to appeal to the blacks and whites alike. He endeavoured to restrain the settlers from attacking and driving the blacks away from their farms whenever they appeared, as had become the custom, but some new outrage by the bushrangers gave a new impulse to the feud, and the settlers were compelled to fight in self-defence. In one of his despatches to the Colonial Secretary Governor Arthur said: "It is not a matter of surprise that the injuries real or supposed, inflicted on the blacks, have been avenged upon the whites whenever an occasion presents itself; and I regret to say that the natives led on by a Sydney black, and by two aborigines of this island, men partially civilised (a circumstance which augurs ill for any endeavour to instruct these abject beings), have committed many murders upon the shepherds and herdsmen in remote settlements...I have long indulged the expectation that kindness and forbearance would have brought about something like a reconciliation, but the repeated murders which have been committed have so greatly inflamed the passions of the settlers, that petitions and complaints have been presented from every part of the colony, and the feeling of resentment now runs so high that further forbearance would be totally indefensible."[3]

[3] *Despatch dated April 17th, 1828.*

The Sydney black here mentioned was known as Musquito. He was transported to Van Diemen's Land for the murder of a black gin (presumably his wife, which is no crime according to native law) in 1823, and having been employed on a cattle station in New South Wales, was appointed stock-keeper. Later, he was employed as a tracker, and aided the soldiers in capturing some of the bushrangers. For this he was so persecuted by his fellow convicts that life became a burden to him. He appealed to the authorities for protection; but, as this was not accorded to him, he became a bushranger himself. "Perhaps taken collectively the sable natives of this colony are the most peaceable creatures in the universe. Certainly so taken they have never committed any acts of cruelty, or even resisted the whites, unless when insufferably goaded by provocation. The only tribe who have done any mischief were corrupted by Musquito, a Sydney black, who, with much perverted cunning, taught them a portion of his own villainy, and incited them after a time to join in his delinquencies."[4]

Knowing, as we do, the general character of the Australian blacks, it seems strange that one of them should prove himself so much superior to the Van Diemen's Land blacks as Musquito is represented to have done. But however that may be, there can be no doubt as to his skill in organisation. Some of his attacks on settlers were so skilfully planned and carried out, that many persons believed that the blacks had been led by a white man. After about two years of bushranging, Musquito and Black Jack, the two leaders, were captured. Musquito was charged with the murder of William Holyoak, and Mr. Gilbert Robertson appeared in his defence. Mr. Robertson urged that the murders committed by Musquito were in self defence. Had he been protected by the Government, as he should have been after the services he had rendered, he would never have taken to the bush. He related many instances to show the skill of the black, and among others, said that he had seen him "cut the head off a flying pigeon with a crooked stick."[5] This seems to indicate that however intimately Mr. Robertson might be acquainted with the Van Diemen's Land blacks he had no acquaintance with the boomerang. In spite of the conciliator's efforts Musquito was convicted and sentenced to death. When the sentence had

---

[4] *Hobart Town Gazette.*
[5] *Report of the Select Committee of the House of Commons, 1838.*

Chapter II

been pronounced Musquito said, "Hanging no good for blackfellow." Mr. Bisdee asked him "Why not as good for blackfellow as for whitefellow?" "Oh," exclaimed Musquito, "Very good for whitefellow. He used to it." Black Jack was convicted of the murder of Patrick Macartney. The only English known by Black Jack was of the "old hands oaths brand." The two blacks were hung in Hobart Town, but "The Black War" continued.

"The deadly antipathy which was excited between the aborigines and the bushrangers of Van Diemen's Land provoked a series of outrages which would have terminated in the utter extinction of the whole race, if the local Government had not interposed to remove the last remnant of them from the island; an act of real mercy, though of apparent severity."* Before proceeding to describe this attempt to save the remnant of the race we may perhaps give a list of the "Atrocities committed by the blacks." It is not a very long one, taking into consideration the time occupied in the war. In March, 1820, forty-nine natives attacked Mr. Broadribb's house. They were divided into several parties which came up from different points simultaneously. One man was speared in the thigh before the blacks were repulsed. They all went away together and stripped Mr. Thomson's house of everything portable. They then proceeded to Mr. E. Denovan's and robbed his place. On April 1st John Raynor was speared and dreadfully beaten at Spring Bay. On May 18th a party of blacks attacked two men employed by Mr. Lord. One was dangerously speared and the other beaten. The hut was stripped. On June 1st Mr. Sherwin's hut, at Weasel Plain, was plundered, and on the 15th, Den Hut, at Lake River, was stripped bare, and Mary Daniels and her two children murdered. On August 7th, S. Stockman's hut, at Green Ponds, was plundered. On the 9th, some muskets, powder, and shot were stolen from the huts of Mr. Sharland, a Government surveyor. On the same day the Government hut, between Borthwick and Blue Ash, was robbed, several horses stolen from Mr. Wood and Mr. Pitcairn, and a man wounded at Mr. Purvis's. This party consisted of about forty blacks. They were met by Mr. Howell's party, and the blacks were driven off after a fight. A woman living near was wounded with a spear. On the 23rd, the huts of Mr. J. Connell and Mr. Robertson were attacked, and the latter plundered; Mr. Sutherland's shepherds were robbed of their arms and one of them wounded; some arms were taken from Mr. Taylor's hut.

The next day James Hooper was killed, and his hut plundered. The huts of Lieutenants Bell and Watts were attacked, but the blacks were repulsed. On September 8th Captain Clark's shepherd was attacked, but contrived to escape. On the 13th one man was killed and another wounded on the banks of the Tamar River. On the 14th a man working at the Government lime kilns at Bothwell was attacked, but escaped. On the 18th a private of the 63rd Regiment was speared and two other soldiers wounded. One of the savages was killed. On the 27th Francis Booker was killed with spears,. and on the next day three men at Major Gray's hut were wounded. On the same day two men were killed at Mr. G. Scott's place and their bodies thrown into the river. A third man was wounded, but escaped into the bush. The house was stripped of everything. This robbery was so systematically carried through that it was believed that the blacks had been led by white men. A hut on the opposite side of the road was also stripped. On October 16th the settlement at Sorell was attacked, one man being killed and another severely wounded. Four houses were stripped. On the 18th Captain Stewart's shepherd was killed and a settler, Mr. Gilders, was also speared and died. On the 19th, Messrs. Gatehouse and Gordon's house was attacked, but the blacks were repulsed. They were also driven away from Mr. Gaugel's place, but not before he was severely wounded. On November 29th two huts were robbed on the Ouse River. Captain Wight's shepherd was killed and dreadfully mangled. His body was found later. On the 27th a hut on the Esk River was stripped bare. On February 3rd, 1821, an attack was made on Mr. Burrell's house on the Tamar River. Mr. Wallace was severely wounded in several places, and a child was also wounded by a spear. L. Knight's hut was plundered, three horses belonging to Mr. Sutherland were killed and three others were wounded. His hut at North Esk was also plundered. Mrs. McCaskell was killed near Westbury, and her hut plundered of everything. An attack made on Mr. Stewart's house was repulsed. On March 8th, two sawyers: were wounded, and two huts near New Norfolk were plundered. On the 12th, Mrs. Cunningham and her child were severely wounded, and her hut at East Arm plundered.[6]

Mr. Lawrence's servant was wounded, and three men were wounded on Norfolk Plains. On April 5th, T. Ralton was killed with a spear while split-

[6] *Report of the Select Committee of the House of Commons, 1838.*

ting wood. On the 16th, Mr. Fitzgerald was sitting at the door of his hut reading, when a blackfellow sneaked up and drove a spear through him, after which his cottage was plundered. On the 17th, another attack was made on Fitzgerald's house. On May 10th, the Government store at Patrick Plains was burned down. Mr. Kemp's establishment at Lake Sorell was attacked by a large mob of blacks. Two men were killed, one wounded, the buildings were burned down and the firearms carried away. On June 6th, several huts were attacked at Hunter's Hill. Mrs. Triffet was speared and her house plundered, the huts of Messrs. Marnetti, Bell, and Clark were robbed, and Mrs. N. Long was killed. On September 5th, Thomas Smith was killed at Tapsley, and his hut plundered; John Higginson was killed and his hut robbed, and a sawyer's hut was plundered. On the 7th, Mr. B. B. Thomas and his overseer, Mr. Parker, were murdered near Port Sorell, while endeavouring to carry out the conciliatory policy of the Government. Mr. Stocker's hut was attacked, a man named Cupid killed, and a child wounded. On the 27th, Mr. Dawson's hut on Bushy Plains was attacked, and a man severely beaten. On the 23rd, Mr. Dawson's man Hughes was again beaten with waddies and nearly killed. On October 13th, the natives, armed with muskets, attacked and robbed the house of Constable Reid, and afterwards that of Mr. Amos Junior.[7]

This report covers only a portion of the time during which the war lasted, but it sufficiently indicates the character of the war. When the blacks attacked the cottages, or huts as they are called in Australia, of shepherds, sawyers, splitters, and other workers, they were frequently successful, but were generally repulsed when they attacked the residences or houses of the employers. The manner in which the blacks fought struck terror into the hearts of the settlers. No one was safe. At any time, day or night, a party of blacks might sneak up and, with wild yells, spear men, women, and children, old or young, without warning. Their patience in tracking was indomitable. If they could not effect a surprise they withdrew and waited. No doubt, as the advocates of the cause of the blacks said, the number of whites killed was much smaller than the number of blacks slaughtered by bushrangers in their lust and by settlers and soldiers in defence. But it can be readily understood that the position of the settlers was intolera-

[7] *Despatch from Governor Arthur to Earl Bathurst, dated October 13, 1831.*

ble. Every attempt to drive the blacks away from the settled districts only provoked fresh reprisals, while every attempt at conciliation failed until at length it became evident that the blacks must be either captured or killed. It was therefore with a view to saving the blacks that Lieutenant Governor Arthur urged the necessity of capturing and removing them from Van Diemen's Land to one of the Islands in Bass's Straits. In his despatches to Governor Bourke and to the Colonial Office, he said that it was utterly impossible to restrain the colonists, so great was their rage at the murders of peaceful citizens, and especially of women and children, while all his attempts at conciliation had failed in consequence of the continual outrages committed on the blacks by the bushrangers. Mr. Gilbert Robertson said: "One day a settler was riding across his grounds looking for cattle. He jumped his horse over a log, and while doing so caught the sparkle of a pair of eyes gleaming from the shadow of the log. He pulled up, wheeled his horse round and dismounted, thinking he had found a kangaroo, but on pulling some brush away saw a poor cowering black trying to hide himself, but there was no mercy in the heart of the settler. He cocked his gun and shot the black in cold blood."[8]

The story is a very pathetic one, but perhaps the settler had had reason to know that "the poor cowering black" was sneaking up to the settlement to murder any unsuspecting man, woman, or child he might come across. Hiding behind logs, crawling through brush, was the ordinary method of fighting employed by the Van Diemen's Land aborigines, and had he not been on the war path he would not have resorted to this secret manner of travelling but would have stood out boldly. The blacks are not cowards, and are not afraid of showing themselves, as a rule, after their first superstitious fear of the white man passes away. This being the general experience of bushmen, the settler may have been justified in killing the black. He may have been simply treating him according to the blackfellow's own rule in war time. But although we may acquit the settler of blame by such reasoning, the existence of such conditions as to necessitate such a war is not the less deplorable. The whites all carried arms when travelling, and even while working about their homes. Shepherds and other workmen went in pairs. There was no safety anywhere outside the cleared lands round the

[8] *Report of the Select Committee of the House of Commons, 1838.*

larger towns. Reviewing the whole situation from our present standpoint, it is difficult to say what other measures could have been adopted than those tried by the Government. The authorities were apparently incapable of controlling the bushrangers, nor could they prevent convicts from running away, and these outlaws appear to have always considered the blacks as fair game. Mr. Robertson tells us that a convict known as "Carrots" boasted shortly before his death that, "having killed a native in his attempt to carry off the black's wife, he cut off the dead man's head and obliged the woman to go with him carrying it suspended round her neck."[9]

Is it any wonder that even such "passive and inoffensive creatures" as the Van Diemen's Land blacks are said to have been, should have been aroused to fury by such methods? But although the Government had no control over the convicts in the bush, and such outrages as this were not known of until long after they had occurred, it can scarcely be said that even Governor Arthur, in spite of his earnest desire to protect the blacks, was altogether blameless. The whole policy of the Government in relation to the blacks was weak and vacillating. Governor Arthur promised a native, known as Teague, a boat on condition that he should assist in the capture of some bushrangers. The black performed his share of the work, but he never got his boat, and is said to have fretted himself to death in consequence. The Sydney black, Musquito, was forced "into the bush" by the failure of the Government to protect him against the persecution due to the manner in which he had been employed in the service of that Government. In September, 1826, two blacks were hung in Hobart Town "to impress the others." Nothing could be more absurd than this, and it was far more barbarous a method of reprisal than the shooting of a "poor cowering black." But the Government was not even consistent in its savagery. At the trial of Eumarrah Mr. Robertson pleaded that the black was justified in resisting the invaders of his country in any and every way; and, on his undertaking to remove Eumarrah to Flinders Island, where he had collected about thirty-eight blacks under the charge of missionaries, the plea was accepted and the prisoner was handed over to him. By this time, however, the war had become so vindictive that even the authorities in London recognised that the blacks must be captured or annihilated, and consequently permission

[9] *Report of the Select Committee of the House of Commons, 1838.*

was granted to Governor Arthur to put in practice the most extraordinary project perhaps ever attempted.

In April, 1828, a proclamation was issued which, after describing the state of tension which existed between whites and blacks, exhorted all well-disposed persons to assist the Government in attempting to establish peace and order. The proclamation went on to explain that a cordon was to be drawn round the disturbed area and that this was to be gradually contracted until the natives were either captured or driven across the narrow isthmus which connects Tasman's peninsula with the main portion of the island. "But I do, nevertheless, hereby strictly order, enjoin, and command, that the actual use of arms be in no case resorted to, by firing against any of the natives, or otherwise, if they can by other measures be captured."

The force employed in this gigantic scheme is said to have been about two thousand two hundred men, of whom five hundred and fifty were soldiers belonging to the 63rd, the 57th, and the 17th regiments. The whole force was divided into parties of about ten each, and one of these was appointed a leader. On October 7th, a chain of posts was established from St. Patrick's Head along the rivers St. Paul, South Esk, Macquarie, and Meander, under the command of Major Douglas, of the 63rd regiment. A similar chain of posts was formed from the Derwent River along the River Dee to the Lakes, under Captain Wentworth, of the 63rd regiment. A third party, under Captain Donaldson, of the 57th regiment, was stationed in the rear to capture any blacks who might escape through the front line. Captain Moriarty, R.N., in charge of a party, was appointed to scour between the lines and to drive the natives forward or capture them. Mr. Gilbert Robertson and other friends of the blacks acted with this group of parties with the object of persuading such natives as they might meet to surrender quietly. For about three weeks the posts were advanced slowly, and frequent reports were circulated that the beaters had seen parties of blacks and that they were going in the desired direction. On the 25th Mr. Walpole reported that he had come on a camp of blacks and saw them lighting their fires and cooking as if nothing unusual was going on. He watched all night, and just before daybreak crept up slowly and found five blacks asleep. He seized one and held him after a desperate struggle, during which the black bit

Chapter II

him severely on the arm. A boy of about fifteen was captured by another settler who was with Mr. Walpole, and these two were handed over to the authorities and conveyed to the nearest police station to be kept until the remainder were captured. On the 26th Lieutenant Ovens saw a black with a firestick apparently trying to sneak through the lines. He ran forward and the black retreated into the bush. Several other blacks were turned back from other points in the line. These also carried firesticks. On the 27th the cordon had been drawn so close that the escape of the blacks within the line was considered impossible, but as no reports had been made for some time of any blacks having been seen, some discontent was manifested by the hunters. On the 30th an order was issued from the camp at Sorrell rivulet to close in, and hopes were expressed that no blacks would be permitted to escape in the final rush. The following day the lines closed in, and no blacks escaped. There was none there to escape. They had slipped through the lines as soon as they became aware that they were being hunted, and the man and boy caught by Mr. Walpole's party were the only blacks captured. A proclamation was published next day, in which the Governor thanked the settlers for their services, and regretted that their efforts had not been more successful. In a despatch sent to the Colonial Secretary, Governor Arthur said, "I regret to report that the measures which I had the honour to lay before you terminated without the capture of either of the native tribes,"[10] and that was all that was said about it officially. It has been estimated that the scheme cost the colony some £35,000, but no particulars were published, and therefore all estimates of cost are mere guesses.

From a humanitarian point of view it is to be regretted that it did not succeed, but the fact that it could be attempted proves how little was known of the blacks by the authorities. The fact that the blacks, who were said to be endeavouring to escape through the lines, held firesticks in their hands proves that they were then unaware of the intention of the whites, and they were probably outside the lines very shortly after it had been thus intimated to them that they were being hunted. But it is doubtful whether the race could have been preserved if they had been removed in large numbers from Van Diemen's Land. Mr. Gilbert Robertson and his successor, Mr. G. A. Robinson, succeeded in removing about 130 blacks to

[10] *Despatch dated June 27th, 1835.*

Flinders Island, where, although they were under the care of missionaries, they gradually died off. It was not recognised in those days that compelling the blacks to wear clothes induces skin diseases which soon prove fatal. The only way to preserve the Australian blacks is to leave them alone, and the knowledge of this fact came too late to save the Tasmanians.

Three

PIERCE THE CANNIBAL; A TERRIBLE JOURNEY; A SHOCKING CONFESSION; ESCAPES FROM "THE WESTERN HELL"; THE RUFFIAN JEFFERIES; BRADY THE BUSHRANGER; ESCAPES FROM MACQUARIE HARBOUR; STICKS UP THE TOWN OF SORELL; THE GOVERNOR'S PROCLAMATION; BRADY LAUGHS AT IT; THE FIGHT WITH COLONEL BALFOUR; BETRAYED BY A COMRADE; CAPTURED BY JOHN BATMAN; SYMPATHY AT HIS TRIAL; END OF THE EPOCH.

In a despatch to the Colonial Secretary in 1822, Lieutenant Governor Arthur said that bushranging had been "totally suppressed in Van Diemen's Land during the past three years," or since the breaking up of Howe's gang. But the happy conditions suggested by this report were not destined to last. There was still a number of runaways or bolters in the bush, but bushranging had by this time come to mean the commission of more serious crimes than petty larceny, and it was in this sense that the Governor made use of the term. We have, however, not yet arrived at the time when others, besides highwaymen, can be excluded. The next illustration is, perhaps, the most terrible of all the events connected with bushranging, although it concerns only the bushrangers themselves. On September 10th, 1822, Alexander Pierce, Bob Greenhill, Mathew Travers, Thomas Bodenham, Bill Cornelius or Kenelly, James Brown, John Mathers, and Alexander Dalton made their escape from the recently-founded penal station at Macquarie Harbour. According to Pierce's confession it appears that they "made it up for to take a boat" and proceed to Hobart Town. Greenhill being at work at the mines, "we had to call for him, he being a good navigator." Greenhill smashed up the miners' chests with an axe, and took all their provisions. "We then put out all the fires with buckets of water, so that the miners could not signal our escape; but, when we were a quarter of a mile out we saw fires all along the beach, so we could not have put them all out. We thought a boat would be despatched after us, so we went a little further and then landed. We knew it was no use trying to go by water, so we broke up the boat. We then proceeded to the side of the mountain right opposite the settlement. We were afraid that Dr. Spence or the Commandant would see us with the spy glass, the settlement being so plain to us. So we agreed to lie down until the sun went round. When the sun was behind the hill we went to the top, kindled a fire, and camped all night. Next morning we started again, and walked all day. Little Brown, who came back, and died in the hospital, was the worst walker of all. He was always behind, and kept cooeying. So we said we would leave him behind if he did not keep up. We kept off Gordon River for fear the soldiers might be after us. We travelled from daylight till dark night over very rough country for eight days. We were very weak for want of provisions. Our tinder got wet and we were very cold and hungry. Bill Cornelius said 'I'm so hungry I could eat a piece of a man.' The next morning there were four of us for a feast. Bob Greenhill said he had 'seen the like done before and it ate much like pork.' Mathers spoke out and said it would be murder; and perhaps then we could not eat it. 'I'll warrant you,' said Greenhill, 'I'll eat the first bit; but, you must all lend a hand, so that we'll all be equal in the crime.' We consulted about who should fall, and Greenhill said, 'Dalton, he volunteered to be a flogger. We will kill him.' We made a bit of a breakwind with boughs, and about three in the morning Dalton was asleep. Then Greenhill struck him on the head with an axe and he never spoke after. Greenhill called Travers, and he cut Dalton's throat to bleed him. Then we dragged him away a bit and cut him up. Travers and Greenhill put his heart and liver on the fire and ate them before they were right warm. The others refused to eat any that night, but the next morning it was cut up and divided and we all got our share. We started a little after sunrise. One man was appointed each day to walk ahead and make a road. He carried nothing but a tomahawk. The others carried the things. This morning Cornelius and Brown said they would go ahead together and carry the pots. We had not gone far when the leaders were missing. We went back to look for them, but could see no signs of them. We said, 'They will go back and hang us all,' but we thought they would not find the way, so we went on. We walked for four days through bad country, till we came to a big river. We thought it was the Gordon. We stopped a day and two nights looking for a place to cross. We felled trees, but the stream was too strong and carried them away. Travers and

Chapter III

Bodenham couldn't swim, but at last we got over and cut a pole thirty or forty feet long and reached it across, where there was a rock jutting out into the river, and pulled them across. We got up the hill with great difficulty, it was so steep. The ground was very barren on the other side, and covered with scrub. We were very weak and hungry. A consultation was held as to who should be the next victim. Bodenham did not know anything about it, and it was resolved to kill him. Me and Mathers went to gather wood, Travers saying, 'You'll hear it directly.' About two minutes after Mathers said, 'He's done; Greenhill hit him with the axe and Travers cut his throat.' Greenhill took Bodenham's shoes and put them on, for his own were very bad. We ate only the heart and liver that night. Next day we camped and dried the meat. We travelled on for three days, and saw many emus and kangaroos, but could not catch them. Mathers and me went away together, and Mathers said, 'Let us go on by ourselves. You see what kind of a cove Greenhill is. He'd kill his own father before he'd fast for a day.' We travelled on for two days more. We boiled a piece of the meat, and it made Mathers so sick that he began to vomit. Greenhill started up and hit him on the forehead with the axe. Although he was cut, he was still stronger than Greenhill. He called out, 'Pierce, will you see me murdered?' and rushed at Greenhill. He took the axe from him and threw it to me. We walked on till night, and then Travers and Greenhill collared Mathers and got him down. They gave him half an hour to pray. When the half-hour was up Mathers handed the prayer-book to me and Greenhill killed him. When crossing the second tier of mountains Travers got his foot stung by an insect and it swelled up. On the other side we got to a big river and camped for two nights. Me and Greenhill swam across and cut a long wattle, and pulled Travers over as he could not swim. Here the country got better and we travelled well for two days. Then Travers' foot got black, and he said he couldn't go any further. He asked us to leave him to die in peace. When we were a little way away, Greenhill said: 'Pierce, it's no use for to be detained any longer; let's serve him like the rest.' I replied, 'I'll have no hand in it.' When we went back Travers was lying on his back asleep. It was about two o'clock in the day. Greenhill lifted the axe and hit him on the head, and then cut his throat. We crossed the third tier of mountains and got into fine country, the grass being very long. Greenhill began to fret, and said he would never reach a post. I watched Greenhill for two nights and thought that he eyed me more than usual. He always carried the axe and kept it under his head when lying down. At length, just before day-break, Greenhill dozed off to sleep, and I snatched the axe and killed him with a blow. I took a thigh and one arm and travelled on four more days until the last was eaten. I then walked for two days with nothing to eat. I took off my belt meaning to hang myself, but took another turn and travelled on till I came to a fire with some pieces of kangaroo and opossum lying beside it. I ate as much as I could and carried the rest away. Some days later I came to a marsh. I saw a duck with ten young ones. I jumped into the water and the duck flew off, while the little ones dived. Two of them came up close to my legs and I caught one in each hand. Next day I saw a large mountain, and thought it was Table Mountain. Then I came to a big river and travelled down it for two days. I came on a flock of sheep belonging to Tom Triffet, at the falls, and caught a lamb. While I was eating it the shepherd came up and said he would tell. I threatened to shoot him. Then he got friendly and took me to the hut, and fed me for three days. Then he told me that the master was coming up and I'd have to go. I went to another hut and stayed three weeks. Then I fell in with Davis and Cheetham and they said I could join them. They had 126 newly-marked sheep and said they were going to select some more. I shepherded the mob while they were away. They continued robbing the stations until the soldiers came. The soldiers captured the gang except Bill Davis, who snatched up his gun and ran away, Corporal Kelly followed and called on him to stop. As he kept on Kelly fired and missed, when Davis turned round and said, 'I've got you now.' Kelly cried out 'Murder,' and the other soldiers ran forward and fired. Davis was wounded in the arm and gave in."

The confession may here be very much abridged, as the account he gives of his acts is very rambling. About 250 sheep, a gold watch, two silver watches, and a number of other articles were found at the camp. Several of the gang were hung and the others sentenced to long terms of penal servitude. Pierce denied having taken any active share in the robberies, and as he was merely found in charge of the stolen, or as he euphoniously calls them "the selected," sheep, he was sent back to Macquarie Harbour to be

Chapter III

dealt with as a bolter. On November 16th, 1823, Pierce again absconded from Macquarie Harbour in company with Thomas Cox. On the 21st, as the schooner Waterloo was sailing down the harbour, a man was observed standing on the shore and signalling with smoke from a fire. These signals had also been observed from the settlement, and a boat was despatched from there. The boat sent by Mr. Lucas from the schooner reached the place at the same time that the boat from the settlement arrived. On landing it was found that Alexander Pierce had made the fire, and he was immediately arrested by Lieutenant Cuthertson. Pierce said that he had killed Cox and eaten part of the body. He volunteered to show where the remainder was. On going to the place it was found that all the fleshy parts had been cut away, leaving the bones and viscera. It is impossible that Pierce could have committed this murder through want of food. He had only been away from the settlement for a few days, and some flour, a piece of pork, some bread, and a few fish, which Pierce and Cox had stolen from a party of hunters, were found at the camp. Before his trial Pierce said that he had been so horror-struck at the crime he had committed that, when he signalled, he did not know what he was about. After his conviction, however, he said that man's flesh was delicious; far better than fish or pork; and his craving for it had led him to induce Cox to abscond so that he might kill and eat him. He was wearing the clothes of the murdered man when he was captured. Although he made no secret of his cannibalism after his conviction, but boasted about it, he is believed to have very much toned down his share in the murders perpetrated during that terrible journey across the Western Tiers. Possibly Greenhill may have been the moving spirit in these atrocities, but we have the fact that Pierce was the sole survivor, and he gives but a very brief account of the last struggle between himself and Greenhill. We can conceive something of it. Pierce was the larger and stronger man, but Greenhill was active though small, and moreover he carried the axe. The two men probably pretended to be actuated by friendly feelings towards each other; each one endeavouring to put the other off his guard; but each knew that the other was only watching for an opportunity to slay him. For two days they walked side by side at a safe distance apart; each afraid to let the other get behind him, or near enough to spring upon him; and each was also afraid to allow the other to get out of sight because of the certainty that he would merely dog him through the scrub until an opportunity to strike occurred. For two nights they sat facing each other, a short distance apart, each afraid to go to sleep or to allow the other to go out of sight. If one rose up the other started to his feet immediately. Every slight movement of one caused the other to be on the alert. The tension must have been fearful. At length, when the second night was drawing to a close, Greenhill could bear up no longer. He dozed, and Pierce sprang on him at once. That is something like the tradition handed down among the "old hands," who knew nothing of Pierce's confession, but who had heard the tale from companions of the cannibal himself. There was a time when it was frequently told round the camp fire in rough, coarse language, plentifully intermingled with profanity, but the old hands have died out and it is heard no longer. Pierce, the cannibal, has been almost forgotten, and yet the story has its moral. It affords us an example of the terrible depths of degradation to which men can be reduced by brutal treatment, and it is not good that the story of Alexander Pierce should be forgotten as long as any remains of the old prison discipline which produced such men continues to exist, either in Australia or in any other civilised country.

The settlement at Macquarie Harbour, "the Western Hell," as the convicts called it, was opened as a penal station on January the 3rd, 1822, and from that time until its removal to Port Arthur in May, 1827, one hundred and twelve prisoners ran away. Of these, seventy-four are reported to have "perished in the woods." The remains of a number of men have been found at various times; but, as a rule, too late for identification, and therefore the official records do not assert positively that these men did perish, but only that, as nothing had been seen or heard of them for long periods, and remains supposed to be theirs had been found, it was reasonable to assume that they had perished. Two returned, as related by Pierce, namely Bill Cornelius or Kenelly and James Brown. On both these men portions of the murdered man Dalton were found, and Cornelius was punished as a bolter. Brown, however, was too ill, and was admitted to the hospital, where he died. Eight of the hundred and twelve runaways from Macquarie Harbour are reported to have reached Port Dalrymple or some other settlement, but in each case the official report bears the significant note, "wants confirmation." Five men were eaten as related. Three were picked up in a wretched condition on the beach by the steamer Waterloo, three others of the same gang being included among those who perished. Two were shot; two found dead. This leaves sixteen, and these are known to have reached the settled districts. Of these, Pierce was one. Every precaution was taken at Macquarie Harbour to prevent bolting. A line of posts was established across the neck of land between Pirates' Bay and Storm Bay, and fierce dogs were chained at these places to give notice when any one passed or approached. This use of dogs gave rise to a report in England that bloodhounds were used in Van Diemen's Land to track runaway convicts or bushrangers. This, however, was shown not to be true. The dogs were used as watch dogs and not as hunting or tracking dogs.[1]

Three other men who ran away from Macquarie Harbour were Jefferies, Hopkins, and Russell. Like Pierce and his mates they started to cross the Western Tiers. They lived fairly well for several days, Jefferies having a gun and ammunition which he had stolen, it is supposed, from a soldier, but at length their provisions failed and they could find no game. They therefore agreed to toss up to decide who should die to save the others. Russell lost and was immediately shot by Jefferies. The two men lived on the flesh for five days, when they carne to a sheep station. They immediately threw away about five pounds weight of Russell's flesh and killed two sheep. The shepherd ran forward at the sound of the shots, when Jefferies told him that if he interfered he would "soon be settled." They only wanted "a good feed." Jefferies and Hopkins appear to have adopted bushranging as a profession. Of Hopkins we hear little, but Jefferies established a character for brutality which has been rivalled by few and surpassed by none. When he bailed up Mr. Tibbs's house he ordered Mr. and Mrs. Tibbs and their stockman to go into the bushes with him. The stockman refused and was immediately shot. The other two then went across the cleared paddock towards the timbered country, Mrs. Tibbs carrying her baby and Jefferies walking behind. When near the edge of the timber Jefferies ordered Mrs. Tibbs to walk faster. The poor woman was weeping bitterly. She sobbed out that she was walking as fast as she could with the baby in her arms. Jefferies immediately snatched the baby from her and dashed its brains out against a sapling. Then he asked her "Can you go faster now?" Mr.

[1] *Report of the Select Committee of the House of Commons on Transportation, August, 1838.*

Tibbs turned round and rushed at the bushranger, who shot him, and then walked away, leaving Mrs. Tibbs with her dead and dying. At Georgetown Jefferies stuck up and robbed Mr. Baker and then compelled him to carry his knapsack. They had not, however, walked far along the read when Jefferies, who was behind, shot Mr. Baker without warning and for no apparent cause. Jefferies was captured by John Batman, a native of Parramatta, New South Wales, and afterwards one of the founders of the city of Melbourne, Victoria. Batman had taken several Australian aborigines to Van Diemen's Land and was engaged by the Government to track and capture bushrangers. He caught Hopkins and several others. A man named Broughton, who had been captured a short time before, was convicted of murder and cannibalism shortly before Jefferies and Hopkins were brought to trial.

It is quite a relief to turn from these monsters in human form to Mathew Brady, the central figure among the bushrangers of this epoch. Brady was a gentleman convict: that is, he was an educated man. He was transported to "Botany Bay" for forgery, the capital sentence having been commuted. In Sydney he soon "got into trouble" for insubordination and was retransported to Van Diemen's Land. He was one of a gang of fourteen who effected their escape from Macquarie Harbour. His companions in this enterprise were James Bryant, John Burns, James Crawford, James McCabe, Patrick Connolly, John Griffiths, George Lacey, Charles Rider, Jeremiah Ryan, John Thompson, Isaac Walker, and John Downes. They stole a whale boat on June 7th, 1824, and pulled round the coast until they came to a favourable place for landing, from whence they walked to the settled districts. Here they were joined by James Tierney, and for some two years they defied the authorities. In company with the "notorious Dunne," Brady stuck up Mr. Robert Hobart house near obart Town when the males of the family were away. In the evening Mr. Walter Bethune and Captain Bannister returned from the city on horseback, and Brady went out to meet them. He told the two gentlemen that they were prisoners and that resistance was useless. They were taken by surprise, and unarmed, and surrendered at once. Brady called one of his men to "take the gentlemen's horses to the stables and see that they were cared for," and then conducted the gentlemen into the parlour as if he were, the host and they merely visitors. The ladies of the family and the servants, except the cook, were already gathered there, and Brady ordered dinner and invited those present to take their seats at the table. He himself sat down, while his companions had food taken to them at the stations where he had placed them on guard. When the meal was over Brady made a collection of watches, rings, money, and other valuables, and then, after profusely thanking Mr. Bethune for his hospitable treatment and the kind reception he had given them, the whole gang mounted and rode away. On the following evening he rode into the little town of Sorell. The soldiers stationed there had been out kangarooing, and were cleaning their muskets. Taken completely by surprise, they were easily overpowered, and were locked up in the gaol, the prisoners being released. Mr. Long, the gaoler, contrived to make his escape, and ran to the residence of Dr. Garrett. Here he found Lieutenant Green, who was in command of the military stationed at the town. The doctor and the lieutenant walked together to the gaol, and the doctor was seized by Brady's orders and placed in a cell. Green refused to surrender, and was shot in the arm by one of the bushrangers and overcome. The bushrangers made a good haul from the houses in the town, and then left quietly. The only personal injury inflicted was the wound received by Lieutenant Green, who was forced to have his arm amputated.

On August 27th, 1824, Governor Arthur issued a proclamation offering rewards for the capture of Brady, McCabe, Dunne, Murphy, and other bushrangers, and calling upon all Crown servants and respectable citizens to aid the soldiers in their capture.

By way of reply, Brady and his gang paid a visit to Mr. Young's house at Lake River. It was late at night, but the bushrangers soon roused the inmates up. After having secured the men, Brady enquired whether there were any ladies inside, and on being told that there were he issued an order to them to get up and dress at once, and to go into any room they pleased, pledging his word that they should not be interfered with. While this was being done Brady sat on the verandah chatting with Mr. Young. Among other things he spoke of the Governor's proclamation, and asked whether Mr. Young had seen it. He laughed heartily at the idea of the soldiers capturing him. While the chief was thus employed the other members of the gang searched every room of the house, and collected everything they thought worth taking. The ladies had all gone into one room, and when the rest of the house had been searched they were requested to leave that room and go into another.

One day Brady walked alone into a house close to the town and "made a swag" of all that was valuable. He then called two of the convict servants and ordered them to take up the bundles and carry them for him into the bush. He was obeyed because it was believed that his gang was not far off, and the owner of the property saw it carried away without making an effort to preserve it. On another occasion Brady ordered an assigned servant to leave his master's house and join the band. The man refused. Brady walked to the sideboard, filled a glass with rum, and asked the man whether he could drink that? The man said he never took strong liquor. "Well, you will this time," exclaimed Brady, pointing his pistol at the servant's head. "Now choose." The man took the glass and swallowed the rum. Brady laughed heartily as he staggered away. However, the next morning, the unfortunate man was found lying in the bush some distance from the house. His dog was lying beside him licking his face. He was still drunk. His employer, who found him, tried to rouse him up, and after he had shaken and called for some minutes the man opened his eyes, called out "Water, for God's sake, water!" and rolled over dead. When Brady was informed some time after of the man's death, he said he was very sorry. He had made him drink the rum as a joke and without any thought or desire to injure him.

Brady stuck up the Duke of York Inn, and finding Captain Smith there, knocked him down, having mistaken him for Colonel Balfour. On discovering his mistake the bushranger apologised. He then threatened to shoot Captain White, but on Captain Smith saying that White had a wife and family Brady told the two officers to go away. He "hated soldiers" and did not know what he might do if they stayed.

Colonel Balfour, of the 49th regiment, with a strong party of soldiers, had been beating the bush for some time in hopes of capturing Brady and his gang. A report spread abroad that the gang intended to break open the Launceston gaol and torture and shoot Mr. Jefferies. The threat was treated with derision, but about 10 a.m. a man came into the town and said that the bushrangers had taken possession of Mr. Dry's place, just outside the

CHAPTER III

town. Colonel Balfour, with ten soldiers and some volunteers, started out and a fierce fight took place. Ultimately the bushrangers were driven off, but not before they had secured Mr. Dry's horses. The soldiers followed, and the bushrangers fired from behind the trees. Suddenly a report spread that the attack on Dry's place was a ruse to draw the soldiers from the town, and that a party of bushrangers under Bird and Dunne had gone to attack the gaol. Colonel Balfour sent half his force back to protect the town. The report was found to be partly true. The bushrangers had entered the town and had robbed Mr. Wedge's house, but had not gone to the gaol. At Dr. Priest's house some shots were exchanged, and the doctor was wounded in the knee, but the soldiers coming up at the time the bushrangers made off.

The following day the gang made an attack on the farms of the Messrs. Walker. They burned the wheat-stacks and barns belonging to Mr. Abraham Walker and also those of Mr. Commissary Walker. They had Mr. Dry's two carriage horses, which they had stolen the day before. Brady was wearing Colonel Balfour's cap, which had fallen off in the fight at Launceston. On the next day they burned down the house of Mr. Massey at South Esk, having sent him a letter a day or two before informing him of their intention.

Two of the gang called on Thomas Renton, and shouted for him to come out. On his doing so, they charged him with having attempted to betray them. Renton denied the charge. A wrangle took place, during which one of the bushrangers shot Renton dead. It is highly improbable that Brady was aware of this outrage. He boasted loudly on every available occasion that he never killed a man intentionally, and he is known to have quarrelled with members of his gang who were too ready with their firearms. Thus he drove McCabe out of the gang on account of his brutality, and McCabe was captured and hung shortly afterwards.

The gang held almost complete control over the roads, and resistance was very rarely offered when they ordered a man to "bail up."[2] One of the

[2] *The first supply of horned cattle for Australia was obtained from Capetown, South Africa, big-boned, slab-sided animals, with enormous horns. These animals are much more active than the fine-boned, heavy-bodied, short-horned, or other fine breeds, but they can never be properly tamed. It is always unsafe to milk one of these cows unless her head is fastened in "a bail," and her leg tied. When driving the cows into the bail it was the custom to order them to "bail up." It was also usual for bullock drivers when yoking their teams to call out "bail up" to the bullocks, although no bail was used for this purpose. The words were in constant use all over Australia, and were adopted by the early bushrangers in the sense of "stand."*

customs established by the gang was to order their witnesses to remain where they were for half an hour, and the order was rarely disobeyed. Any person who declined to promise to remain was simply tied to a tree and left for any chance passer-by to unloose. In by-roads, or in those cases where the prisoners were marched some distance off the high road into the bush before being plundered, being tied up was a very serious matter. Cases are known to have occurred in which men have remained bound to a tree until they have died of starvation. From this time forward tying up the victims was a common practice with bushrangers, though some like Brady accepted the promise of the victims to remain where they were left for a certain time to allow the bushrangers time to get away.

At length about the middle of 1825 a convict named Cowan or Cohen was permitted to escape from an iron gang with broken fetters on his legs. He was found by some of the gang and was taken to a friendly blacksmith who knocked his irons off for him. He joined the gang and more than once led them into conflicts with the soldiers out of which only the skill and bravery of Brady delivered them. Cowan was no doubt a clever man in his way; he completely hoodwinked Brady and his mates; he fought bravely in their skirmishes with the troops and was always eager in looting houses or other places attacked. He professed to rob "on principle." He is said to have murdered the bushrangers Murphy and Williams while they slept, but there is no proof of this. He betrayed the camp to Lieutenant Williams of the 40th regiment, who was out with a party of soldiers in search of bushrangers. A terrific fight took place in which several were killed on each side; some of the bushrangers were captured while others escaped, but the gang was broken up. Cowan is said to have received a free pardon, several hundreds of pounds reward, and a free passage home for his services.[3]

Brady made his escape in the bush and was followed by Batman and his black trackers. The bushranger had been wounded in the fight and could not travel fast. Batman came up to him in the mountains and called on him to surrender. "Are you an officer?" asked Brady, coolly cocking his gun. "I'm not a soldier," replied Batman, "I'm John Batman. If you

[3] *History of Van Diemen's Land in the Launceston Advertiser, 1840.*

CHAPTER III

raise that gun I'll shoot. There's no chance for you." "You're right," replied Brady, "my time's come. You're a brave man and I yield; but, I'd never give in to a soldier." Brady was taken to the nearest lock-up, where, as it happened, Jefferies, the cannibal, had been lodged some days before, and much to Brady's disgust the two men were conveyed to Hobart Town in the same cart. Brady, however, refused to sit on the same side of the cart as Jefferies, and kept as far from him as possible during the journey.[4]

The trial of Mathew Brady excited great interest. He and his gang had kept the country in a ferment for twenty-two months. Many of his companions had been shot or captured, but the leader had escaped. One of his mates, James Crawford, who had escaped with him from Macquarie Harbour, but who had been shot by the soldiers some time before the break up of the gang, was said to have been a lieutenant in the army.[5] Numerous stories were told to illustrate his reckless bravery, his skill in strategy, or some other trait of his character. On the day of his trial a number of ladies were in the court, and when the verdict of guilty was returned, and the judge put on the black cap, they showed their sympathy by weeping so loudly that the judge had to pause until order was restored, and sentence of death was pronounced amid signs of sorrow by all present.[6]

At the same sessions Jefferies, Hopkins, Bryant, Tilly, McKenny, Brown, Gregory, Hodgetts, and Perry were sentenced to death for bushranging, cattle, horse, and sheep stealing, and for murder. Some of these had been "in the bush" with Brady. The last of the batch was hung on April 29th, 1826, the prisoners being hung two or three at a time at intervals of a few days.

The remnant of the gang under the command of Dunne continued for a time to commit depredations. In one of their journeys they saw a tribe of blacks camped on the other side of the river. Dunne swam across and attacked them. He fought them for some time driving them back until he seized one of the women, when he turned back forcing her to accompany him across the river. He had this black girl with him when an attack was made on Mr. Thomson's house, but she escaped. On the following day two men were quietly driving in a cart along the road when the blacks attacked

---

[4] *Hobart Town Gazette, 1826.*
[5] *Launceston Advertiser, 1840.*
[6] *Hobart Town Gazette.*

and speared them, killing one and wounding the other. The blacks went on and burned the hut of Mr. Nicholas. They attacked Mr. Thomson's place, and speared a man named Scott. The woman who had been stolen by Dunne was present urging the blacks on when Scott was killed. The troops were sent out to drive the blacks back, and while so engaged came across the bushrangers and shot Dunne. One or two were captured and hung as related.

The Hobart Town Gazette, of the 29th of April, 1826, said that for some months the roads had been safe, and with the executions to take place that day, the colony might be congratulated on having at length stamped out the crime of bushranging. As a fact, it was only the close of the first epoch; the first act in the great bushranging tragedy which was to close so sensationally more than fifty years later.

Four

BUSHRANGING IN NEW SOUTH WALES; MANUFACTURING BUSHRANGERS; EMPLOYING BUSHRANGERS; THE FIRST BANK ROBBERY IN AUSTRALIA; MAJOR MUDIE AND HIS ASSIGNED SERVANTS; TERRIBLE HOLLOW; MURDER OF DR. WARDELL; THE STORY OF JACK THE RAMMER; HALL MAYNE AND OTHERS.

Bushranging of the more serious character with which we are concerned, appears to have begun in New South Wales in about 1822. In that year thirty-four bushrangers were hung in Sydney. The crimes for which these men were executed were generally of a petty description. Robberies of articles from the farms had become so prevalent that it was deemed expedient to adopt severe measures, but beyond removing so many evil-doers and preventing them from continuing their depredations, this severity of the judicial authorities does not appear to have had much effect. Bushranging not only continued, but the bushrangers became bolder and operated over a wider area. On March 16th, 1826, a desperate fight took place between a party of mounted troopers and seven bushrangers near Bathurst. The Blue Mountains had only been crossed thirteen years before, and the settlement was a very small one. The leader of the gang, Morris Connell, was shot dead by Corporal Brown, and the other bushrangers ran away into the bush.

The Sydney Monitor of September 22nd reports that a shepherd on Mr. H. Macarthur's run at Argyle ran away into the bush. He was captured, and taken to Goulburn to be tried for absconding. He complained that he had not received his proper allowance of rations, and had gone to seek for food. He was of course found guilty, and, when sentenced to be flogged, he sulkily said, "It's in the power of the likes of me to have revenge when lambing time comes round." For this threat he was sent to Liverpool for trial. He was convicted, and as a warning to other shepherds he was sentenced to receive five hundred lashes and to be transported to a penal settlement for life. The Monitor denounced this sentence as being "unduly harsh," and spoke of the heavy sentences given whenever the Rev.

Samuel Marsden, Principal Chaplain of New South Wales, took his seat on the Bench. The chaplains were at that time all ex officio magistrates, and the Rev. Samuel Marsden was said to be very active in the discharge of this portion of his duties. It is of Mr. Marsden that Mr. J. T. Bigge says "His sentences are not only more severe than those of other magistrates, but the general opinion of the colony is that his character, as displayed in the administrations of the penal law of New South Wales, is stamped with severity."[1] Judging from the sentence under notice, it does not appear that the reverend gentleman had become any more merciful since Commissioner Bigge compiled his report some years before. The Monitor charged him with "helping to manufacture bushrangers." In this connection I may mention that the opinion expressed by the "old hands" was that the clerical magistrates were generally far more cruel and brutal than the lay magistrates, and this opinion was crystallised into a cant phrase which was current among the old hands many years later. It was "The Lord have mercy on you, for his reverence will have none." This phrase was used on all occasions, whether it was appropriate or not to the subject under discussion or the circumstances of the time.

In the Windsor Court on February 10th, 1827, Mr. McCarthy was fined £14 10s., including costs, for having employed a returned bushranger instead of handing him over to the police for punishment. About the same time a bushranger was charged in Sydney with having bailed up a settler's house and compelled him to hand over some money and a bottle of wine. Taking the wine was an aggravation of the offence which was more than the worthy magistrate could stand. "What right," he demanded of the delinquent, "have you to drink wine? Do you not know, you rascal, that when you were convicted you forfeited all rights?"

"Yes, your honour," replied the culprit, "But, I didn't forfeit my appetite."

The robbery of the Bank of Australia does not properly, perhaps, come under the head of bushranging, but as the later bushrangers made bank robbery a feature of their depredations the record would not be complete if this, the first and in some respects the most remarkable of the bank robberies which have taken place in Australia, was omitted. The Bank of Australia was established in 1826 and was spoken of as the "new bank" to

---

[1] *Commission of Enquiry into the state of New South Wales, 1822.*

distinguish it from the older Bank of New South Wales. It was also sometimes called "the squatters' bank." Its president was Mr. John Macarthur, the first of the squatters. It was situated in George Street, Sydney. The strong room was constructed under ground, and had walls nine feet thick. Near the foundation of the bank was a large drain or shore, one of the openings of which was on an unoccupied plot of ground on the opposite side of the street to that in which the bank stood. The other end of the drain terminated on the shore of the harbour. Into this drain the thieves must have entered, and judging from the amount of work done and the quantity of the remains of provisions found afterwards they must have been at work for a week or more. As they were too deep underground for the strokes of their picks or hammers to be heard, they may have worked night and day. However that may be, they took the bricks out of the side of the drain facing the bank and then dug a tunnel until they reached the foundations of the bank. How they disposed of the earth dug out is not known, but it was surmised that they carried it away in bags. With great labour they dislodged a stone at the corner of the foundations, and then gradually enlarged the hole until there was sufficient room for a man to get through. Having effected an entrance in this way into the strong room, they found there forty boxes each containing £100 worth of British silver coins; a smaller box containing two thousand sovereigns; a box containing one thousand dollars, and another containing five hundred dollars. But the robbers took only the two boxes containing dollars and seven of the forty boxes containing British silver; leaving thirty-three boxes of silver and the box of sovereigns. They took also some bundles of bank notes, amounting to between ten and twelve thousand pounds worth. The forty boxes of silver weighed a ton, and it was believed that the thieves had been disturbed by some noise before they had time to remove so great a quantity. The locks on the boxes left in the vault were found to have been so rusted by damp as to be useless. No arrests were made and no traces of the robbers could be found. Notifications were issued denying that the loss, heavy as it was, would affect the stability of the bank, but it appears that it never recovered. In 1833 it was re-organised. In 1845 the Government passed a Lottery Bill to enable the bank to raise money, but to no purpose. The bank failed in 1848 and caused a great many other failures and much distress. The robbery was discovered on September 15th, 1828, and was reported in the Monitor of the 10th October.

There has been much speculation in Sydney from time to time as to what became of the money stolen, and it has been reported that the thieves buried it somewhere on the shores of Snail's, or White Bay, or some other place on the opposite side of the Harbour to Sydney, but although several persons have searched for the hidden treasure, it has not yet been found. There is a somewhat similar legend of buried treasure at North Sydney. The story is, that a sum of money variously stated at one thousand and two thousand guineas, sent out in early times from England to pay the troops, was stolen from the ship while she lay at her anchor and was buried either near Mosman's Bay or Great Sirius Cove. This also has been searched for at various times but hitherto without success. What truth there is in these legends it is now impossible to say.

John Poole, James Ryan, and James Riley, assigned servants of Mr. John Larnack, son-in-law of Major James Mudie, of Castle Forbes estate, Patrick's Plains, Hunter River district, took to the bush on November 4th, 1833. Three other assigned servants, Anthony Hitchcock, alias Hath, Samuel Parrott or Powell, and David Jones, were sent away the following morning, in charge of constable Samuel Cook, to Maitland, under sentence of twelve months, in a chain gang for insubordination About half-a-mile from Castle Forbes, Poole, Ryan, and Riley, and another man named John Perry, who had been in the bush for some time previously, met the constable and called on him to stand or they would shoot him. Cook only had a pistol with him and he snapped it at the robbers and then surrendered. The robbers took the pistol from him, led him some distance off the road and tied him to a tree. Parrott refused to go with the bushrangers and was tied to a tree near Cook. The robbers went back to Mr. Larnack's house which they reached about noon. They called upon Mrs. Larnack to stand, but she and one of the female servants jumped through a window and ran. Perry followed them and brought them back, threatening to blow Mrs. Larnack's brains out if she refused to do as she was told. The robbers took a double-barrelled gun which was always kept loaded in Mr. Lamack's room, and some guns and fowling pieces from the dining-room. Hitchcock brought the shearers from the shed, walking behind them and threatening to shoot any man who resisted. The robbers broke open the door of the store and put the shearers inside. They emptied a chest of tea into a bag, took bags of flour, sugar, and other provisions from the store, and fastened up the door leaving Perry on guard. They took a quantity of pork from the kitchen, a bucket of milk from the dairy, and the silver-plate and Other valuables from the house. Then, having made the shearers secure in the store and locked Mrs. Larnack and the female servants in the kitchen, they went away after having told Mrs. Larnack that they were sorry "the old ——," the Major, was not at home, as they wanted to settle him. One of them also expressed sorrow at the absence of Mr. Lamack, and added that when they could catch him they would "stick his head on the chimney for an ornament." As soon as the news of the robbery became known, a party was organised to follow the bushrangers. Mr. Robert Scott, mounted trooper Daniel Craddige, and a party of five came up with the robbers at Mr. Reid's station, Lamb's Valley. Some shots were exchanged and then Jones and Perry ran away. Constable Craddige followed them and called on them to stand, and they did so. He took them back and by that time Mr. Scott and the rest of the pursuing party had captured Hitchcock, Poole and Riley. The boy Ryan got away in the scrub but was discovered and caught next day. Alexander Flood, overseer to Messrs. Robert and Helenes Scott, with two constables, took charge of the prisoners, and conducted them safely to Maitland for trial. Mr. John Larnack then said that on the morning of the 5th of November before the attack was made on the house, he was at the sheep-wash. The prisoners came up and said to the washers, "Come out of the water, every one of you, or we'll blow your —— brains out." Lamack jumped into the water among the washers. Hitchcock fired at him shouting, "You'll never take me to court again, you ——." He called on the washers to get out of the way and let him shoot the ——. Poole also said, "I'll take care you never get another man flogged." Larnack scrambled out of the wash-pool on the opposite side to where the robbers were, and ran to the timber. He went on to Mr. Danger's farm, and remained there till next day. He was only ten yards distant when Hitchcock fired at him. Shots from the other bushrangers struck the water within twelve and eighteen inches of him, but none of them hit him. The robbers had four double-barrelled guns, two single-barrelled fowling pieces, a musket, and two pistols, when they were captured. When asked what they had to say in defence, Hitchcock called Ensign Zouch and other gentlemen to speak as to his character. It appears that until he was assigned to Major Mudie and Mr. Larnack, he had always been well behaved. The prisoners complained that they were given short rations, that the flour was mouldy and the meat bad, and that they were repeatedly flogged. Some of them had been flogged for refusing to work on Sunday. Hitchcock had been sentenced to work in an iron gang, for an offence of which he knew nothing. Whatever punishment was threatened by the master was sure to be inflicted by the Bench. Jones was acquitted of the capital offence, but was sent to Norfolk Island for life. The other five prisoners were sentenced to death, Hitchcock and Poole being hung at Maitland, and Ryan, Perry and Riley at Sydney. An enquiry was held as to the alleged ill-usage of their assigned servants, by Major Mudie and Mr. Larnack, and they were acquitted by Governor Bourke of the charges of tyranny and ill-treatment, but Major Mudie's name was removed from the Commission of the Peace. On his return to the station after the result of the enquiry had become known, he was greeted with cries of "No more fifties now, you bloody old tyrant."[2]

The beautiful valley of Burragorang is enclosed on all sides by precipitous mountains, there being only one practicable entrance, which, in early times, before a government road was cut into it for the convenience of the farmers who now occupy the valley, was easily blocked with a few saplings, so that sheep, cattle, or horses turned into the valley could not escape. Precisely how the entrance to this extensive enclosure was first found is not known. It is believed, however, that it was discovered by a party of bushrangers, who endeavoured to discover a road over the Blue Mountains, in order to reach a settlement of white men, which was popularly supposed to lie somewhere in that direction. Whether this supposed settlement was a Dutch or an English settlement does not appear, but as I have already said, there was a wide-spread belief that some of these settlements were at no very great distance from Sydney, and could be reached overland. The valley is situated only about fifty-four miles from Sydney, and for many years was an absolutely secure hiding-place for bushrangers and

[2] *Select Committee of the House of Commons on Transportation.—July, 1837. Major Mudie's evidence.*

Chapter IV

their plunder. Later on the valley came to be known, from the horrible tales told of the convicts who made use of it, as "Terrible Hollow," and under this name it is introduced by Rolf Boldrewood in his "Robbery under Arms." Among the old hands themselves it was known as "The Camp," "The Shelter," or "The Pound." Bark huts were erected in this valley by the bushrangers, and here they retired when hard pressed or when wounded. When the secret of the entrance was betrayed to the soldiers, who were out in search of a party of bushrangers, it was evident that the valley had been long in use by the bushrangers. Cattle and sheep were running wild there, numbers of broken shackles, handcuffs, and other relics were found, and, besides these, evidences that several murders had been committed there; but there are no records of these events, and only the recollections of the legends which have been handed down among the old hands remain to explain why this beautiful valley should have been called "Terrible Hollow." One of these legends may be told somewhat as follows: A settler was reported to have received a large sum of money. This became known to the bushrangers and they determined to rob him of it. They bailed up his place, tied his assigned servants, and searched everywhere for the money but could not find it. The settler declared that he had not received the money, but was not believed. He was threatened with death if he refused to disclose its hiding place. He persisted in his assertion that he had no money, and a consultation was held by the bushrangers to decide what should be done with him. Some were for shooting him there and then; but, this was so evidently not the way to extort money, if he had any, that it was resolved to take him to "the camp," and there force him to say where the money was hidden. When they got him there they tied him to a sapling, built a circle of bushwood round him at some distance away, set fire to it, and slowly roasted him to death. His screams are said to have been fearful, but no one heard them in that solitude except the fiends who were torturing him, and they had been rendered too callous, by treatment little less fiendish by the authorities, to heed his agonised cries. Whether this story is literally true or not it is impossible to say, but certainly charred remains of human bones were discovered in the valley when it was searched, though whether the bodies had been burned before or after death could not, of course, be determined.

It was to this valley that Will Underwood and his gang were said to retire when hard pressed or when they required a rest. Underwood operated on the roads about Campbelltown, Liverpool, Penrith, and Windsor, sometimes sticking-up people, and robbing farms on Liberty Plains and other places between Parramatta and Sydney. The gang was a large one and continued to operate in the more populous districts for some two years. Among the members of this gang were Johnny Donohoe, Webber, and Walmsley. Donohoe was shot by a trooper named Maggleton, near Raby, in September, 1830. Webber was shot a month later, and Walmsley was captured in another skirmish between the troopers and the bushrangers. Walmsley was sentenced to death, but was reprieved for disclosing the names of "fences," or receivers of stolen property, and his revelations caused quite a sensation, a number of hitherto highly respected persons being implicated. Underwood was shot in 1832, and shortly afterwards a "traitor" is said to have led a party of soldiers into Terrible Hollow. There was a fight between the troops and the bushrangers found there at the time, and several of the bushrangers were captured and the gang was broken up. The evil reputation which the valley had acquired, at first prevented settlement there, but when the bushrangers and their doings had been forgotten, the Government threw the valley open for selection, and a number of farms were taken up or purchased. More recently, a line has been surveyed for a railway to the valley, but this line has not yet been constructed. In the meantime, a good road has been opened into the valley through the one practicable entrance, and those who visit the valley now for the first time, can scarcely credit the horrible stories which have been told in connection with it.

One Sunday in September, 1834, Dr. Robert Wardell, a practising barrister in Sydney, and editor of The Australian, was riding across his park, which stretched from the Parramatta road, where the municipality of Petersham now stands, to Cook's river, to look after his herd of fallow deer, of which he was very proud. He jumped his horse over a log and found himself confronted by three armed men. Thinking they were poachers after his deer, he reined his horse in and cried, "What are you doing here, you rascals?" The reply was a shot from one of the guns, and the doctor fell. His horse galloped to the house and alarmed the family. Men were despatched in all directions to seek for the doctor, who it was believed had somehow been thrown and injured. The search was continued all day and night, but with no result. The next day his body was found covered over with boughs, apparently to prevent the dingoes from tearing it rather than to hide it. John Jenkins, Thomas Tattersdale and Emanuel Brace were arrested on suspicion and charged with the murder. Evidence was produced that they had been seen in the neighbourhood, and they were committed for trial. Brace was a lad who had only recently been sent to the colony, and before the day of trial he consented to turn King's evidence. From his testimony it appeared that Jenkins was the man who had fired the gun. But both he and Tattersdale were hung for the crime, and it was said that they had been guilty of various acts of bushranging. After the doctor's death the herd of fallow deer was neglected. Some were sold, and their descendants may still be seen in the park at Parramatta, and elsewhere. A large number, however, escaped, and the late Mr. Charles Hearn, for many years landlord of the Stag's Head Inn, on the Parramatta road, about five miles from the Sydney Town Hall, used to boast that he shot the last of Dr. Wardell's deer about where the Callan Park Lunatic Asylum now stands.

The story of Jack the Rammer illustrates the relationship which sometimes existed between the bushrangers and the assigned servants, and indicates the difficulties with which law-abiding citizens had to cope. Jack had been living by robbery in the Manaro district for some time. One day Mr. Charles Fisher Shepherd, the overseer of the Michelago sheep station, said something about all bushrangers being cowards. One of the assigned servants on the station, named Bull, replied, "They'll be here next." "If they come here," exclaimed Shepherd, "I'll give them a benefit." A few nights afterwards Shepherd was asleep in his hut. He was awakened by someone calling on him to come out. After a time he did so, and saw Jack the Rammer and a man named Boyd standing at the door. Jack cried out to him, "Keep your hands down." They stood for a second or two regarding him, and then Jack said, "What a benefit you're giving us." The two bushrangers then walked away. Although he felt convinced that Bull was in league with the bushrangers and had reported his speech to them and that he probably could not expect any assistance from the other assigned servants on the station, Shepherd loaded his gun with No. 4 shot, the largest he had, and started off after the bushrangers. It was about daybreak on a beautiful December morning in 1834, probably between three and four o'clock, and the air was soft and balmy as he made his way through the bush in the direction in which the bushrangers had gone. After travelling some distance he came on a sort of a camp, and saw Boyd through the trees. He kneeled down and fired, but missed. He was about to fire the other barrel when Bull stepped from behind a tree close by, and said "Don't shoot him, sir." "By G—, I will," exclaimed Shepherd. "If you fire, by G—, I'll shoot you," returned Bull. Before Shepherd could reply another bushranger named Keys fired at him from behind a tree, and wounded him. Shepherd rushed forward, and was about to close with Keys when Boyd ran up and fired, wounding Shepherd in the head. Keys seized him, but Shepherd shook himself free, and ran back to the station. He went to the house, roused up the owner, and said to him, "Good God, Catterall, I'm shot all to pieces, and you never help me." "What's the good?" returned Catterall. "What can I do?" Just then the bushrangers came up, and Catterall went in and shut the door. Shepherd rushed across to his own hut, and tried to shut himself in, but Boyd thrust the barrel of his gun in in time to prevent him. Shepherd seized the gun and tried to wrench it out of Boyd's hands, but Keys pushed the door open and struck Shepherd on the head. Shepherd fell, and Boyd put the muzzle of his gun close against his chest and pulled the trigger. The bushrangers, including Bull, then went away. It was some hours later when Shepherd regained consciousness, and yelled out as loud as he could. He continued calling for some minutes, and at last Catterall came out of the house and went to the hut. "Why," he said, as he looked at Shepherd, "I thought you were dead." He went away, but soon returned with several of the station hands, and had Shepherd carried into the house and put to bed. He sent for a doctor and the police. When the doctor arrived he took fourteen slugs and bullets out of various parts of Shepherd's body. He recovered, and lived for many years afterwards. In the meantime the police followed the bushrangers, and shot Boyd as he was trying to escape by swimming across the Snowy River. Keys and Bull were captured, and were subsequently hung. Jack the Rammer escaped for a time, but was shot a few months later.

CHAPTER IV

On September 24th, 1838, the bushrangers Hall and Mayne stuck up Mr. Joseph Roger's station at Currawang, near Yass. As they approached the kitchen door the men inside rushed out, and the bushrangers fired among them. A lad named Patrick Fitzpatrick was struck in the mouth, the bullet coming out at the crown of his head. Three of the men were wounded. The bushrangers appear to have regretted their act as soon as it was done. They made no attempt to get away, but assisted to carry the wounded men into the kitchen. Hall had been captured previously, but had succeeded in escaping from the Goulburn Gaol shortly before this attack on Mr. Roger's station. When sentenced to death, he said, "I've been all over the country in my time without taking the life of any one. I've been baited like a bull dog and I'm only sorry now that I didn't shoot every —— tyrant in New South Wales." When taken from the court-house to the gaol, he said to the crowd assembled there, "I've never had anything to say against the prisoners, but I've a grudge against every —— swell in the country. I'll go to the gallows and die as comfortably as a biddy and be glad of the chance." The trial took place on May 15th, 1839, and between then and the date fixed for the execution, Hall made a desperate attempt to escape from Darlinghurst Gaol. He failed and was hung on June 7th, with Michael Welsh, Donald Maynard, and his mate, Mayne.

In January, 1839, Mr. Bailley was returning to his home on the Parramatta Road, Sydney, when he was knocked down and beaten by three men near his own door. They took a roll of bank notes from his pocket, but a vehicle driving rapidly approached and frightened them so that they dropped the notes and ran. Mr. Bailley picked them up and went indoors.

Five

John Lynch; Murder of Kearns Landregan; Lynch's Trial and Sentence; His Terrible Confession; Murder of the Frazers, Father and Son; Murder and Cremation of the Mulligans; His Appeals to Almighty God.

John Lynch is usually regarded as the most callous and brutal of the bushrangers of New South Wales. He was transported from Cavan, Ireland, in October, 1831. For some months after his arrival in the colony he worked in a road gang in the neighbourhood of Sydney and was then assigned to Mr. Barton as a farm servant. Soon after his arrival at the farm, near Berrima, he appears to have exercised his ingenuity in stealing any articles which he could find and of selling them to any person who would buy them. In 1835 he was arrested and tried at Berrima on a charge of having stolen a saddle from his employer but was acquitted. He "bolted" into the bush and a few days afterwards a man named Thomas Smith, who had been witness in a case of highway robbery, was found dead in the scrub. Several bushrangers were arrested, Lynch being among them, on suspicion of having decoyed Smith from his hut and beaten his brains out with clubs as "a warning to traitors," as all those were called who gave evidence against bushrangers. Lynch was again acquitted, but two others were hung for the murder. During the following two or three years he was sentenced to twelve months' imprisonment for having harboured bushrangers, and on February 21st, 1841, he was arrested at "Mulligan's Farm" and charged with the murder of Kearns Landregan. On the 19th, Mr. Hugh Tinney was travelling to Sydney with his bullock dray and camped for the night at Ironstone Bridge. The next morning his driver walked along the creek bank to look for the bullocks. He noticed some freshly cut scrub piled up, and, being curious to know what it had been placed there for, he pulled some branches away and discovered the newly-murdered body of a man. On examining further, he found that the. head had been fearfully cut and battered. Round the neck was a piece of string, and to this were attached an Agnus Dei and a temperance medal.

Mr. Tinney sent Sturges, the bullock-driver, to Berrima to give information, and he returned with Chief Constable Noel, Mr. James Harper, the police magistrate, and Dr. McDonald. On search being made, signs of a camp were found not far away. A small fire had been lighted as if to boil a quart pot of tea, and some remains of hay were found, showing that a horse had been fed there. It was noticed that grey hairs were scattered about where the horse had rolled, and therefore it was evident that the horse was of that colour. During the day investigations were made by the police, and the following morning Chief Constable Chapman, Sergeant Freer, and Mr. John Chalker, landlord of the Woolpack Inn, Nattai, went to Mulligan's Farm, Wombat Brush, and identified John Dunleavy, as John Lynch, a prisoner illegally at large. When arrested on the charge of having murdered Kearns Landregan, Lynch exclaimed: "I am innocent, I leave it to God and man. I don't blame you, Chapman, but Chalker is interfering too much in what doesn't concern him."

A grey horse was found at the farm, and Chalker identified this as the horse which Lynch had been driving when he stopped at the Woolpack for dinner. Lynch had "shouted" for Landregan and the landlord before leaving, and Chalker gave him a bundle of hay for the horse. The hay was rye grass, similar to that found at the camp.

Lynch was tried at Berrima on March 21st, 1842, before the Chief Justice, Sir James Dowling. Mary Landregan said that the body found was that of her husband. The temperance medal had been given to him by Father Mathew before they left Ireland. They were both teetotallers, and had come to Australia as free immigrants. Her husband had about £40 when he left his last place and started to look for another job. She had not seen him since, but he had sent word, by Susan Beale, servant at Mr. Chalker's hotel, that he had engaged to put up fencing and do other work for Mr. Dunleavy for £15.

A leather belt on which the words "Jewish Harp" had been scratched, apparently with the point of a knife, was found at the farm, and was identified as the property of Kearns Landregan by his brother, who said that Kearns had promised to meet him at a public-house of that name in the neighbourhood, and had scratched the name on his belt so that he might remember it.

Further evidence showed that Lynch had purchased, at the Post Office Stores, Berrima, on the 10th February, a merino dress, some women's caps, a pair of child's shoes, and some tobacco. He was served by Mrs. Mary Higgins and gave her a £5 note in payment. From the store he went to Michael Doyle's, White Horse Hotel, and bought two gallons of rum, four gallons of wine, half a chest of tea, and a bag of sugar. He gave his name as John Dunleavy, Wombat, and said he had taken Mulligan's farm. He gave six £1 notes and a note of hand for £5 2s. in payment. The goods were placed in a cart drawn by a grey horse. Some of the Bank notes were identified as having been among those carried by Landregan.

There were a number of witnesses, and the case against the prisoner with regard to the murder of Landregan was very clear. It was also stated that Mr. and Mrs. Mulligan and their two children had disappeared suddenly, and that there was a suspicion that they had been murdered. Lynch produced a letter dated from Wollongong purporting to have been signed by Mulligan, but the writing was said to be unlike that of Mulligan. Several other mysterious disappearances were also spoken of. When asked what he had to say Lynch replied that he had met Landregan on the road, and Landregan asked him to carry his swag for him. Landregan said he had been gambling at McMahon's public-house, and must have left his money there. Lynch told him to get up and ride as far as he was going his way. When they reached Bolland's, Lynch asked Landregan to have a drink, but Landregan refused, saying that his wife was there, and that he did not want her to see him. When they got a little further along the road Landregan got down, took his swag, and walked away into the bush, and he had not seen him since. Lynch complained that he had been treated very unfairly. He had, he said, been sent out for seven years, but had been treated as a "lifer." He had served his time fairly, but he could not get his rights. When his father died in Ireland he had left him between £600 and £700. That was how he bought Mulligan's farm.

Lynch was found guilty, and, in passing sentence, his Honour said: "John Lynch, the trade in blood which has so long marked your career is

Chapter V

at last terminated, not by any sense of remorse, or the sating of any appetite for slaughter on your part, but by the energy of a few zealous spirits, roused into activity by the frightful picture of atrocity which the last tragic passage of your worthless life exhibits. It is now credibly believed, if not actually ascertained, that no less than nine other individuals have fallen by your hands. How many more have been violently ushered into another world remains undiscovered, save in the dark pages of your own memory. By your own confession it is admitted that as late as 1835 justice was invoked on your head for a frightful murder committed in this immediate neighbourhood. Your unlucky escape on that occasion has, it would seem, whetted your tigrine relish for human gore—but at length you have fallen into toils from which you cannot escape." His Honour quoted from the evidence at length, and said that the prisoner had "spared neither age nor youth in gratifying his sordid lust for gain." The disappearance of the Mulligans had not been accounted for, but there could be little doubt that the prisoner knew what their fate was. He concluded his exordium by saying that too much praise could not be bestowed, "not merely on the police, but upon the inhabitants of the neighbourhood, in unravelling the dark mystery of Landregan's death, and bringing his blood home to your door." He then pronounced sentence in the usual form.

The prisoner listened throughout with an unmoved countenance, and when the Judge had finished he said he hoped his Honour would order that the small amount due as wages to the Barnetts should be paid. They were innocent of any complicity in the offence with which he had been charged, and he hoped they would soon be released from gaol. There was also £1 due to a boy who had been working on the farm, and he hoped this would also be paid. Whatever had happened at the farm it had happened before either the Barnetts or the boy went there, and they knew nothing about it. For some days after his sentence John Lynch continued to assert that he was innocent, but finding, as is supposed, that there was no hope of a reprieve, he asked to see the Rev. Mr. Sumner on the day before that fixed for his execution, and in the presence of the police magistrates and the minister, made a very extraordinary confession, of which the following is a brief summary:—

He arrived in the colony in 1832 in the Dunvegan Castle. The entry on his indent was:— "False pretences; sentence, life." This was wrong. He had only been sentenced to seven years' penal servitude. He had applied to the authorities at the Hyde Park Barracks for his free papers, but had been kept waiting a fortnight without getting any satisfaction. So he returned to the Berrima district, where he had been assigned. He went to John Mulligan for advice and assistance. Mulligan had a lot of goods and valuables, which Lynch is supposed to have stolen and left at the farm. He wanted to sell them, but Mulligan refused to give a fair price for them. Lynch had made up his mind to live honestly, but this treatment disgusted him. He complained bitterly of the dishonesty of men who were in a good position and who "ought to have known better."

He left Mulligan's and went to T. B. Humphrey's farm at Oldbury and stole eight bullocks, which he had himself broken in, and started with them for Sydney, with the intention of selling them, so that he might "start honest." At Mount Razorback he fell in with a man named Ireland, who was in charge of a loaded team belonging to Mr. Thomas Cowper. The load was a valuable one, consisting of wheat, bacon, and other farm produce. Lynch thought it would pay him better to kill Ireland and take possession of the dray and its load than to sell Mr. Humphrey's bullocks. He therefore camped with Ireland that night, and "they were very friendly." In the morning a black boy who accompanied Ireland went to look for the bullocks, and Lynch followed and killed him. He returned to the camp without his absence having been noticed by Ireland, and watched for a chance. Ireland had no suspicion of foul play, and Lynch soon got near enough to him to strike him a blow with his tomahawk. Lynch hid the bodies in a cleft between two rocks, and piled stones over them.

He remained at the camp two days. On the second day two other teams arrived at the camp in charge of men named Lee and Lagge, and they all agreed to travel together for company. When near Liverpool Mr. Cowper rode up and was surprised to find a stranger in charge of his dray. Lynch told him a plausible story to the effect that Ireland had been taken suddenly ill, and had asked him to take the team on. The black boy had stayed behind to nurse Ireland, and they were to follow as soon as Ireland got well enough. Mr. Cowper believed him and was satisfied, and after making enquiries as to where Ireland was stopping, arranged with Lynch

Chapter V

where they should meet in Sydney. The time and place having been agreed on, Mr. Cowper rode away. Lee and Lagge were bound for Parramatta, and therefore, when they reached the junction of the Dog Trap Road with the Liverpool Road, they parted company with Lynch, who kept straight on. Left by himself, Lynch drove on night and day, reaching Sydney two days before the time appointed for him to meet Mr. Cowper. He hired a man who was half drunk to sell the loading, and as soon as he had received the money for the loading he started away with the team on the Illawarra Road.

When near George's river he met Chief Constable McAlister, of Campbelltown, and fearing that he might have been recognised, he turned off the road on to a cross track leading towards the Berrima road. He knew there would soon be a hue and cry after him and feared that McAlister would report having met him on the Illawarra road. He travelled on until he came back to Razorback, near where the murder had been committed. Here he met the Frazers, father and son, driving a horse team owned by Mr. Bawten. He kept company with them and they camped together at Bargo Brush. Another horse team with which there were two men and their wives also camped there. After their supper Lynch was lying under his dray when a mounted trooper rode up and asked Frazer some questions about a dray which had been stolen, and which belonged to Mr. Cowper. The Frazers were unable to give him any information and the trooper rode away without noticing Lynch, who was lying under the very dray he was enquiring about.

This narrow escape gave Lynch a terrible shock. He lay awake all night thinking of the danger he was running by keeping this dray. He "prayed to Almighty God to assist and enlighten" him in this emergency, and feeling much strengthened he resolved to kill the Frazers and take their dray. Having arrived at this decision he became calmer and thought out the details of his plan carefully. In the morning Lynch left the camp under the pretence that he was going to look for his bullocks, but in reality to drive them away. On his return he reported that he could not find them and spoke of the trouble bullocks gave by their wandering habits. He asked the Frazers to help him to pull his dray into the bush where he could leave it safely until he could return with another team of bullocks and take it home. There was nothing surprising in this, as bullocks frequently stray away home as soon as they are unyoked and will travel astonishing distances, even when hobbled, before morning. The Frazers, therefore, helped Lynch to drag the dray away from the road to where there was a clump of trees, and then yoked up their horses. Lynch put such few things as he had in the dray into Frazer's cart, and they all started together. That night they camped at Cordeaux Flat.

In the morning young Frazer started to find the horses, and Lynch accompanied him. Lynch wore a coat because, he said, it was rather cold. As a fact, it was to hide his tomahawk. When they were in the bush, out of sight of the camp, Lynch found "no difficulty in settling him." He struck one blow, and "the young fellow fell like a log of wood." Lynch returned to the camp leading one horse, and said the lad was looking for the other. This made Frazer very uneasy, not on account of his son, but because he had never known the horses to part company before, and feared that some one must have stolen the other horse. He "fidgeted about" until Lynch, who had been watching for an opportunity, got behind him and "struck him one blow and killed him dead." Lynch buried the two bodies a little way off the road and remained at the camp all day.

The next morning he drove through Berrima to Mulligan's farm. He told Mrs. Mulligan that the dray and horses belonged to a gentleman in Sydney. He asked her for the £30 which he said her husband owed him for the articles which he had left at the farm, and which he had obtained by burglary and highway robbery. Mrs. Mulligan assured him on oath that all she had in the house was £9. Lynch felt sure she was only "putting him off," and felt very much discouraged. He walked to Mr. Gray's, Black Horse Inn, about three miles down the road, and bought two bottles of rum. On his return he gave some to Mr. and Mrs. Mulligan, but "took very little" himself. He sat down on a log near the fence, and thought, "This man passed me by as if he didn't know me when I was in the iron gang in Berrima. He never offered me a shilling though he has made pounds out of me, and I risked my life to obtain it. It would be a judgment on him to take all he's got for the way he's treated a poor prisoner. Oh, Almighty God, assist me and direct me what to do." After praying he felt strengthened and returned to the hut. Mrs. Mulligan told him that she had dreamed that she had a baby and that he had taken it away and killed it. "It was all covered with blood and looked horrible." Lynch joked with her about this dream; but, at the same time, he "felt very frightened." He believed that "she could foretell things," and he knew that "she could toss balls and turn cups." He went away again and prayed to God to enlighten him, and at last made up his mind to "kill the lot." He returned to the hut and "talked pleasantly." Then he asked young Mulligan, who was about sixteen years of age, to "come and cut some wood" for the fire. The boy went with him, and as they walked along Lynch spoke to the lad of the fine property he would have "when the old man died;" adding, "Ah, Johnny, you don't know what's in store for you." They chopped up several sticks and then, when the boy was stooping, Lynch swung the axe round and "hit him on the head." He threw a few branches over the body, and then, picking up an armful of the wood they had cut walked back to the house.

Mrs. Mulligan asked him where her boy was, and Lynch replied that he'd "gone to the paddock with the horses." Mrs. Mulligan was very uneasy and asked Lynch to fire his gun off, as a signal to the boy to return. Lynch said this might bring the police round and he didn't want them "to see that dray." Mulligan also objected to the gun being fired. Both Mulligan and his wife were greatly excited. The old man paced up and down in front of the house, while the old woman, after asking Lynch several times what he had done with her boy, started up the path to look for him. Then said Lynch, "I knew it was time for something to be done." He got his tomahawk without being seen, walked up to the old man and cried "Look!" Mulligan turned round and looked up the road where Lynch pointed, Lynch struck him "one tap" and he "fell like a log." Lynch then followed Mrs. Mulligan, tripped her up and killed her.

He walked back to the hut and saw the daughter, a girl of fourteen, standing behind the table with a large butcher's knife in her hand. She was trembling violently. He said to her "Put down that knife." She hesitated to obey him, and he cried louder, "Put down that knife." Then she put it down. He walked round the table and took her hand. He said he did not wish to hurt her, but if he let her live she would "only put him away." He told her to "pray for her soul," as she had "only ten minutes to live." She sobbed bitterly and he tried to comfort her, talking very seriously, and telling her that life was full of trouble, and that she would be better dead. Then he took her into the inner room, and after having violated her, brought her out again and killed her with the tomahawk.

He dragged the four bodies together, heaped firewood over them and set fire to the heap. "I never seen nothing like it," he said. "They burned as if they was bags of fat." He threw the greater part of their clothing on to the fire and burned it. He stayed at the farm all next day, and then, when he had "made things right," he went to Sydney.

Here he inserted an advertisement in the Sydney Gazette to the effect that Mrs. Mulligan having left her home without his consent he would not be responsible for any debts she might contract. This was signed "John Mulligan." He returned to the farm and wrote letters to those people to whom he knew Mulligan owed money, informing them that he had sold the farm to John Dunleavy, who would pay their accounts. These letters he also signed "John Mulligan." Lynch then engaged Terence Barnett and his wife to work on the farm, and stayed there quietly for six months. The stories he told in the neighbourhood induced the belief that Mulligan had taken him in with regard to the farm, and that he had paid more for it than it was worth.

At the end of six months Lynch paid another visit to Sydney, and on his return journey met with Kearns Landregan, who said he was looking for work. Lynch engaged him to put up some fencing. Landregan agreed and got into the cart. Lynch drove on until they were passing Crisp's Inn. Here Landregan crouched down as if to hide himself. Lynch asked him what he did that for. Landregan replied that he had summoned Crisp for stealing a bundle of clothes from him and didn't want a row about it then. Lynch felt sorry that he had engaged Landregan and determined to get rid of him. He decided to camp at Ironstone Bridge and, when Landregan was sitting on a log near the camp fire, Lynch crept up behind him and struck him with the tomahawk. In his confession Lynch was very particular in pointing out that in all his previous murders he had not struck any one of his victims more than one blow with the tomahawk or axe. Landregan, however, was a big powerful man, who boasted that he had never met his match in wrestling, and Lynch felt afraid of him. He therefore departed from his rule and struck Landregan twice. He attributed his "ill-luck" in being caught and convicted to this breach of the rule he had laid down for himself.

Lynch seems to have persuaded himself that he was acting under Divine inspiration in committing his murders. He was very emphatic in his assertions that he never committed a murder, without having first prayed to Almighty God to assist and direct him, until he felt sufficiently strengthened to carry out his intentions. He appeared to believe that he was justified in taking life. Whatever may be thought of his confessions, however, there can be no doubt that the main facts were correct. After his death a search was made at the places where he said he had hidden or buried his victims, and in all cases the remains were found as he had stated they would be. With regard to the Mulligans, a large heap of ashes was searched and found to contain human remains. The confession only included his more serious crimes. He said nothing about the numerous robberies he had committed at various times, nor of his relations with other bushrangers, with whom it was known he was on cordials terms during at least a portion of his career.

Lynch was hanged at Berrima on April 22nd, 1842. At that time he was only twenty-nine years of age. He was about five feet three and a half inches in height, of fair complexion, with brown hair and hazel eyes. There was nothing ferocious in his appearance.

Six

Jackey Jackey, the Gentleman Bushranger; His Dispute with Paddy Curran; Some Legends About Him; Jackey Jackey Always Well-dressed and Mounted; His Capture at Bungendore; His Escape at Bargo Brush; Jackey Jackey Visits Sydney; His Capture by Miss Gray; Paddy Curran's Fight with the Police; Re-captured and Hung; John Wright Threatens to Make a Clean Sweep.

William Westwood, better known as Jackey Jackey, was the darling of the old hands. He was only an errand boy in England, and was transported for some small peccadillo when he was sixteen years of age. He landed in Sydney in 1837, and was assigned to Mr. Phillip Gidley King, at Gidley, in the Goulburn district. He stayed at the station for nearly three years, and then, in company with a notorious scoundrel named Paddy Curran, stuck up and robbed his employer's house. The partnership between Jackey Jackey and Curran, however, did not last very long. Curran disgusted Jackey Jackey by his brutality to women. In one of their mutual enterprises Curran criminally assaulted a woman, the wife of the farmer whose place they had stuck up. Jackey Jackey was furious. He declared that even if a man was a bushranger he might be a gentleman, and added that he would never see a woman insulted. He threatened to shoot Curran unless he left at once, and stripped him of his horse, arms and ammunition.

This story furnishes the key-note to Jackey Jackey's character. To the old hands he was always the gentleman bushranger. The stories told by them about the Jewboy and other bushrangers, and even about Mathew Brady, were generally coarse and sometimes brutal, but Jackey Jackey was always polite and well-behaved. More legends have collected round the name of Jackey Jackey than round that of any other of the bushrangers, and many of them are obviously variants of the stories told of the historical highwaymen of England. For instance, Jackey Jackey is said to have bailed up the carriage of the Commissary. When he discovered that the Commissary's wife was inside he dismounted, opened the door and, sweeping the ground with his cabbage tree hat, as he bowed low before her, he invited her to favour him with a step on the green. He rode incredible distances in incredibly short periods of time. He is represented as bailing up a man near Goulburn and telling him to note the time by his watch and then racing away and bailing up another man at Braidwood or some other place a hundred or a hundred and fifty miles away in a few hours and asking that person to note the time. Many of the popular stories told about him are so evidently apocryphal that little notice can be taken of them. But one thing is certain and that is that he was always well mounted. He scorned to steal an inferior horse and would travel miles to secure a racer. He stole racehorses from Mr. Murray, Mr. Julian, and many other gentlemen in the districts over which he ranged.

Although he appears to have been of humble origin he is credited with having been highly educated. This point was especially insisted upon by his eulogists among the old hands. By them he was always represented as being "able to hold his own," in conversation, with "the best of 'em." I remember one old fellow telling me that when Jackey Jackey met Governor Gipps (of which meeting, however, I can find no record) the governor and the bushranger had a long conversation and parted mutually pleased with each other. "You and me," said the old chap, "couldn't have understood what they said though it was all English; but, they talked grammar." What his precise meaning was I had no idea, but I have always thought that he intended to suggest that their conversation was all carried on in what he might have called "dictionary words;" that is, words not used by the uneducated. But everything said of Jackey Jackey redounds to his credit from the old hand point of view. He was emphatically "a good man." The meaning attached to words is purely conventional, and is therefore liable to vary with the conventionalities. The point of view of the convict being entirely different to that of the law-abiding citizen, the terms "good" and "bad" changed places in their vocabulary. Thus the clergy, the magistrates, the free men, were generally "bad men," while those who resisted authority, who fought against law and order, were "good men." Even the cannibal Pierce was a good man from their point of view, however strongly they might condemn his methods. But Jackey Jackey, although he continued the fight to the bitter end, and ended his life on the gallows when he was only twenty-six, never did anything mean or brutal or unworthy of a gentleman bushranger, until he was almost goaded to madness by the cruel discipline of Norfolk Island.

Paddy Curran was "out in the bush" several months before Jackey Jackey joined him, and he was not the only bushranger at work in the district. On December 31st, 1839, the station of the Rev. Mr. Cartwright was stuck up and robbed. On the same day a skirmish between the police and seven mounted bushrangers took place near Yass. One of the police horses was killed, and the police were compelled to retreat. On the same day, Mr. Heffeman's house, not far from Goulburn, was stuck up and robbed of £21 in money, a case of duelling pistols, a valuable mare, and other property. Mr. Israel Shepherd also lost a valuable horse, besides some money, and Mr. Charles Campbell was reported to have been shot dead. This is a heavy record for one day, and as the robberies took place so far distant from each other, there must have been at least three separate parties concerned in them. About the same time it was reported that Scotchy and Whitton were plundering the stations on the Lachlan River in all directions, and that Mr. Arthur Rankin had left his station and retired to Sydney in consequence of the insecurity in the country districts. The robberies continued all through the year 1840, and a great part of 1841.

On January 13th of the last-mentioned year a man ran into the township of Bungendore, and said that Jackey Jackey had followed and fired at him A few minutes' later Jackey Jackey himself, mounted on a splendid mare, which he had stolen from the Messrs. Macarthur, hove in sight on the plains. He was dressed in a fine suit of clothes which he had obtained when he stuck up and robbed the store at Boro a few days before. He stopped to speak to a man near Eccleton's. In the meantime Mr. Powell, the resident magistrate, and his brother, Mr. Frank Powell, promptly mounted and went towards the bushranger, and were joined by Richard Rutledge, who, however, had no arms. As they approached Jackey Jackey wheeled round and fired at them, but failed to hit any one. Mr. Balcombe and the Rev. Mr. McGrath drove up in a gig, and Mr. McGrath jumped down and presented his gun. Jackey Jackey seeing himself surrounded, surrendered. He explained that his mare had come a long journey and was unfit to travel, and that his musket was out of order and would not go off. He was conducted to the inn and placed in a room, two ticket-of-leave men being placed there to guard him. Jackey Jackey sat very quiet for some time. Then he jumped up suddenly, knocked down one of his guards, snatched his musket, jumped through the window, and ran across the plain. Frank Powell, who was close at hand, followed him, and with the assistance of Dr. Wilson's postman, recaptured him. Among other exploits previous to this capture Jackey Jackey had robbed the Queanbeyan, Tarago, and other mails, stuck up Mr. Julian, Mr. Edinburgh, and a number of other people on the roads at various times and places, stolen horses from all the principal owners and breeders in the district, fired at .the driver of the Bungendore mail, who escaped, and had robbed the Boro Creek store of clothing, money, provisions, and other articles, on the Tuesday before his capture. For several months Lieutenant Christie and the whole of the mounted police of the district had been trying to capture him, and he had more than once escaped only by the superior fleetness of his horses. As soon as possible after his capture he was handed over to Lieutenant Christie, who conducted him to Goulburn, where he was lodged in the lockup. The following day he was being taken to Bargo Brush, on the road to Sydney, when he made a desperate attempt to escape on foot, running for a mile before he was recaptured. He was then tied on the horse and the journey was resumed, but at night he broke out of the Bargo lock-up, taking with him the watch-house keeper's arms and ammunition. He soon procured a horse, and on the following day stuck up Mr. Francis Macarthur on the Goulburn Plains. He robbed Mr. Macarthur of his watch, money, and other valuables, and took one of his carriage horses because it was better than the animal he was riding.

In the meantime the other bushrangers in the district had not been idle. In September, 1840, a fight took place between the police and the bushrangers near Wellington. One of the bushrangers was shot dead, and a mounted trooper was wounded in the shoulder. A few days later another encounter occurred, when a constable was shot dead within two miles of the township.

On October 3rd, Mr. Robert Smith's station, Newria, was attacked by four armed bushrangers and plundered of everything worth carrying away. Mr. Aarons had recently arrived from Sydney, with the intention of opening a store in Wellington. The bushrangers threatened to throw him into the fire unless he handed over his money. They got upwards of £400 from him. Mr. McPhillamy rode up at the time, and was invited by one of the bushrangers to dismount and come in. He dismounted, and then, discovering the class of men he had to deal with, quickly jumped on his horse again and started. The bushrangers fired at him, and one of the bullets so severely injured his hand that it had to be amputated. A reward of £200 was offered for the capture of these men.

On Tuesday, May 18th, 1841, a gentleman, mounted on a spirited horse, pulled up at the tollbar on the Parramatta Road, Sydney, and asked the tollkeeper if he could oblige him with a pipe of tobacco. The tollkeeper gave him a piece, and the gentleman dismounted and filled his pipe. As he stood at the door of the tollhouse he remarked a firelock hanging over the mantelpiece, and asked what it was for. "For bushrangers," replied the toll man. "But there are none now. I've never seen it taken down since I've been here."

"Did you ever hear of Jackey Jackey?" enquired the gentleman. "Oh, yes," replied the toll man, "but he's a long way away. He never comes to Sydney. If he did he'd soon be caught." "Not at all," replied the gentleman laughing. "They don't know how to catch him, nor to keep him when they do catch him. I'm Jackey Jackey." He raised the lappels of his coat as he spoke and showed a brace of pistols stuck in his belt on each side. The tollman looked very much alarmed, but the bushranger said to him, "Don't be frightened, I am not going to hurt you, I've been in Sydney for three days and I'm going back to Manaro." He informed the tollman that he had taken a horse in Sydney, but that he was too old and stiff, so he had taken the liberty of exchanging him for the one he had with him at Grose's Farm. "Ain't you afraid of being took?" asked the tollman. Jackey laughed. "I'd like to see who'll stop me while I've these little bull-dogs about me," he said, tapping his pistols. He stood chatting while he smoked regardless of the fact that Grose's Farm, now the grounds of the Sydney University, was within a stone's-throw of the toll-bar. He offered the tollman some money and asked him to go to the public-house for some rum. The tollman replied, "I can't leave the bar."

Chapter VI

"All right," returned Jackey, "then I'll get it myself." He went away to Toogood's Inn and returned in a few minutes with half-a-pint of rum. He gave some to the tollkeeper and took a stiff glass himself. Then he shook hands with the tollman, mounted his horse, and rode on towards Parramatta.

On the 8th of July a great commotion was caused in George Street, Sydney, by a soldier arresting a well-dressed man and asserting that he recognised him as Jackey Jackey. A large number of people assembled and there were plenty of them quite ready to assist in the capture of the noted bushranger. On the prisoner being taken to the police court proof was soon forthcoming to show that he was a free man. He was discharged and the soldier was censured for being too officious. Since the visit of the bushranger in May had become known a constant look-out had been kept in case he should repeat his visit.

Jackey Jackey did not long maintain his freedom, however. He one day went into Gray's Black Horse Inn on the Berrima road, called for some refreshments, went into a sitting room, and threw himself on the sofa. He was served by Miss Gray, and while he was drinking she pounced on him and screamed. Her father and mother came to her assistance, but Jackey Jackey fought with so much determination that he would no doubt have got away. A carpenter named Waters was working near, however, and hearing the noise he rushed in and struck Jackey Jackey on the head with his shingling hammer. Knocked senseless, the noted bushranger was easily secured. It will be remembered that Gray's Black Horse Inn was about three miles from Mulligan's farm, and was the place where Lynch had bought the rum to treat Mr. and Mrs. Mulligan just before he murdered them. The capture of Jackey Jackey was effected for the purpose of securing the reward of £30 offered for him dead or alive. He was tried for the robbery of the Boro store, and was sentenced to penal servitude for life. He was first confined in Darlinghurst Gaol, Sydney, but being detected in an attempt to escape, he was transferred to Cockatoo Island at the mouth of the Parramatta River. While here he organised a band of twenty-five prisoners, and made a desperate attempt to escape. The gang overcame and tied a warder, and then jumped into the harbour with the intention of swimming to Balmain. The water police, however, were apprised of the mutiny and captured the whole gang. It has been asserted that no prisoner has escaped from Cockatoo Island. The distance from the island to the shore is not very great, certainly less than half-a-mile to the nearest point, but all who have tried to swim it have either been retaken by the police or eaten by sharks.

The gang was tried for this attempt at escape and were sentenced to be sent to Port Arthur, Van Diemen's Land. Being such a desperate lot of scoundrels they were chained down in the hold of the brig, in which they were forwarded, for safety; but, in spite of this precaution, they contrived to get loose and were only prevented from capturing the brig by the hatches being put on and battened down. They reached Port Arthur in an almost suffocated condition, and were nearly starved, as they had had no food for several days; the captain of the brig not daring to remove the hatches, either to let in air, or to pass food to the prisoners.

Jackey Jackey succeeded in escaping from Port Arthur and immediately resumed his bushranging career. He was captured, however, after a very short run and was sent to Glenorchy Probation Station for milder treatment. Probably this attempt at reformation came too late, but however this may have been, it had little beneficial effect. Jackey Jackey made his escape and again began bushranging. He was captured in a house in Hobart Town and was sentenced to death. The sentence, however, was commuted to penal servitude for life and he was sent to Norfolk Island, where we shall hear of him again later on.

In the meantime, Jackey Jackey's old mate, Paddy Curran, continued to rob as before. He went to Major Lockyer's station and entered the men's hut while they were having their Christmas dinner, in 1840. He had a pair of handcuffs hanging at his belt, and was therefore thought to be a constable out on the spree. He helped himself freely to the good things on the table, and behaved generally so as to induce the idea that he had been drinking. One of the men, however, said he did not believe that the visitor was "a drunken trap," and Curran immediately knocked him down with the butt of his gun. The man jumped up at once and rushed at Curran. There was a struggle for a time, and the man got Curran down. He was, however, too much exhausted to hold him, and Curran got up. The other men, who were all assigned servants on the estate, looked on and applauded the wrestlers, but not one of them made any motion to assist his mate, otherwise Curran might easily have been captured. After his wrestling match Curran walked out of the hut, mounted his horse, and rode away. On the following day Curran again went to the station, and found Mr. North, son-in-law to Major Lockyer, and another man in the store. He called on them to bail up, and both men held their hands up. Curran was about to enter the store-door when he was pinioned from behind. Mr. North and his store-keeper rushed forward, and after a severe struggle, during which the bushranger tried hard to get his gun free, he was captured and tied. The man who had pinioned him was the man with whom he had had the wrestling match the day before. Curran was taken to Goulburn for examination, and was remanded to Berrima to take his trial, "where," said the Port Phillip Herald, "it is to be hoped he will be more securely confined, and not allowed to escape, as he did before."

Paddy Curran and James Berry, another bushranger, were sent to Berrima for trial in charge of Constables McGuire and Wilsmore. They stopped at a hut on the road for a rest and food. After they had finished their meal Constable Wilsmore left the hut, and stayed away for some time. At length Constable McGuire went to the door of the hut to call him, and Berry and Curran, taking advantage of his action, immediately rushed upon him. They were handcuffed together, and this no doubt hampered their movements. McGuire fought hard. The bushrangers had seized the guns, and each held one. McGuire endeavoured to wrest the gun from Curran with one hand, while he held Berry's gun off with the other hand. He yelled for Wilsmore, but Wilsmore did not come. At length Berry got his gun loose and shot McGuire in the back of the head and in the shoulder. At this moment Constable Wilsmore returned, and seeing his mate dead and the prisoners in possession of the guns, ran away again. Curran and Berry beat McGuire about the head until he was dead, and a "fearful spectacle to look upon." Then they searched his body, and finding the key of the handcuffs, released themselves and made off. The two bushrangers continued their depredations for only a few months, however, as they were tracked down by the police and captured. Curran was tried on September 15th, 1841, for the murder of Mr. Fuller. He afterwards confessed to this murder. He said he was in company with two other bushrangers on the road near Bungendore when he heard two men quarrelling. Curran and his mates went towards the road and hid behind trees. Presently two men, riding on one horse, came in sight and appeared to be having a dispute about something. They were talking loud and swearing at each other. Curran stepped out from behind the tree and called on them to stop. Instead of doing so they wheeled the horse and began to gallop away. Curran fired and both men fell, while the horse bolted along the road and soon got out of sight. One of the men jumped up as soon as he fell and ran into the bush and they did not see him again. The other man was Mr. Fuller, and he was either dead or at the point of death. "I turned him over and took about £11 in money and a pocket knife out of his pockets," said the bushranger.

Curran was also tried for having committed a rape on Mary Wilsmore. He went to the hut occupied by Wilsmore on the 8th of February. It was near Bungendore. He ordered Mrs. Wilsmore to get him some tea. A bushranger, named White, was with him. Mrs. Wilsmore went outside to get some wood to make up the fire and Curran followed her, knocked her down, and dragged her away to some scrub where he committed the offence. He was found guilty of both crimes and was sentenced to be hung. There were another case of rape, several cases of murder, and numbers of robberies and burglaries charged against him, but none of these were heard.

James Berry was tried for the murder of Constable McGuire, and was sentenced to death.

At the same sessions John Wright, another bushranger, was also sentenced to death. The case against him was as follows:—On May 17th, 1840, Mrs. Margaret Foley, living at Long Swamp, about thirty miles from Bathurst, was going from her house into the detached kitchen at the rear, when three armed men appeared. She shouted "Here's the bushrangers" and ran into the kitchen. Mr. Cunningham, Mr. Foley's partner in the farm, came out of the house and fired both barrels of his gun at the intruders, but failed to hit any of them. The leader of the gang followed Mr. Cunningham, who went back into the house; and saying, "It'll be a long time before you and Steel (son of Captain Steel) hunt us again," shot him dead. Wright then went to the kitchen, pushed the door open, and asked where Foley was?

Chapter VI

On being informed that he had gone to Bathurst, he replied "I'm sorry for it. I'd 'a served him the same as Cunningham if I'd 'a caught him." He swung his gun about in such a reckless manner that one of the assigned servants in the kitchen requested him to be careful, adding "Recollect that there are women and children here." Wright told him to mind his "own —— business and be ——" to him. He continued to swear about Foley's absence and declared that he'd a "good mind to make a clean sweep." He became cooler afterwards, and having collected all the jewellery and other valuables, went away. In passing sentence the Chief Justice commented on the great number of robberies which had been committed by Wright and his gang and said there was no hope of mercy. Wright thanked his Honour and then coolly asked whether he might have a candle in his cell, as it was very dark.

Seven

The Jewboy Gang; "Come and Shoot the Bushrangers;" Constable Refuses to Leave His Work to Hunt Bushrangers; Saved by his Wife; Robberies in Maitland; Bushrangers in High Hats; The Bullock-driver Captures the Bushrangers; An Attempt to Reach the Dutch Settlements; Mr. E. D. Day Captures the Gang; Assigned Servants' Attempt at Bushranging; Some other Gangs.

One of the most notorious of the early bushrangers of Australia was Edward Davis, commonly known as The Jewboy. Next to Jackey Jackey and, perhaps, Mathew Brady, more yarns have been told about this hero of the roads than of any other bushranger in the pre-gold digging era. The Jewboy gang varied in numbers from time to time, no doubt from the cause already noted in the cases of Mike Howe and Mathew Brady. Numbers of runaways joined the gang for a time and then returned to what was called civilisation, gave themselves up as ordinary runaways, and "took their fifties like men." Others were shot or captured, and either hung or sent to a penal settlement to continue their careers there. The Jewboy appears to have commenced his depredations in 1839 in what were then the northern districts of the colony of New South Wales. His range extended from about Maitland to the New England ranges, he having taken possession of the Great Northern Road, but he was not particular and, therefore, either he or other members of his gang, or, perhaps, independent bushrangers who were only supposed to belong to the Jewboy gang, travelled considerable distances from the road. On January 12th, 1839, Mr. Biddington's servant was stuck up and robbed near Mr. Wightman's station on the Namoi River, some distance lower down than Tamworth. The servant sent an invitation to Mr. Wightman to "come and have a shot at the bushrangers." The Sydney Gazette, of April 3rd, said: "The country between Patrick's Plains and Maitland has lately been the scene of numerous outrages by bushrangers. A party of runaway convicts, armed and mounted, have been scouring the roads in all directions. In one week they robbed no less than seven teams on the Wollombi Road, taking away everything portable. They also went to Mr. Nicholas's house, and carried away a great quantity of property after destroying a great many articles which they did not want. Mr. Macdougall, late Chief Constable of Maitland, and a party of volunteers set out in pursuit. The Wollombi district constable is a tailor by trade, and he refused to leave his work to accompany the party on the plea that it would not pay him." This reminds us that the ordinary police force of the present day did not exist in Australia at that time. In the larger towns there were paid constables and watchmen who devoted their whole time to guarding the citizens and their property; but, in country districts, a tradesman was paid a small sum per annum for acting as constable. There was, however, a mounted patrol force which is frequently spoken of as a police force. The police duties in Sydney, Parramatta, and other large towns were discharged by soldiers.

Major Sutton was stopped on the road by armed men, and robbed on his return from attending the Maitland police sessions, and a hut belonging to Mr. Windeyer, near Stroud, was broken into and robbed. Robberies were very frequent about Maitland, and in the Upper Hunter and Patterson River districts, and these were all credited to the Jewboy gang, which was just coming into notoriety. On June 17th, 1839, four bushrangers were captured near Murrurundi. They had a black gin and a black boy with them. These were supposed to be part of the gang which had bailed up Lieutenant Caswell's place on the 9th. When challenged Lieutenant Caswell refused to stand. One of the bushrangers fired at him, but his wife rushed forward and struck up the barrel of the gun in time to save her husband's life. For doing this another of the gang knocked her down. They searched the place and took away about £400 worth in money, jewellery, and other property. They held the road for a day between Green Hills and Maitland, and robbed every person who passed. The next day they went to Mr. Simpeon's house in West Maitland. A man employed there, however, fired at them, and they made off. On the following day Mr. Michael Henderson was knocked down and robbed near Wallis' Creek, on the road between East and West Maitland. Mr. Cotham came up at the time and was seized, thrown down, and robbed. As soon as news of these robberies were reported, Lieutenant Christie with a party of mounted troopers started in pursuit. From Maitland the gang is supposed to have travelled northwards, and on the 15th Mr. Fleming received a note requesting him to get his horses up early on the following morning. Instead of complying with this insolent order, Mr. Fleming sounded his men, and believing that he could trust them distributed arms among them and stationed them at various advantageous points. When the bushrangers arrived the men fired at them. The robbers returned the fire and ran to a hut, which they took possession of. A regular siege ensued, and the black gin proved herself to be an expert in loading guns. She was said to have acted as guard over men bailed up, while the bushrangers were waiting to stop other travellers. The bushrangers were dressed as gentlemen in clothes which they had stolen from some of their victims. They were well armed and had plenty of money. One of them, Thomas Maguire, was said to be a free man.

During the year 1840, the Jewboy gang committed numberless depredations. They robbed Mr. Deake's house at Wollombi, stole his horses, took horses from several other stations, and held the roads at various places for a day at a time, and robbed every one who passed along. The head-quarters of the gang were at Doughboy Hollow in the Liverpool Ranges, and it was said that any man riding along the road near Murrurundi or Quirindi, or between these places and Tamworth, was "almost certain to lose his horse and whatever property he might have about him, and be compelled to walk to the next stage and perhaps further, while the bushrangers were riding his horse to death harrying other honest people."

One of the stories told of the Jewboy was that he "rounded up" the chief constable of the district with a party of constables and volunteers who had gone out to seek for him, and after having "yarded them like a mob of cattle," took their horses, arms, and whatever money they had, and rode away laughing. However, sometimes the tables were turned on the bushranger. A bullock driver named Budge was bailed up by two of the gang. Budge had a little boy with him, and one of the bushrangers stood over Budge and the child while the other was ransacking the dray. Budge kept his eye on the sentry and, noticing him look round to see how his mate was getting on, sprang on him, snatched the pistol from his hand, and knocked him down. Then he ordered the other bushranger to get off

Chapter VII

his dray, and made the two stand side by side. He kept them standing thus for about two hours in hopes that some travellers would pass along and assist him to take them to the nearest lock-up, but unfortunately no one came, and he was forced at length to let them go. He, however, kept their arms and saddles, and these he delivered to the Commissary on arriving at his destination. There were two guns and four pistols, all loaded. One of the saddles was owned by Mr. Joliffe and was returned to him. In connection with this it is said that Budge, when he was an assigned servant on Mr. Potter's Marquesas Estate, some years before, had bolted with six or seven other servants on the estate, and started to walk northward with "the hope of reaching the Dutch settlements at Timour."

They travelled for three days, during the last forty-eight hours of which they had nothing to eat. Budge therefore left them and returned towards the Hunter River. He was so exhausted, however, for want of food, that he fell. He was discovered by a stockman who was out rounding up the cattle on the station. Budge was taken into the station in a deplorable condition, and for a time was not expected to live. He recovered, however, and continued to work in the district. Of his companions nothing was heard for some years, but later, when the country northward was explored, remains were found which were believed to be theirs. From these it was conjectured that, after Budge left, one man had been killed "to save the lives of the others." There was evidence that one man had been cut up, it was supposed for food; but this had not saved the others. That at least is what the evidence pointed to. The remains had been so torn about by dingoes, crows, and hawks, as to make it impossible to identify them. The bodies were scattered over a wide area, some of them being several miles away from the others; and it is not even certain whether the whole number were ever found.

Nine men were arrested in Sydney and charged with being runaways. Eight of them proved that they were free men, and the constable who arrested them was censured. The case was cited as an instance of the arbitrary character of the Bushranging Act. One of the men, however, proved to be James Jackson, who had absconded from the estate of Mr. Turner, of Maitland. He was sent back to Maitland and convicted of bushranging, and was sent to penal servitude for life. He was said to have taken part in some of the robberies committed by the Jewboy gang, having been at large since the middle of 1840.

On Sunday, September 26th, some of the gang bailed up the mail man between Muswellbrook and Patrick's Plains, and are supposed to have taken some £250 from the letters. After this robbery one of them bolted from his mates, taking the greater part of the proceeds of their industry with him. He made his way to Sydney, where he passed himself off for a time as a free immigrant. He was arrested under the Bushrangers' Act and charged with being illegally at large. Then news of the mail robbery reached Sydney, and the fellow was sent to Muswellbrook, where he was identified by the mail man, and was sentenced to penal servitude.

The gang afterwards went to Scone and stuck up Mr. Danger's store and Mr. Chiver's Inn. The storeman in charge, named Graham, fired at the bushrangers and then ran for the soldiers, but one of the bushrangers followed him, and before he reached the watchhouse, shot him dead. They hastily made a bundle of such articles as took their fancy, and left the town. They went to Captain Pike's station and seized the overseer, taking him with them. When they were far enough in the bush they formed themselves into "a court," and tried him "for want of feeling." He was found guilty and sentenced to receive three dozen lashes, "which he got in good style."

On Sunday, December 21st, 1840, Captain Horsley, of Woodbury, Hexham, on the Hunter River, about five miles from Maitland, was awakened and alarmed by the violent barking of his dogs. He rose twice during the night and went out on to the verandah of the house, but could see nothing. As the noise continued he went out for the third time, when three men rushed at him. They threatened him with their guns and compelled him to surrender. They then took him back to his bedroom, made him get into bed, lie down, and cover his face with a pillow. The captain and Mrs. Horsley were told that if either of them moved, they would both be shot instantly. The robbers demanded the keys, and on being told where to find them they opened the drawers, cabinets, and cupboards, and made bundles of the clothes, jewellery, plate, and money. They collected all the

CHAPTER VII

guns and pistols in the house, using the most violent and profane language during their search for plunder. It is supposed that they were disturbed in their work, as they left very suddenly and dropped two gold rings and two silver candlesticks in their flight; as these articles were picked up the following day outside the house. On hearing of this outrage, Mr. Edward Denny Day headed the soldiers and followed the bushrangers. They received tidings of them at several points on the Great Northern Road, the robbers bailing up people as they went along. They crossed the Page River at Murrurundi and came up to the bushrangers near Doughboy Hollow. Here the Jewboy made a stand. The fight was a desperate one, but ultimately the bushrangers were beaten and Edward Davis (the Jewboy), John Everett, John Shea, Robert Chitty, James Bryant, and John Marshall were captured. Richard Glanvill, the remaining member of the gang, made his escape, but was so closely pursued that he was captured in the scrub on the following day, the 24th December. They were tried and convicted and were hung on March 16th, 1841.

In January, 1841, a public meeting was held in Maitland, and a vote of thanks was passed to Mr. E.D. Day for the service he had rendered the district in ridding it of such a desperate lot of villains as those which constituted the Jewboy gang. It was also resolved that a subscription should be taken up with the object of presenting Mr. Day with a handsome testimonial, and this was duly carried out. But the capture of the chief members of this formidable gang by no means rid the northern district of bushrangers, although no doubt it paved the way towards that desirable end. Of those who remained it is impossible to say whether they were members of this gang or not. Some of them had no doubt acted with it occasionally, while others may have always operated independently, though many of their depredations were credited to the gang by the public.

Charles Vaut and Henry Steele, two of the assigned servants of Mr. George Furber, worked in the field all day on Saturday, April 24th, 1841, and were seen in the kitchen at eight o'clock at night. On the following Sunday evening the Rev. John Hill Garvan, residing at Hull Hill, four miles from Maitland, was sitting at tea just after sunset, when two men came to the door, presented their guns at him, and said, "Don't stir." Mrs. Garvan was so much alarmed that she nearly fainted, and Mr. Garvan asked that she might be allowed to retire to the bedroom. "Sit still," cried the robber, "or I'll blow your brains out and put your wife on the fire." Mr. Garvan then struck the smaller man, Vaut, who was nearest to him, and he snapped his gun at the minister, but it missed fire. The bigger man then ordered Mrs. Garvan to "go and sit on the fire." "Oh, don't, pray don't, make me sit on the fire," cried the poor woman, but the ruffian took her by the shoulders and forced her back on to the burning logs. At that moment a dray was heard coming along the road, and Steele let her go. She was more frightened than hurt, but her stockings were scorched.

The two men then ran away, and went back to their beds at Mr. Furber's. They were arrested on the following day by Chief Constable George Wood, of Maitland. A pistol was found under the sheet of bark which served them for a bedstead. When brought up for trial, Judge Stephen (afterwards Sir Alfred Stephen), said the law of England on burglary made no provision for such an outrage as this, committed in a dwelling before nine o'clock. If they were convicted they could not be sentenced to more than fifteen years' imprisonment. The jury found them guilty, and they were sentenced to the term mentioned. They were afterwards charged with shooting at Mr. Garvan with intent to do grievous bodily harm, and were found guilty and sentenced to transportation to a penal settlement for life. It is more than probable that these men, and many others like them, assisted the bushrangers whenever an opportunity occurred—that is, when the bushrangers operated in the neighbourhood in which they were assigned servants, but without actually becoming members of the gang. There was a sort of freemasonry among the convicts which impelled them to assist each other in their war against society, and even in cases where it was obviously to their interests to stand by and assist their masters, their sympathies with the bushrangers and their hatred of all forms of authority impelled them irresistibly to take the opposite side, to their own individual detriment. But the principal gang having been broken up in this district, robberies of the kind described gradually ceased, and it was some years before this district was again disturbed as it had been. In other districts, however, the bushrangers were still active.

Mr. Michel, of Kurraducbidgee, was travelling to Port Phillip in February, 1840. He went into an inn near Yass for food and refreshment and

Chapter VII

found the place in the hands of the bushrangers. Fourteen men were bailed up and Michel was compelled to take his place in line against the wall of the bar. The bushrangers handed him a pannikin full of tea before they took his money. Knowing what was coming, he held the pannikin as if the tea was too hot to drink and, when the bushranger in charge was looking away, dropped his roll of bank notes into it. He stood very quietly and when the bushranger came to feel his pockets there were only a few shillings in them. They appeared to be quite satisfied and, on his saying that he had important business to attend to, he was allowed to go. He carried the pannikin out with him, took the money out and put it in his pocket without being observed, and threw the tea away. Then he mounted his horse, rode to the nearest police station and gave information. The police started for the hotel immediately, but the robbers had decamped and no information could be obtained as to the direction in which they had gone.

William Hutchinson, who had run away from the prisoners' barracks at Hyde Park, Sydney, in July, 1836, was captured on June 28th, 1840, at the corner of Market and George Streets. He had been out with a gang in the Windsor district and a reward of £25 had been offered for him.

In January, 1841, six armed men called at the lock-up at Appin, and asked Constable Laragy who was in charge to put them on the right road for Campbelltown. They said that they had come from Kings Falls. The constable stepped back for his gun, when one of them presented his gun at Laragy and told him not to be a fool. They didn't want to hurt him. As there was no one there to assist him he answered "All right," and showed them the road, which they probably knew as well as he did. It was said that this was merely a ruse de guerre to let the police know that they were out.

On Sunday, October 24th, 1841, a man entered the house of a soldier in Parramatta and offered to pay half-a-crown for a night's lodging. The offer was accepted, but the host afterwards, noticing that his lodger carried pistols, became suspicious and went to the police station. A constable accompanied him back and identified the lodger as a bushranger who "was wanted." It was said that he had stuck up Mr. Frazer and several other persons just outside the town. The constable made an attempt to seize him and was promptly knocked down. The bushranger ran towards the river, and was followed and caught after a severe struggle. He walked quietly back towards the lock-up until he came to the corner of Macquarie Street, when suddenly wrenching himself free from the two men who were holding his arms, he exclaimed "This is my road," and "bolted." He was seen two days later at Longbottom, about halfway between Parramatta and Sydney, and was chased, but succeeded in eluding capture in the scrub at Five Dock.

In February, 1842, the house of Mr. Gray in Balmain was stuck up. The bushrangers collected the watches, rings, money, and other valuables, and then compelled Mr. and Mrs. Gray and the servants to drink tumblers full of sherry wine to their success. They were very merry, and drank Mr. and Mrs. Gray's healths. When they departed they took a dozen and a half of sherry and a dozen of bottled ale with them to "have a spree in the bush."

In the same month Colonel and Mrs. Gwynne, Major Woore, and Mr. Thomas Woore, J.P. with the Chief Constable of Goulburn, and another constable, were driving near Bargo Brush. The party was in two carriages, with the constable on horseback. They were stopped by a gang which it was said had just robbed the Goulburn mail. The constable on horseback was the only one of the party who carried a gun, and he bolted as soon as the bushrangers appeared, dropping his musket. The robbers took £11 14s and the gun, but after holding a consultation among themselves they returned three one-pound notes and the fourteen shillings so that "the gentlemen might drink their healths." Then, wishing the party good-day, they departed.

In January, William Gunn and John South were arrested as runaways from the station at Port Macquarie. It was said that they had been at large for more than a year and had been with the Jewboy. They robbed the northern mail near Scone and were followed and captured. They wore black coats and vests, beaver hats and clean white shirts, "as if they had just come from an inn or a gentleman's residence."

In March, 1842, John Wilkinson alias Wilton escaped from Towrang stockade, carrying away with him Captain Christy's double-barrelled gun and a fowling piece. He was joined by another runaway named John Morgan, and on March 10th they took possession of the Sydney Road near Berrima and bailed up every person who passed. They plundered several drays and stopped the mail-man. They searched the mail bags, but finding

Chapter VII

no money in the letters, they permitted the mail-man to gather them up and proceed on his journey. They took seven pounds from a passenger named Jones, but on his saying that he would have no money to pay for his board and lodging while in Sydney, they returned him two pounds. At Red Bank they stole a horse belonging to Mr. Post to carry their plunder. Further along the road towards Sydney, they met a trooper and a constable, and told them that they were in pursuit of a woman who had run away from her husband and had taken his spring cart and horse and some of his property. They pretended that they expected to overtake her before she reached Liverpool. At Crisp's Inn they had some champagne. Not far from there, still going towards Sydney, they tried to bail up Dr. McDonald, but he rode away. They fired at him but failed to overtake him. They slept that night in the little church at Camden. The following day they rode straight into Sydney, put up at a first-class hotel and remained there for several days, "living like gentlemen."

By some means, however, they excited the suspicions of the police and became alarmed at the enquiries made about them. They therefore left suddenly and returned towards Berrima. Mr. Post, who had been away from home when his horse was stolen, started out in company with his son-in-law, Tom Howarth, to follow the bushrangers. The rapidity of their motions, however, threw him off the scent. On their return to the district in which he lived he met them and tried to bail them up, but the bushrangers rode away. The following day Chief-Constable Hildebrand, of Stone Quarry, and Tom Howarth saw the bushrangers near Bargo Brush. Hildebrand pretended to be drunk, and rolled about on his horse as if he was going to fall off, and Howarth started singing to heighten the illusion. This put the bushrangers off their guard and they allowed the constable to come close up. As soon as he was near enough Hildebrand pulled out his pistol and called upon them to surrender. They were taken by surprise and yielded at once. Howarth boasted that these two made eighteen bushrangers whom he had helped to capture. The two men were tried at Berrima, and sentenced to penal servitude for life. They narrowly escaped being charged with murder, as one of the bullock drivers stuck up on the 2 oth had been severely wounded for forcibly resisting the ransacking of his dray. He recovered, however.

Mr. Harrison, a jeweller and watchmaker, of Sydney, went to Glen Rock, and walked from thence to Berrima, to call on the settlers along the road to solicit orders. He was bailed up by three men, who threatened to cut his throat with a razor. They tied his handkerchief over his eyes, took three £1 notes, a cheque for £1, and an order for £10 from his pockets. They returned the order saying it was "no good to them." A bullock driver and another traveller were bailed up, and then the bushrangers went into the road to stop a gig, and Mr. Harrison bolted into the bush.

Mr. Campbell was travelling along the Dog Trap Road when he was bailed up by three men and robbed. He returned to Parramatta and gave information to Chief Constable Ryan, who dressed in private clothes and with another constable similarly disguised started to drive along the road in Mr. Campbell's gig, Between Anlezack's Inn and Liverpool three men came out from behind trees and called on the constables to stand. Ryan immediately pulled up, and presenting his pistol at the men called on them to surrender in the Queen's name. The other constable jumped out of the gig and also presented his pistol, and the robbers capitulated. They were identified as John McCann and William Lynch, escapees from Norfolk Island, who had landed from a whale boat some months previously, and James O'Donnell, alias William McDonald, who had absconded from the Hyde Park Barracks a short time before, in September, 1842. A considerable amount of property was recovered when their camp was searched.

Mr. F. E. Bigge, a settler in the northern district, started to take a drove of horses across the country to Moreton Bay. He was assisted by Alexander McDonald and two assigned servants. When between Schofield's and Brennan's stations, near Tamworth, they were called upon to halt by three armed men, known as Wilson, Long Tom or Coxen's Tom, and Long Ned. The order was obeyed, and then Mr. Bigge was ordered to strip. He refused, and one of the bushrangers called to another of them to knock him down with the butt of his gun; but, observing that Mr. Bigge was trying to get his pistol out of his belt, he fired. The first shot was said to have been fired by Long Tom, but Wilson fired immediately afterwards and wounded Bigge in the shoulder. McDonald, having no arms, rode away to Schofield's for assistance. In the meantime Bigge succeeded in getting his pistol out of his belt and fired at the nearest bushranger, who fired in re-

Chapter VII

turn, the other two also firing. Bigge drew his second pistol and fired, and the bushrangers having expended their ammunition ran away. Bigge then mounted and rode to Brennan's. Finding no one there he went on, and his horse bolted and threw him. He then walked to Nillenga, where he found Dr. Jay, who dressed his wounds, which wefe not considered dangerous. In the meantime, McDonald, when he started to go to Schofield's, met Mr. Kayes and another gentleman, but they refused to go with him to assist Bigge. McDonald went on to the station, but not being able to obtain any arms or assistance there, he rode back again, and found the bushrangers' horses and some baggage, which they had left behind when Mr. Bigge put them to flight. McDonald collected the horses, which had been scattered, and drove them to Tamworth, where Mr. Allman soon organised a large party to go in pursuit of the bushrangers. Wilson had been captured by Mr. Robertson only a few weeks before and had been sent to the chain gang at Maitland, from whence he had effected his escape. They were all three caught and were sent to penal servitude.

Eight

Bushranging in South Australia; The Robbers Captured in Melbourne; A Remarkable Raid in Port Phillip; Going Out for a Fight with Bushrangers; A Bloody Battle; Cashan and McIntyre; The Fight with the Mail Passengers; Cashan Escapes from the Lock-up; Is Re-captured; McIntyre Caught at Gammon Plains.

Three bushrangers named Wilson, Green, and another, robbed the settlers in the vicinity of Lyndoch Valley, South Australia, and extorted heavy contributions from their victims in the latter part of the year 1839 and the beginning of 1840. These robberies had been going on for some months before news of them reached Adelaide. The colony had been only founded a little more than three years before, and communication was difficult and very irregular. There were no roads and the police provisions were not yet of a character to enable the authorities to cope effectually with such an outbreak as this.

The robbers called at Mr. Read's station and knocked at the door of the house. The woman opened the door and was immediately knocked down by one of the robbers without any notice being given or question asked. Another robber fired his musket at her at so close range that the wadding of the gun bruised her cheek, but the slugs with which it was loaded did not injure her. Immediately on hearing of this outrage, Mr. Inman, superintendent of the police, left Adelaide with a party of mounted troopers, and as he proceeded on his way, news of other robberies were spread about. The movements of the police, however, appear to have been known to the bushrangers, as they were fired at when passing through some scrub. Not knowing how many men there might be in the gang, Mr. Inman intrenched himself, and sent to Adelaide for more men, and in a few days parties of mounted police arrived from Gawler and Mount Barker. The district was thoroughly searched, but without success. About the middle of February, three men on horseback arrived in Melbourne, Port Phillip. Their principal place of resort was the Royal Highlander Inn, in Queen

Street, where they spent money freely and drank heavily. One of the men was recognised by the police as a convict from Van Diemen's Land, free by service. He was arrested on suspicion of having stolen the horse he rode, from Mr. Cox, but as Mr. Cox's superintendent could not swear to the animal, although he bore the station brand, the man was discharged and immediately left Melbourne. On Sunday, February 23rd, Wilson was arrested for drunkenness and rowdyism, and was fined 5 shillings next morning at the police court. While there he was seen and recognised by two South Australian policemen who had been to Sydney with some prisoners, and were on their way home. Wilson and Green were both arrested that evening and charged with the robbery at Mr. Read's station, South Australia. They were detained until warrants could be obtained from Adelaide, when they were sent there and convicted. The robbers had travelled from South Australia to Melbourne, via Portland Bay, and had probably stolen the horses and perhaps some other property on the road. The third man, whose name is not given, was searched for, but was not found, and it was supposed he had crossed the Murray into New South Wales.

What is generally said to be the first highway robbery in the Port Phillip district took place in April, 1842. A gang, composed of John Ellis, alias Yanky Jack, Jack Williams, Young Fogarty, and a "Van Demonian" named Jepps, bailed up Mr. Darling and a friend as they were riding to an out-station on the Dandenong run to brand cattle. The robbers took £2 and a silver watch from Mr. Darling, and one shilling and sixpence from his friend. Mr. Darling was riding a thorough-bred horse, and Jack Williams remarked that he was a fine beast, and ordered Mr. Darling to show off his paces. This was a blunder on the part of the bushranger, who should have tried the horse himself, and Mr. Darling was not slow in taking advantage of it. He did not wish to lose his horse, and therefore jerked the bit, rolled about in the saddle, and pretended that he had as much as he could do to keep his seat while the horse was cantering. Williams watched as the horse went past him a couple of times, and then said, "That'll do. He seems to be a —— rough 'un." He contented himself with the horse the friend was riding, giving him his knocked-up horse in exchange. The bushrangers handed Mr. Darling his watch, asked for it again, and returned it a second time after passing it round for each to look at. Then as the gang was going away Williams turned back, asked Mr. Darling to let him see what the time was, and when that gentleman again showed him the watch he took it and put it into his pocket. He then produced a bottle of rum, and after having taken a swig himself passed it to Mr. Darling and his friend with the remark that "a drop of grog was good on a cold day." Then he took five shillings from his pocket, gave this also to Darling to "drink their healths with at the next public-house," said "good day," and rode on after his mates. The gang went along the main road up the Plenty River robbing the stations on either side of the road as they came to them. They stuck up Messrs. Serjeantson, Peet, Bond, Langor, Marsh, Fleming, Rider, Bear, and Captain Harrison, collecting a goodly assortment of watches and chains, mostly silver, and some money. It was after dark when they finished at Mr. Bear's house, and they camped by the creek within sight of the house for the night.

Early next morning the gang took to the road again and robbed Messrs. Sherwin, Roland, and Wills. At about nine o'clock they reached Mr. Campbell Hunter's station as the family was sitting down to a breakfast of roast duck, kippered herrings, and coffee. Williams walked into the room pistol in hand and cried, "Put up your hands." He was immediately obeyed. Then looking round he said "Gentlemen, you must make room for your betters." Those present were Messrs. Campbell Hunter, Alexander Hunter, Streatham, Rumbold, Boswell, and Dr. Grimes. They were made to stand up against the wall while the roast ducks and other good things were removed to a slab hut used as a store room. The bushrangers had, however, only just begun their breakfast when a large party of armed men galloped up.

News of the robberies of the previous day had reached Melbourne in the evening, and Messrs. P. Snodgrass and H. Fowler, of the Melbourne Club, had resolved to "go out for a hunt." They got their arms and horses, and started, and were joined by several other gentlemen, among whom were Mr. Sergeantson, and others who had been robbed, to the number of about thirty. The bushrangers hastily made the Messrs. Hunter and their other prisoners promise not to take part in the coming fight, and then took up positions behind the fence. Undeterred by this show of resistance, Mr.

Chapter VIII

Gourlay jumped his horse over the fence, alighting close to Jack Williams, so close, in fact, that the flash from the bushranger's pistol, which was fired immediately, singed his whiskers and burned his cheek. The bushranger dashed his pistol down on the ground with an oath, and drew another, but Mr. Snodgrass, leaning over the fence, shot him in the head before he could make use of it. Thinking he had killed his man, Snodgrass turned to Yanky Bill, when Williams jumped up and fired point blank at Gourlay, who shouted, "Tell my friends I died game," and fell. Mr. Chamberlain shot Williams through the head and killed him. Much to the surprise of those near, Mr. Gourlay jumped up again almost as quickly as he had fallen, and it was soon discovered that the pistol bullet had smashed his powder flask and glanced off, inflicting only a severe bruise.

On the death of their leader the bushrangers rushed to the hut, and took shelter there, pointing their pistols through the openings between the slabs, and a fierce fusilade took place, during which Mr. Fowler was severely wounded. Then there was a pause. It was believed that the ammunition of the robbers had been expended, and a horse dealer residing in the neighbourhood, named John Ewart, but usually known as Hoppy Jack, volunteered to go in and speak to the bushrangers. At first this was objected to as being too dangerous, but Hoppy Jack insisted, and said it would be "all right." He advanced towards the hut waving a white handkerchief, and after a few words at the door was admitted. The result of this embassy was that the bushrangers agreed to surrender provided that their captors would sign a petition to the judge to deal leniently with them. This was readily agreed to, and the men came out and gave themselves up just as a party of mounted police appeared on the scene, and the prisoners were handed over to them.

This raid was principally remarkable for the boldness and rapidity with which it was executed. The bushrangers travelled directly from one station to the next, taking the shortest route, which was generally along the main road. The robberies were effected in very short time at each station, the bushrangers contenting themselves with money, watches, rings, and other property carried on the person. There was no time wasted in breaking open boxes or drawers, and there was no necessity to spare their horses, a knocked-up horse could be exchanged for a fresh one almost whenever the robbers pleased. Mr. Gourlay was little the worse for his bruises and bums, although the powder marks on his face remained; but Mr. Fowler died a few days after the fight. The prisoners were tried and convicted, and in spite of the recommendation to mercy duly signed by their captors and forwarded to the judge, were sentenced to death for the murder of Mr. Fowler. Jepps confessed that it was he who had fired the fatal shot, but he also said that he had refused to join in an attempt to murder Judge Willis, the resident judge in Port Phillip. They were all hung in Melbourne, in May, 1842.

During the following two years there was little bushranging in any part of New South Wales, but in 1844 McIntyre and Cashan, alias Nowlan, held the roads between Hartley, Bathurst, and Mudgee for several days, robbing all who passed. On December 2, 1845, they stopped the mail at Bowenfels, on the main Sydney road at the foot of the Blue Mountains, on the western side. They called on the passengers to hand over their money and valuables, but two of them resisted and drew their pistols. A fight took place, and the bushrangers were worsted, Cashan being captured, while McIntyre ran away into the bush. Cashan was taken to Bathurst, tried, convicted, and sentenced to be transported for life. He was being taken to Sydney, in April, to be sent to Cockatoo Island, when the escort stopped at Weatherboard Hut for the night, Cashan being lodged in the lockup. He broke out during the night, and could nowhere be found. He travelled to Gundagai, where he stuck up Mr. Nicholson's station, taking clothes, provisions, horse, saddle, and bridle. Mr. Andrews, who was in charge of the station, and who was absent when Cashan called, on hearing of the robbery followed the bushranger. He rode to Charles Simpson's station, but was told by Messrs. Edwin and Alfred Tompson, who resided there, that no bushranger had been seen. While they were talking a man on horseback came in sight, and Andrews recognised him as the robber from the description that had been given of him and the horse he was riding. Andrews retreated into the house out of sight, and Cashan rode up, dismounted, and asked for refreshments, but he was immediately seized by the Tompsons and told that he was a prisoner. He asked, "How dared they insult a gentleman in that manner," and struggled hard to escape; but, finding that this was no use, he became quiet, and said he was ready to go wherever they wished him to. They took him towards the house, which was only a few steps distant, when suddenly he broke away with a laugh, ran down the bank, and plunged into the Murrumbidgee River. The river was in flood at the time, and was therefore twice its ordinary width, and running strongly. Cashan, encumbered with a great coat, and perhaps with other stolen property, could make no headway against the current. He sank at once, rose some distance lower down, and succeeded in grasping the pendulous branches of a swamp oak (Casuarina) hanging over the water. After a severe struggle he contrived to haul himself out of the water, and took a seat in the fork of the tree. He was still on the same side of the river as Simpson's station, and at no great distance from the bank, although the flood waters prevented Alfred and Edwin Tompson from getting close to him. However, Edwin Tompson covered him with his pistol, and threatened to shoot him if he moved. They talked for some time, and the bushranger, seeing no chance of escape, agreed to give himself up. He dropped into the water, swam to the bank, and walked quietly to the house, where he was tied and made secure for the night. The next day he was taken to Yass by the Tompsons and Andrews, and in spite of his frequent attempts to break the handcuffs and make his escape, he was safely lodged in the lock-up. He was identified as one of the men who had burned Dr. Bell's house at Braidwood, and robbed the Braidwood mail. When robbing the Braidwood mail in company with McIntyre, he nearly committed murder, one of the passengers having been dangerously wounded. He was convicted and sentenced to be hung.

In the meantime, his former partner had not been idle. On the 21st April, 1846, the two brothers Cutts were travelling towards Sydney with a number of horses, when they were stopped at Meadow Flat, less than a quarter of a-mile from Howard's Inn. They were compelled to dismount, place their money on the ground, and retire. They deposited £3 18s. in notes and silver and a watch on the ground, and then stepped back several paces as they had been ordered to do. William Cutts begged that a seal attached to his watch might be returned to him, as it was a present from his dead wife, and he valued it accordingly. The bushranger, who was supposed to be McIntyre, told him that "if there was any more palaver" he would get his brains blown out. The robber took up the money and watch, mounted his horse, and rode away. As soon as information of the robbery was received in Bathurst the mounted troopers started in pursuit of the bushranger.

On Monday, August 11th, two men went to the Golden Fleece Inn, Gammon Plains, and remained drinking till Friday. On that day the landlord, Mr. Perfrement, received his copy of the Maitland Mercury, and saw in it a list of the numbers of the bank notes recently stolen from the Singleton mail. He compared the numbers with those of the notes he had received from his two guests, and finding that some of them corresponded, he went to the police station and gave information. The inn was not a large building, but there were several out-houses and the bushrangers were in some of these. Perfrement and the police went to one of these huts at the rear of the inn and found McIntyre there. Perfrement put his hand on the bushranger's shoulder and said "You're a prisoner." "Am I," exclaimed McIntyre jumping backwards, "Come on." Constable Barker rushed in and a fierce wrestling match begun and lasted for some minutes. Then McIntyre got on top and tried to get his pistol out from his belt. Mr. Perfrement, who had snatched the other pistol from him when the wrestling first began, now threatened to shoot him if he did not surrender, but as the bushranger took no notice Perfrement endeavoured to twist the other pistol out of his hand. While this struggle was going on Barker wriggled from under the bushranger, got up, and struck him so heavily with his fist as to stun him. McIntyre lay still for several minutes before he regained consciousness, and by that time his hands were tied. His companion was found fast asleep in another hut and was easily captured. They were tried in Maitland, and McIntyre was subsequently hung, while his companion was sent to penal servitude.

Nine

Bushrangers and Pirates; Capture of H.M. Brig Cyprus by Bushrangers; A Piratical Voyage; Stealing the Schooners Edward and Waterwitch; Mutiny of Prisoners on H.M. Brig Governor Phillip at Norfolk Island; The Trial of the Mutineers at Sydney; How Captain Boyle Recaptured the Vessel.

The connection between bushranging and piracy may not at first seem very apparent, but the bushrangers stole more than one vessel, and started a career of crime on the high seas instead of on the high roads, and our story of the bushrangers would be incomplete were no reference made to thefts of vessels and boats, and their use as vehicles for robbery. It is not very surprising that so many convicts made their escapes from Macquarie Harbour, Port Arthur, and Norfolk Island, in whale boats which they stole, long as the voyages made were. The whale boat has played a conspicuous part in Australian exploration. Lieutenant Bass made his memorable voyage from Sydney, when he discovered the straits which bear his name, in a whale boat in which he started to explore the coast. Flinders and many others also made long voyages and many discoveries in whale boats; for the Pacific, the largest of the oceans of the world, however stormy it may be at times, fully deserves the name bestowed upon it by early navigators, for several months in the year. Hence a voyage in a whale boat from Norfolk Island or from Van Diemen's Land is not so dangerous as the distance to be travelled might suggest. We know that even now it is no very uncommon occurrence for convicts to steal boats and sail or row from New Caledonia to some part of the coast of Australia, and we know also that the Australians have at times entertained no very friendly feelings towards France for persisting in maintaining a penal settlement so near their shores. It is not with the capture of whale or ships' boats that we now have to deal, but with the seizure of larger vessels.

In August, 1829, the Government brig Cyprus, commanded by Captain Harris, left Hobart Town for Macquarie Harbour with thirty-three convicts on board, the crew consisting of twelve, including the Commander, and there were also some soldiers under the command of Lieutenant Carew, and some women and children, numbering eleven altogether. The brig put into Research Bay on the south coast of the island, and anchored, but a gale arose and the brig was driven from her moorings, and lost her anchor and cable. She put back to Hobart Town, obtained a fresh anchor, and started again. On reaching Research Bay she was again anchored, and the anchor and cable lost a few days before were recovered.

At about six in the evening, while the men on board were having supper, Lieutenant Carew, Dr. Williams, a soldier, and Popjoy (the coxswain), with two or three convicts, started in the long boat to catch some fish. They had not rowed very far when they heard shouting and some shots on board the brig, and Lieutenant Carew exclaimed: "Oh, my God The convicts have taken the ship." They pulled back as rapidly as possible, and Carew tried to climb on board, but was threatened with a musket by one of the prisoners. When the trigger was pulled the gun flashed in the pan (misfired) and Carew again tried to get on board, but was pushed back into the boat. He then asked the convicts who were clustered round to give him his wife and children, and these were passed into the boat. Mrs. Williams, her servant, and the wives of a couple of the soldiers were also put into the boat. It appears that when the long boat left there were only Captain Harris and two soldiers on deck, the rest of the crew and passengers being below at supper.

Suddenly five heavily ironed prisoners made a rush, and knocked down the captain and two sentinels. Others rushed to the hatchway, and began to put the hatches on, when the soldiers and crew, fearing that they would be suffocated, agreed to surrender. They gave up their arms, and as they came on deck they were conducted to one of the boats, in which several prisoners who had had their irons taken off seated themselves at the oars. Popjoy was compelled to go on board, as it was said his services would be required for navigating the vessel. Then the captain, the lieutenant, and doctor, with the women, the soldiers, and the crew, were rowed to an island in the bay and landed. Seventeen of the prisoners were also landed, the mutineers only numbering sixteen of those on board. The boats were hoisted in, the sails lowered, and the ship got under way. But as she started Popjoy jumped overboard and swam ashore. As the brig went down the bay the men on board shouted "Hooray! the ship's our own, hooray!" The captain and others landed on the little island in the bay, with no means of reaching the mainland, suffered great hardships. For several days they had nothing but a few mussels and other shellfish which they picked up on the beach to eat. Popjoy, however, came to the rescue. He made a sort of canoe of bark and sticks, and sailed out into the open sea. Here he saw the barque Zebra, and made signals. He was taken on board, and a couple of boats with provisions were sent in to feed and bring off the fugitives. For these services Popjoy, who was a convict with a ticket-of-leave, received a free pardon.

What became of the brig and its crew of mutineers was for some time a matter of conjecture. It was reported in Australia that she had been seen at Valparaiso. Then it was said that she had foundered at sea owing to the ignorance of navigation of the men on board. However, in the beginning of March, 1830, the Committee of Supercargoes at Canton were informed that four persons with a ship's boat had landed. They represented themselves as part of the crew of an English merchant vessel which had been wrecked on the China coast. The story was not believed, as no such wreck had been reported, but enquiries were made and a man calling himself William Waldon, of Sunderland, was examined. He represented himself as having been the commander of the brig Edward, which left the London Docks in December, 1828, bound for Rio de Janeiro. On his return voyage he had called at Valparaiso and the Sandwich Islands. At Japan his ship had been fired at from a battery and much damaged. He sailed for Manilla, but had to abandon the brig near Formosa, as she leaked heavily. He and the fifteen men of the crew had taken to the boats and all had been lost except himself and the three men with him. The boat bore the name:—" The Edward, of London—William Waldon." Although some doubt was still entertained the Committee arranged for the four men to be taken to England in the Charles Grant.

A few days after their departure another boat with three men on board arrived at Whampoa. The leader, Huntley, represented himself as having been wrecked in the brig Edward, but said the captain's name was James Wilson and that she had left London in June, 1828, and gone straight to the Cape. When near the Ladrones he had quarrelled with Wilson and run away. As the two accounts differed so materially the former suspicions were revived and Huntley was sent home under arrest in the Killie Castle, and on the arrival of the Charles Grant in London the three men on board, John Anderson, Alexander Telford, and Charles Williams, were arrested. Waldon had landed at Margate, and thus escaped for the time, but was arrested in London a week or two later. The four men were brought up at the Thames Police Court on September 22nd, 1830, for examination, and were charged with piracy. The principal witness was Popjoy, who had returned to England on receiving his pardon. He identified Huntley as George James Davis, a convict who had been sentenced to death at Hobart Town for highway robbery, but whose sentence had been commuted to penal servitude at Macquarie Harbour. Davis was one of the leaders of the mutiny when the brig Cyprus had been seized. Alexander Stevenson, sometimes called Stevie, who now appeared as Telford, had been convicted in Glasgow in 1824, and had been reconvicted for bushranging in Australia. John Beveridge, alias Anderson, was sentenced in Perth in 1821, and was further sentenced in Hobart Town to seven years' penal servitude for having robbed Mr. Peachey. William Watts, alias George Williams, was known in Van Diemen's Land as Wattle. He ran away from a chain gang and took to the bush. He had stabbed one man and had attempted to shoot another. Of Swallow, Popjoy knew nothing, but had seen him on board the Cyprus before the mutiny. The boat which had been sent from China to England was identified by Popjoy as one belonging to the Cyprus, the names Edward and Waldon, having been painted on it since the mutiny.

The prisoners were tried at the Admiralty Court, on November 4th. Popjoy, under cross-examination, admitted that he had been transported to New South Wales for horsestealing. He had been assigned to a master, and had run away. He had received two hundred lashes at Botany Bay, but this was "only a few." He had been sent to Van Diemen's Land, and had been charged with highway robbery near Hobart Town, but had "proved his innocence." He had "buried in oblivion all the charges" made against him in the colony. He went to Macquarie Harbour in the Cyprus as a volunteer. Dr. Williams, surgeon, said that he was on board the Cyprus when she was seized by convicts in Research Bay, in August, 1829. He had gone in

Chapter IX

the long boat with Lieutenant Carew to fish, and when the boat was some distance from the brig they had heard a clashing of arms. They put back, and Lieutenant Carew tried to get on board but was repulsed, and a pistol was snapped at him. He then asked for his sword, but a convict named Ferguson, who had it, refused to give it up. When Mrs. Carew and Mrs. Williams were put into the boat, Swallow came to the side of the vessel and said, "Gentlemen, you see I'm a pressed man. I am unarmed, and surrounded by armed men." In consequence of this testimony, Swallow, alias Waldon, was acquitted, but was subsequently sent to the colony to serve his original sentence. Davis, alias Huntley, Watts, alias Williams, Stevenson, alias Telford, and Beveridge, alias Anderson, were sentenced to death.

On January 13, 1840, six bushrangers were captured at Woolnorth, near Circular Head, and were charged with having attempted to seize the schooner Edward, the property of the Circular Head Shipping Company of Launceston, Van Diemen's Land. The object with which this vessel was seized was to enable the bushrangers to escape to one of the South Sea Islands, where they intended to settle.

The schooner Waterwitch was seized at the Forth River by three bushrangers on January 27th. The robbers told the captain that they did not wish to do him or his vessel any harm, but that they were determined to go to Sealers' Cove. If he liked to take them, well and good; if not, they would take the vessel there themselves and turn her adrift. The captain agreed. He took the bushrangers to, where they wished to go, and parted with them very amicably.

From time to time several small vessels disappeared, and it was supposed that their captors had succeeded in navigating them to some of the Islands, but as nothing further was ever heard of them, it is supposed that they either foundered at sea, or that if the bushrangers reached the islands, their predatory habits or brutal violence embroiled them with the natives, and they were killed in the fights which took place, but it is impossible to do more than conjecture their fate, and to speculate as to whether their acts of aggression were the cause of some of the apparently unprovoked attacks of the savages on the crews or passengers of other vessels. This subject has never been adequately investigated, and there is too little evidence available to enable us at present to do more than refer to the subject as one worthy of enquiry.

The case which attracted the most notice in Australia, perhaps, was the capture of H.M. Brig, the Governor Phillip. On October 15th, 1842, John Jones, Thomas. Whelan, George Beavors, Henry Sears, Nicholas Lewis, and James Woolf, alias Mordecai, were charged in the Criminal Court, Sydney, with that they did on the 21st June, 1842, on board the brig Governor Phillip, the property of Our Sovereign Lady the Queen, assault one Charles Whitehead, with intent to murder. There was a second count charging, the prisoners with piracy. The brig was lying out in the roads, at Norfolk Island, discharging cargo and taking in ballast. The prisoners were sent from the shore with a boat load of ballast and slept on board the vessel. Two of them were called up at about four a.m. to bale the boat out, and Jones asked William Harper, one of the sailors, if he could navigate? Harper replied "Yes, if I had a slate and pencil." No notice was taken of this incident at the time, but afterwards it was deemed to have been an indication that a conspiracy to seize the vessel had been formed among the prisoners.

At seven o'clock the remainder of the boat's crew was called up to begin work, when Bartley Kelly rushed at one of the sentries and knocked him down with a belaying pin, while Lewis knocked down another. Then there were cries of "Jump overboard, you ——" and "Throw the —— overboard and they'll tell no tales." Charles Whitehead was sergeant of the guard in charge at the time. Henry Sears struck him. It was not known whether the soldiers jumped or were thrown overboard, but one sentry who was missing had been thrown over by two of the mutineers. The noise roused the soldiers who were below and they attempted to gain the deck, but were driven back by the prisoners, who shouted "Keep down, you ——, or we'll kill you." They also called for "Hot water to scald the —— soldiers." Captain Boyle, who was in command of the vessel, was in his cabin at the time when the mutiny occurred; Christopher Lucas, the second mate, being in charge of the deck. Lucas had been knocked down in the first charge, but he contrived to slip away and went to the captain's cabin and reported the mutiny. He also went to the soldiers' quarters and roused them up, but by that time the prisoners had control of the deck and prevented the soldiers

Chapter IX

from ascending the hatch gangway. Lucas had received several very severe blows on the head with belaying pins and had been left for dead. The captain also tried to mount the gangway but did not succeed. He then went to the men's quarters and ordered the carpenter to cut away the fore and aft piece of the hatchway which the mutineers had closed. By this means he was enabled to raise the hatch slightly and shot a prisoner named Moore. Bartley Kelly had also been severely wounded by one of the sentries and was unable to rise. Another prisoner named McLean came to the hatchway and told Captain Boyle that if he would consent to leave the brig with the soldiers they would all be put on shore. The captain refused. McLean then told him to give up his arms. The captain fired at him by way of reply and McLean fell dead. The death of the leaders seemed to have a depressing effect on the other mutineers. Beavors asked the captain "for God's sake" not to fire any more. Encouraged by this appeal for mercy, Captain Boyle forced the hatchway open and went on deck, followed by the soldiers, and the mutineers, having lost their leaders, surrendered. The vessel was under the control of the mutineers for about a quarter of an hour. Beavors, alias Berry, and Jones, alias Jack the Lagger, were the least active of the mutineers. It was Sears who had struck Whitehead, the sergeant of the guard, immediately after Whitehead had shot Kelly. Kelly died from his wound the following day, but Whitehead recovered, although, at one time, his life was despaired of. The brig was 180 tons burden, and there were on board eighteen men, including an officer and eleven men of the 96th regiment.

The Chief Justice, Sir James Dowling, before whom the case was tried, said that had Sergeant Whitehead died he could have held out no hopes for the prisoners. The jury which had found them guilty had recommended them to mercy, and he agreed in that recommendation for all except Henry Sears. It was his duty to pronounce the death sentence, but with the exception named he would not deprive them of hope. As a result Sears was hung, while the sentences on the other prisoners were commuted to penal servitude for life.

Ten

Van Diemen's Land Again; A Hunt for Bushrangers in the Mountains; Some Brutal Attacks; "Stand!" "No, thanks, I'm very Comfortable Sitting;" A Degrading Exhibition; A Determined Judge; Cash, Kavanagh, and Jones, an Enterprising Firm; The Art of Politeness as Exhibited by Bushrangers; A Bushranger Hunt in the Streets of Hobart Town; The Capture of Cash; Break Up of the Gang; A Doubtful Mercy.

For some years the roads in Van Diemen's Land had been comparatively safe, very few highway robberies being recorded, and the newspapers generally asserted that bushranging, in its worst form, had been stamped out. This assertion, however, is not altogether borne out by the evidence, and the most that can be said is that bushranging was not nearly so prevalent as in former times, and no bushranger had exercised his calling for a sufficiently long time to earn notoriety, but even this comparatively happy condition did not last very long.

The bushrangers James Regan, William Davis, James Atterill, alias Thompson, and Anthony Bankes having committed a number of depredations on the settlers, the Government resolved to make a decisive effort to capture them. Consequently, on February 21st, 1838, Captain Mackenzie, with three privates of the 21st Fusiliers, two constables of the Field Police, and two prisoner volunteers, went to Jerusalem, where he was informed by the Police Magistrate of Richmond that another house had been robbed by the bushrangers, who had retired to the Brown Mountain. A guide, well acquainted with the Tiers, was found, and the party started the following morning. They struck into the bush a short distance beyond Mr. Tomley's, and at two o'clock came to a hut where the stockman, an intelligent lad, informed them that the bushrangers had robbed his master's house on the previous night at ten o'clock, taking a horse to carry the robber Bankes, who had been wounded. The lad was taken as a guide, and led them up a ravine, which soon became too steep for the horses. They reached the summit of the Brown Mountain about dusk, but without seeing any fire or other indication of a camp. They reached Mr. Ree's house, on the Richmond side, about midnight, and returned to Jerusalem at six on Friday morning, having been marching for twenty-three hours over very rough country. After six hours' rest Captain Mackenzie took Wesley, one of Mr. Johnson's shepherds, as guide, and resumed the search. They reached Mr. Stokell's house at dusk, and approached it with great caution. Finding no one there, Captain Mackenzie left two sentries, and pushed on to Romney's, where they arrived at about half-past one.

The moon was shining brightly. The hut was surrounded, and Captain Mackenzie called for three volunteers, telling the men that it was a forlorn hope, as the robbers would probably shoot two out of the three, the moonlight being so bright. The captain called on Regan by name to surrender, but received no answer. He then walked up to the window, and said to the occupant of the hut, "Tucker, you old blockhead! why don't you open the door?" There was a rattle of musketry, and the captain stepped back into the shadow of the hut. Captain Mackenzie called out to his men not to fire unless the bushrangers did, or unless they rushed out and tried to escape. Then Constable Peacock advanced to the window and looked in. Captain Mackenzie said if the door was not opened he would fire, and after waiting a minute or so told Private Cockburn to shoot, but not too low. Cockburn fired into the window when the door was opened, and a man came out. The captain cried "Lie down, or you die." "I'm Tucker," said the man, "don't shoot," and threw himself on his face. The captain went to the door and looked in, when Private Cockburn cried, "Take care, captain, the fellow is going to fire. They are all armed." This raised a cheer among the soldiers, who now knew that their men were there. Regan it appears had tried to bring his musket to bear on the captain, but could not do so without exposing himself. The captain gave the word to fire, and a volley was poured into the hut. Then the captain asked Regan to surrender, promising not to hurt him. Regan endeavoured to induce the captain to promise not to prosecute them, but he refused, saying it was more than he could do. Finally, they consented to surrender, and Atterill crawled out naked. He was tied. Regan was then called, and he refused to come out on his hands and knees, saying that he would sooner be shot than be treated like a dog. The captain told him he might walk out if he came without arms and held his hands up. He did so, and the police then went in and brought out the other two. The prisoners were handcuffed and placed in a cart. About £14, found in their clothes, and their guns and pistols, were carried in another cart. Tucker was employed by Mr. Romney and was considered the best guide in the district. The robbers had taken possession of his hut and intended to make him show them the way across the mountains on the following day. The party reached Richmond on Saturday night, and early next day the bushrangers were lodged in the gaol at Hobart Town. The prisoners were tried and convicted of several acts of bushranging, ranging from highway robbery to burglary. They were all sentenced to death, but only Regan was hung. The Cornwall Chronicle said "His inquisitors were conscious that, had he been permitted to give his dying attestation to the treatment he had received from his master, it would have been so appalling and horrible as to leave the guilt of his crimes, in the estimation of an impartial public, not on his own head, but on theirs." "The Government," said the paper, "is afraid to hear the dying statements of the condemned."

On September 8th, 1840, two armed men entered the Post Office at Ross, and bailed up the post-mistress, who was also a store-keeper. They took from her about £16 in cash and a quantity of wearing apparel. A large sum of money which was enclosed in a letter ready for despatch was missed by the robbers. The police were informed and at once followed on the track of the bushrangers, but failed to arrest them. On the following evening the bushrangers went to a hut on the station of Mr. Joseph Penny, of Ashby Cottage, and tied the shepherd, telling him that if he was quiet and did as he was ordered they would not hurt him; but that if he refused to obey they would shoot him. They went to the gardener's lodge and compelled the gardener to give them some food. While they were engaged in eating a man who had previously agreed to go out opossum hunting with the shepherd called at the hut and shouted. He received no answer, the shepherd believing that the bushrangers were "trying" him. The friend knocked again and shouted, but receiving no reply went in. He was surprised to see the shepherd lying down tied and quickly untied him. The two men then went to the house and informed Mr. Penny of what was going on. Quickly arming himself and the two men Mr. Penny went to the gardener's lodge and surprised the bushrangers before they could get their pistols and guns ready. They were tied and conducted into the town, and were subsequently convicted and sent to penal servitude.

James Leverett, while driving a cart belonging to Mr. James Cox, of Clarendon, was attacked by a bushranger and brutally beaten. The bushranger struck him on the head from behind and stunned him. He stopped the horse and battered Leverett about the head. Then he searched his pockets and decamped. The constable stationed at Morven happened to pass along the road, and seeing the horse and cart standing went over to ascertain what was the matter. Finding Leverett lying in the cart insensible the constable took him to the police station and sent for a doctor. He then followed the tracks of the bushranger, but failed to find him. Another man, a servant of Mr. Stephenson, of Curramore, was beaten and robbed in a similar manner. It was said that these assaults were committed by ticket-of-leave men, who were thrown out of employment by the arrival of a large number of free immigrants.

On the 15th April, 1841, James Broomfield and Jonas Hopkins bailed up and robbed Henry Atkins, Bonney, taking seven five pound notes from him. In company with James McCallum the same two bushrangers went to the house of Thomas Bates, at Norfolk Plains, about midnight, and woke him up, demanding something to drink. Bates told them that there was plenty of water in the cask. This, however, did not satisfy them, and they broke into the kitchen. They took some flour and grain from the cask and made a damper. While this was baking they took a watch, some money, and a quantity of clothes out of the bedroom. When they had had a meal, they left with their plunder, but were followed and captured. They were convicted of robbery with firearms and were sentenced to death; their sentences were, however, commuted to imprisonment for life.

John Gunn, George Griffiths, William Lambeth, Samuel Harrison, and Thomas Hurn stuck up and robbed Daniel Ddwnie on the 5th September, 1842, of clothing and money. They were followed by Constables Patrick Flynn and George Marsden, and a volunteer named Joseph Masson. The bushrangers were armed with a fowling-piece and a musket. They went next morning to the hut of James Thompson, and told him not to be frightened as they did not intend to hurt him. They took his money and were walking away, when the constables came up and called on them to stand. They surrendered and were taken to gaol. When they were convicted, sentence of death was recorded against each of them, but they were not hung.

On May 4th, 1843, Mr. Thomas Massey, of Ellerslie, South Esk River, was sitting on his verandah when John Conway came up, presented a gun at his head, and cried "Stand."

"No, thank you," replied Mr. Massey, "I'm very comfortable sitting down. What do you want?" Conway then asked where the man was. Mr. Massey replied, "Out in the kitchen." A man named Riley Jeffs was standing a short distance away with Henry Blunt and a man named Pockett, both of whom had their hands tied behind them. Jeffs left the two tied men and went round to the kitchen, while Conway demanded money and firearms. Jeffs returned with the manservant and tied his hands. The robbers then took two double-barrelled guns, a single-barrelled fowling-piece, with a shot belt and powder flask, some tea, sugar, flour, and a gallon of rum. After they had gone Constable Thomas Connell, of Campbelltown, with Joseph Masson, Matthew Perry, Edward Quin, Aaron Dunn, and Stephen Wright followed the bushrangers to Blunt's hut, when two men ran away. One of them was lame and was soon caught. It was Jeffs, who said he had accidentally wounded himself the day before, after he left Mr. Massey's. The other man, Conway, was captured after a brisk run. At their trial, Mary Bryan, servant at Mr. Massey's, said she recognised Conway by his big nose. "How many inches? Did you measure it?" asked Jeffs, but the question was ruled out of order by Judge Montagu. The prisoners were then tried for the murder of Constable William Ward. They went to Mr. James Gilligan's house, Clifton Lodge, Break-o'-day Road, and asked Sarah Vasco, the servant, whether any one was at home. She replied, "Only master and mistress and a gentleman." They had four men with their hands tied behind them. Jeffs stopped with these at the kitchen door, while Conway walked into the passage. When he reached the parlour door he presented his gun and cried, "Stand, or I'll blow the contents of this through you." Ward, who was sitting near the door, jumped up and grappled with the bushranger. They struggled together into the passage. Mrs.

Chapter X

Gilligan pushed her husband to prevent him from going out, and slammed the parlour door. Mr. Gilligan heard the struggle along the passage, and then a gun went off. He got the door open at last and went out. He saw Ward lying on the floor of the kitchen. Jeffs and Conway and the four men whose hands were tied were looking at him. Conway said to Gilligan, "You go back into your room, old man, or I'll mark you." In the fight in the passage both of the men had endeavoured to obtain possession of the gun, but between them they let it fall and it exploded without injuring any one. Conway then broke away and ran into the kitchen. Ward followed him and was grappled by Jeffs. While they were wrestling Conway drew a pistol and watched for a chance, and when Ward was on top holding Jeffs down Conway deliberately put the pistol to his shoulder and fired. Ward rolled over dead, and Jeffs got up. The robbers then demanded money, and Mrs. Gilligan went to the bedroom upstairs to fetch some. Conway accompanied her. Mrs. Gilligan said, "It's a great pity, Mr. Ward had a large family." "Well," replied Conway, "why didn't he keep out of our road? We tried to shoot him before."

The prisoners were convicted of wilful murder. In his summing up the Judge said that the four men who were present appeared to be accomplices, although they were tied. They had prevaricated so much in their evidence that it was worthless or worse. He would consider whether it was advisable to prosecute them for perjury. Conway was very violent while in gaol. He threw a loaf of bread at the gaoler, and threatened that if he got out he'd "do for him." Jeffs and Conway were hung at Launceston in July. The census of the town had been taken a short time before, and showed that the population was 4458 souls. The Launceston Advertiser said that there were more than a thousand men, women, and boys present to see Jeffs and Conway hung. Numbers of people took their blankets with them and slept in the square all night. They were singing songs and making a great noise. The paper says the scene was a disgraceful one, and doubts whether such exhibitions can have any beneficial effect.

John Price and Thomas Roberts were tried for highway robbery. Judge Montagu said that if the robbery had been committed at night, or if any undue violence had been used, he would have cast them for death without hope of mercy. It appeared, however, that they had been followed and captured at once, and therefore, although the death sentence would be recorded against them, they would be sent to a penal settlement, and he hoped they would reform.

John Fletcher and Henry Lee stuck up and robbed Daniel Griffin at Cocked Hat Hill, on November 6th, 1844. In passing sentence of death, Judge Montagu said that he was determined to put down robbery on the high road between Hobart Town and Launceston, and especially about Cocked Hat Hill. It was a horrid place. No man was safe there. The residents were fortunate in having so active and energetic an officer stationed there as Constable Harvey. He would sentence the prisoners to transportation for life. When they were being removed from court, Lee said, as he was passing Constable Harvey: "I'll rip your —— guts out, you ——, if ever I get out."

On the 10th July, 1841, Hogan and Armytage visited the Travellers' Rest Inn, within four miles of Launceston. There were eight men in the bar and they took all the money they could get, some grog, and provisions. Hogan said he was tired of the bush, and wished "it was all over." Armytage looked ill and miserable. The police followed them as soon as news of the robbery was conveyed to Launceston, but without success, as the bushrangers were too well acquainted with the country round there.

On January 8, 1841, a bushranger went to a shepherd's hut on Mr. Frank's station, Lake Crescent, and tied the shepherd, telling him that he would shoot him if he got loose. The robber only got a few shillings. The robber went away, but soon returned, and seeing the shepherd still tied, cautioned him again and went away. The man remained tied for several hours before he attempted to untie the rope. It was said that this was the man who had robbed Mr. McCrae's station, and murdered a shepherd on Mr. Brodribb's station.

On the following day, Hogan the bushranger walked into a public-house kept by Mrs. Bonny at Deloraine, and asked for two case bottles of rum. On these being given to him, he took a ham and a pudding and walked away, saying that he wanted them for his mate, who was ill. Although there were five or six men in the bar at the time, no attempt was made to detain him. Nothing further is known about Armytage, who is supposed

Chapter X

to have died in the bush; but Hogan was captured and sentenced to penal servitude on Norfolk Island.

On April 2, 1842, it was reported that Martin Cash, the notorious bushranger who had for so long a time defied the police, had been captured in a house in Harrington Street, Hobart Town, by Constables Kirby and Williams. He was lodged in the lock-up, but during the night succeeded in making his escape.

On March 25, 1843, the bushrangers Martin Cash, Lawrence Kavanagh, and Thomas Jones, armed to the teeth, bailed up Mr. Panton at Broad Marsh, and fired at Dr. Macdonald. The police started in pursuit. On April 18th, the gang visited Mr. Hay, who was in his barn overlooking five shearers who were at work. They were ordered to stand up and put down their shears. Then the men were forced to tie each other. While the bushrangers were plundering the house, Mr. Ward came up. He was ordered to stand, but instead of obeying he ran away. Cash followed and fired his pistol, the shot grazing Ward's ear. Ward, however, kept on and got behind a tree, and the bushrangers decamped, taking very little plunder with them. On the 19th they captured Mr. John Clarke and his overseer, Mr. Denholme, and compelled them to accompany the bushrangers to the late Mr. Allardyce's house on the Clyde River. They went into the parlour, and after arranging the chairs, invited the gentlemen to sit down. Then they called for brandy and glasses. The servant brought in a bottle of brandy and a tin pannikin. Cash was in a great rage. He swore at the servant, and asked him in an indignant tone, "Is that a proper thing for gentlemen to drink out of? Take it away and bring glasses." When they had had some refreshments, Cash sat talking to Messrs. Clarke and Denholme, while Kavanagh and Jones collected the plunder. The bushrangers were said to be very haggard in appearance and not well dressed.

On May the 18th they invited themselves to visit Captain McKay, on the Dee River, and dined with him in the most amicable manner. After dinner they loaded two horses with clothing, provisions, and other articles from the store. Then, taking Captain McKay with them, they went to Mr. Gellibrand's, where they loaded a third horse. With this the bushrangers appear to have been satisfied, as they went away.

"Messrs. Cash & Co.," as some of the Van Diemen's Land papers called the gang, visited Mr. Christopher Gatenby, of the Isis, on July 1st, and politely apologised for their intrusion, They as politely asked for a supply of provisions, which they said were necessary owing to the police having recently captured their camp and taken away all that they could find there. Mr. Gatenby opened the store and gave them what they required, and then Cash said he should feel extremely obliged if Mr. Gatenby and four of his servants would carry the provisions to their new camp. He politely explained that this was necessary, as the police had taken their horses. The invitation was so pressing that Mr. Gatenby could not refuse. He therefore took up a portion of the swag, while his servants shouldered the rest, and escorted by the three bushrangers they started into the bush. After walking for about two miles Cash said he would not trouble Mr. Gatenby to go any further, as he thought that they could manage without him. The load he was carrying was distributed among the bushrangers, and Mr. Gatenby returned home, after having been profusely thanked for his generosity in giving them the provisions and his kindness in carrying them so far. The servants were taken two or three miles further into the bush, and were then allowed to deposit their loads under a gum tree and return home. Cash denied that the gang had had an encounter with the Campbelltown constables. He said that the constables found their hiding place when he and his mates were absent.

On August 22nd two men dressed as sailors were seen by the constables in Hobart Town enquiring for the residence of a well-known suspicious character. One of the constables stepped forward, and gave them the address they required. Then one of the sailors walked away, while the other remained standing near the constables as if in bravado. The constables held a consultation, and decided to arrest the sailor as a suspicious character. Two of them went towards him, when the sailor drew a pistol, fired, and then ran. The shot took no effect, and the constables gave chase. Charles Cunliffe, a carpenter, was standing at the door of his house as the sailor passed, and hearing the constables chasing him and crying "Stop, thief!" he joined in the chase. As they went down Brisbane Street Constable Winstanley came out of the Commodore Inn on hearing the hullabaloo, and attempted to seize the sailor, but the sailor drew a pistol from his belt and

Chapter X

fired. The ball passed through Constable Winstanley's chest, but nevertheless he grappled with the sailor and held him until Cunliffe came up, when Winstanley fell. Cunliffe and the sailor had a terrific struggle for a few minutes, Cunliffe being much bruised, but he held on until the other constables arrived and secured their man. The sailor was taken to the Penitentiary, where he was identified as Martin Cash. It was believed that the other sailor was Lawrence Kavanagh, but although search was made for him, he could not be found. Constable Winstanley died from the effects of his wound two days later.

Martin Cash was tried for the murder of Peter Winstanley on September 15th, and was found guilty. He said he had been standing quietly in the street when a constable came up and cried out, "It's Cash, blow his brains out." He had then fired and run. The constables were all cowards. They thronged round him when he was down, but they would never have caught him if it had not been for Cunliffe. Judge Montagu said in reply that he could see no proof of cowardice in the action of the police. They were not such fast runners as the prisoner. Charles Cunliffe was the more active, and consequently he had caught the prisoner first. For this he deserved credit, but the police had arrived at the spot without delay and were also to be complimented for their share in the capture of so dangerous a character as the prisoner. He then sentenced the prisoner to be hung on Monday, the 18th instant.

Cash, however, was not hung, but was sent to Norfolk Island for life. Rewards of one hundred acres of land or one hundred sovereigns, in addition to the rewards previously offered of fifty sovereigns, with a free pardon for convicts and a free passage to any post in Her Majesty's dominions, were offered for the capture of Kavanagh and Jones, dead or alive.

Thomas Jones, in company with John Liddell and James Dalton, stuck up Catherine Smith's house on December 6th, at Effingham Banks. They tied the servants and went into Mrs. Smith's bedroom. The lady requested them to go out while she dressed, and they complied. When Mrs. Smith got up the bushrangers ordered the servants to get them some supper, telling them that they need not be afraid, as nobody would hurt them. They made the servants sit down while they ate. After their meal they opened the drawers and took out clothes and other articles which suited them, and went away. On December 11th they stuck up a hawker named John McCall. They drove his cart half a mile into the bush off the road, and tied McCall to a tree. Then they made a bundle of the articles they wanted in the cart, and went away. On December 30th Thomas Jones, "late with Messrs. Cash & Co.," with another man named Moore, dressed as sporting gentlemen, went to Mr. William Field's, and enquired if he was in? They were answered in the negative, and they then went to the men's hut and bailed up the two men there. As the others came in they were compelled to stand in a row against the wall. When Mr. Shanklin, the overseer, came in, Moore told him to kneel down and say his prayers, as he intended to shoot him. The men interceded for the overseer, saying that he always had treated them well. Moore asserted that Shanklin had "got him an extension of time," and he meant to have revenge. He was very violent in his language. Jones had been looking on very quietly, but he now said, "Oh, let the —— go, and let him beware how he behaves in future." Moore at first objected, but gave way, and Shanklin was made to stand up with the assigned servants. The robbers broke open Mr. Field's escritoire, and took £50 out of it. They also took tea, sugar, flour, and other things from the store.

In the meantime the police had not been idle. They had had several brushes with the bushrangers, and had captured Kavanagh, Liddell, and Dalton. After this last robbery Jones and Moore were followed, and Jones was captured. They were all convicted and sentenced to death, but were told that probably their sentences would be commuted to penal servitude. On hearing this Liddell exclaimed, "I don't want mercy from you or any one else. I've been eleven years at Port Arthur and I don't want to go there again. I'd rather die than live." Judge Montagu said that this statement showed a deplorable frame of mind and exhorted Liddell to think of the future. Dalton complained that he had been knocked down by Thompson, the gaoler. Mr. Thompson said that the prisoner was a very desperate man. "But you'd no right to put irons on my neck," cried Dalton. The Judge said it was the duty of the gaoler to prevent escape. If he deemed it necessary he had a perfect right to put irons on the neck of a prisoner as well as on his hands and feet. He should report the behaviour of the prisoners in the proper quarter and he could not recommend either Liddell or Dalton to mercy. "I don't care a —— what you do," exclaimed Dalton. George Cumsden, who had also been associated with Jones in some of his robberies since the capture of Cash and Kavanagh, was also sentenced to death, "without the hope of mercy." He had threatened to "blow a hole through" any witness who appeared against him.

There was again a lull in bushranging in Van Diemen's Land, and again the papers asserted that the crime had been stamped out. The majority of those convicted had been sent to Norfolk Island, and this, it was said, would act as a deterrent to other evil doers. Norfolk Island was feared more than death.

Eleven

Norfolk Island: Its Founding as a Penal Station; The Terrible Discipline, in Norfolk Island; An Attempt to Ameliorate it; Its Failure; The Rigorous Treatment Restored; The Consequent Riot; Jackey Jackey's Revenge; An Unparalleled Tale of Ferocity; The Soldiers Overawe the Rioters; Thirteen Condemned to the Gallows; Jackey Jackey's Remarkable Letter; The End of Several Notorious Bushrangers.

Norfolk Island, lying some seven hundred miles from the coast of New South Wales, was first utilised as a penal settlement in 1788, when it was decided that convicts who committed crimes in New South Wales should be transported there for more severe treatment. Early in the nineteenth century a rumour spread in Australia that Napoleon the First intended to fit out a fleet to search for Admiral La Perouse, and to found colonies in the south seas. The truth of this rumour seemed to be affirmed by the activity of the naval authorities in New South Wales. Settlements were made at Port Essington in the north, King George's Sound in the west, and the Derwent River in Van Diemen's Land. Shortly afterwards, in 1805, the prisoners were removed from Norfolk Island to Hobart Town, apparently for the purpose of strengthening the settlement in Van Diemen's Land. When Van Diemen's Land was made independent of New South Wales, in 1825, Norfolk Island was again made a penal settlement of the mother colony, and it so continued until transportation to New South Wales ceased in 1842, when Norfolk Island was transferred from the jurisdiction of the Governor of New South Wales to that of the Governor of Van Diemen's Land. The treatment of the prisoners in the island was rigorous in the extreme, and may aptly be described as savage. When the enquiry of the House of Commons, by Select Committee, was made in 1837 and 1838, as to the condition of the convicts in the penal settlements, the few particulars published about the evidence in the English newspapers had some effect on public opinion, and in 1841, Captain Maconochie, one of the witnesses examined who said that the prisoners might be governed with less harshness, was appointed Commandant of Norfolk Island, with instructions to try the mild reformatory treatment he advocated. Captain Maconochie and his supporters in England do not seem to have realised that human beings who have been under demoralising influences until they have reached the adult age, and their characters have become set, are not amenable to civilising influences. These should have been applied during the impressionable years, and the younger they are applied the more successful they are likely to be. This fact, however, does not yet seem to be known sufficiently in England, and therefore small blame attaches to Captain Maconochie, if he was not aware of it sixty years ago. The new Commandant abolished Sunday labour as a punishment, shortened the hours of labour on week-days, and granted holidays for good behaviour. He allowed the men to build huts and to cultivate small patches of ground, and thus to provide themselves with vegetables. He also gave them tins to cook in, and served out rations individually, instead of giving the rations out in messes. It does not appear that the prisoners became unduly riotous under this treatment, and no such murders as were mentioned by Judge Forbes and other witnesses before the Select Committee, in which men had killed their mates for the purpose of being hung "out of their misery," took place. One of these murders which occurred only a short time before Captain Maconochie took charge may be mentioned here.

Stephen Brennan was sent to the island for bushranging. He was tried there and found guilty of the murder of another convict. There had been no quarrel between the two men, who were as friendly as circumstances permitted under the rigid discipline, nevertheless Brennan suddenly struck Patrick Lynch a blow with a stone-breaker's hammer, and then stabbed him with a knife. The murder was committed avowedly so that the perpetrator might be hung, and thus escape the harsh treatment he was subjected to, and it is not improbable that it was committed with the consent of the victim, for although there is no evidence of this in this case, it is well known that men had actually drawn lots in Norfolk Island, to decide which should murder the other and get hung for the crime. In place of crimes like this, there were quarrels and some rowdyism, but this was sufficient for the opponents of the new experiment. Paragraphs appeared in the Van Diemen's Land papers jeering at the "plum pudding policy" of Captain Maconochie, and asserting that Queen's birthday rejoicings only led to increased disturbances in Norfolk Island. Whether these paragraphs were inspired by the prison officials, who feared that if Captain Maconochie was successful there would be an end of "the system" which they had organised, it is impossible to say, but after a three years' trial, the mild treatment was pronounced a failure, and Major Joseph Childs was appointed to supersede Captain Maconochie, as Commandant of Norfolk Island, and reached the island on February 8th, 1844. Major Childs landed with orders to revert to the old rigid discipline, and he appears to have endeavoured to carry these orders out to the best of his ability.

The hours of work were increased, holidays abolished, and all the old punishments re-established. These alterations were made very gradually. As I have already said, the prisoners had been supplied with rations individually, and were allowed their own pots and pans to cook them with. In July, 1846, new regulations were issued that rations were to be issued in bulk and to be cooked in the general mess house. The rations on the island had always been notoriously bad, and consisted generally of salt beef and maize. Captain Maconochie had allowed them to grow potatoes. The privilege was abolished on January 1st, 1846, when the garden plots were taken from the prisoners and laid waste. The prisoners refused in a body to go to work unless some equivalent was given them for their potatoes, and half a pint of peas daily was promised them. After three days the peas in stock gave out, and another mutiny took place. Numbers of the prisoners were flogged, but this did not quieten them, and Commandant Childs promised them that eight ounces of flour should be served out in place of the peas. In a few days, however, the stock of flour was exhausted, and then, "incredible as it may appear, an old order, issued in May, 1846, after the gardens were taken away from the prisoners, stating that two pounds of sweet potatoes should form part of the daily rations, was posted up; although it must have been known to the superintendent that it would be utterly impossible to serve out a single ounce of sweet potatoes a man daily for a week."[1] The sweet potatoes in the island had been grown by the men, and had been most unjustly taken away from them when their gardens

[1] *Launceston Chronicle.*

Chapter XI

were laid waste. It was well-known that there were no sweet potatoes in the island, and the reposting of this old and obsolete regulation was an outrage on truth. The prisoners were not slow in showing their indignation, nor very particular as to the words they used in expressing it. And it was during the dissatisfaction consequent on the posting of this old order, that the new regulation calling in the kettles on July the 1st was posted. When the order was first posted, the majority of the prisoners were in their cells.

A few were attending school, and among these was Jackey Jackey, who was doing a sum when the soldiers came round to collect the kettles. Hearing the rattling of the tins, he raised himself up, pencil in hand, and listened intently. Then he pushed the slate away, folded his arms, and sat as if in deep thought. The other prisoners present were whispering together, trying to conjecture what was being done with their tins. On the following morning, July 2nd, the prisoners were all mustered for prayers, a practice only recently introduced along with the repressive measures of the new superintendent. During the service the men kept whispering and paid but little attention. Several times order was called for, but this only produced a lull for a time. When the prayers were over the men marched to the Lumber Yard and read the new regulation. Then they found that their tins had already been removed. There was silence for a moment, followed by fierce and eager whisperings, then the whole body marched to the Barrack Yard, broke open the store, and took out all the tins they could find. They marched back to the Lumber Yard, and then Jackey Jackey made the following speech:—"Now, men, I've made up my mind to bear this oppression no longer; but, remember, I'm going to the gallows. If any man funks let him stand out. Those who wish to follow me, come on."

A policeman named Morris was standing in the archway or entrance to the yard, Jackey Jackey rushed forward, struck him a fearful blow with an enormous bludgeon, and knocked him down. A large mob of the prisoners snatched up such weapons as came to their hands and followed him. Many of the prisoners only had sticks, some large, some small. One had a reaping hook and another a pitchfork. As soon as the sentry fell under the blow from Jackey Jackey, the other prisoners were upon him, beating, stabbing, and cutting until the man was a fearful sight to look upon. Jackey Jackey then led the way to the cook-house, where Stephen Smith, the police overseer, was in charge. Smith was something of a favourite among the prisoners, but this good feeling availed him nothing at this time. When Jackey Jackey came rushing towards him, Smith cried out in a piteous tone, "For God's sake don't hurt me, Jackey? Remember my wife and children!" "Damn your wife and children," shrieked Jackey Jackey, as he crashed in one side of Smith's head with his bludgeon. Jackey Jackey passed on, leaving those who followed him to finish his bloody work if necessary.

Near the gate of the Barrack-yard John Price, overseer of work, and a man named Ingram were standing together. Jackey Jackey rushed towards them and aimed a blow at Price, but he dodged back and the club struck Ingram, nearly killing him. Jackey Jackey raised his club for another blow at Price, when the surging crowd behind pushed him forward, and Price escaped and ran for the soldiers. The prisoners behind Jackey Jackey now raised the cry of "Barrow! Barrow!" and from this it is conjectured that their main object was the murder of the Stipendiary Magistrate of the Island, Mr. Barrow, who was believed by the prisoners to be the cause of much of their misery. Jackey Jackey turned from the Barrack-yard and led the way towards Government House. On their road they came to the limekilns, and Jackey Jackey, who had by this time exchanged his club for an axe, opened the door of the hut there. Two policemen were stationed there and they had not yet risen from their beds. One named Dixon was still asleep, and Jackey Jackey smashed the axe through his skull as he lay. The other, Simon, sprang from his bed on to the floor, but was immediately knocked down by a ferocious blow aimed at him by the bushranger, his brains and blood spattering the walls of the hut. Jackey Jackey immediately left the hut, and while his followers crowded in to strike at, or jeer at, their dead enemies as their humour prompted them, he coolly stood aside and lighted his pipe. After drawing a few whiffs he said in a loud calm voice, "Now, boys, for the Christ killer," and the crowd responded with shouts of "Hooray! Now for Barrow's." "To Barrow's." "To Barrow's." They started off, but had not gone far when the soldiers with muskets loaded and bayonets fixed barred the road.

At this time there were about eighteen hundred prisoners on the island, and of these, sixteen hundred were among the rioters. The soldiers numbered only about three hundred, but their discipline enabled them to over-

Chapter XI

awe the vastly superior force, numerically, opposed to them. Perhaps the habits of obedience and submission, so long enforced on the prisoners, may have had some influence. Perhaps, even among this herd of desperate and reckless men, the sight of the soldiers standing firmly with their guns presented ready to fire may have instilled some fear. However this may have been, there was no fight. The rebels retired slowly and unwillingly to the Lumber Yard, where they permitted the soldiers to arrest them one after the other without making any show of defence until one thousand one hundred and ten of them were placed "on the chain." Perhaps Jackey Jackey and the more violent of his followers may have thought that they had done sufficient to ensure them that death on the gallows which was the avowed object of their rising, while the majority had been so demoralised by official brutality as to be utterly indifferent as to what might become of them.

Among those arrested were Jackey Jackey, the bushranger with a continental notoriety, and Lawrence Kavanagh, the Van Diemen's Land highwayman. John Gardner, John Jackson, William Duncan, Abraham Farrer, and John Booth, some of them convicted bushrangers, were also conspicuous for their support of Jackey Jackey in the murder of officials. Another New South Wales bushranger engaged in this riot was Michael Houlihan, who had been captured by Commissioner Brigham in September, 1842, in the Lachlan district, and transported to Van Diemen's Land for highway robbery and horse-stealing, and had been sent from thence to Norfolk Island for similar offences committed near Hobart Town. Besides these there were John Price, and many others named in Chapter X., who were among the insurgents and who more or less actively supported the leaders. On the other hand, Martin Cash, the companion of Kavanagh, refused to take part in the rising. He retired from the Lumber Yard when Jackey Jackey announced his intention, and remained in his cell during the whole time of the riot. Some speculation has been indulged in as to his reason for so acting. It is certain that he was not deterred by fear. Possibly, having been for so long the leader of a gang of bushrangers, he objected to serve under another and a younger man. He, however, was almost the only well-known bushranger confined in the island at the time who did not follow Jackey Jackey.

As soon as news of the riot and its suppression reached Van Diemen's Land, Judge Brown was sent to Norfolk Island by the Lieutenant-Governor, Sir W. T. Denison, to try the prisoners, and Jackey Jackey, Henry Whiting, William Pickthorne, William Scrimshaw, Kavanagh, Gardner, Jackson, Duncan, Farrer, Booth, and three others, making thirteen in all, were arraigned on the charge of murdering John Morris. They were convicted and sentenced to death. They were all executed on October 13, 1846.

The following letter was written by Jackey Jackey to a former chaplain at Port Arthur, and was published in the Cornwall Chronicle. The spelling of many of the words has been corrected, but the style has not been interfered with:—

H.M. Gaol, Norfolk Island.

Condemned Cells, 1846, October the 8th.

Reverend Sir,

As in duty bound to you for the kindness you have shown to me, and the interest I have always seen you take in those that have ever been under your spiritual care, whatever may be their fate, I have been induced to write to you, hoping this may find you in good health, and in the enjoyment of all God's choicest blessings. I have to inform you, that long before this letter reaches your hands, the hand that wrote this will be cold in death. I do not grieve that the hour is fast approaching that is to end my earthly career. I welcome death as a friend;—the world, or what I have seen of it, has no allurements in it for me. 'Tis not for me to boast; but yet, Sir, allow a dying man to speak a few words to one who has always shown a sympathy for the wretched outcasts of society, and ever, with a Christian charity, strove to recall the wretched wanderer to a sense of his lost condition. I started in life with a good feeling for my fellowman. Before I well knew the responsibility of my station in life, I had forfeited my birthright. I became a slave, and was sent far from my dear native country, my parents, my brother, and sisters—torn from all that was dear to me, and that for a trifling offence. Since then I have been treated more like a beast than a man, until nature could bear no more. I was, like many others, driven to despair by the oppressive and tyrannical conduct of whose whose duty it was to prevent us from being treated in this way. Yet these men are courted by society; and the British Government, deceived by the interested representations of these men, continues to carry on a system that has and still continues to ruin the prospects of the souls and bodies of thousands of British subjects. I have not the ability to represent what I feel on this subject, yet I know from my own feelings that it will never carry out the wishes of the British people! The spirit of the British law is reformation. Now, years of sad experience should have told them, that instead of reforming—the wretched man, under the present system, led by example on the one hand, and driven by despair and tyranny on the other, goes on from bad to worse, till at length he is ruined body and soul. Experience, dear bought experience, has taught me this. In all my career, I never was cruel—I always felt keenly for the miseries of my fellow-creatures, and was ever ready to do all in my power to assist them to the utmost, yet my name will be handed down to posterity branded with the most opprobrious epithet that man can bestow. But 'tis little matter now. I have thus given vent to my feelings, knowing that you will bear with me, and I know that you have and will exert yourself for the welfare of wretched men. It is on this account that I have strove, though in but a feeble manner, to express my feelings. The crime for which I am to suffer is murder. Reverend Sir, you will shudder at my cruelty, but I only took life—those that I deprived of life, though they did not in a moment send a man to his last account, inflicted on many a lingering death—for years they have tortured men's minds as well as their bodies, and after years of mental and bodily torture, sent them to a premature grave. This is what I call refined cruelty, and it is carried on, and I blush to own it, by Englishmen, and under the enlightened English Government. Will it be believed hereafter, that this was allowed to be carried on in the nineteenth century? I will now proceed to inform you what has happened since I left Port Arthur. I was sent to Glenorchy Probation Station. I was then determined, if possible, to regain my freedom, and visit my dear native country, and see my parents and friends again. I took to the bush, with two men; one of them said that he knew the bush well, but he deceived me and himself too. Our intention was to take a craft from Brown's River; we were disappointed—there was no craft there. We then turned to go to Launceston, thinking to get one there, and to cross to the

Sydney main. But after leaving New Norfolk, I lost one of my mates, and the same night the other left me at the Green Ponds. I was soon after taken and sent to Hobart Town. I was tried and sent to Norfolk Island, and this place is now worse than I can describe. Every species of petty tyranny that long experience has taught some of these tyrants is put in force by the authorities. The men are half-starved, hard worked, and cruelly flogged. These things brought on the affair of the first of July, of which you have, no doubt, heard. I would send you the whole account, but that I know you will have it from better hands than mine. I am sorry that this will give you great pain, as there are several of the men that have been under your charge at Port Arthur concerned in this affair. Sir, on the 21st of September, 1846, Mr. Brown arrived in the Island with a commission to form a Court, and try the men. On the 23rd of September he opened the Court. Fourteen men were then arraigned for the murder of John Morris, that was formerly gate-keeper at Port Arthur. This trial occupied the Court nine days. The Jury retired, and returned a verdict, and found twelve out of fourteen guilty of murder. On the 5th of October the sentence of death was then passed on us, and to be carried into effect on the 13th of October, 1846. Sir, the strong ties of earth will soon be wrenched, and the burning fever of this life will soon be quenched, and my grave will be a haven—a resting-place for me, William Westwood. Sir, out of the bitter cup of misery I have drunk from my sixteenth year—ten long years—and the sweetest draught is that which takes away the misery of living death; it is the friend that deceives no man; all will then be quiet—no tyrant will there disturb my repose, I hope, William Westwood.

Sir, I now bid the world adieu, and all it contains.

WILLIAM WESTWOOD, his writing.

Beneath the letter is printed as follows:—

The Dying Declaration of Gillian Westwood, alias "Jackey Jackey."

I, William Westwood, wish to die in the Communion of Christ's Holy Church, seeking mercy of God through Jesus Christ our Lord and Saviour.—Amen.

I wish to say, as a dying man, that I believe four men now going to suffer are innocent of the crime laid to their charge, viz.:—Lawrence Kavanagh,

Chapter XI

Henry Whiting, William Pickthorne, and William Scrimshaw. I declare that I never spoke to Kavanagh on the morning of the riots; and these other three men had no part in the killing of John Morris as far as I know of. I have never spoke a disrespectful word of any man since my confinement. I die in charity with all men, and now I ask your prayers for my soul!

WILLIAM WESTWOOD, aged twenty-six years.

Jackey Jackey, at the time of his death, was twenty-six years of age. He was 5 feet 9 inches in height, with fair hair, blue eyes, and a ruddy complexion.

Shortly after the death of these men, Mr. John Price, superintendent of Port Arthur, was sent to Norfolk Island with instructions to break up the settlement and remove the prisoners to Van Diemen's Land, and this was gradually effected. Two or three years later the Government of the Island was again transferred to the Governor of New South \Vales, and in 1859, about two hundred of the Pitcairn Islanders—the descendants of the Mutineers of the Bounty were landed there and have remained unmolested to the present time, and the later history of this beautiful island may be summed up in the one word "peace."

Twelve

The Third Epoch of Bushranging; the Gold Digging Era; Influx of Convicts from Van Diemen's Land; Passing of the Criminals' Influx Prevention Act; Attitude of the Diggers Towards the Bushrangers, and Other Thieves; The Nelson Gold Robbery; Some Pitiful Stories; A Rapid Raid; Insecurity of the Melbourne Streets.

Before entering upon the next stage in the story of the bushrangers, it may be advisable to say something of the vast change which suddenly took place in the conditions in Australia about this time. In 1842-3 the colony of New South Wales was plunged into a financial crisis, about which it is unnecessary to say much here, but from which the colony was only beginning to recover in 1851. Wages were still very low, and numbers of men were out of work. In April, 1851, the news that gold had been discovered at Summerhill Creek, in the Bathurst district, roused something like a ferment in the colony. Men employed in Sydney threw down their tools to "go to the diggings." There was a general exodus from the coast cities and towns to the ranges, then considered far away in the interior. Wages jumped from about one shilling per day for labour to ten or more, meat rose from one penny per pound, for the best cuts, to sixpence. The roads leading to Orange, the Turon, and other early goldfields in New South Wales, were thronged by men, either going to the diggings to seek their fortune, or returning disappointed. In July, 1851, the Port Phillip district of New South Wales was erected into the independent colony of Victoria, and in August the news that gold had been struck in the Ballarat district of the newly-established colony turned the tide of gold-seekers in that direction. The police establishment, with which the new colony started, was merely that of an outlying district of a huge sparsely-populated colony, and was wholly inadequate to the requirements.

There were two gaols in the colony; one at Melbourne, the other at Geelong; neither of them very large. The Geelong gaol, in fact, was little more than a lock-up, and it was only within the past two years that the gaol had been enclosed within a high wall. In 1850 it stood out on the hill, a short distance from the banks of the Barwon River, an ordinary-looking brick building, with the Governor's House and other offices grouped near it, and all opening out directly on the level flat which stretched from the top of the banks of the Barwon River to the hill on which the main portion of the town of Geelong was situated. On the top of this hill, the last building in that direction, in "old Geelong "—as it was called, although it had only been founded about twelve years before—was the court house, and there was no other building along Yarra Street, on the southern side of the hill and across the little flat (a distance altogether of about half-a-mile) until the gaol was reached. The Melbourne gaol stood on what was then the boundary of the city of Melbourne. It was a larger and more imposing building than the Geelong gaol, but still wholly inadequate for the requirements; and therefore one of the first duties of the Legislative Council of the new colony was to provide accommodation for evil doers, who could no longer be sent to the gaols of Sydney to serve out their terms of punishment. This was done by the establishment of "stockades" at Collingwood and Pentridge, both near Melbourne, and the purchase of two old trading vessels, the President and the Success, in September, 1852, to be converted into convict hulks for the safe keeping of the more desperate of the malefactors. Subsequently three other hulks were added to the list, and these were in use for many years after large prisons had been erected at Melbourne, Geelong, Ballarat, Bendigo, and other centres of population.

Looking back from the present time it appears to me that the Colonial Office was guilty of a serious tactical blunder in appointing Mr. Charles Joseph Latrobe, as the first Governor of Victoria. He had been appointed Resident Magistrate, or Superintendent, of the Port Phillip District in 1839; and, during the agitation for the separation of that district from the huge colony of which it was a part, Mr. Latrobe, very naturally perhaps, did all that he could to prevent the inhabitants from gaining their end. As a consequence, he was perhaps the best hated man that has ever lived in Australia. He was usually called "the Governor's poodle," and was denounced in no measured terms by the advocates of separation. When that was carried, and Mr. Latrobe became Lieutenant Governor, his harsh treatment of the diggers nearly drove them into rebellion. This is not the place to give the history of the Ballarat riot, but some reference to it is necessary. A most exorbitant licence fee was imposed on all residents on proclaimed gold-fields, and this tax was collected in a most arbitrary and brutal manner. There were no gaols nor lock-ups on the diggings at the time, and men arrested for all 'sorts of offences—murder, bushranging, stealing, or the non-payment of licence fees—were simply fastened with hand-cuffs to a bullock chain attached to a tree stump by a huge staple. Later some boxes, made of corrugated iron, were put up as cells and these were known as "the Dutch ovens," or "the sardine boxes," and prisoners confined in them on hot summer nights suffered tortures, and begged to be put "on the chain" as a relief. Mr. Latrobe, therefore, soon came to be as cordially hated by the new comers as he had been by the older inhabitants of the district. But whatever may be said as to the harshness of his treatment of the gold diggers, the efforts he made to check the lawlessness rampant in the colony cannot be too highly commended. He and the Legislative Council organised a fine body of police in a very short time. The horse police were as well-disciplined and mounted as any similar body in any part of the world, but allowing for their efficiency, it would have been impossible for them to repress lawlessness so rapidly and completely as they did, had they not been assisted by the attitude of the general public. I may be wrong perhaps, but it has always appeared to me that the antagonism between the free and the convict elements in the population of which I have already spoken was continued long after the abolition of the convict system, and even passed on to these who landed in the country during the rush to the diggings. There was a general tendency at the time to credit all sorts of misdeeds to the convicts. No doubt, among the enormous crowds which landed in Victoria in the early years of the rush to the diggings, there was a fair admixture of rough and reckless characters who were not convicts, but it was the custom to assume that all crimes were committed by the "old hands," and that any man arrested for any criminal offence had been "sent out." Thus, when Mr. Lachlan McLachlan was appointed police magistrate of Bendigo, he merely expressed openly the opinion held by other magistrates, and the public generally, when he declared that nearly all thefts were perpetrated by "old hands." He asserted that he could distinguish a convict from a free man at a glance. He would order the police

Chapter XII

to make the prisoner walk down the court, and would exclaim: "Turn him round again, sergeant. Ah! I thought so! I can see the marks of the irons on his legs."* By which he meant that the man had acquired a sort of limp through wearing irons, and that he could detect it.

All such men were sent to gaol for six or twelve months, not so much for the crime or offence with which they stood charged, as because they were ex-convicts. And generally the public endorsed this apparent injustice. "It's a pity we ain't got more magistrates like Bendigo Mac," was an expression frequently heard in all parts of the colony. It is not impossible that the fashion of crediting all crimes and offences to convicts, however unjust it may have been, tended to prevent others from committing crimes. Whether this was so or not, it is certain that the diggers, rough and careless as the majority of them were, steadily set their faces, as a class, against crime, and never hesitated, even during the height of their dispute with the authorities, to hand over to the police any person detected in stealing. Probably they were forced into this attitude in self-defence. The diggings were merely huge camps, everybody living in tents or "houses" made of wooden rafters and uprights, covered with calico or canvas. Even the big hotels and theatres were calico structures. It was so easy for an evil-disposed person to rip open a tent and thrust his hand under the pillow or into any other place where he thought gold might be concealed. But such thefts, although numerous, constituted only a minority of the crimes committed on the goldfields. All round were holes twenty or thirty feet deep, and the paths from one part of the field to another wound in and out between these holes, so that it was dangerous for a stranger in the locality to travel about after dark. In such a place it was so easy to stab a man and throw his body down a hole that the very facilities offered operated as a temptation to murder. Scarcely a day passed without a body being found murdered and

* "Mr. Lachlan McLachlan, or 'Bendigo Mac,' as he was more familiarly styled, administered the law with a vigour and severity which brought upon him censure from many quarters... but 'desperate evils require desperate remedies.'...When an old hand happened to be among the prisoners, he would be terrified by the fierce reprobation of 'Bendigo Mac,' or by the glare which shot from that inevitable eyeglass...At other times he would say to a prisoner, 'This district is not big enough for both you and me. One of us must leave—which shall it be?' The prisoner would feel, of course, that there was very little doubt about the matter, and would promise to make himself scarce, requesting probably a couple of days' grace to wash up a bit of washdirt." History of Bendigo, by George Mackay, chap. III.

rifled, and thus a peculiar sort of morality was developed on the diggings, and the diggers, while resisting the police, jeering at them and showing their hatred of them in every possible way, still assisted them in capturing thieves and other criminals. It was the custom to call public meetings for political and other purposes, by sending men to all the various camps each carrying a tin dish. These heralds would beat their tin dishes and yell, "Roll up! roll up!" Frequently a "roll up" was called for the purpose of organising a party to hunt down thieves or other evil-doers, and very soon the "roll up" carried terror through the ranks of tent thieves and other robbers. Sometimes the delinquent when caught was cuffed and beaten and ordered off the diggings on pain of death, but, as a rule, he was marched to the police camp, popularly known as "The Camp," and handed over for trial. It was perhaps because of this attitude of the diggers, that "Lynch law" did not become an institution in Victoria, as it had in California. On more than one occasion, it was proposed that thieves, robbers, and murderers should be summarily dealt with by their captors, but such resolutions were not endorsed at the "rolls up"; although, on more than one occasion, it was said that if the Government could not protect the diggers from bushrangers, the diggers would have to protect themselves. Some of the old names, now rapidly disappearing, record the character which the neighbourhood once bore. Thus "Murderer's Flat," the old name of a portion of the Mount Alexander Goldfield, is almost forgotten. The flat is now a portion of the pretty little mining and agricultural town of Castlemaine. It was the custom here in the "roaring fifties," for the diggers to fire off their guns and pistols every night after sundown, and ostentatiously reload them, as a caution that any person seen prowling round the tents during the night would be shot without further notice. In many of the outlying gullies on the Bendigo and Ballarat Goldfields the same ceremony was performed nightly. Beyond the limits of the goldfields the roads were infested by footpads and bushrangers, who hated the diggers for their antagonism to their class. To these the digger was fair game. It was popularly supposed that these bushrangers were all convicts from "Van Diemen's Land," hence they were known as "Van Demonians," "Derwenters" from the River Dement, and "Tother siders." The newspapers were full of references to their doings. The Geelong Advertiser of June 2nd, 1851, warned the public that

Chapter XII

"large numbers of men—half bushranger, half gold-seeker—are travelling along the roads, especially the Sydney road, robbing all who are unprotected." These were said to be Van Demonians who had landed in Geelong or Melbourne, and who were making their way to the goldfields of New South Wales. In the same month the Melbourne Herald published several articles calling the attention of the authorities to the large "influx of Van Diemen's Land expirees who are thronging into Port Phillip." These "villains," it was said, were travelling along all the roads which led to the diggings on the Sydney side, and lived by plundering honest travellers. On June 23rd the mail coach was bailed up at Bruce's Creek, between Portland and Geelong. The coach, with three passengers on board, was going down the hill to the crossing-place, when two men stepped from behind gum trees, presented their pistols, and cried "Bail up." The driver, William Freere, instead of complying, began to flog his horses, but before they could respond their heads were seized by one of the bushrangers, while the other put his pistol to Freere's head; and threatened to blow his brains out. The coach was taken some distance off the road, and its occupants were tied to trees. The robbers went very leisurely through the letters, and when all that was of value had been abstracted one of the bushrangers took a saddle and bridle belonging to one of the passengers (Mr. Thomas Gibson) and set it aside with the remark, "Ah, this is just what I wanted." This bushranger was dressed "in a black suit of fashionable cut, and wore black kid gloves." He was afterwards identified as Owen Suffolk, while his companion was Christopher Farrell. Suffolk took one of the coach-horses, put the saddle and bridle on, and mounted. Farrell jumped on the other horse bare-backed. The tied men begged hard to be let loose, offering to swear that they would not give information to the police, or move from the spot until their captors were away, but their supplications were only laughed at. The road was at that time but little frequented, and the next mail, which might possibly be the first vehicle to pass, would not come for a week. Moreover, they were out of sight of the road. The struggle to get free was therefore a struggle for life, and it was a severe one. Mr. Gibson was the first to get one hand loose. After this the rest was comparatively easy. In less than an hour they were all free, and they walked straight to the township at Bruce's Creek to tell the police. The robbers were caught in Geelong a day or two later. Suffolk was strolling along the beach near the wharf, and Farrell was found in a boardinghouse not far away. They were sentenced to ten years' penal servitude, the first three in irons.

James Mason and John Brown, two diggers, were sitting at their camp at Bendigo having supper, when a man named William Scott passed along, going towards the "township." They invited him to "sit down and have a feed," as he looked tired, and he did so. But while eating he slipped his hand under the edge of the tent and took out a bag containing 100 ounces of gold. The gold was missed before he was out of sight, and he was followed immediately and captured. He was taken to "the camp," and subsequently sent to gaol for five years.

On January 28, 1852, the Melbourne Herald reported that "a gang of Vandemonians have kept the road between Bendigo and Eaglehawk Gully for three days, robbing all who passed." The police were sent out and the gang was broken up. One was shot and three others traced to Halliday's Inn at Kyneton, where they were captured. They had thirty-three pounds weight of gold in their possession, and were taken on to Melbourne for trial.

Such reports were so frequent that the Legislative Council was compelled to take action, and as a consequence the Act known as the Criminals' Influx Prevention Act (18 Vic., No.3) was passed in November. This Act was specially designed to keep ex-convicts out of the colony. It was impossible to prevent those from New South Wales from crossing the Murray River, but it no doubt checked the influx of the more desperate criminals from Van Diemen's Land, where transportation was continued for many years after it had ceased to New South Wales. But although the Act prevented ex-convicts from landing at Victorian ports it could not prevent them landing at Sydney or Adelaide and walking overland to the Victorian diggings. In spite of this, however, the Act was undoubtedly very efficacious in checking the landing of criminally-minded persons. There were, however, so many in the colony previously to the passing of the Act that the police had plenty of employment in hunting them down.

On February 6th, Corporal Harvey, of the mounted police, was searching some boxes at the Police Barracks, Buninyong, to ascertain whether they contained gold. A man named Goldman threatened to shoot him if he touched his box. The trooper simply replied "I must do my duty," and opened the box. Goldman shot him at once. This crime was a purposeless one. The trooper had been ordered to remove gold from all boxes left at the station so that it might be sent down to Geelong by escort. The only excuse which can be made for Goldman is that the diggers were very sensitive where their gold was concerned and were also very ready to protect it even at the risk of murder. But the boxes were left there in charge of the police, and any man who objected to his box being searched had no right to take it there. However, Goldman was convicted of murder and hung.

On February 23rd, Elliott Aitchison, a squatter, was robbed near Buninyong. The robber took horse, saddle, bridle, saddle-bags, watch, a bill of exchange for £30, and some money. The bushranger was identified as a man named Edward Melville, who had been working for a neighbouring squatter, Mr. Winter, of Winter's Flat, and was well known in the district. A reward of £30 was offered for his apprehension.

The ship Nelson arrived at Geelong from London in March 1852, where she landed her passengers and cargo and took on board some cargo for her return voyage. She was then taken round to Hobson's Bay to fill up. On the night of April 1st she was lying off Liardet's Beach, near where the South Melbourne pier now stands. There were on board Mr. Draper, the mate in charge, Mr. Davis, second officer of the Royal George lying at anchor near, three seamen, three passengers, and the cook. At about two a.m. they were roused by loud calls, and as each one came out of his cabin to ascertain what the row was about he was seized and lashed to the bulwarks. When all had been secured the robber who appeared to be the leader untied Mr. Draper and ordered him to show where the gold was. The mate refused. The robber fired and wounded him in the side. He then threatened to shoot him dead next time he refused. Another of the gang prodded Mr. Draper behind with a sword, and, realising that resistance was useless, he led the way to the lazarette. The door was soon broken down, and twenty-three boxes containing 8183 oz. of gold, valued at about £25,000, were taken out and carried on deck. "I say, mates," exclaimed the leader, "this is the best —— diggings we've seen yet." The boxes were lowered over the vessel's side into boats, and then the men tied to the bulwarks were unloosed, their hands tied behind them, and they were marched into the lazarette. The entrance was closed up with the broken boards nailed across. When the stevedore and his men arrived some hours later to go on with their work the prisoners in the lazarette were released, and information was given to the police. The robbers were said to have numbered about twenty. A search proved that two of Mr. Liardet's boats had been removed from their moorings. They were found far away along the beach, and it was conjectured that these boats had been used by the robbers. A reward was offered by the Government of £250 for the capture and conviction of the robbers, and this was supplemented by a further reward of £500 offered by Messrs. Jackson, Rae & Co., the consigners of the gold. Within a few days John James, alias Johnston, was arrested in Melbourne, and shortly afterwards James Morgan and James Duncan were found at the Ocean Child Inn, Williamstown. They were in bed, and when the police entered the room Morgan exclaimed: "If we'd known you was —— traps we'd a' blown your —— brains out." When taken to the lock-up he said: "We may be sentenced, but we'll live to dance on your —— grave, and have 2000 a nob to ride in our carriages." At the trial it was said that they had been concerned in several highway robberies on the Keilor Plains and in the Black Forest, but these cases were not gone into. They were convicted of having stolen the gold from the Nelson, and sentenced to fifteen years' hard labour, the first three in irons.

The winter of 1852 was an exceptionally severe one, and snow fell heavily in the ranges. A bullock driver who was looking for his bullocks near Buninyong was bailed up by three armed men. Although it was snowing at the time they stripped him and tied him to a tree while they searched his clothes. Finding only about five shillings in his pockets they cast him loose, gave him his clothes and money, with the remark that they thought he "was a —— digger from Ballarat." A few miles further along the road they met a party of real diggers and took from them 8 oz. of gold and an escort receipt for 84 oz. more.

Such robberies as these were reported daily on the roads round Ballarat, Bendigo, and Mount Alexander. Perhaps the worst places were the Stoney Rises, on the road from Geelong to Ballarat, and the Black Forest, between Melbourne and Mount Alexander. But the conditions even in Melbourne

Chapter XII

were not much better than elsewhere. On August 6, 1852, a digger who had just returned from Bendigo was knocked down in Little Collins Street, Melbourne, and the pocket of his trousers cut out. He, however, lost only a few shillings, while the robbers missed 3lb. weight of gold which he held clutched in his hand.

Judge Barry and Mr. Wrixon, the barrister, left the Supreme Court House together on August 11, at about half-past eight p.m. When they were near St. Francis' R. C. Church, Lonsdale Street, they heard a shout for help. Ploughing through the deep mud they stampeded three robbers who had got a man down in the gutter. At that time the streets of Melbourne were not paved as they are now and the judge and the barrister nearly got bogged while pulling the digger out of the mud hole in which he was nearly smothered. The robbers escaped, but the digger found his gold safe.

Mr. John Scraggs was going home to his house in Richmond one evening. When passing a corner near his own residence he received a blow on the head and fell stunned. When he recovered consciousness his watch, chain, ring, and purse had disappeared. The next day he purchased a revolver, loaded it carefully, and carried it in his hand ready for use as he went home. He was specially vigilant when he approached the corner where he had been knocked down before. Probably he was rather too vigilant on one side. However that may be, he received a blow on the other side which "stretched" him again. That time the robbers only got a revolver, and Mr. Scraggs swore that they should get no more firearms from him.

It was about this time that the Melbourne Herald reported a case of a captain of a vessel lying in Hobson's Bay. The captain had been to the theatre and was walking to Liardet's Beach to get a boat to take him on board his ship, when he was knocked down in Flinders Street and dragged into a right-of-way. Here he was stripped stark naked and left insensible. It was early morning when he regained his senses. After some hesitation he walked towards an hotel, hoping to be able to borrow some clothes there, but he was pounced on by a vigilant policeman and taken off to the lock-up. His story was not believed and he was taken into court and charged with "indecent behaviour," which was adding insult to injury, and the magistrate remanded him till next morning, to allow enquiries to be made, bail being refused. Later on, when it was ascertained that he really was the captain of a vessel, he was discharged. The Herald cited this as an instance of the vagaries of police magistrates, and charged the police with being unable to protect the public against robbers.

But to return to the knights of the road. A pitiful story was told of an old man and his son who had left their work in Melbourne, and gone to the diggings to "make their pile." They were unsuccessful, like a good many more, and started to walk back to Melbourne, to return to their ordinary work. They were bailed up on the edge of the Black Forest. The bushrangers refused to believe that they had no gold. It was a stale trick, they said, to throw a bag of gold behind a log and swear they hadn't got any, and then go back and pick it up, when the bushrangers had gone away. It was in vain that the old man swore that he had had no gold to throw away. One of the bushrangers compelled him to hold out his hand and fired a bullet through the palm. As he continued to declare he had no gold the bushranger was about to shoot through the palm of the other hand, when the boy made a rush at him and was shot dead by the other bushranger. The old man was then allowed to go on his sorrowful way. Bushranging was the common subject of conversation. Little else was talked of and even the children played bushranger. Two young lads, who were old enough to know better, thought it would be good fun to "stick up" their father. He was a farmer living on the Barrabool Hills, about eight or nine miles from Geelong. He went into town with some produce and was returning at nightfall when, at about half a-mile from his own gateway, he was ordered to "bail up" by two persons on horseback. Without hesitation he snatched up a gun from the bottom of the dray and fired. One of the bushrangers fell and the other cried out "Oh, father, you've shot Johnny! We were only in fun." It was too late. The father's aim had been too sure and the boy was taken home to his mother dead.

On October 24th, 1852, Henry Johnston, John Finegan, John Donovan, Charles Bowe, and John Baylie, known as the Eureka gang, were tried for highway robbery in Melbourne. William Cook said he was riding from Melbourne to Bendigo, on August 4th, when near Aitken's Gap he was bailed up by Finegan and Donovan. Three other men sat on their hors-

Chapter XII

es some distance away along the road, but did not interfere. One of the bushrangers held a pistol to his head, while the other stripped him naked and searched his clothes. He also felt him all over, under the armpits and elsewhere. They took £2 14s. and a pistol from him. Finegan wanted to take everything, but Donovan would not agree to that, but gave him back his clothes. Then he returned one of the £1 notes and the fourteen shillings in silver. Wesley Anderson identified Baylie and Donovan as the two men who had robbed him on a Sunday in August, near Buninyong. The proceedings were very similar to those in the first case. All the other prisoners were identified in a similar way by other witnesses. The robberies were effected over a wide range of country, and were all of a similar character. When asked what they had to say in defence, one of the prisoners asked the Judge whether he thought they were crows? "Here's one man," he continued, "says we stuck him up at Aitken's Gap, another at the Porcupine, another near Mount Egerton, and others at other places, and the police says they caught us in the Crown Hotel, Buninyong. Why, your Honour, horses couldn't get over the ground in the time." The jury, however, seemed to have formed a better opinion of the power of the bushrangers' horses than the bushranger himself. Perhaps this was due to the fact that some of them at least had exchanged horses with their victims. However that may be, they were all found guilty. Finegan and Donovan, who appeared to have been the leaders, and to have taken part in the majority of the robberies, were sent to gaol for twelve years, and the others for six years each.

The Geelong mail was stuck up in December 1852, between the old Burial Ground and the Flagstaff Hill, now in the very heart of Melbourne. The robbers took watches, rings, and money from the passengers, but did not dismount from their horses nor interfere with the mail bags. Probably it was too close to the city.

On December 26th two diggers returning to Melbourne were robbed near Keilor by three armed men on horseback, who took a large parcel of gold dust and an escort receipt for more. On the same day a man was brutally beaten on the Sydney road, about fifteen miles from Melbourne, and robbed of his watch, some gold specimens and nuggets, and his money.

Thirteen

Captain Melville Takes to the Road; He Ties and Robs Eighteen Men; He Goes to Geelong for a Spree, and Boasts of His Exploits; His Sensational Capture; Sent to the Hulks; Murder of Corporal Owens; Melville Removed from the Hulk Success to the Gaol; Murder of Mr. John Price and Mutiny of the Convicts; Melville Attacks Mr. Wintle; Death of the Noted Bushranger.

Of all the bushrangers of the "roaring fifties" none was more talked of than Frank McCallum, alias Captain Melville. Every now and then, during the latter half of the year 1852, stories were told of daring robberies committed by Captain Melville, and rewards were offered for the capture of the captain, dead or alive, or any person who aided and abetted him. On December 18th, 1852, he rode up to a sheep station near Wardy Yallock and asked Mr. Wilson, the overseer, who was the owner? "Mr. Aitcheson," was the reply. "Is he at home?" asked Melville; and on being answered in the affirmative he expressed a wish to see him. Mr. Wilson having no suspicion as to who the civilly spoken visitor was went into the house and returned with Mr. Aitcheson. Melville drew out a pistol, pointed it towards them, and ordered them to "put up" their hands. The two gentlemen complied at once and were marched to the wool shed. Here they found the sixteen shearers and other workmen sitting in a row down the middle of the shearing floor and William Roberts, Melville's mate, standing sentry over them pistol in hand. Aitcheson and Wilson were conducted to the head of the row and ordered to seat themselves, which they did. Melville then searched about until he found a rope. This he cut into lengths and then mounted guard while Roberts called the prisoners out one by one and tied them to the fence. Mr. Aitcheson asked Melville what he wanted? and the bushranger replied, "Gold and horses, and we're going to get them." When all the men were securely tied the bushrangers cautioned them not to attempt to get loose until permission was given, and then walked to the house. Melville told Mrs. Aitcheson not to be afraid, as he never interfered with ladies any more than was necessary. He told all the women and girls to go into one room. One of the women was told to get some food ready, and part of this was taken, with two bottles of brandy, to the men at the shed. Melville and Roberts both ate heartily. They searched the house thoroughly, and took all the money and jewellery they could find. They picked out two fine horses with saddles and bridles, and when mounted they stopped at the wool-shed to bid good-bye to Mr. Aitcheson and their "other friends," and to inform them that Mrs. Aitcheson would come and untie them as soon as he and his mate were out of sight along the road.

The boldness with which this robbery was conceived and carried out caused quite an excitement throughout the colony. The idea of eighteen men permitting two to tie and rob them without a struggle caused as much amusement perhaps as wonder. People talked of little else for days, and everywhere the question was asked, "What next?" This, however, was not all. After leaving the station the bushrangers only travelled a few miles and camped in the bush. The following morning they stuck up two diggers, Thomas Wearne and William Madden, on the Ballarat Road, and robbed them of £33. After taking the money, Melville asked them where they were going. "To Geelong to see our friends, and spend Christmas. But now we shall have to go back to the diggings," was the reply. Melville drew Roberts apart, and after a brief conversation he came back, handed the diggers a £10 note, and hoped that would be sufficient to enable them to enjoy their holidays. During the next few days the bushrangers stuck up and robbed a large number of travellers on the Ballarat Road, travelling themselves towards Geelong at the time. On the morning of the 24th, they stuck up and robbed a man near Fyan's Ford, about five miles from the town, and then rode straight into Geelong. They put up at an hotel in Corio Street, where they had dinner and saw that their horses were fed. Then they went to a house of ill-fame, a little off the street, and not far from the Corio Street lock-up. One of the women was sent to a public-house in Moorabool Street for some bottles of brandy, and the spree began. The liquor opened Melville's mouth, and he informed one of the women who he was, and boasted of his exploits. This woman told the others, and as there was a hundred pounds reward offered for "such information as would lead to his apprehension," the chance of making money was too good to be missed. One of the women put her arms round his neck and talked to him, while another slipped out by the back door and went to the police station to inform the police as to the character of their visitors.

Somehow Melville became suspicious. He suddenly pushed the woman away, and called to Roberts to go and fetch the horses, swearing that he would leave the town at once. Roberts, however, was too drunk to heed him. He was asleep with his head resting on the table. Melville jumped up and shook him, but finding that he could not rouse him, resolved to go alone. He opened the front door and saw a woman with two policemen just entering the gate. Slamming the door to hurriedly, he rushed across the room, and seizing a chair, dashed it through the back window. Then, jumping clear through the opening thus made, he raced down the yard to the back fence and climbed over in time to meet another constable, who was hurrying up towards the back of the house. Without a moment's hesitation Melville knocked the policeman down, and ran across a piece of vacant land. His first intention had, of course, been to go for his horse, but on reaching Corio Street after this enforced detour, he knew he would have to pass the lock-up to reach the stable where his horse was. This was too dangerous, and he took the opposite direction.

On its western side Geelong proper—that is, the older part of the town—is separated from its western portion by a deep gulley, which in early times was closed up by a dam. The water thus penned back spread over a flat, and served to supply the first settlers with water. In 1852 the dam was still there, and formed the roadway which connected Geelong with Ashby, Kildare, and other suburbs. It was across this dam that all the traffic on that side of the town passed. At short distances away the Melbourne and Ballarat roads branched off, the one along the banks of the bay, and the other towards the Bellpost Hill. A few years later the dam was cut away, and a handsome iron bridge erected across the deep gulley, while the space formerly covered with water was converted into a park or garden.

The dam was in a line with Malop Street, and Melville raced away across the vacant lots to that street, followed by several policemen. It was near sundown, and as Melville came to the dam Mr. Guy was returning from

Chapter XIII

his afternoon ride. Mr. Guy was a young gentleman who had not been long in the colony. He was lodging at the Black Bull Inn, Malop Street, where the most extensive stables in the district were. The Black Bull was a great sporting house and there were always some race horses there, either in training or waiting for engagements; and, as Mr. Guy was an excellent horseman, he frequently took one or other of these horses out for an airing. On this occasion he had been for a gallop across the plains to Cowey's Creek, and was walking his horse quietly back to allow him to get cool. When crossing the dam a man suddenly rushed up and seized him by the leg. He was lifted out of the saddle, and half fell, half jumped to the ground. He landed on his feet and rushed round the horse in time to collar the man who was trying to mount. The horse was a spirited animal and objected strongly to this summary change of riders, otherwise, perhaps, the bushranger would have got away. He reared and plunged and prevented the bushranger from mounting. Guy seized the bushranger, and received a heavy blow for his trouble, but he held on gamely, and in the struggle the horse broke away and galloped off to his stable. A moment later the police came up, and Melville was captured. Mr. Guy was highly complimented for his plucky fight with so redoubtable an opponent, but he usually replied that he wasn't going "to lose a horse in that manner if he could help it." Of course, he was intensely surprised when he was informed that he had captured the notorious bushranger, Captain Melville. Melville and Roberts were lodged in the "old gaol" in "South Geelong," and I remember going to see "the bushrangers" conveyed across the flat and up the hill to the court-house to stand their trial. They were seated in a dray, heavily ironed—there was no "black Maria" in Geelong in those days—and drawn by two horses. There were several armed policemen on the dray, and others marched before and behind. The courthouse, of course, was crowded, and, as boys were not admitted, I was not present.

It may perhaps be of interest to-notice that at that time there were stocks outside the Geelong Court-house. They were converted into firewood about two years later when the foundations for the new and larger court-house were laid. I believe these were the last stocks seen in Victoria, the Melbourne ones having been destroyed some time before, when the court-house there was enlarged.

Melville was convicted on three charges of highway robbery, and was sentenced to twelve years' penal servitude on one and to ten years each on two other charges, making in all thirty-two years. A number of other charges were withdrawn. Similar sentences were passed on Roberts, but they were made concurrent. Melville was taken by boat from Geelong to the hulk President in Hobson's Bay, "until the devilish spirit he had for so long a time exhibited appeared to be broken," to quote the Melbourne Herald. Rather more than a year later he was removed to the hulk Success "for milder treatment," and was permitted to go ashore to work in the Government stone quarry at Point Gellibrand. At that time Melville was engaged in translating the Bible into the language of the Australian aborigines, "in which he could converse fluently." For more than two years the public heard nothing of Captain Melville.

On October 22nd, 1856, a launch with fifty or sixty convicts on board was being towed from the hulks Success and Lysander to the landing-place near the quarry, when Mr. Jackson, the officer in charge, observed that the prisoners were crowding towards the bow of the launch. He shouted to them to go back and trim the launch. Some obeyed, but those nearest the bow seized the tow-rope and rapidly pulled the launch up to the stern of the boat which was towing it. Then the prisoners began jumping into the boat. Mr. Jackson was hurled into the water. Corporal Owen Owens' head was smashed, and he and John Turner, one of the rowers, were thrown overboard. The other rowers jumped, some on to the wharf, the others into the water. The convicts seized the oars and pulled rapidly down the bay, Captain Melville standing up in the boat, waving the hammer with which it was said Owens had been killed, and shouting "Adieu to Victoria!" The desperadoes, however, were not to be allowed to escape so easily as they imagined. The guard on the hulk Lysander fired at them as they passed, and the water-police from Williamstown soon followed and overtook them. Being threatened with muskets at close range, and having no arms themselves, they surrendered and were towed back quietly to the Success. Nine of the conspirators were tried for mutiny, Melville at his own request being placed first at the bar alone. In the charge sheet he was described as Thomas Smith, alias Frank McCallum, alias Captain Melville, and was said to have been transported to Van Diemen's Land in 1838. This

CHAPTER XIII

contradicts the many rumours which gained currency about him during his bushranging career. That most generally received was that he had come to the colony in charge of an emigrant ship from England, and that he and his crew had deserted her and gone to the diggings, where, being unlucky, he had taken to bushranging. This report was frequently denied, but still it was extensively believed, especially in the Geelong district. After hearing the evidence, the jury were unable to agree on a verdict of murder in the first degree, as there was a doubt as to who struck the blow which killed Corporal Owens. The Judge ruled, however, that if, in an attempt to escape from lawful custody, any person is killed, all of those attempting to escape are guilty of murder. In consequence of this ruling Melville was found guilty and was sentenced to death. The other prisoners were acquitted. The sentence was afterwards commuted to imprisonment for life, and when Melville was informed of the "mercy" which had been extended to him, he remarked quietly, "Well, you'll be sorry for it."

On March 26, 1857, Mr. John Price, Inspector General of Convicts in the Colony of Victoria, attended at the quarry near Williamstown to hear any petitions or complaints which the convicts might have to present. Convict James Kelly was the first called and he asked for a ticket-of-leave. Mr. Price replied that he was unable to accede to this request. As he walked away Kelly was heard by Captain Blatchford to mutter "Bloody tyrant, your race is nearly run." He appeared to be in a furious passion, but very little notice was taken of him at the time. Several of the prisoners pressed forward and began to crowd round Mr. Price, loudly complaining that they had not received the due amount of rations. Some exclaimed that they were being cheated. Mr. Price stepped back and said in a loud voice, so as to be heard above the din, that these complaints must be given in proper form, when full enquiries should be made. If the charges were true the abuses should be rectified, but if they were false or unfounded, those making them would be punished. Suddenly a rush was made. Kelly threw a heavy stone, shouting at the time, "Down with the bloody tyrant." The stone struck Mr. Price and he reeled. The convicts pressed forward shouting "Give it him, give it him," and a volley of stones was sent flying through the air. Captain Blatchford was struck several times and rushed off to summon the guard, which was stationed on the other side of the quarry tramway, behind a large heap of stones. A convict named Bryant was said to have struck Price with a heavy navvy's shovel. He then shouted "Come on. He's cooked. He wants no more." When Captain Blatchford returned with the guard the convicts had placed Price's body on a hand barrow, which they held up in their hands. The remainder stood round as if waiting for orders. The face of the murdered man was calm, even pleasant to look at, but the back of his head was terribly battered, and the heap of stones was covered with his blood and brains. The guards surrounded the convicts, who offered no resistance, and they were marched away to the wharf and taken on board the Success. Soon afterwards shouts of "The bloody tyrant's done for, hooray," and much cheering were heard on board of this vessel and on the Lysander. Fearing that a general mutiny of convicts might take place, the harbour defence vessel Victoria, with her guns shotted and the crew at their quarters, was laid alongside the Success ready to sink her if necessary. The convicts, however, were very quiet and allowed themselves to be conducted to their cells without opposition.

Fifteen convicts were placed on trial for this murder, but each one exercised his full right of challenge, so that the panel was exhausted without a jury being secured. On the next day the Crown Prosecutor withdrew three prisoners and the jurors to whom they had objected were recalled. This manoeuvre was repeated until at length a jury was obtained to try three prisoners, Thomas Malony, Thomas Williams, and Henry Smith. They were found guilty and sentenced to death. On the day following Richard Jones, William Jones, John Williams, and James Kelly were placed at the bar, and after a lengthy consultation the jury returned a verdict of "Not guilty." This verdict was condemned in the strongest terms by the judge, the press, and the general public. The acquittal of Kelly, who was said to have led the assault and struck the first blow, caused general indignation. The remainder of the prisoners were charged in two batches, and they were all found guilty and sentenced to death. Their names were Francis Brannagan, Richard Bryant, William Brown, John Young, alias Lowe, James Anderson, Henry Smith, alias Brennan, Daniel Donovan, and John Chesley. The majority of them had been condemned to penal servitude for bushranging and robbery, and the last on the list was Chesley, who was executed on April 30th, 1857.

CHAPTER XIII

Melville had been removed from the hulks to the Melbourne gaol a short time before because it was believed that he had been planning a general mutiny, and now it was said that the murder of Mr. Price had been included in his scheme. During the first two or three months of his residence at "Wintle's Hotel," as the Melbourne gaol was facetiously called, Melville behaved very quietly, and was treated as an ordinary prisoner. On July 28th, 1857, he made a savage attack on Mr. Wintle, the Governor of the gaol, and was afterwards confined to his cell. Later it was reported that for weeks he would behave in the most exemplary manner, but would suddenly and unexpectedly break out into a paroxysm of fury, during which he would destroy everything destructible. At these times the warders and officers were ordered to keep away from his cell, and leave him to himself. He was placed under medical surveillance, with a view to ascertain whether he was sane or not, great care being taken, it was said, not to excite him. On August 10th he was locked up as usual, and appeared to be in his normal condition as regards health and spirits, but, on his cell being opened next morning, he was found lying dead on the ground. A blue handkerchief with red spots, which he had brought with him from the hulks, was tied round his neck with a slip knot and twisted up tightly. Dr. McCrae was called in immediately, and said that death was due to strangulation. Life had been extinct some three or four hours. He was of the opinion that the prisoner had tied the knot himself. A verdict of *felo de se* was returned by the coroner's jury which heard the case. A variety of opinions were expressed as to this verdict. So far as is known, there is no evidence to prove that Melville came to his death in any other way than that stated at the inquest, but there were numbers of people who asserted their belief that the bushranger was strangled by the gaolers.

As a rule these people did not blame the gaolers for this act. The opinion generally expressed was that Melville was little better than a wild beast, and was better dead than alive. They also asserted that it would have been more satisfactory if the bushranger had been hung openly instead of being murdered secretly, and they blamed the Governor and the Judge for having been so "soft-hearted" as to commute his sentence when he was condemned to the gallows. There appears, however, to be no evidence in support of this view. The records of the inquest are brief, but they seem clearly enough to prove that the most noted bushranger of the gold-digging era took his own life in one of the paroxysms to which he was liable. Whether these paroxysms were due to his harsh treatment on the hulks is another matter, but we are not in the "Fifties" now. The hulks have been destroyed or sold, and the prisoners are treated as humanely now in Australia as they are in any other civilised country.

The treatment of the bushrangers all through the later developments of that crime tend to prove that the Australians considered bushranging as a sort of exotic introduced into the country with the convicts sent from England, and only to be wiped out by the suppression of the convict element in the population. We see the influence of this view in New South Wales, Van Diemen's Land, and elsewhere, as well as in Victoria. In this colony the appointment of Mr. John Price as Inspector General of convicts was an expression of the popular belief. Mr. Price had had a long experience among convicts, and the very fact that his treatment of them was harsh was a recommendation in his favour. He had been superintendent of the convict station of Port Arthur, where he was known to the convicts placed under his charge as "Bloody Tyrant Price." When that establishment, of the character of which the late Marcus Clarke gives us an idea, but an idea only, in his story, "For the Term of his Natural Life," was broken up, in consequence of the cessation of transportations to Van Diemen's Land, in 1853, Mr. Price was specially chosen for the position he held in Victoria because of his knowledge, not merely of convict character, but of the personal appearance of a large number of the criminals who were disturbing the peace of the colony, because the majority of them had already been under his charge in Van Diemen's Land.

The Victorians desired above all things to keep the convicts out of their colony, and as a means to this end they endeavoured to make their prisons a "holy terror" to this class of immigrant. When that object had been achieved, or the convict element in the population had died out by the effluxion of time, they modified their prison discipline in accordance with the growth of humanitarian ideas. Whether they have done all that is possible in this direction may be doubted, but this is not the place to discuss this question. The evidence so far as it has been collected and considered tends to show that the chief remedy for crime is education. It is impossible to believe that even the worst of the bushrangers would have grown up to be such scourges to society had they been properly cared for during the impressionable period of their lives, and many of them amid all their savagery show traces of qualities which might, under happier circumstances, have fitted them for useful positions in the world. It may be added here that Mr. John Price is popularly supposed to have been the prototype of "Maurice Freere" in Marcus Clarke's novel, which should be read by every student of Australian history.

Fourteen

Murder of a Bullock-driver; Sticking Up in the Melbourne Streets; Stealing £100,000 in Bank Notes; Want of Efficient Police Protection; Murders and Robberies at Ballarat, Bendigo, Mount Alexander, and other Diggings; The Robbery of the McIvor Gold Escort; A Bushranger Intimidated by a Bottle of Brandy; Robbery of the Bank of Victoria at Ballarat; Capture of Garrett in London; Prevalence of Horse-stealing; The Doctor's Creamy.

The arrest of Captain Melville, although it removed the central figure in this the third bushranging epoch in Australia, by no means put a stop to the crime. Melville had been a specialist, a true highwayman, while the others were merely general practitioners who were not very particular what crimes they committed so long as they secured booty. On January 24th, 1853, the driver of the mail coach from Colac to Geelong was ordered to bail up near Mr. Dennie's station. The driver kept on. One of the bushrangers reached out to grasp the reins, while the other fired at the driver. The report frightened the horse of the man who was trying to seize the reins, and it bolted, throwing the rider. The mail-man whipped his horses into a gallop and got safely away.

Richard Bryant and William Mack walked into Mr. J. Jackson's store at Fryer's Creek, Mount Alexander, and ordered the storeman to bail up. They took all the money that was in the till, a quantity of gold dust, and a bundle of the most valuable articles they could find. They were arrested by Constable Bloomfield in a house in Melbourne and sentenced to twelve years' imprisonment.

On May 7th, a carrier named William Morgan left Melbourne with several passengers, each of whom had agreed to pay him £14 to carry his "swag" to the Mount Alexander diggings. Besides these swags Morgan had some goods for the conveyance of which to the diggings he was to receive £29. The first day's journey was a short one, the party camping near the Lady of the Lake Inn. The passengers, who, it may be as well to explain, had to walk, had a tent with them which they took off the dray. They were erecting this when Morgan and the driver of another dray camped there, named Pilcock, walked to a blacksmith's shop near the hotel to get some small jobs done. Pilcock returned alone and informed the company that Morgan had walked on to "Tulip" Wright's to try and purchase an extra pair of bullocks to strengthen his team. The following morning Pilcock yoked up Morgan's team as well as his own, and asked one of the passengers to drive it, adding that Morgan would join them somewhere along the road. They were about to start when a little boy, travelling with his parents by another dray, ran up crying out that there was "a man's head sticking out of the ground." A rush to the place was made and the child's statement proved to be true. The body was dug up and identified as Morgan's. From the appearance of the ground about half-way between the camp and the blacksmith's shop it was apparent that a fierce struggle had taken place. The ground was trampled and torn up as if with a wrestling match. A pool of blood was discovered with a track leading from it to where the body was found, showing that it had been dragged there. Some wonder was expressed that so severe a contest should have taken place without any sound having been heard at the camp, which was not more than a quarter of a mile away. But there were some fifty or sixty people at the camp, and some of these had been amusing themselves by singing, while others had been playing concertinas and other musical instruments. The noise thus made had no doubt drowned the noise of the deadly contest which was taking place so close at hand. Pilcock was arrested at once, and was subsequently convicted and hung. Had his project succeeded, he would have made quite a nice little haul with the money for the loading on the two drays.

So prevalent was crime at this time, that even the streets of Melbourne were not safe. One afternoon, David Clegg and Henry Jones were driving home in a spring cart from Melbourne, to the huge encampment on Emerald Hill, known as Canvas Town. They had just crossed Prince's Bridge, over the Yarra Yarra, when they were ordered to bail up. Clegg caught up a double-barrelled gun from the bottom of the cart, but before he could make any use of it, it was snatched from his hands by one of the robbers, who cried out: "Stand aside till I blow his —— brains out." A second robber said: "Oh, let him go." While these two were disputing as to whether

Clegg should be shot or not, a third robber struck the horse and started him off. During the next few days the Canvas Town mob, as it was called, committed several robberies in the neighbourhood of Prince's Bridge, and at length the police made an effort to protect travellers between Melbourne and Canvas Town (now known as South Melbourne). One day, Chief Constable Bloomfield and Mr. Farrell were walking together near the bridge, when Bloomfield exclaimed: "Hulloa! there's a man I want for uttering a £5 note." He crossed the street and said: "Well Hammond." "What the —— do you want?" asked Hammond. "Oh, you needn't be afraid, I won't hurt you," replied Bloomfield. "I don't care whether you do or not," cried Hammond, walking beside the policeman in bravado. Bloomfield delayed making the arrest in hopes that another constable would appear, until Hammond turned away, when he grabbed him. Farrell shouted, "Look out, Bloomfield," and the constable turned, but not quickly enough to avoid a blow aimed at him by another man. Bloomfield fell, but did not relax his grip on Hammond, and two other constables appearing at the time, both Hammond and Edwards were secured. James Hammond and William Edwards were identified as the men who wished to shoot Clegg, and were sent to gaol for ten years, the first three in irons. Another man, named Smith, who had prevented Hammond from firing at Clegg, was let off with six years.

Another batch of this gang of scoundrels which infested the river side at Melbourne was secured in connection with the stealing of a consignment of bank notes with the face value of £100,000. These notes were brought to Melbourne in the ship Strathedon, consigned to Messrs. Willis,

Merry & Co. as agents for the Union Bank of Australia. The notes were for £15, £10, £5, and £1. They were unsigned and were therefore non-negotiable. They appear to have been taken from the ship and dumped down on the wharf, pending the arrival of a dray to take the case to the warehouse of Messrs. Willis, Merry & Co. When the dray arrived, however, the box could not be found. The loss caused great excitement and the police were notified of the robbery. Some days later an unsigned £10 note was passed on Messrs. Brasch & Sommerfeld, Collins Street, in exchange for clothing, and this led to the arrest of William Young. During the following week William Layworth, William Simpson, William Rogers, and Thomas

Chapter XIV

Stroud were detected in attempts to pass unsigned notes on various hotel and boarding-house keepers, store-keepers, and others, and were arrested. Stroud's residence was searched and a number of the unsigned notes were found there. His wife was arrested, but was acquitted. Layworth turned Queen's evidence and escaped punishment, but Young, Simpson, Rogers, and Stroud were sentenced to long terms of imprisonment. The jury commented on the carelessness shown by the bank and its agents in leaving the box unwatched on the wharf. The manager of the bank expressed his regrets and promised that more care should be taken in future.

John Atkins went into the Cross Keys Hotel in Melbourne and called for a drink. George Ellison, who was in the bar, asked him what he had done with the gold he had brought from the diggings. Atkins replied that he had none. Ellison called him a liar, and said that if he had not come from the diggings his trousers would not be the colour they were. Everybody knew a digger, because his moleskin trousers were always coloured by the clay he worked in. A row started, and the landlord interfered and told Atkins to leave. He did so, but was followed by Ellison and another man, who knocked him down and robbed him of his gold. Ellison was arrested next day and was sent to gaol.

The Geelong Advertiser of March 5th says:—"The shameful want of adequate protection along the main roads leading to the diggings has repeatedly been exemplified in the robberies, assaults, and murders committed by bushrangers upon, a number of luckless wayfarers, with the grossest and most notorious impunity. These unavenged offences against society and the public peace have been excused by some, on account of the difficulty of keeping afoot such an extended line of patrol as would effectually intimidate marauders…When we are in possession of the fact that the Sydney Executive could and did accomplish such protective arrangements over a hundred and fifty miles of country, we may be allowed to doubt the alleged inability of the Victorian Government to render equally efficient aid out of a revenue probably ten times as great as that derived by the sister colony from the same source; at least we might reasonably suppose that townships between Melbourne and Mount Alexander, Geelong and Ballarat, would be supplied with police, mounted or otherwise, to act in a radius of ten miles or so when called upon…A gentleman well known to the public, from his long connection with the newspaper press, has been the victim of a murderous assault. His story is that while at Ballan, a township about twenty miles this side of Ballarat, on the Melbourne road, a man attacked him with an iron poker. The gentleman raised his arm to protect his head and it was broken. But for this the blow might have fallen on his head and proved fatal…Two days were wasted at Ballan and four at Bacchus Marsh waiting to find a magistrate to issue a writ for the arrest of his assailant… The gentleman having been robbed of his money had to make his way to town for medical aid by the charity of persons along the road. Fortunately some kind friends supplied him with means to obtain food and carriage."

At the time the police were too busy harrying the diggers for the exorbitant licence to attend to the roads, but later in the year, when the Melbourne papers backed up the demand for better police protection, police stations were established at the larger camping places where villages or, as they are called in Australia, townships had grown up. In the meantime numbers of murders were committed without the perpetrators of the crimes being discovered. Thus Mr. and Mrs. Skinner were travelling from Bendigo to the new rush at McIvor and camped for the night on the banks of Eve Creek. In the morning Skinner went to look for his horse while his wife prepared breakfast. When she went to the lagoon to fill the billy to make the tea, she saw the half-immersed body of a man. When her husband returned he drew the body out of the water, and saw that the head had been fearfully battered. A pocket-knife, pipe, tobacco, and a silk handkerchief were found in the pockets, but no gold or money. An enquiry was held in this case, and a verdict of murder was pronounced against some person or persons unknown, and that was all; but there were hundreds of such cases in which no enquiry was held.

John Shannon was travelling from Ballarat to Geelong, and stopped for the night at an inn at Batesford. He called on Mr. White, a butcher, and had tea and was about to return to his inn, when three men stopped him at the door. One of these men asked, "Is this the butcher's shop?"

"Yes," replied Shannon. "Ah! you're just the bloke we want," exclaimed the man. The three men then hustled Shannon back into the shop and compelled him to stand with his back to the wall and his arms stretched

CHAPTER XIV

out. White was placed in a similar position, and made to stand while the robbers emptied the till. They then searched Shannon's pockets, and took out a parcel of gold and some money. He objected, and one of the men who had been standing on guard at the door drew a pistol, put the muzzle close to Shannon's breast, and pulled the trigger. Shannon fell. The man who had been searching him turned the body over, and then said, "Barry, it's finished; we'll be off." The three men then left, no attempt being made to detain them. An inquest was held on the body, and a verdict of wilful murder was returned against three men whose names were unknown. The jury added: "We cannot separate without expressing a strong feeling with regard to the unprotected state of the road between Geelong and Ballarat, which is overrun with bad characters. We would respectfully but firmly urge on the Executive the immediate necessity of erecting intermediate police stations between the two places, with patrols to traverse the road from station to station, and we would also point out the necessity for strenuously enforcing the Vagrant Act." Three men were arrested and charged with this cold-blooded murder, but were acquitted.

The great bushranging event of the year was the sticking up and robbing of the Gold Escort from the McIvor Goldfield. The escort was a private one travelling from McIvor to Kyneton, where it met the Government Escort which conveyed gold from Bendigo and Mount Alexander to Melbourne. It started, as usual, on July 28th. At about fifteen miles from McIvor and three miles from the Mia-Mia Hotel, there was a sharp bend in the road round a point of rocks which jutted out from the range. At the bend a mia-mia, or shelter such as is made of boughs by the blacks, had been constructed, and opposite to it a big log was drawn across the track. This compelled the driver of the escort cart to pull his horses off the track and drive very close past the mia-mia. The road was very rough, and the cart swayed about badly. Just as it was passing the mia-mia a volley was fired from it, and the three troopers on the cart as well as the driver fell. The horses on which Mr. Warner, in charge of the escort, and Sergeant Duins were mounted were both wounded. Although they were wounded, the troopers returned the fire as speedily as possible, but could see nothing to shoot at except the bushes. The bushrangers fired again, and the troopers were compelled to fall back, when about a dozen men rushed from behind the mia-mia, seized the two boxes which contained the gold, and rushed back into the scrub. Mr. Warner sent Sergeant Duins to the nearest police camp for assistance, and then followed the bushrangers, who fired at him. He replied with the three shots remaining in his revolver, and then retired. Then Mr. Warner galloped as fast as his wounded horse could go to Patterson's station for help. On his return with some of the station hands he found a man putting the wounded troopers into the cart, and arrested him on suspicion of being one of the robbers. The driver, T. Flooks, was the most seriously hurt, and he died a few days later. He and the troopers, S. B. Davis, J. Morton, and R. Boeswetter, were taken to the hospital at the police camp on the McIvor goldfield as quickly as possible, and the man who had been arrested, having proved that he had no connection with the bushrangers, but had been acting from purely humanitarian motives, was discharged. A party was organised to pursue the robbers, and on going to the place where the attack had been made three horses with packsaddles were found tied to the trees. It was conjectured that the robbers had been disturbed before they could pack the gold on the horses by the approach of the pursuing party, and had made off on foot into the ranges. Some time passed away, and then a man named John Murphy was arrested on board the ship Madagascar, lying in Hobson's Bay. He had taken a passage in her on the eve of her departure for England. When charged he admitted that he had been one of the party, and promised to turn approver. He gave some information, which led to the arrest of others of the gang, but he then seems to have repented of his decision, as he committed suicide. His brother, Jeremiah Murphy, however, was arrested in Queensland, and gave the desired information, thereby escaping punishment. The gold stolen was valued at about £5000, and very little of it was recovered. George Wilson, George Melville, and William Atkins were charged with the murder of Thomas Flooks, and were found guilty. They were hung in Melbourne, on October 4th. Atkins died as soon as the bolt was drawn, but Wilson and Melville struggled for several minutes. The hangman was compelled to "draw the legs of Melville down with considerable force" before life was extinct.

Alfred Stallard and Christopher Goodison went to a tent at Bendigo Creek, and entered into conversation with Mrs. Roberts, who lived there.

Chapter XIV

They offered her a glass of rum which she drank. It is supposed that the liquor was drugged, as she became insensible, and the two men "made a pack" of everything valuable in the tent, including five ounces of gold, and walked away. On his return to his tent, William Roberts was informed of what had taken place and gave information to the police. The robbers were followed and were captured near the Loddon River. When they were asked at their trial whether they had anything to urge as a reason for mitigating their punishment, Goodison complained that they had been chained to a tree for three days at the Loddon. They were forced to walk to Mount Alexander, and were then chained to a log in the Camp Reserve for ten days. They were marched to Kyneton, where they were kept in the lock-up for five days on bread and water. From thence they were conveyed to Melbourne by coach. They received little sympathy, however, because it was well known that diggers whose only crime was inability to pay a heavy licence fee were treated no better.

Occasionally the tragic events of the year were lightened by a touch of comedy, as when a resident of Ashby was returning home from his business place in Geelong. It was dark when he was crossing the dam, when a man presented a pistol at him and called "Bail up." The suburbanite was taking home with him a bottle of brandy, which, in accordance with the custom of that time, was not wrapped in paper. Paper was too dear in Australia to be used for wrapping articles which would keep together without. When challenged, the suburbanite brought the bottle from under his coat, presented it at the head of the bushranger, and cried, "You bail up." The would-be robber, taken by surprise, dropped his pistol and turned to run, but the suburbanite cried "Stop, or I'll fire," and the fellow stopped. The suburbanite thought for a moment whether he should take the "bushranger" to the lock-up or not, and decided that it would only entail a "lot of trouble," so he punched his head and let him go. He kept the pistol as a trophy, and carried home his bottle intact. About the same time Edmund Taylor was found in the bush dead. His body was terribly mutilated. He had left Eureka, Ballarat, to travel to Burnt Bridge, and was known to have taken with him a bank receipt for £200 and a £10 note.

Arthur Burrow and William Garroway called at the hut of William Henry Mitchell, at Pennyweight Flat, Ballarat, and asked the way to the township. Mitchell told them and was then asked to "shout." Mitchell refused, when Garroway struck him with a pick handle, while Burrow drew out a pistol and presented it. They took what gold they could find and walked on. They were joined by two other men, and stuck up and robbed Alexander McLean. They were followed and arrested.

William Bryan and John Douglass were also convicted of highway robbery at Muddy Creek and other places between Geelong and Ballarat, and sent to gaol for five years. James Nugent and four others stopped Benjamin Napton on the road near Modewarre. They pretended they were policemen in search of bushrangers. Nugent was anxious to take care of Napton's gold for him, but Napton refused to entrust it to him. They walked together to Kildare, where they went into the Sportsman's Arms and had drinks. When they came out, Napton missed his gold, and Nugent was arrested. A knife was found on him, and this had some soil sticking to it. At the police-court investigation the magistrate recommended the police to dig in the yard of the hotel near where Nugent had been standing. They did so, and found a bag containing 9 oz. of gold. Two nuggets, which Napton said were also in it, could not be found.

Roberts, who had been convicted of complicity in the robbery of gold from the ship Nelson, but who had been pardoned on a question of identity having been subsequently raised, was captured, and charged at Buninyong with highway robbery. He, with ten other men, was being conveyed to Geelong to serve the ten years to which' he had been sentenced, and were halted at Ray's Hotel, on the road, for refreshments. Roberts begged to be allowed to write a letter to a magistrate in the neighbourhood, and his request being granted, his right hand was freed from the handcuffs. The other prisoner to whom he was chained managed to slip his hand out of the handcuff, and Roberts being thus free, jumped through the window and bolted for the bush. Only one constable had been left in the room in charge of the prisoners, and he could only shout out an alarm. However, Roberts ran almost into the arms of the foot policeman, who had recently been stationed at this point, and he held the bushranger until the other constables came up.

On December 14th, 1854, Thomas Quinn, a stonemason, started from

Chapter XIV

his home in Geelong and rode to Ballarat. He left his pony at Mrs. Smith's, about three miles from the diggings, and walked in. He stopped at the tent of John Boulton, and played cards with Boulton and his mate, Henry Marriott. Later on the three men went to the tent owned by Henry Beresford Garrett at the Big Gravel Pits. They took their revolvers, but no powder and shot, and walked across Main Street to the Bank of Victoria on Bakery Hill. They had formulated a plan to rob the bank, and Quinn had been induced to join on the understanding that no violence was to be used. Hence the unloaded pistols. They put new caps on to the revolvers and some paper in the muzzles to "make them look as if they were loaded." Garrett and Boulton entered the bank, Marriott stopped at the door inside, while Quinn remained outside on watch in the street. They ordered the cashier and teller, Messrs. Buckley and Marshall, to "bail up." Then they tied the hands of the two bank officials, and collected the spoil. As soon as they were outside they separated, one going down Bakery Hill, another along the Melbourne Road, and the others by different routes across the Eureka Plateau, having previously agreed to meet at Garrett's tent. They had taken with them notes, sovereigns, and silver to the amount of £14,300, besides about 350 ounces of gold. When they had divided the loot Marriott returned to his lodgings in "the township," now known as the City of Ballarat. He lodged at a boarding-house in Lydiard Street. Garrett disposed of his tent and tools, and went by coach to Melbourne, from whence he shipped direct for London. Quinn and Boulton went to Geelong. They stayed one night at Quinn's house in Chilwell, and went by boat next day to Melbourne, where they sold their share of the gold at the London Chartered Bank in Collins Street. They returned next day to Geelong, and again stopped at Quinn's house for a night, and then went back to Boulton's tent on the diggings. They took good care not to mention the robbery before Mrs. Boulton, because "she was a good woman." On the following day Boulton went to the bank from which the money had been stolen and asked for a draft on London for £1450. With an infatuation difficult to account for he tendered in payment for this draft some of the stolen bank notes, among those which he had received for the gold in Melbourne. This was almost like asking plainly to be arrested. Of course the notes were recognised at once. He was kept waiting on some frivolous pretext while the police were sent for, and was then arrested. One of the stolen £10 notes was produced at the trial and identified as part of the money advanced by Boulton in payment of the draft. Quinn and Marriott were speedily arrested, and Quinn turned approver. The other two were sentenced to ten years' penal servitude. Detective Webb followed Garrett to London and found him in fashionable lodgings near Oxford Street. The detective watched him for some days before he made up his mind that the fashionably-dressed man was the bank robber he was after. One day he saw Garrett come out of his lodgings and followed him into Oxford Street. Suddenly Webb shouted "Garrett," and Garrett, taken by surprise, stopped and half-turned round. That was enough to convince the detective that he was right. He walked up to the robber, slapped him on the shoulder, and said "How do you do, Mr. Garrett?" "I don't know you," replied Garrett. "Perhaps not," returned the detective, "but I know you. You've just arrived from Melbourne in the Dawstone. I've a warrant here to arrest you for robbing the Bank of Victoria at Ballarat. Will you come quietly?" Garrett saw that the game was up and surrendered. He reached Melbourne in August, 1855, and was speedily sentenced to keep his former mates company for ten years.

Sufficient has, I think, been said to indicate the state of the country and the character of the crimes committed during this epoch. How many men were shot while prowling about the tents on Ballarat, Bendigo, Mount Alexander, and other diggings it is impossible to say. Many of the bushrangers, after having made a haul on the roads or on the diggings, went to Melbourne or Geelong and spent their ill-gotten gains in riot and debauchery, and then committed crimes in these towns for which they were captured and punished. Others returned to New South Wales or to Van Diemen's Land and ended their careers there. It was rarely known how many crimes even those who were captured had committed. They were placed on trial for their last offence. In some cases it was said that the prisoner had been guilty of other crimes, but the difficulty of finding witnesses in a population which was continuously shifting from one end of the country to the other, as new goldfields were opened, made it impossible to prosecute for crimes committed a few months before. It was the custom therefore to inflict long terms of imprisonment to keep the evil-disposed out of mischief

CHAPTER XIV

for a time. When a prisoner was tried and convicted for more than one crime the sentences were usually made concurrent, so that there was no encouragement for the police to pile up a record of crimes against a prisoner. Captain Melville was the one exception to this rule.

The sole motive for the robberies of this epoch was a sordid lust for gold, which seems to have seized many men who but for the gold discoveries might have lived out honourable lives. The case of George Hanslip may be cited as an instance of this. He was a confidential clerk employed by Mr. Spence, draper, of Collins Street, Melbourne. He was sent by his employer to pay some accounts and purchase goods in Sydney, at that time the emporium of Australia. For convenience of carriage, in days when communication was difficult and bank drafts rare, he was entrusted with 1400 ounces of gold and some jewellery, and was instructed to offer the gold to Messrs. C. Newton & Co., of Pitt Street, on his arrival at Sydney. He reached Sydney by boat at nine a.m., but did not call at Messrs. Newton's store until three p.m., when he reported that he had been robbed of the gold. He seemed very excited, saying to Mr. Newton "Oh, what shall I do?" He asked Mr. Newton to go with him to Malcolm's Adelphi Hotel, and Mr. McKeon, one of the partners in the firm, did so, and saw a carpet bag which had been ripped open. Hanslip said he felt certain that the gold had been taken to Hobart Town, and asked Mr. Newton for the loan of £50 to enable him to go there to seek for it, but whether Hanslip overdid his part or not, Newton began to be suspicious of him, and refused to lend the money. One thing that tended to make him doubt that the money had been stolen as Hanslip said, was that Hanslip was spending money very freely. Enquiries were made, and it transpired that Hanslip had called on a Mr. Marks and offered to sell him the gold before he called on Mr. Newton. Marks had agreed, and sent a man with Hanslip to the Adelphi to fetch the gold, so that it might be weighed. On their arrival Hanslip had fumbled about with his key for several minutes and could not open the door of his room. He said he believed the door must have been nailed up. He got it open at last, and when they went in the first thing they saw was the ripped bag and a few grains of gold scattered about on the hearthrug. Another carpet bag had been turned out, and the clothes scattered about the room. It was after this that Hanslip went to Mr. Newton's, who advised him to give notice to Mr. McLerie, the Police Superintendent. Hanslip went to Mr. McLerie's office, and afterwards had a handbill printed offering £1000 reward for the recovery of the gold. Information was to be addressed to "George Hanslip, Esq." The result of the police enquiries was that Hanslip was himself arrested and charged with having stolen the gold. On enquiries being made, it was discovered that he had left the jewellery entrusted to him at his lodgings in Melbourne. He was convicted, but in consequence of his previous good character he was let off with a comparatively light sentence.

But for the unfortunate dispute between the Government and the diggers over the licence fee, it is probable that the bushrangers might have been disposed of in less time than they were. That dispute culminated at the end of 1854, in a fight between the more violent section of the diggers and the military. Although the military won in the conflict on the Eureka, the diggers were the actual victors, and during the year 1855 they were granted all that the moderate party had previously asked for. With the settlement of this vexed question the police were relieved from their task of harrying the diggers, and devoted their time to the suppression of bushranging so successfully, that in the latter half of 1855 the Government proposed to make a considerable reduction in the police force. The Ballarat Times, the Bendigo Advertiser, and the various newspapers in Melbourne and Geelong protested strongly against this proposed reduction. The gold digging organs predicted an immediate increase in bushranging and other forms of lawlessness, but when the reduction was made in 1856, these predictions were not fulfilled. No doubt many of the bushrangers were captured and punished as horse-stealers. The two crimes have always been intimately related in Australia. Horses were a necessity to bushrangers, and a man who would steal a horse would not be likely to hesitate to stick up an unarmed man if money or gold might be obtained by that means, and they were quite as liable to be arrested while stealing a horse as when robbing a man. For two or three years it was almost impossible for any honest man to keep a horse. Perhaps one of the most daring and impudent of this class of offence, was the stealing of Dr. Bailey's "Creamy," in 1855. Dr. Bailey was perhaps the best known man in Geelong. He was elected the first mayor of the town when it was incorporated in 1849, and was re-elected for several consecutive years. He was very wealthy, rather pompous, and highly respected. He had given up general practice, but had an office, where he received a few patients and friends, at the rear of Mr. Poulton's chemist's shop in the Market Square. One morning he rode to his office as usual, hitched Creamy, which was as well known in Geelong as his master, to a post in Moorabool Street, the busiest portion of the town, and went into his office. Almost as soon as the doctor disappeared, a man in shirt sleeves unhitched the horse, threw himself carelessly into the saddle and rode slowly away. He nodded familiarly to the policeman at the corner, who, like the numerous persons about at the time, thought the fellow was the doctor's groom sent to take Creamy back to the stable. The man rode very slowly up Moorabool Street until he turned into Ryrie Street, but once out of sight of those who saw him mount he must have travelled much faster. He had barely turned the corner when the real groom rode up, and he was much surprised to find that Creamy was already gone. Of course, the excitement was intense. The idea that anybody would dare to steal the doctor's horse had never entered the head of the most imaginative person in Geelong. Why, even a burglary at Buckingham Palace would not have been more astonishing. Crowds collected to stare at the hitching post on the kerb opposite the doctor's office. Parties of mounted police and civilians started to hunt for the robber in all directions, but no traces of the missing Creamy could be discovered, and it was not until some months later that he was discovered in Ballarat. The daring scoundrel had ridden him straight to the diggings, and had sold him in Mr. O'Farrell's newly-opened "Horse Bazaar."

Fifteen

An Escape from Norfolk Island; Stealing a Government Boat; The Convicts of New South Wales; A Terrible Indictment; Thomas Willmore; Murder of Philip Alger; Murder of Malachi Daly; Fight between two Bushrangers; Hunting down Willmore; His Capture while Asleep; The Last of the Van Diemen's Land Bushrangers; Wilson and Dido; Some Minor Offenders; An Unfounded Charge; Change of Name to Rid the Island of Evil Associations.

The rush of men of all sorts from all parts of the world to the great goldfields of Victoria, although it no doubt attracted the majority of the desperate characters from the neighbouring colonies, did not entirely free them from bushrangers. It is necessary, therefore, to devote our attention to these, and Norfolk Island claims first place. On March 15th, 1853, a few months before the penal settlement on the island was finally broken up, a number of convicts were employed in loading the store ship Lord Auckland. The ship lay off in the roads, and the goods were taken out to her in boats rowed by convicts, under the charge of soldiers. One boat, manned by the convicts Dennis Griffiths, James Clegg, Thomas Clayton, Robert Mitchell, Joseph Davis, Patrick Cooper, Jeremiah O'Sullivan, John Naisk, and "Ginger," was on its way to the ship with a load. When it was at about a quarter of a mile from the shore the convicts suddenly rose up, rushed the soldiers, and threw them overboard. No other boat was near, and this gave the convicts the opportunity they had been looking for. One constable was left on board, and Bordmore, the coxswain, seized the gunwale of the boat and held on. The convicts resumed their oars and pulled as hard as they could, but as Bordmore refused to let go, and stopped the way of the boat, he was taken on board again and set to his old work of steering. He was, however, ordered on pain of death to steer for the main land. On April 11th they reached Stradbroke Island, off Moreton Bay, but in taking the boat through the surf she stranded.

The men on board, however, all got safely on shore. The constable and coxswain, with convict Mitchell, were left near the landing-place while the other eight walked along the coast to seek for food, of which they were much in need. They found the hut of Ferdinand Gonzales, a fisherman, and tried to induce him to lend them his boat to take them to the mainland. They represented themselves as having been shipwrecked, but Gonzales did not believe them, and refused to trust them with his boat. They went away, and Gonzales walked to where they had said their boat had been capsized to ascertain whether their story was true or not, and during his absence they returned, stripped his hut of all that was eatable or of value, and stole his boat. They pulled round the coast out of sight, and then sent Clegg and Griffiths to fetch the constable and the others, but the two officers had in the meantime secured Mitchell, and now arrested Clegg and Griffiths. The other six runaways waited for a time, and then started for the mainland.

On the Monday following a fisherman named Thomas Duffy went from the mainland to the island, and he consented to land the constable, the coxswain, and their three prisoners at Moreton Bay, from whence they marched to Brisbane, where the prisoners were lodged in gaol. In a few days complaints of robberies having been committed along the coast were received, and the Customs boat, with six armed constables on board, was despatched to capture the runaways. They were told to call at Cleveland Point to pick up the Chief Constable, who had gone to the coast by land. When near the mouth of the Brisbane River, on passing a patch of scrub, the constables suddenly became aware that another boat was alongside, and that they were threatened by six men armed with pistols. This completely turned the tables. The constables were compelled to hold up their hands, and were towed into the scrub, where they were forced to land and strip. The convicts took the constables' clothes and gave them their own rags in exchange, and then, having made them get into Gonzales' old boat, ordered them to "be off."

There was nothing else to be done, and the would-be captors returned to Brisbane as rapidly as they could, only to be arrested as the runaways. However, they soon established their identity, and were released. In the meantime the runaways, being decently dressed and having a first-class boat, pulled to the barque Acacia, which was lying at the mouth of the river waiting for the mails, before beginning her voyage to Sydney. They told their old story about being shipwrecked mariners, and were believed and invited on board, where they were hospitably feasted. The constables were blamed for not having given notice to the vessels lying at the mouth of the river, of the fact that these convicts were at large, but they had not yet reached that part of the river when they were captured themselves, and if they had gone to these vessels in Gonzales' battered boat and in the tattered raiment of the runaways, they would not only not have been believed, but might have been detained or sent to Brisbane as the runaways they resembled. It was a very trying and difficult position in which they were placed.

When the convicts left the Acacia where they had been so well entertained, they pulled to the house of Mr. Watson, the chief pilot, and robbed him of provisions, a gold watch and chain, and about £40 in money. They stove in his boat to prevent him from going to the mainland to report, but left him a bottle of rum out of his store to "keep his spirits up a bit." Mr. Watson, however, managed, when they had gone away, to patch up his boat so as to enable him to cross the narrow strait which separated Pilot Island from the mainland, and very soon several boats, manned by constables and volunteers, were searching the scrubs and islands near the mouth of the river in hopes of being able to capture the runaways. On May 12th, Eugene Lucette was rowing near the mouth of the river, when he discovered the stolen Customs Officer's boat among the mangrove bushes. He towed the boat up the river and restored it to its proper owners. Mr. W. A. Duncan, J.P., Mr. Shendon (the customs officer), Mr. Sneyd (the chief constable), and a party of the water-police constables started in pursuit. They had some black trackers with them, and these soon found a camp among the mangroves where the convicts had recently been staying. The tracks were patiently followed by the blacks for some distance, and at length the party was found near the Cleveland Road, about eight miles from Brisbane. They were in a very weak condition, having had no food, they said, for four days, and were easily captured. They had tried to make a living by bushranging along the coast, having landed at several points and robbed the few settlers there were there then. At Wide Bay they had come on a large camp of natives who appeared so hostile that the convicts had been afraid to land, and had therefore worked their way back to Moreton Bay with the intention of going up the country to look for work, as they were tired of living by robbery. They had a number of watches and other articles of value, two guns and two pistols, all loaded. They were tried on two charges, viz:—stealing the Customs Officer's boat, the property of Her Majesty, &c., and stealing a boat belonging to Ferdinand Gonzales, fisherman, and were convicted. They were sentenced to fifteen years' penal servitude.

These men had been sent to Norfolk Island for bushranging and other crimes committed in Van Diemen's Land, and therefore had nothing to do with New South Wales until they landed at Moreton Bay as escapees. Griffiths, Clegg, and Mitchell were sent back to the island in charge of the constable and coxswain who had captured them, and who were officials under Mr. John Price, Commandant of the island. The six convicted of stealing the Government boat at Brisbane were not retransported to the island, but were accommodated in the gaol at Moreton Bay.

It may be as well to state here that transportation to New South Wales ceased in 1841, and only two vessels conveying convicts reached that colony afterwards. These conveyed some prisoners who were supposed to be reformed characters, and were known in Australia as "Pentonvillains," from the name of the Reformatory in London through which they had passed. They were sent out in consequence of an agitation on the part of the wealthier settlers for the revival of transportation, but so much indignation was aroused among the mass of the colonists that no further attempts of that kind were made. The agitation was supported by the Governor, Sir Charles A. Fitzroy, who said in his despatch to Earl Grey, that "out of about 60,000 persons transported hither, 38,000 are reformed and respectable members of the community. Of the residue, deaths and departures from the colony will account for the greater part; and I am enabled to state that only 372 out of the whole are now undergoing punishment of any kind." At the date of this despatch, January 6, 1850, the colony of New South Wales included the whole of the eastern side of Australia, Victoria being then the Port Phillip District, and Queensland the Moreton Bay District of this colony. The southern portion, or Port Phillip District, was erected into an independent colony about a year later, and I have dealt with the bushranging there during the gold digging era. In New South Wales robberies were also very frequent, although the condition of the colony was never so desperate as that of Victoria.

In August, 1853, the Bathurst Free Press said:—"For some time past the neighbourhood of King's Plains has been adding to a murderous notoriety...There bloodshed in its most awful shape, murder, appears to be reduced to a science, and the stereotyped phrase *Murder will out* has lost its meaning. An unfortunate old man, remarkable for nothing so much as his hospitality, is slaughtered like a sheep and deposited under a heap of stones...Some fifteen years have rolled over his grave, his death is still enveloped in mystery. A woman in the prime of life is shot dead in her house; the walls being bespattered with her blood. A helpless old shepherd...who had excited the cupidity or revenge of some miscreant, is discovered in the bush, so cut, bruised, mangled, and disfigured that words are wanting to describe the tigrish bloodthirstiness of the murderer... A resident of Bathurst...starts for that bloodstained region one day in perfect health... and the only evidence of him, living or dead, are the merest fragments of calcined bones...and a few hairs which have been pronounced to be those of a human being."

The indictment was a terrible one and was no doubt true, and the paper was perfectly justified in urging the Government to make more strenuous efforts to stamp out bushranging. Nevertheless the murders spoken of here belong to a bygone age, the perpetrators having probably been attracted, like the majority of their class, to the Victorian goldfields. That was the focus to which all such enterprising scoundrels were drawn, and there the majority met the fate they so richly deserved. A few robberies were committed on the roads in the Bathurst district and in other parts of the colony, but the greatest number of such crimes took place in the Manaro district and along the road leading to Victoria. The only bushranger in New South Wales who became notorious at this time was Thomas Willmore. He had been under butler to a gentleman in England, and at the age of fourteen was transported to "Botany Bay," for having stolen a number of silver spoons and other plate from his employer. He was first sent to Pentonville and was then sent to the colony as a reformed character, being

Chapter XV

among th4 last of the English convicts sent to New South Wales, where he and his companions were known as "Earl Grey's pets." He was granted a ticket-of-leave soon after landing and was assigned as servant to a settler in the Wellington district. Soon after reaching the place he quarrelled with a fellow servant and fired a pistol at him. The bullet struck a button and glanced off, and the man escaped, while Willmore, to avoid a trial, took to the bush.

He gained a living by highway robbery for some months. One day he met Philip Alger, near Tomandra, on the Big River. Alger was riding a very fine horse and Willmore claimed it as one which had been stolen from him, and for which he said he had offered a reward. He demanded that the horse should be given to him at once. Alger swore he had purchased the horse honestly, and from a man whom he knew, and declined to part with it. Willmore ended the dispute summarily by drawing a pistol and shooting Alger in the stomach. Willmore was aware that Alger had a considerable quantity of gold on him, as the man had foolishly shown it in a hut where both had lodged during the previous night; but Willmore did not search the body and the gold was found on it when it was discovered. He seems to have been satisfied with the horse. He mounted it and rode towards Wellington.

At Montefiore he bargained with Malachi Daly for a cart, offering for it a quantity of gold dust, which he had no doubt stolen from some other victim, in exchange. They could not come to an agreement, but continued their journey towards Wellington together the next day. At about nine miles from Wellington on the road to the Big River the road goes down a very steep hill, and both men dismounted to lead their horses down. Daly was just starting when Willmore stepped before him, pistol in hand, and demanded his money and gold. Daly protested that he had left it at his hut, and Willmore called him a "liar." They disputed for a few minutes, and then Willmore shot Daly through the head. On searching the body Willmore found only thirty shillings and a deposit receipt for £11, which was of no value to any one except the depositor. Later on Willmore boasted that he got £40 from Daly; but, in his last confession, he said he had only asserted that he had found £40 on Daly's body because he did not wish it to be known that he had "killed a man for thirty bob." Willmore was only just riding away from where Daly's body was lying when he was ordered to bail up by another bushranger. Instead of complying with this request Willmore drew his pistol and fired, both men shooting at the same time. Willmore's horse bolted, and ran for some considerable distance before he could pull him up. When he had once more brought him under control Willmore wheeled his horse round, and galloped back to the scene of the encounter.

He tracked his late opponent for a mile or more. He felt certain that he had not missed, and expected to find the body lying somewhere in the bush. Gradually he became convinced that he had been mistaken, and that the bushranger had escaped, and gave up the search, feeling "very sorry" that he had not fired straighter. During the following three or four weeks he stuck up and robbed a number of people on the roads between Wellington and Mudgee, until at length it was resolved at a public meeting to hunt him down.

A large party assembled by appointment, and this was divided into several smaller bands, each of which was to travel through the district by a specified route, and all were to meet again at a certain time and place and report. One party, under the leadership of Mr. Cornish, got on his track and followed it for two days. On the third day they discovered him asleep on Ponto Island in the Macquarie River, where he had made a camp among the scrub. He was conveyed to Bathurst, tried and convicted of murder and hung.

Great satisfaction was expressed at his capture having been effected without further loss of life, and Mr. Cornish and the men under him were highly complimented for the skill they had shown in tracking him to his lair and their caution in effecting his capture without waking him, as it was highly improbable that he would have surrendered without a fight, and his skill and coolness were such as to make it almost certain that one man at least would have been shot. In reporting his trial the Sydney Morning Herald compared him with "that monster Lynch," and congratulated the colony on having got rid of "such a savage."

In Van Diemen's Land the interregnum between the two bushranging eras was shorter than in New South Wales. In fact, in spite of the assertion

Chapter XV

that bushranging had been suppressed with the breaking up of the Cash and Kavanagh gang, robberies took place occasionally with only short intervals between them. As a rule, however, there was nothing very remarkable in them, and only a few seem worthy of notice here.

On February 19th, 1846, Henry Ford and Henry Smart stuck up and robbed a small farmer named Robert Stonehouse, on the Tamar River. They then compelled Stonehouse, under threats, to accompany them to the next farm and call out his neighbour, John Joynes. When Joynes opened the door the bushrangers rushed in. They tied Joynes and Stonehouse and ransacked the house, taking everything of value. When they left they walked along the road and robbed every one they met. On March 5th they went to Mr. Philip Oakden's house and rang the bell. Mr. Oakden went to the door and was immediately confronted with a gun and ordered to stand. Mr. Oakden informed the robbers that Mrs. Oakden was very ill and requested them not to make a noise. He said he would give them all he had in the house if they would go quietly and not alarm his sick wife. He gave them three £1 notes and some silver. The robbers insisted on going in and searching the drawers for jewellery, but took nothing. They then asked Mr. Oakden for his gold watch. He gave it to them and they left, taking Mr. Oakden with them. They stopped at the Rev. Dr. Browne's house and made Mr. Oakden enquire whether his friend was at home. On Dr. Browne coming to the door he was bailed up, and Ford asked him "How much money have you got?" "None," replied Dr. Browne. "Take care I don't find you out in a lie," cried Ford; "where's your money?" They went in and began searching the drawers and cupboards, and while they were thus employed Chief District Constable Midgeley, who had heard that the bushrangers were in the town, came in with another constable, and taking the bushrangers unawares captured them, though not without trouble. When called on to surrender Ford tried to get out his pistol, but Midgeley said, "If you stir you'll be settled quick." Ford and Smart were convicted of highway robbery and death was recorded against them, but the sentences were commuted to imprisonment for life.

A carrier was stopped on the Brighton Road by two armed bushrangers on Sunday, December 6th, 1846. A carpet bag, containing some dress clothes belonging to Lieutenant Lloyd, of the 96th Regiment, which were being sent to Hobart Town for safety, was stolen. The coat and vest buttons were faced with gold. Several other articles were taken from the carrier's cart. For this robbery Richard Gordon was apprehended by District Constable Goldsmith and Constable Daley. On the following day Henry Jenkins, alias "Billy from the Den," was also captured by the police. Billy had broken out of Oatland's Gaol about three months previously, and had been living by highway and other robberies since. The clothes were offered to Mr. Roberts, a pawnbroker in Hobart Town, and he, suspecting that they were stolen, communicated with the police, who also arrested Michael Cogan, a marine store dealer, as an accomplice.

On December 31st, a party of constables out seeking for bushrangers found a boat containing provisions, wearing apparel, &c., on the east bank of the River Tamar, about eight miles from George Town. Another boat was reported to have been stolen from Mr. Coulson. The police watched by the boat all day and night. On the next morning, Sunday, they saw two men pulling another boat towards the spot and hid themselves in the scrub. When the men landed, the constables appeared and the men ran away. The constables followed, and ran down one man named Jones. The other bushranger, George Jamieson, was captured by Mr. Hinton and his crew at the Marine Station, near the Heads. Jamieson was seen in the scrub, near the station, and one of the men, in accordance with Australian custom, invited him into the hut to have some food. Jamieson accepted the invitation and, while he was eating, Mr. Hinton came in and recognised him. When Mr. Hinton said that he should arrest him Jamieson replied, "I'll be —— if you do," and took a tomahawk from under his jumper. He was immediately seized from behind by one of Mr. Hinton's men and was handed over to the police.

The bushrangers Wilson and Dido were the most notorious about this time. They were watching Mr. James Clifford's house, at Piper's River, on September 16th, 1846, and when Mr. Clifford came out they rushed upon him, took him inside, tied him, and took wearing apparel, ammunition, and other articles out of the drawers and boxes. In January, Mr. Rees and Mr. Stevenson started from Campbelltown in a gig for St. Patrick's Head. On reaching the fourth gate on the road, known as Davidson's gate, they saw two men with guns. At first they took these men for constables. Ste-

Chapter XV

venson got down to open the gate, and while he was doing so Rees became aware of the character of the two armed men who were approaching, and called out to Stevenson, "Make haste! Here's the bushrangers!" Stevenson tried to jump into the gig, but before he could do so the men were upon him. They presented their guns and called upon the travellers to surrender. They then ordered Rees to drive the gig off the road into the timber. Mr. Rees objected, and the bushrangers told him he need not fear, as they intended to act honourably. "But what do you want?" asked Rees. "We want to rob you; we want your money," was the reply. "Then," said Mr. Rees, "why not take it here and let us go on?" The bushrangers made no reply, but took the horse by the head and led him away. When the gig was in among the timber the robbers took £18, a gold watch and chain, and a gold pencil case, from Mr. Stevenson; and £8 and a silver watch from Mr. Rees. They also took two dress suits and two top coats from the gig, and then ordered the gentlemen to take off their boots. "What for?" asked Mr. Rees. "Because we want them," was the reply. "But," cried Mr. Rees, "how are we to get home?" "Oh, you're all right. You can ride while we have to walk," said the bushranger. "But—" began Mr. Rees, when he was interrupted with, "Oh, no more nonsense. If you don't make haste we'll strip you." Stevenson took off his boots, and Rees thought it prudent to follow his example. They returned to their homes in Campbelltown two and a-half hours after they had left, and deferred their visit to the Heads to another day.

On the 27th the police were informed that Dido, the bushranger, had been seen in a hut in Prosser's Forest. A party of constables started immediately, and reached the place at one a.m. Everything was quiet, and the constables walked very cautiously, fearing that if they stepped on a stick and broke it, the noise would waken the bushranger should he be there. The constables took up positions round the hut to prevent escape, and then District Constable Davis, who was in command, suddenly burst in the door. Dido sprang out of the bed and fell on his knees on the floor begging for mercy. He was secured without resistance. In the hut were a double-barrelled gun and a pistol, both loaded ready for use. Mr. Rees's watch and some of Mr. Stevenson's clothes were found in the hut. When brought up at the police court Dido said he had been transported in the name of William Driscoll, but his proper name was Timothy. Mr. Tarleton, the magistrate, made some remarks on the folly of men taking to the bush. Dido replied that he should have been happy enough if he had not been betrayed. He might have lived in luxury for life. The man who betrayed him had been his best friend, but he became jealous and gave him up. He had been sixteen times in Launceston. He had been drinking about town all day on Christmas Day. He had been hocussed and had not been well since. Wilson and he had quarrelled and they had parted. Wilson was all right. He had a nice little patch of cultivation, with plenty of flour and some sheep. He was not likely to be taken. In spite of this assertion, however, Wilson was captured a few days later while drinking at Pitcher's Inn on the Westbury Road. He showed a pistol and this excited suspicion, so Mr. Pitcher sent a servant to inform the police. Constable Leake came and found the man asleep in a hut at the rear of the public-house. He handcuffed him and took him to Launceston in a cart. He was identified as Dido's mate and was committed for trial at the same time.

Robberies of a similar character to these took place from time to time, but after the discovery of gold in Australia in 1851 the great object of the disaffected in Van Diemen's Land was to get to the mainland. No doubt many of these men made their way across the Straits in stolen boats, but the majority paid their passages out of the proceeds of their robberies. Probably it was in consequence of this exodus that no bushrangers became notorious in Van Diemen's Land at this time, and a few examples of the crimes committed during the later days of the epoch will suffice.

About the beginning of 1853 a desperate attempt was made by nine bushrangers, who had been convicted and were being taken from Launceston to Hobart Town, to escape from the two constables who had them in charge. The prisoners had been very rowdy since leaving Launceston, and when the party was near Bagdad, Convict John Jones suddenly snatched the musket from Constable Doran and felled the constable with a blow. Jones then shouted "Now we'll fight for it." Constable Mulrooney rushed at Jones and endeavoured to wrest the musket from him, but the other prisoners forced him back. The prisoners were handcuffed together in threes, and this no doubt hampered their movements, but they contrived to get Mulrooney down and beat him with their handcuffs. Convict Mc-

Chapter XV

Carthy presented the musket at Mulrooney and pulled the trigger, but finding that the gun was not loaded he, in a rage snapped the stock across his knee. In doing this the bayonet fell off and both sides struggled to obtain possession of it. At this moment two men appeared along the road, and hearing the noise they hastened forward. One of them was an assigned shepherd of Captain Chalmers and was armed with a double-barrelled gun. Constable Mulrooney was shouting "murder," and the shepherd came to his assistance. The convicts then gave up the struggle and fell into rank. They were taken to Bagdad, and from thence a stronger guard was sent with them until they were safely confined in the Pentonville gaol.

The bushrangers Dalton and Kelly stuck up and robbed the Halfway House near Campbelltown in January, 1853. On the following day they went to Mr. Simeon Lord's house, Bona Vista, near the river, and bailed up about thirty people, including the District Constable of Avoca, the watchhouse keeper, and another constable. The watchhouse keeper was shot dead. There were several ladies in the house, and these were ordered to go into one room and stay there. The robbers ransacked the house in their search for jewellery and other portable property. They collected between £100 and £200, besides several gold and a number of silver watches, rings, &c. When they had obtained all that they could they compelled Mr. Frank Lord to accompany them to the stables, where they selected two of the finest horses, with saddles, bridles, and spurs. Mounting these horses, the robbers rode away to Mr. Duxbury's Inn at Stoney Creek, where they bailed up twelve men, including two mounted constables. They collected about £50 more and Mr. Duxbury's gold watch. On leaving the inn they went along the road, and met Mr. Sykes, recently returned from Melbourne. They robbed him of about £75, returning the odd six shillings to enable him to continue his journey. They told Mr. Sykes that they intended to rob Captain Creer's and other houses along the Esk Valley, and, when they had collected all they could, to go to the diggings in Victoria. On the following day they visited Vaucluse, but Mr. and Mrs. Bayles were away from home and they got no money. They, however, took some jewellery from the drawers and some provisions from the kitchen. During the following week they continued their depredations and then went to the coal mines on the river Mersey, and stole a whale boat. They impressed four men at work there into their service and put to sea, but the wind was so tempestuous that they were driven back and landed on the coast near Port Sorell, where they were captured.

In February, 1853, a man named Robinson, who had recently returned from the Victorian diggings, shot a shoemaker named William Moonan, while he was waxing a thread. The murderer dragged the body from the hut to the Swan River and threw it in, and then returned to steal what little money there was in the place. The bushrangers Maberley, Hickson, and Poulston committed a number of daylight burglaries in the neighbourhood of Sandy Bay, robbing the houses of Messrs. Stacey, Frodsham, Power, and Dunkley. From Dunkley's they took more than twenty pounds' worth of goods. They had supper at Mr. Winter's and then went to camp in the bush not far away.

Moses Birkett and Peter Perry were captured in a cave about this time. The cave was on the shores of Lake Crescent, and a large quantity of stolen property was found hidden there. Besides the guns and pistols, a couple of sheep shear blades, mounted on long wooden handles were found, and it was supposed that these had been used in the murder of George Kelsey, at Lemon Springs.

Thanks to the activity of the police and the assistance they received from the civilians, such malefactors were gradually captured and dealt with. Some of the Victorian papers charged the Government of Van Diemen's Land with conniving at the escape of expirees from the island to Victoria, but there does not appear to be any foundation for this charge. It is quite possible that neither the authorities nor the public were sorry to be relieved from their company, but we have merely to read the accounts published at the time, to realise that all was done that was possible to suppress bushranging in Van Diemen's Land at this time, and that the escapes of these criminals across the Bass's Straits could not very well be prevented. It was in 1853 that transportation to the island ceased. A few years later, responsible government was established, and the name of the island was changed from Van Diemen's Land to Tasmania, with the object of getting rid as much as possible of old associations. Very shortly afterwards, the papers once more said that bushranging had been stamped out in the island, and this time they were justified in the assertion. No doubt the larger settlements on the mainland offered better chances to the enterprising Tasmanians, whether they were "old hands" or not. Tasmania has, perhaps in consequence of this custom of young men going to seek their fortunes in Melbourne or Sydney, progressed less rapidly than some of the other colonies, but it has progressed, and this progression has been as peaceful and as innocent as possible under present social conditions, and the island which was once infamous has for many years been remarkably clear from criminal offences.

Sixteen

The New Bushranging Era; Fallacy of the Belief that Highwaymen Rob the Rich to Enrich the Poor; The Cattle Duffers and Horse Planters; The Riot at the Lambing Flat; Frank Gardiner, the Butcher; Charged with Obtaining Beasts "on the cross," he Abandons his Butcher's Shop; Efforts to Establish a Reign of Terror in the District; A Letter from Gardiner; The Great Escort Robbery.

Hitherto the bushrangers of Australia had been, as the records prove, drawn almost exclusively from the ranks of those who "left their country for their country's good." Those who took the most prominent share in the next outbreak of the "epidemic" were generally native-born Australians. The sequelae of the old disease were not yet worked out. As I have already said, there were numbers of the "old hands" scattered about the bush, some of them with farms or small cattle or sheep stations of their own who lived fairly honest and useful lives, but even among these, whatever may have been their station in life, there was the old antagonism to "law and order," and their sympathies were all with those who waged war against society. Their children imbibed these ideas, and wherever there was a neighbourhood where this class had collected together, morality was at a low ebb. But besides these settlers there were numbers of nomads, men who worked as shepherds, bullock-drivers, splitters and fencers, shearers, and so on, and as long as the old hands formed a majority, or even a considerable minority of the bush-workers, it was the custom for men to work from shearing to shearing, or from harvest to harvest, and then "draw their cheques," make for the nearest public-house, and indulge in a wild spree, until they were informed by the landlord that the money which their cheques represented had been expended. There were some respectable inns in the back country where they got fair value for their money perhaps, but in too many of these "bush pubs," as they were called, the object of the landlord was to "lamb them down" in the shortest possible space of time. Perhaps when the character of the liquor sold in these places is taken into consideration, this method of cheating was not altogether an evil. It prevented the bushmen from swallowing such large quantities of the deleterious stuff as they might have done if they had received full value for their money. During the time when they were working their principal mode of amusing themselves was telling or listening to tales of the convict days. Some of these stories told by the old hands were of too revolting a character for repetition, but no doubt they were founded on fact. Nothing is too horrible or obscene to have been true of the convict times. The stories, however, which appear to have had the greatest influence over the minds of a certain class of Australian youth were those told of the bushrangers. In these stories there was of course much that was apocryphal, to put it mildly. Many of the exploits of the historic highwaymen of old were told as actual facts in the careers of some Australian bushrangers, with just sufficient variation to adapt them to local purposes. One of the ancient superstitions introduced into Australia by these story-tellers was that the highwaymen robbed the rich to give to the poor. I have no desire to raise any doubts as to the generosity and benevolence of Robin Hood, but I can find no evidence of any such beneficence on the part of any of the Australian bushrangers. No doubt they got their money easily, and spent it recklessly. But they did not pause to enquire whether the person they robbed was rich or poor. There was no such class distinction in the colonies as there is and always has been in England; no very poor class not worth robbing and ready to bless anyone who gave them a penny, and no hereditary wealthy class. Every one had to work somehow for his living, though some were more successful in piling up wealth than others. But the poor had opportunities which have never existed in England, and if they neglected them it was more or less their own fault if they were poor.

The tendency in Australia, as elsewhere, is to build up a wealthy class, but this class did not exist in convict times, and is only just beginning to appear now. The Australian bushranger in fact had to obtain money or go under. He was compelled to share his ill-gotten gains with those who supplied him with food and information. He was a mark for the blackmailer, and he was compelled to find money to bribe those who were in a position to lead the troops or the police to his hiding place. But the convict bushranger was not so well off as the native-born bushranger. There was a strong feeling of camaraderie, an *esprit de corps*, among the convicts, which tended to prevent numbers of men from betraying him, even though they received no bribes. But the new bushranger was more fortunate than the old one. He had his parents, his brothers and sisters, his cousins and his aunts and uncles, who sympathised with him for family and other reasons, and who were bound to help him. It was from among these relatives and friends that the "bush telegraphs," who informed the bushranger of the whereabouts of then police, were drawn, and it soon became apparent that if bushranging was to be abolished these sympathisers and "bush telegraphs" must be dealt with.

There were several localities in New South Wales where the conditions were favourable for bushranging; places where the morality was low and where the police, as representatives of authority, were hated with all the hatred of the "old hand." One of these localities was in the spurs of the Great Dividing Range, in the neighbourhood of Burrowa. All round this district were a number of small squatters, principally cattle breeders, and among these no man's beast was safe. These small squatters were the terror of the big sheep and cattle breeders in the plains, and their principal industry was "duffing." Duffing was not stealing. If a moralist had remonstrated with a Burrowa man whom he found branding his neighbour's beast, the Burrowa man would have replied "I'm only trying to get back my own. He's duffed many a head of my cattle." Sheep could be duffed as well as cattle, but the ranges were generally too steep for sheep. One sheep breeder of the district, however, adopted, as his distinguishing mark, the plan of cutting off both ears, and he was a most successful duffer, because his recognised ear-mark enabled him to remove the ear-marks in his neighbours' sheep. It was no uncommon occurrence for a man to find that a calf sucking his cow had been branded by one of his neighbours, so that it might be claimed as soon as it was weaned. In such a case, if he had complained, his neighbour would probably have accused him of having "mothered" the neighbour's calf on his cow for the purpose of cheating him out of it.

In such a neighbourhood it was impossible for any stranger to travel with horses with any degree of safety. Horses bred in the district could be duffed like sheep or cattle, and horses travelling through could be "plant-

Chapter XVI

ed." If a man, who knew anything of the characteristics of the settlers in this district, camped for the night there, and failed to find his horses next morning, he did not waste time in looking for them himself. He realised at once that one of "the boys" had driven them off into some inaccessible ravine in the ranges, and "planted" or hidden them there until a reward should be offered for their recovery. He would therefore go to the nearest station and enquire whether his horses had been seen. The answer would be "No." Then the traveller would say that he was willing to pay "a note" for their recovery. The reply of the native would probably be that horses always went astray about there. There was such a get-away for them, and the warrigals came down and enticed them off. The story of the warrigals, or wild horses, tempting working horses away was a common fiction. Hobbled horses could not keep up with the warrigals across the ridges. But it was sufficiently plausible to serve. If the working horses broke their hobbles they might perhaps go with the wild horses, but even then it is uncertain. However, after a few minutes' conversation, the native would probably say that if any one could find the horses it was "Jack the Kid," or some other local character, as he knew every gully in the ridges. The wide-awake traveller could understand that "Jack the Kid" was the man who had planted his horses, and would not return them for less than "a note," that is £1, and on this reward for villainy being promised the traveller might go to his camp with the certainty that the horses would be brought to him in about an hour. It would be useless to look for them, because the planter would be on the watch, and if the owner was seen approaching the gully where they were the horses would be driven over the ridge into the next gully. Cases have happened where a traveller has persisted in refusing to be blackmailed and has lost his horses. It would be only necessary to cut the hobbles. Then the traveller, if he wanted his horses, would have to engage two or three expert stockmen to run them in. It was useless to complain to the police. The horses had not been stolen. They were there. Let the owner come and fetch them. Nobody would prevent him and some kind settler would even offer the use of his stock-yard if the owner could drive them into it.

This was the state of the district when the rush to the newly-discovered Lambing Flat goldfield took place in 1860. Early in the following year there was a great "roll up" of the diggers to drive the Chinese off the field, and the military were sent up from Sydney to restore order. In this riot the peculiar morality of the diggers, of which I have already spoken, was illustrated in a remarkable degree. The leaders of the riots strictly forbade robbery, and any person found stealing gold or any other property from the Chinese was to be handed ever to the police; but burning the humpies, tents, and other property of the unfortunate Chinkies, cutting off their pigtails, beating or otherwise ill-treating them, as an inducement for them to leave the field, were justifiable if not meritorious acts. In after years many of the "flash diggers" wore sashes made of Chinamen's pigtails, sometimes with just as much of the scalp attached as would prevent the hairs from scattering. However, the riots did not last long and the leader, William Spicer, was sent to gaol.

There were, of course, many of the young men of the district in the goldfields and, as far as is known, these conformed to the rules laid down by the diggers with regard to property. But this did not affect their own peculiar notions as to the ownership of cattle, sheep, or horses, and the attention of the police was early drawn to the district. Warrants were soon issued for numbers of the youths on charges of horse or cattle stealing, and several were arrested. Later it was said that many young fellows, who might have remained at home, were "driven on to the roads" by the police. That is to say that, because they were interfered with in their favourite amusements of duffing and planting, they turned bushrangers.

Among the residents on the diggings was Frank Gardiner, who opened a butcher's shop on Wombat Flat. Gardiner was born at Boro Creek, near Tarago, in the heart of the district in which Jackey Jackey had first won his notoriety as a bushranger, and the morals of that district were very similar to those I have described as prevalent in the Burrowa district. Gardiner went to the diggings in Victoria in the "Fifties," was arrested near Ballarat, and tried at Geelong for horse-stealing. He was sent to gaol for five years. He escaped from the Pentridge stockade and returned home. Shortly afterwards he was convicted of horse-stealing at Goulburn and sentenced to seven years' imprisonment on two charges, the sentences being made concurrent. He served half the term and was granted a ticket-of-leave. His butcher's shop at Burrangong, to give the diggings its proper name, was

Chapter XVI

said to be the resort of all the worst characters among the young natives of the district, and the majority of the beasts he slaughtered and sold were said to be obtained "on the cross." Becoming aware that a warrant had been issued for his arrest he abandoned his shop and took to the mountains. Here he organised a band of bushrangers, and shortly afterwards reports of people being stuck up and robbed on the roads round the diggings became frequent.

In 1861 the young Australian had not taken to cricket and football so enthusiastically as he did later, and perhaps there were few opportunities for him to get rid of his superfluous energy. Whether this is so or not, it is certain that Gardiner's example had an enormous influence. Not only were those against whom warrants had been issued for cattle and horse-stealing ready to join the gang, but numbers of young men and lads who had hitherto led blameless lives became so excited that they turned out and tried their hands at bushranging.

The first robberies were in the immediate neighbourhood of Burrangong, but very soon the area over which the bushrangers operated was enlarged, and finally embraced the whole colony, and even overflowed into the neighbouring colonies. At first, however, Gardiner and his gang claim our attention, but there were many young men who began as independent bushrangers who made their way to the Burrangong district to join the gang, and others who intended to do so who were captured on the road. It is a difficult matter to decide who did and who did not belong to this gang, as the personnel changed so rapidly. Some actual members of the gang acted independently of it for a time, and made raids into other districts, while others, after having a flutter with Gardiner, left the gang to start elsewhere. The bushrangers did not confine their attentions to travellers on the roads. They robbed whenever and wherever an opportunity occurred. Thus on August 19th, 1861, Henry Keene, Michael Lawler, and William Watson went to Mr. Brennan's station, on the Billabong, and called out "All hands in, or we'll blow your brains out." Mr. and Mrs. Brennan and a number of men who were working at the station were gathered about the verandah of the house smoking and talking. Mrs. Brennan cried out in alarm, "They're going to shoot." James Laurie, one of the men, replied, "Let them shoot away." However, the men went inside, as they were told, and Lawler dismounted and followed them. Keene took his place as sentry at the door, and Watson remained on horseback outside. Laurie said to Lawler, "You're the man that was looking for a gray mare."

"What if I was? What is it to you?" returned Lawler. Laurie picked up a big stick from the fire and made a blow at Lawler, when a shot was fired, presumably either by Keene or Watson, and Laurie fell. He cried out for water, and Mrs. Brennan told her little daughter to go out and fetch a glassful, but Lawler would not permit her to leave the room. Lawler was very violent. He threatened to shoot any one who opposed him, and to "put a firestick to the house" if Mrs. Brennan did not give him her money. One of the bushrangers went to a hawker named Isaac Lavendale, camped close by, and made him go into the house. Lavendale gave the wounded man some milk and spilt some on his face. He said, "I'm dying—don't let them—don't let—" and then he died. Keene fired a ball through the roof of the house and said: "I —— quick took the flashness out of that man. He won't be so flash again." The robbers collected all the money they could, and took clothes and other articles from the hawker's cart. The robbers were subsequently captured by the police, and on March 23rd, 1862, were convicted at Goulburn and sentenced to death. Sir Alfred Stephen told them to prepare to meet their God, when Keene and Lawler both said that they were ready. They were innocent. Watson said: "I don't care if it's tomorrow; I hope you won't keep me like you did Johnson." When taken from court, Watson shouted, "Well, good-bye."

Charles Ross, William Mackie, and John McMahon, alias McManus, robbed the mail at the Chain of Ponds, on the Great North Road, on October 17th. They searched the letters, took a gold and a silver watch, two gold chains, and £55 in notes and coin from Mr. Jonathan Snell, £23 from Mr. Thomas Lumley, and smaller sums and valuables from the other two passengers. On the 30th, Constable Leonard saw Mackie in a public house at Lochinvar, near Maitland, and challenged him. Mackie attemped to run, but was followed and captured. He threw away a gold watch, which was picked up and identified as one stolen from Mr. Snell. Ross and McMahon were discovered not far away and were arrested. When tried they were convicted, but Ross was recommended to mercy on account of his previous good character. He was sentenced to five years' imprisonment, his companions being sent to gaol for seven years.

Chapter XVI

Michael Henry Davis, Aaron von Ehrstein, and Robert Smith, stopped the mail coach on January 6th, 1862, about six miles from Burrangong. Ensign Campbell Morris and Sergeant O'Grady, of the 12th regiment, which had been engaged in suppressing the riot, were passengers going to Cowra. Another passenger, a Frenchman, refused to surrender, and Davis fired at him. After this no further resistance was made, and Ehrstein, who searched the passengers, took £9 13s. from the Ensign and other sums from the others. The police started in pursuit immediately on receiving information of the robbery, and the prisoners were captured without much trouble. They were convicted and sent to gaol for ten years.

Benjamin Allerton and another man walked one day into the bar of the Wakool Hotel on the lower Billabong and called for nobblers like ordinary travellers. They were served by Mr. Talbot, the landlord. They then went into the dining room and had supper. As soon as the meal was over the two men rose, and one of them drew a pistol and said, "Excuse us, gentlemen, this is our business." David Elliott, who was employed at the hotel, was sitting next the bushranger, and made a snatch at the pistol. The bushranger, however, was on the alert, and jumped aside. Then he fired and Elliott fell wounded. Mr. Talbot rushed in from the bar and said that he didn't want any more damage done. "Take the money in the till," he cried, "and go." The bushrangers took some seven or eight pounds from the till, a saddle and bridle, a canister of powder, and some clothing, but they took nothing from the other persons who had been at supper with them. They said that they were going to join Gardiner and "make it hot for the traps." Information was at once given to the police, and they were followed, but only Allerton was found and captured. He was tried at Goulburn on March 27th, and found guilty, the jury pronouncing the verdict without leaving the box, and the judge sentenced him to death. Benjamin Allerton and Henry Keene were hung at Goulburn on May 5th. Another bushranger named Regan was hung there in June. The sentences on Lawler and Watson were commuted to fifteen years' imprisonment.

These were outsiders who intended to join the gang, but in the meantime the gang itself had not been idle. John Peisley was a well-known settler in the district, and his house was said to be the resort of the bushrangers, and was closely watched by the police. On December 27th, 1861, Peisley and

James Wilson were drinking at Benyon's Inn, about a mile from Bigga, when Peisley challenged William Benyon to run, jump, or fight for £10. Benyon declined, and Peisley struck him several light blows on the chest and called him a coward, until at length Benyon said he would wrestle. They went into the yard, leaving Wilson, who was drunk, on the seat in the bar. Stephen Benyon, who was at work in the barn, and several others, collected in the yard to see the wrestling match. The men stripped, and grappled, and Peisley threw the publican and then struck him in the face. Stephen Benyon called Peisley a coward, rushed forward and threw Peisley. On getting up Peisley rushed into the house swearing he would "do for Bill." He seized a knife, when Mrs. Benyon cried out "My God! are you going to kill my husband?" and grappled with him. Stephen Benyon picked up a spade and struck Peisley on the arm. Peisley then threw away the knife and said it was all right. The row seemed to be all over and Peisley walked into the bar and asked Wilson where his vest was. He had taken it off when he went out to wrestle and left it beside Wilson. Wilson said he had not seen it. Then Mrs. Benyon announced that she had hidden it because she found two revolvers rolled up in it. She offered to tell Peisley where it was if he would promise to go away quietly. Peisley said all right, and Mrs. Benyon showed him where she had hidden the vest in the garden. Peisley walked out, picked the vest up from under a bush, and went back again. He began to examine the revolvers, when William Benyon said, "Surely you don't mean to shoot us?"

"You never knew me do a mean action in my life," replied Peisley, "and I'm not going to begin now. Shake hands. We're all friends." They shook hands all round and Peisley put on his vest and went away. As soon as he was out of sight, William Benyon loaded his gun and took it to the barn, where his brother Stephen had returned to his work. William gave the gun to his brother and told him to take care of it, as Peisley was not to be trusted. About half-an-hour later, when William Benyon was in the bar, Peisley came galloping back, hitched his horse to the fence, and went into the barn. Stephen Benyon picked up the gun and Peisley said, laughing, "Why, you're not going to shoot me, are you?"

"I was told you were going to shoot me," returned Stephen. "Nonsense," cried Peisley, "I never did a cowardly action in my life, and I'm not going

Chapter XVI

to now. Shake hands." Stephen put the gun down and shook hands, and Peisley immediately seized the gun and fired, wounding Stephen in the arm. Stephen ran out of the barn and towards the house, and Peisley, taking careful aim, again pulled the trigger, but the cap missed fire. Peisley ran to the corner of the house, and asked William Benyon's son which way his uncle went. The child pointed in the wrong direction, and Peisley ran to the other corner of the house. Not seeing Stephen anywhere he returned. He was in a great rage, and struck a man named George Hammond with the gun, which exploded without doing any damage. Peisley threw the gun away, and drew a revolver. He ordered William Benyon, Wilson, Hammond, and the servant girl into the barn. Then he said to William, "I've got a bullet here for you. You've had your game, now it's my turn." The servant went between Benyon and Peisley, and begged the bushranger not to hurt her master. Peisley told her to go away unless she was tired of her life. Suddenly Benyon rushed at Peisley, who fired and wounded him in the neck, and as he fell Peisley rushed out to his horse, mounted, and galloped away. William Benyon died a week later, and a warrant was issued for the apprehension of Peisley, who left his house and joined the gang.

On January 15th Constables Morris, Murphy, and Simpson were searching for bushrangers in the Abercrombie Mountains, when they saw Peisley near Bigga. The bushranger was splendidly mounted. He rode up, and coolly informed the police that he was the man they were looking for. He added, "I'd like to have a turn up with Morris if he will get down, and put his gun aside." Morris replied, "All right," and immediately dismounted, and placed his gun against a tree, expecting his challenger to do the same. But Peisley laughed, turned his horse round, and cantered away. Morris drew a revolver from his belt and fired. The bullet passed just under the neck of the bushranger's horse. He turned in his saddle and said "That was a good one. Try again." The police gave chase, but the superiority of the bushranger's horse enabled him to escape easily About a week later Peisley was captured by Messrs. Mackenzie and Burridge after a severe struggle. He was tried at Bathurst, and sentenced to death for the murder of William Benyon, and was hung on April 25th, 1862. When on the scaffold he said that he had never used violence during his bushranging career until he had had that row with Benyon. He had never taken a shilling from or done violence to a woman. He denied that he had had anything to do with the attempt to bribe Constable Hosie to let Gardiner escape. He was aware that the money offered was £50. He also knew that there was a cheque for £2 10s. in the collection, and that that made the amount up to £52 10s. He had spent five or six pounds in the spree at Benyon's. Wilson wanted him to sing and Benyon to dance, but he refused. Benyon then asked him to put on the gloves, but he declined because he knew it would lead to a row. At this point, said the Bathurst Free Press, one of the clergymen on the scaffold whispered to Peisley, and he immediately said that he would say no more on that subject. He concluded with "Good-bye, gentlemen. God bless you." Peisley did not appear to suffer much, but a black-fellow, known as Jacky Bullfrog, who was hanged at the same time for the murder of William Clarke, suffered terribly, his body being frightfully convulsed for several minutes. Peisley was twenty-eight years of age, five feet ten inches in height. He is described as a fine-looking man at a distance, but when examined closely there was a shifty, disagreeable look about his eyes.

In April Gardiner, with three companions, stuck up Pring's Crowther station and then went on to Crooke's, and bailed up all hands there. At Pring's, one of the bushrangers played the piano while the others danced. At Crooke's one played the concertina and another sang "Ever of thee."

On March 10th, Mr. Horsington, a store-keeper on the Wombat, was driving with his wife in a spring cart to Lambing Flat, and Mr. Robert Hewitt, store-keeper at Little Wombat, riding beside them. Suddenly, James Downey, with three other bushrangers, barred the road and ordered the travellers into the bush. The two store-keepers had a large quantity of gold with them which they had purchased in the course of business, and were taking to the bank at Lambing Flat, the main centre of the Burrangong Goldfield. Mr. Horsington had a parcel containing forty ounces in his pockets, and another of two hundred ounces in the cart. The robbers took some £1100 worth from Mr. Horsington in gold and money, and about £700 worth from Mr. Hewitt. When pocketing the plunder, Downey said: "You're the best gentlemen I've met this month, and I've stuck up twenty already."

Sergeant Sanderson, with detectives Lyons and Kennedy, left the Lach-

CHAPTER XVI

lan Goldfield (Forbes), on April 11th, in charge of three bushrangers who had been arrested, and who were being taken to Burrangong for the police court examinations. Near Brewers' Shanty, three horsemen, with two led horses, were observed, and on seeing the coach these horsemen turned into the bush. The two detectives followed them on foot, when the horsemen turned round and fired. The police returned the fire, and the horses of two of the bushrangers bolted. The third bushranger remained and fired again. The police replied and the bushranger fell. He was identified as a man named Davis. He had received four wounds, none of which was very serious. He was placed in the coach with the other prisoners, and was subsequently sentenced to death. This sentence was, however, commuted to imprisonment for life.

It was at this time that the Burrangong and other papers in the disturbed area accused the Government of neglect in consequence of the non-arrival in the district of Captain Battye with his troop of black trackers. It was said that without this aid the police might ride round for months, but could not penetrate the ranges. No doubt this outcry had the effect of stirring up the authorities, because the blacks speedily arrived and were set to work without delay.

The Lachlan Miner of April 19th, 1862, inserted the following paragraph:

"We have received the following letter, purporting to be from the hand of Frank Gardner (sic), the notorious highwayman, of Lachlan and Lambing Flat roads. The circumstances under which we became possessed of the documents can be known, and the original copies, with the envelopes and seals, seen by the curious, on application at this office, and they can then use what judgment they choose as to the genuineness of them. We give it to our readers as we received it:—To the Editor of the Burrangong Miner, Lambing Flat. Sir,—Having seen a paragraph in one of the papers, wherein it is said that I took the boots off a man's feet, and that I also took the last few shillings that another man had, I wish it to be made known that I did not do anything of the kind. The man who took the boots was in my company, and for so doing I discharged him the following day. Silver I never took from a man yet, and the shot that was fired at the sticking-up of Messrs. Horsington and Hewitt was by accident, and the man who did it

I also discharged. As for a mean, low, or petty action, I never committed it in my life. The letter that I last sent to the press, there had not half of what I said put in it. In all that has been said there never was any mention made of my taking the sergeant's horse and trying him, and that when I found he was no good I went back and got my own. As for Mr. Torpy, he is a perfect coward. After I spared his life as he fell out of the window, he fired at me as I rode away; but I hope that Mr. Torpy and I have not done just yet, until we balance our accounts properly. Mr. Greig has accused me of robbing his teams, but it is false, for I know nothing about the robbery whatever. In fact I would not rob Mr. Greig or any one belonging to him, on account of his taking things so easy at Bogolong. Mr. Torpy was too bounceable or he would not have been robbed. A word to Sir W. F. Pottinger. He wanted to know how it was the man who led my horse up to me at the Pinnacle, did not cut my horse's reins, as he gave me the horse. I should like to know if Mr. Pottinger would do so? I shall answer by saying no. It has been said that it would be advisable to place a trap at each shanty on the road, to put a stop to the depredations done on the road. I certainly think it would be a great acquisition to me, for I should then have increase of revolvers and carbines. When seven or eight men could do nothing with me at the Pinnacle, one would look well at a shanty. Three of your troopers were at a house the other night and got drinking and gambling till all hours. I came there towards morning when all was silent. The first room that I went into I found revolvers and carbines to any amount, but seeing none as good as my own, I left them. I then went out, and in the verandah found the troopers sound asleep, satisfying myself that neither Battye nor Pottinger were there, I left them as I found them, in the arms of Morpheus. Fearing nothing, I remain, Prince of Tobymen, Francis Gardner (sic), the Highwayman. Insert the foregoing, and rest satisfied you shall be paid."

The spelling of the name appears to be a typographical blunder. Mr. Torpy was a well-known resident of the district. This letter throws some light on the methods pursued by the bushrangers, and tends to prove that although Gardiner might not be present on some occasions, the robberies were committed under his directions. And some fresh outrage was reported almost every day, until in June, the report that the Government gold escort from the Lachlan diggings had been stuck up and robbed, caused

Chapter XVI

a commotion throughout the colony. The escort started from Forbes on June 15th with 2067 oz. 18 dwt. gold and £700, owned by the Oriental Bank; 521 oz. 13 dwt. 6 grs., owned by the Bank of New South Wales, and 129 oz. and £3000 in cash, owned by the Commercial Banking Company, making about fourteen thousand pounds worth in all.

The report of this robbery caused intense excitement throughout the colony. Nothing like it had been heard of since the old gold digging days in Victoria. Large bodies of police were sent out to scour the country near the scene of the outrage. One of these parties of police under Sergeant Saunderson, when in the ranges near Wheogo, saw a man on horseback who rode away as they approached. The police followed him up the steep gully, and when he was near the top four other men joined him from behind the trees and made off too. The police followed so rapidly that a packhorse which one of the men was leading broke away and they had not time to recover him. The police seized the packhorse, but the men got away. On the captured horse were found about 1500 oz. of gold, a policeman's cloak, and two carbines which were identified as having been among those with which the troopers of the escort had been armed. It may be remarked en passant that no more of the property stolen in this robbery was ever recovered.

Some weeks later the police succeeded in apprehending Alexander Fordyce, John Bow, Henry Manns, John McGuire, and Daniel Charters, and these were committed for trial for having been concerned in the escort robbery. Charters turned approver, and his evidence given at the trial may be taken as a substantially true account of the method by which the robbery was effected; although, of course, due allowance must be made for the apparent efforts of the witness to minimise his own share in the crime.

Charters lived with his parents at Humbug Creek and knew the country well. One day Frank Gardiner met him near the Pinnacle and compelled him to lead the way across the ranges to Eugowra. Johnny Gilbert and Alick Fordyce were driving several spare horses which the gang had collected. They camped near the Lachlan River and Gilbert went into the town of Forbes, the centre of the Lachlan River diggings. It was Sunday, and on his return to the camp Gilbert reported that he had had great difficulty in purchasing guns and an axe. There was only one store in the town in which guns were sold, and that was shut. He had knocked the store-keeper up, however, and persuaded him to supply him with what he wanted. On the next morning the gang rode as straight as possible across the ranges, Gilbert going ahead with Charters to cut the fences on Mr. Roberts' sheep run to enable them to pass through. They camped for the night between the Eugowra Rocks and Campbell's station. On the morning of June 15th, 1862, they tied their horses to saplings near the camp and walked down to the rocks. Manns was sent to McGuire's shanty at the crossing place for a bottle of Old Tom, a loaf of bread, and some cooked meat. Fordyce took too much gin and went to sleep, and Gardiner shook him roughly and told him that if he didn't wake up he'd "cut his —— rations short." Later Gardiner sent Charters to see if the horses were all right, and told him to stop at the camp and mind them, adding "You're no —— good here. You're too —— frightened of your skin." Soon afterwards he heard firing and about an hour later the bushrangers came up leading the coach horses. They had packed the gold on these horses. They wiped out and reloaded their guns, and in doing so it was found that Fordyce's gun had not been discharged. Gardiner turned on the young man fiercely and said, "You —— coward, you were too much afraid to fire, —— you. I'll cut your —— rations short for this." They saddled up their horses and started across the ranges.

The escort was under the command of Sergeant Condell. It left Forbes about noon, Constable John Fagan driving. The other constables were Henry Moran and William Haviland. When they came to the Eugowra Rocks, near the crossing over Mandagery Creek, they found two bullock teams so placed across the road, which bends sharply as it approaches the ford, that the escort cart had to be driven close to the rocks. The teams belonged to two bullock drivers who had been made prisoners, and had evidently been there for some time, as the bullocks were lying down chewing the cud. To pass these teams the coach had to approach the rocks at an angle, and as it was passing a volley was fired and Constable Moran fell. The horses, frightened at the noise and flash of the guns, bolted, but the cart was overturned through the wheels colliding with a spur of the rocks. This threw the other constables out and prevented them from making any effective resistance. As the cart capsized, seven armed men, dressed

Chapter XVI

in red shirts and with their faces blackened, sprang from behind the rocks shouting, "Shoot the —— wretches." The police fired their carbines and then surrendered. The robbers having re-packed their plunder were led by Charters to the place from whence they had started, near the Pinnacle, where the gold and money was roughly divided, and the party separated.

Constable Moran had sufficiently recovered from his wound to be present at the trial and to give his evidence. The first jury disagreed and was discharged, but at the second trial on February 23rd, 1863, Fordyce, Bow, and Manns were convicted and sentenced to death. Charters was acquitted according to promise, and McGuire was also acquitted on the charge of being concerned in the robbery, but was afterwards convicted of aiding and abetting the bushrangers, and was sentenced to a term of imprisonment. Subsequently the capital sentences on Fordyce and Bow were commuted to imprisonment for life, and only Manns was hung. The execution was terribly bungled. The rope was too short for a tall, slim youth like Manns, and he struggled violently. Seeing no prospect of death within a reasonable time, Dr. West instructed the hangman to raise the body and let it drop again, and this proved effectual. The prolonged sufferings of the criminal must, however, have been very severe.

From the date of this daring robbery the "Gardiner gang of bushrangers" was the principal topic of conversation in New South Wales. After a lull of several years a new era of bushranging had started, and it lasted altogether for about ten years before it was finally suppressed. For some time the robberies which were reported almost every day were all attributed to Frank Gardiner, but, as was subsequently proved, unjustly. Gardiner had made his coup and retired, but it was some time before either the police or the public became aware of this fact.

Seventeen

Johnny Gilbert; His First Appearance in Australia; Miscellaneous Bushranging Exploits; Mr. Robert Lowe Makes a Stand; Mr. Inspector Norton Captured by the Bushrangers; A Plucky Black Boy; "Mine know it, Patsy Daly like it, Brudder;" A Brave Boy; O'Meally Shoots Mr. Barnes; A Bootless Bushranger; Capture of John Foley; Something about the Foley Family; Ben Hall.

Next to Frank Gardiner, the man most frequently spoken of in connection with bushranging at this time was Johnny Gilbert, alias Roberts. He was one of the gang charged with assisting in the robbery of the gold escort at Eugowra Rocks, but who had not been captured. He was born in Canada, and emigrated with his uncle, John Davis, to Victoria, shortly after the discovery of gold there. Davis, it appears, soon became tired of gold digging, and went to Sydney, where he opened an hotel at Waverley. On April 6th, 1854, he was found dead in his private room, and his nephew, then known as Roberts, about seventeen years of age, was arrested and charged with the murder. He was acquitted and left Sydney. He was arrested in the Goulburn district, some time later, charged with horse-stealing, and sent to gaol. He is supposed to have made acquaintance with Gardiner during their imprisonment on Cockatoo Island. Roberts made an attempt to escape from the island, but was re-captured and was punished by Captain McLerie, the visiting justice. When liberated, after having served his sentence, he disappeared for a time, and was next heard of in connection with the escort robbery. It soon became evident to all thinking persons, that there were more bushrangers abroad than those connected with "the Gardiner gang." Robberies were reported almost every day, and over a wider range of country than it was possible for one gang to travel over. These robberies were of the most varied character.

One day Henry Stephens, innkeeper, near Caloola, was in his bar when three men walked in and called for brandy. He served them. When they had drunk their liquors they went into the breakfast room and sat down. There were present at the table Mr. and Mrs. Stephens, Mr. Young, and the three strangers. While the meal was progressing one of the strangers went out. He returned almost immediately, pistol in hand, driving the man servant in before him. Mr. Stephens jumped up, exclaiming "Hullo, what's up now?" when the bushranger fired and shot him in the mouth. The other two visitors rose, and ordered Mrs. Stephens to "hand out the cash." As she refused they searched everywhere, breaking open boxes, smashing the furniture, and even refusing to allow the poor woman to lift her baby from its overturned cradle, under which it was in danger of being smothered. They took away about £20 in cash, and a few small articles. As soon as they left Mr. Stephens was conveyed to the hospital at Bathurst for surgical treatment. Of course this outrage was attributed to "Gardiner's gang," but it was subsequently proved that the robbers had no connection with the ex-butcher.

On December 10th, 1862, Charles Foley and John Brownlow robbed Daniel O'Brien's inn at Laggan. Another man stood on guard at the door. They tied Mr. and Mrs. O'Brien, and put a bag over O'Brien's head to prevent him from calling out. Foley searched the place, but only succeeded in finding "ten bob." Mrs. O'Brien, hoping to induce them to leave quietly, offered to give them £4 10s. which she had in her pocket, but Foley said "We want more than that." They ransacked the place, and at last found a roll of about fifty £1 notes which Mr. O'Brien had thrown among some empty casks in a back room on seeing them approaching the place. As they were well-known in the district they were soon arrested, and on February 9th, 1863, were sentenced to seven years' penal servitude.

At the same Sessions, Alexander and Charles Ross and William O'Connor were convicted of the attack on Mr. Stephens. They had also robbed Mr. William Webb's store at Fish River, and committed some other outrages. They were condemned to death and were hung in March, 1863.

George Willison and Frederick Britton stuck up the Hartley mail near the Woodside Inn, about five miles from Bathurst, on November 16th, 1862. The driver, Owen Malone, and a passenger, Arundell Everett, were taken off the road, their hands tied behind them, and they were laid on the ground on their faces while the robbers searched the letters. While thus lying side by side, Everett whispered to his companion, "Let's make a rush." Malone however prudently declined, saying, "What could we do with our hands tied behind us? We'd only get shot." The robbers took about £1500 in notes from the letters and immediately mounted and rode into Bathurst to exchange them. They were too late, however. News of the robbery had reached the town, and they were arrested in the Union Bank while cashing the notes. They were sentenced to sixteen years' penal servitude, the first three years in irons. A companion who had kept watch while the mail was being robbed escaped.

The mail coach was stuck up near Mount Victoria by Charles and James Mackay and George Williams. There was nothing remarkable about the robbery, but the bushrangers were closely followed and were captured in a few days. The two brothers Mackay were sentenced to fifteen years' and Williams to ten years' imprisonment.

On January 7th, 1863, the Yass Courier announced that during the week the Binalong mail had been again robbed, and Woodward, the driver, left bound to a tree. He begged hard not to be left to perish miserably through thirst, but the robbers laughed and rode away. He was released by a shepherd who happened to hear him cooeying. He was much exhausted. The robbers took £24 10s. and a pennyweight nugget. On the same day Samuel William Jacobsen, hawker, was stuck up near the Wedden Mountains by John Healy, who ordered him to "bail up and be quick about it unless you want your —— brains blown out." Jacobsen and his assistant, Henry Clok, were stripped and told to remain where they were for an hour under penalty of death. Their clothes were given back to them after having been searched. They dressed, and when they judged that the time allowed them had expired—their watches had been taken away with other property—they walked on. They followed the track of their waggon and came up to it about three miles away. The horses had been turned loose and were feeding near. All the drawers and boxes in the waggon had been broken open and ransacked, and everything of value had been stolen.

During the week ending April 22nd, 1863, a large number of people were stuck up and robbed on the road between Marengo and Burrangong. One of them, William Oakes, a store-keeper, was going on his usual round among the Fish River farms to purchase fiowls, eggs, butter, and other produce for his store. He was successful in hiding his money, but the robbers emptied his horse feed out on the ground, ripped open the saddles and collars of his horses, and broke all the boxes in the cart in their attempts to find it.

On January 14th a woman was stopped at the Cherry Tree Hill, and asked for her money. She refused to give it up. The robbers tried to search her, but, being unable to find her pocket, they tore the skirt off, and, in spite of her cries, carried it away, leaving her to get home without it. They got about £3 in notes and silver. These fellows stuck up the Mudgee mail about an hour later. There were two passengers on board, a man and a woman. The man refused to give up his money, when one of the bushrangers said, "If you don't hand it out we'll strip the woman." As he hesitated the ruffian began to tear off her clothes. The man yielded. It is satisfactory to know that the amount obtained was small.

On April 3rd the Cassilis mail was stuck up at Reedy Creek, near Mudgee, by two armed men. One of them remarked, after the letters had been gone through, "This mail never has nothing in it." Mr. Farrell, schoolmaster at Cassilis, who was riding beside the coach when it was stopped, was robbed of his gold watch and some money. He was also forced to exchange his horse, saddle, and bridle, for a knocked up horse and a very dilapidated saddle and bridle. On the following day Mr. Robert Lowe was driving in a buggy from Talbragar to Mudgee in company with Hugh McKenzie, who was on horseback, when two armed men ordered them to "bail up." Mr. Lowe snatched his gun from the bottom of the buggy, and fired. The bushrangers wheeled round and rode away, but had not gone far when one of them threw up his arms and fell. Lowe and McKenzie went over to him with the intention of taking him to the nearest town for treatment, but he died almost immediately. The two gentlemen then continued their journey to Slapdash, where they gave information to the police and were informed that Messrs. A. Brown, J.P., and Alexander Dean had just reported that they had been robbed near the same place by two men, one of whom was riding Mr. Farrell's horse. Sergeant Cleary and a trooper with two black trackers, Tommy and Johnny Bein Bar, followed the other bushranger for 260 miles and caught him near Coonamble. He was brought to Mudgee, tried and convicted, and sent to gaol for ten years. At the inquest on the man Heather a verdict of justifiable homicide was returned, and Mr. Lowe was highly complimented for his prompt action. He was afterwards awarded a gold medal by the New South Wales Government for his bravery in resisting bushrangers.

One day Master Willie Cadell was sent by his mother on a message a short distance away from Mudgee. He walked his pony up the hill outside the township, and was about to start in a canter when a mounted man dashed in front and shouted "Stop." The pony was frightened by the shout and bolted for a short distance, the bushranger galloping alongside threatening the boy with instant death if he did not pull up. At length the pony was brought under control, when the robber said, "I don't want to hurt you, but you must come with me." He led the boy to a clump of trees where Mr. Smith, of Appletree Flat, and two other men were lying tied on the ground. The bushranger told Willie that he would not tie him if he promised not to run away, adding, "If you break your word I'll put a bullet through you." The boy promised and went and sat down on a fallen tree. The bushranger took Willie's pony "to spare" his own horse. As he walked past Mr. Smith, he gave the tied man a kick, and said roughly, "You stopped me robbing the mail before, but I'll keep you quiet this time." He mounted the pony and went back to the road. Presently he returned with two other men whom he tied and robbed. He fired several shots from his revolver at a mark on a tree, "for practice" as he told Willie Cadell. Then he went back to the road again. He soon returned with two more men, who were treated as the others had been. There were now seven men and a boy held prisoners under the clump of trees by one man. The robber had also stopped Mr. Robinson, with two stock-riders, and had ordered them to round up the mob of fat cattle they were driving and remain on the flat until after the mail passed. Occasionally he would say to his prisoners: "The mail will soon be here now; then you can all go." He kept continually riding from the road to where his prisoners were and back. About half-an-hour after capturing his last two prisoners the mail coach turned off the road and came into the clump of timber, the bushranger riding behind and directing the driver where to go. There were four male and two female passengers. The women were told to go under a tree, and to "sit down and

Chapter XVII

be quiet." The men were searched and tied. Then the bushranger coolly sat down and went through the letters. When he had finished he mounted the pony, and took the bridle of his own horse in his hand. "Youngster," he said to Willie Cadell, "you'll find your pony by the road." He then rode away. Young Cadell, who had replied "All right," began to untie the prisoners as soon as the robber was outside the clump. When all were loosed they walked out to the road. The pony was hitched to a tree and the robber seated on his own horse was waiting a short distance away. He asked them whether they were all right, and on being answered in the affirmative, raised his hat politely, said, "Good evening, ladies and gentlemen," and cantered away. The mail-man stopped to gather up the torn and scattered letters, while Messrs. Smith and Martin walked to Mudgee to inform the police, and Willie Cadell cantered away to perform the errand on which his mother had sent him.

The coolness with which this robber had acted throughout induced the belief among the public that he was no common amateur bushranger, but a member of the Gardiner gang. In fact it was said that he was no other than Johnny Gilbert himself. The Goulburn Chronicle reported about this time that Gardiner and his gang had paid a visit to the Muswellbrook district, and suggested that one of them had committed this robbery on the way back to their own district. This, however, was disproved later, and it was then believed that the robber was one of the numerous young men who "turned out" with the intention of joining the gang and endeavoured to do something on the road to prove themselves worthy of being accepted as comrades by the redoubtable bushrangers. It was the custom of the time to attribute all highway robberies to Gardiner and his gang, but it is doubtful whether any of those recorded in this chapter so far were perpetrated by actual members of the gang. It was a time of intense excitement, and many of the more or less criminally disposed among the youth of the colony felt themselves impelled to take to the road and rob somebody. Some of these were captured; others were disillusionised and went back to their farms; while others either did join the gang or continued bushranging as independent parties. The next story, published a few days later, was that of the sticking up of the Mudgee mail on the Bathurst-Sydney Road, near the Big Hill, about sixteen miles from Bowenfels. Mr. Henry Edward

Kater, manager of the local branch of the Australian Joint Stock Bank, was a passenger, and he had with him £5000 worth of old notes, which he was taking to Sydney to be destroyed at the head office of the bank The bushrangers had received notice from some source that these notes were on the coach, and asked for them. Mr. Kater replied that they were valueless, as the numbers had been cancelled. "Never mind," replied the bushranger. "We can make a bonfire of them as well as you can." Mr. Kater declined to give them up, and stooped down. The bushranger immediately ordered him to "sit up straight and not try to come Robert Lowe on them," or he would be sorry for it. This, of course, was an allusion to the recent shooting of the man Heather by Mr. Lowe, as already related. Mrs. Smith, wife of a publican at Ben Bullen, who was a passenger on the coach, was very much alarmed. She was seated beside Mr. Kater, and screamed loudly. She had £200 in her pocket. The robber told her to get down and stand aside, adding, "We don't rob women." She was only too glad to obey. She sat down on a log beside the road. The other passengers were then ordered to dismount, and were eased of their valuables. When this duty had been discharged the robbers departed, one of them turning back to request Mr. Kater to ask Captain Norton whether "his spurs were getting rusty." The robbers were well-dressed and splendidly mounted. No doubt was entertained anywhere that they belonged to Gardiner's gang. A reward of £500 was offered by the Joint Stock Bank for the recovery of the cancelled notes.

In recording the principal robberies committed at this time by bushrangers who were not known certainly to belong to the gang, I have necessarily omitted to mention the robberies effected by the gang itself. It is now, therefore, time to return to the beginning of the year and take up the history of the gang itself. On New Year's Day, 1863, races were being held at Brisbane Valley on the Fish River, when Frederick Lowry and John Foley made a daring attempt to stick up the crowd, numbering more than one hundred persons. A man named Foran refused to be tied when called on to come out and was immediately shot by Lowry. Although he was wounded in the lungs Foran rushed forward and grappled with Lowry. Several other men came to his assistance, and Lowry was overpowered, while Foley, who had been engaged in tying the men, jumped on his horse and got away. Lowry was locked up in a room behind the bar of the publican's booth, but

CHAPTER XVII

the booth was a mere shell, and he contrived to escape before the police came.

On February 27th Mr. Cirkel, publican at Stony Creek, Burrangong, was called out of his house and shot dead, after having been accused of having given information to the police. It was said that the men who committed this crime were Gardiner, Gilbert, O'Meally, and another whose name was not known. O'Meally was said to have fired the fatal shot. The party of bushrangers rode on to Mr. Myers Solomon's store at the "Big Wombat." Mr. Solomon, seeing them coming, attempted to run away, but was followed and brought back. A lad in the store vaulted over the counter and snatched a pistol from the belt of one of the bushrangers while the dispute was going on as to whether Solomon should be shot for attempting to "betray" them to the police. Another of the bushrangers immediately put his pistol to Mrs. Solomon's head and said to the boy, "If you fire I'll blow her brains out." The boy looked undecided. The bushranger cocked his pistol and swore that if the boy did not return the weapon he had taken the woman should die. The boy then stepped forward, laid the revolver on the counter, and said, "If it wasn't for Mrs. Solomon I'd stop your run anyhow." He was immediately knocked down and kicked.

The Lachlan Observer of March 5th reported that Mr. Inspector Norton, who had recently relieved Sir Frederick Pottinger as head of the police force in the district, had been captured by the bushrangers. Captain Norton had been in pursuit of the robbers, and was returning from a long ride through the ranges, accompanied only by a black tracker known as Billy Durgan. On Sunday, 1st instant, he came suddenly on a camp some three or four miles front Wheogo. Billy, who was riding behind leading a spare horse, saw the fire first, and shouted "Here they are." Three of the bushrangers sprang up, mounted their horses, and came towards the officer. Billy advised him to "bolt," but the captain shook his head and replied "No good, Billy. Horse too much knock up." "Mine stop it too," said Billy. O'Meally and Patrick Daly fired as they approached, and Norton returned the fire until his revolver was empty, when he said "I surrender." Daly cried "Throw down your arms," and as Norton threw away his revolver another man galloped up and fired at him. At that moment Billy, the black boy, seeing the danger Norton was in, gave a yell, jumped off his horse, and threw his empty pistol in the bushranger's face. By this plucky act Billy no doubt saved Captain Norton's life, but the bushranger turned and fired at the black. Billy, however, kicked off his boots, sprang behind a tree, and shouted "Come on, you ———." O'Meally replied, "We'll wallop you, you young ———, when we catch you." At which threat Billy laughed, and replied "Yon catchem first." Daly and the other bushranger chased him, but Billy dodged about from tree to tree with all the agility of the black, pelting sticks at them, and laughingly telling them to "come on." The bushrangers fired at him several times, but with no effect, and at length gave up the chase and returned to where O'Meally was still guarding Captain Norton. After a consultation aside the bushrangers told the captain that they had mistaken him for Trooper Holliston. They intended to "do for" the trooper the first time they caught him. They detained the captain for about three hours, treating him very civilly, and then released him.

A few days later, Daly was arrested by Sir Frederick Pottinger. He was a native of the district, under twenty years of age. When brought up and charged at the police court, Captain Norton failed to identify him, but Billy Durgan exclaimed, when called upon for his evidence: "Mine know it, Patsy Daly like it brudder." Daly was placed on trial for having, in company with others, robbed Myers Solomon, store-keeper, of property, including money, horses, guns, revolvers, clothing, food, &c., to a large amount. George Johnson identified Daly as the man who had knocked the boy down and kicked him when he placed the revolver on the counter. Johnson called Daly a coward, and was told to keep quiet unless he wanted his "— brains blown out." Johnson replied: "I'd like to meet you man to man fairly." Another of the bushrangers asked: "Will you stand up and fight me if I give you a pistol?" Johnson replied, "Yes," and stepped forward. The third bushranger, however, ordered him back, and told his mates to "quit fooling." Johnson and the other men in the store were then made to lie on their faces, with a bushranger over them on guard, while the other bushrangers selected what they wanted, packed it in bundles, and strapped it on the pack horses. While thus employed, the bushranger who had challenged Johnson kicked him in the ribs savagely, and told him to keep still. The other persons present gave their versions of the occurrence, but they differed little from what has been recorded above. Daly was con-

Chapter XVII

victed, and was sentenced to fifteen years' penal servitude.

On March 30th, two men called at James Brown's hut at Wallenbeen and asked for something to eat. Brown told his wife to give them some breakfast. It may be necessary to remark that such hospitality is common in Australia. Having eaten as much as they required, the travellers demanded Brown's hat and boots. After some dispute these were handed over. The boots were too small, and the man who wanted them took out his pocket-knife to cut them, when his mate said, "Oh, come on; we'll get plenty at McKay's." They left the boots, went out, mounted their horses, and rode away. They had only gone a few yards when they met Mr. Barnes, a store-keeper at Cootamundra, and his assistant, Mr. Hanlow, who was in charge of a branch store at Murrumburrah. The travellers ordered Barnes to "bail up." Barnes said, "I know you, O'Meally," and O'Meally replied, "I know you, you ———. Get off that horse; I want him." Barnes wheeled his horse round and galloped away, and O'Meally followed. They galloped round the hill, back past the stockyard, and then down the gully out of sight among the trees. In the meantime, Hanlow was conducted by the other bushranger off the road to the stockyard, where they were soon joined by O'Meally. "Where's Mr. Barnes?" asked Hanlow, as the robber rode up. "Down there," replied O'Meally nonchalantly, pointing down the gully. "You haven't shot him?" inquired Hanlow anxiously. "Oh, no," replied the bushranger coolly, "he hit himself against a tree and tumbled off." Mr. Alexander McKay, the squatter who owned the stockyard, and whose house was not far away, had heard the galloping and shouting, and went on to the verandah of his house to ascertain the cause of the noise. It was then about half-past eleven a.m., and the day was Sunday. He saw one man chasing another, and thought it was a trooper after a bushranger. He watched them gallop down the gully, and saw the one he took to be a trooper shoot the other, and then wheel his horse round and gallop back without waiting to see whether the man who had fallen off his horse was dead or not. As O'Meally came nearer McKay recognised him, and his suspicions were aroused. He started to walk down the gully to the wounded man, when he was stopped by O'Meally who ordered him to go back and open the store, adding, "I want some boots and clothes for my mate. He lost his in a brush with the traps." Mr. McKay went to the store and gave O'Meally the things he had asked for. The bushranger then said he wanted fresh horses. McKay replied that the horses were never brought in on a Sunday and therefore he could not get them. "Ah," said O'Meally, "I had Chance from you. He was a good 'un. Well, I'll come some other time and get one." The bushrangers then went away and McKay and Hanlow walked down the gully to where Barnes was lying. They found that he was quite dead, and sent word to the nearest police station. An inquest was held next day, and a verdict of wilful murder was returned against O'Meally and another man whose name was unknown.

A day or two later Mr. Frank was riding from Lambing Flat (Burrangong) to Yass, when he was stopped by seven men whose faces were hidden by black crape veils. They ordered him to "shell out." "I've only thirty bob, boys," he replied. One of the robbers said "Oh, keep it. You'll want that to take you home again." Some of the others said that they knew him and he wasn't "a bad sort," so he could go. They asked him if he had seen any police on the road, and added that they wished to "meet the —— traps." After several minutes spent in conversation they rode off and Mr. Frank continued his journey.

Shortly after this Constables McDonald, Lee, and Nicholls traced John Foley to Mackay's Hotel, Campbell's River, with the aid of a black tracker. McDonald pushed the door of the bedroom in which he was told Foley had been sleeping, but the man inside leaned heavily against it to prevent it from being opened. After a struggle McDonald forced his revolver through the opening and fired round the corner. He did not hit the man inside, but the shot forced him to give way a little. The constable said, "Come along, Foley. We've got you. You can't get away." After a moment's pause Foley replied, "All right. Don't shoot." He stepped back and the door swung open. The police rushed in and handcuffed him. He was taken to Bathurst, where he was charged with having looted Mrs. Anne Webb's store at Mutton Falls, and with having aided and abetted other bushrangers in several robberies on the highway and elsewhere. During the trial it was noticed that Mrs. Foley, the prisoner's mother, was passing in and out of the court and communicating with the witnesses who had been ordered out of court. She was cautioned, but as she persisted in spite of the efforts of the police, she was ordered to be locked up for contempt of court. Timothy

Chapter XVII

Foley, a brother of the accused, was also committed for contempt of court, and was threatened with prosecution for perjury for his attempts to prove an alibi. The prisoner was convicted and was sentenced to fifteen years' imprisonment, the first three years in irons. Another brother, Francis Foley, was sentenced at the same sessions to ten years' imprisonment for having raided the Chinese Camp at Campbell's River. Henry Gibson was also arraigned for bushranging. He admitted that he had been overseer on Ben Hall's station, but denied that he had ever joined Gardiner's gang. He was acquitted by the jury, and the verdict was received with some applause. As soon as order had been restored, the judge remarked that it would perhaps add to the general satisfaction if he informed the court that the prisoner would not go free in spite of his acquittal. He had before him a document which proved that the prisoner was an escaped convict from Victoria, and would therefore be detained until he could be returned to that colony to finish his sentence.

Hitherto the gang had continued to be known as "Gardiner's Gang," although it had been repeatedly asserted in the press that Gardiner had taken no share in the later robberies, and that in fact he had retired from "the profession" several months ago. It was said that notwithstanding the vigilance of the police, Gardiner had succeeded in escaping from New South Wales, taking with him the wife of a respectable farmer in the Burrangong district named Brown. The reports, however, were very contradictory. Sometimes it was said that he had gone to New Zealand. Then that he had made his way to California or to South America. In the meantime the gang continued to be as active as ever under the leadership of Johnny Gilbert and Ben Hall.

Eighteen

Racers as Mounts for the Bushrangers; The Shooting of Lowry; The Bushrangers visit Bathurst; They hold the Town of Canowindra for Three Days; Burke Shot by Mr. Keightley; Female Bushrangers; Death of O'Meally at Goimbla; A Newspaper Man and his Wife Stuck Up; Lively Times During the Christmas Holidays.

The chief necessity for a successful career as a bushranger was a good supply of race-horses, and hence it was almost impossible for any person to keep a really valuable saddle horse during this "Reign of Terror," as the newspapers of the district called it. Special raids were organised by members of the gang to obtain a supply of horses, and the bushrangers frequently travelled upwards of two hundred miles to secure a horse which had made a naine on the turf. Thus on May 18th Harry Wilson, trainer for Mr. Allen Hancock, was exercising the racer Jacky Morgan, within sight of the police station in the town of Burrowa, when Gilbert rode up and said "I want that horse." "For God's sake don't ruin me, Johnny," exclaimed the jockey. "Hold your —— jaw and get off," was the reply, as the bushranger brought out his ready revolver. The robber specially cautioned Wilson not to "sing out" so that the police could hear, or he'd "be sorry for it," and in spite of his remonstrances the jockey was compelled to dismount and walk home to inform his employer. Mr. Hancock told him to saddle another horse. He then took down his gun carefully, wiped and loaded it, and went away swearing that he would never return until he had recovered Jacky Morgan.

Gilbert also took a racer out of Mr. Hammond's stables at Junee. He stole the racers Chinaman and Micky Hunter from the stables of Mr. J. Roberts at Currawang. When leading Micky Hunter out of his stall Gilbert patted his neck and said, "You're the —— cove we want." Old Cornus and several other horses were taken out of Mr. Iceley's stables at Coombing. The old horse had had a good career on the course, and had been set apart for stud purposes, and Mr. Icely offered a large sum to the bushrangers to leave him alone, but Gilbert said, "There's a good gallop in him yet," and led him away. But the bushrangers did not devote their whole time to capturing race horses. Robberies on the highway continued as frequently as usual. The police, however, were not idle. In August, Sergeant James Stephenson, Constable Herbst, and Detectives Camphin and Saunderson traced Lowry to Thomas Vardy's, Limerick Races Hotel, at Cook's Vale Creek. When asked if there were any lodgers there, Vardy pointed to the door of one of the bedrooms and replied, "Yes, one there." Stephenson knocked at the door, but there was no reply. The sergeant knocked again and called out "Come out Lowry, it's no use." As no answer was returned, the sergeant placed his shoulder against the door, and tried to burst it open. Immediately some one inside fired a pistol, the bullet from which passed through the panel of the door between the two policemen. Stephenson again called on Lowry to come out or it would be "the worse for him," and the bushranger replied "I'll fight you, you ——. All of you." He again fired through the door, and the bullet wounded one of the police horses tied to the verandah. Sergeant Stephenson called on Vardy to take the horses to a safe place, and when they were out of sight, he and Constable Herbst again tried to force the door by leaning their combined weight against it. Suddenly Lowry threw the door open, and the sergeant almost fell into the room.

The bushranger shouted "Come on, you —— I'll fight you fair," and fired. The police returned the fire. Stephenson, who was inside the room, took steady aim and pulled the trigger. The robber fell, saying "I'm done for! Where's the priest?" The police arrested Vardy and all his family, as well as a man named Larry Cummins, who was in the room with Lowry, but who took no part in the fight. When this ceremony had been completed, Lowry was made as comfortable as circumstances permitted while a messenger was sent off to the nearest town for a doctor. For more than an hour detective Camphin sat by Lowry's side reading prayers from a Catholic prayer-book which Mrs. Vardy lent him. The robber gradually grew weaker and died. His last words were, "Tell 'em I died game." The police borrowed a cart from a farmer who lived about a mile away from the hotel, and the body was placed in it, covered with a blanket, and started away for Goulburn, where this extraordinary funeral cortège arrived the next day, Sunday, just as the people were leaving the churches. Frederick Lowry was a native of the district, twenty-seven years of age, and six feet two inches in height.

In the New South Wales Legislative Assembly, on August 18th, 1863, Mr., afterwards Sir James, Martin moved that "the alarming state of insecurity of life and property which has so long prevailed through the country districts is in a high degree discreditable to Her Majesty's Ministers in this colony." Mr., afterwards Sir Charles, Cowper, speaking for the Government, said that the police authorities had full power to take all the troopers that could be spared from the more thickly-populated districts to the disturbed area. The discussion on the motion lasted for a week, when it was negatived by forty-four to eighteen votes. The Government was in fact doing all that it could reasonably be expected to do to preserve order, and this was generally recognised, although the Press continued to urge that more energetic measures should be adopted, and bushranging stamped out at any cost. The success of the bushrangers was largely due to the nature of the country, with the features of which they were perfectly familiar. Had. there been double the number of police in the district it is barely probable that the outbreak could have been put down much more quickly than it was. The police showed remarkable bravery, but they were unable to follow the bushrangers into the ranges, with the intricacies of which they were unacquainted. It was not the number of bushrangers, but their activity, boldness, and more than all their intimate knowledge of the country, which enabled them to keep so extensive an area of the colony in a ferment for so long a time.

The Carcour mail was stuck up at about a mile outside the town of Blaney on September 23rd. A passenger named Garland refused to "hand out" when ordered. He was told that if he persisted in his refusal he would "get a good hiding." One bushranger stood by his side holding a gun close to Garland's head, while another bushranger felt his pockets. They took out two £1 notes. The coach was then taken up the ridge to about 300 yards from the road. Here there was a level spot fairly clear of timber, and in this little plain were eight men sitting in a ring with a robber standing on guard over them. The coach-driver and the two passengers were ordered to take their seats in the ring while the letters were searched. They obeyed,

Chapter XVIII

and were detained more than an hour. One of the prisoners in the ring was a trooper. When the mail had been gone through the bushrangers, one of whom was riding Mr. Daniel Mayne's horse Retriever, told them they might go. Garland said "It's no use going without any money," whereupon a bushranger handed him ten shillings and told him not to growl. It was about five o'clock p.m. when the bushrangers rode off. They were said to be Gilbert, O'Meally, Burke, and another.

A few days later Gilbert and O'Meally went to a cattle station some miles from Burrangong and rounded up the horses. A stock-rider galloped up and ordered them to desist. Gilbert told him that they were troopers and had orders from Her Majesty the Queen to take any horses they required. The stockman then assisted them to catch two of the best.

On Saturday, October 23rd, Hall, Gilbert, O'Meally, Burke, and Vane walked into Mr. Perdrotta's gunsmith's shop in William Street, Bathurst, opposite the School of Arts, and asked to see some revolvers. They were shown a number, but said they were common things and no good. Mr. Perdrotta said he had sold out. There had been a run on revolvers lately on account of the bushrangers, but he expected a new stock up from Sydney in a few days. The robbers laughed heartily, and said that the bushrangers required to be looked after. They promised to call again in a few days. They walked up the street to McMinn's Hotel, and went in as the family were sitting down to tea. Miss McMinn recognised them and screamed. She was ordered to keep quiet, but as this made her scream louder the bushrangers left. The report that the bushrangers were in the town spread like wild-fire, and the streets were crowded with excited people in a few minutes. It was rumoured that the bushrangers had robbed Mr. De Clouett, in Piper Street, and that De Clouett had recognised Johnny Gilbert as a jockey who had ridden for him some years before. The police hastily armed and mounted, when suddenly the bushrangers, mounted on their horses, with revolvers in their hands, dashed through the crowd in Howick Street, shouting, "Two of us is good for forty ——— troopers." The crowd scattered to let them pass. The bushrangers rode through the street at a gallop and left the town in the direction of the timbered country, avoiding the roads. The police followed close behind, but the bushrangers had the faster horses and got away.

On October 17th, Mr. Robinson, of Robinson's Hotel, Canowindra, was awakened at about 1.30 a.m. by a loud knocking. He went to the door and asked, "Who's there?" The reply was, "The police." Robinson opened the door and was immediately ordered to "bail up." The visitors were Hall, Gilbert, and O'Meally, the bushrangers. Mr. Robinson gave them £3, which he took from a drawer, and said that was all the money he had in the house. He begged them to go away. They refused, and insisted on every one in the house getting up at once. After some delay the family and Mr. Kieran Cummings, a lodger, were collected in the dining-room. The bushrangers took charge and served out drinks all round.

When time for opening the house came, the bushrangers stationed themselves, one at each end of the verandah and the third in the bar. They bailed up fourteen bullock-drivers who were camped near the township, and compelled them to leave their teams in the street as they arrived. The robbers took anything they required or fancied from the drays and marched the drivers into the dining-room of the hotel. During the morning, Messrs. Hibberson, Twaddell, and Kirkpatrick drove up to the hotel in a buggy. They were compelled to alight and go into the dining-room.

Ben Hall, seeing that Mr. Kirkpatrick carried a revolver, requested him to "oblige by handing that thing over. Not that we want it, you know; but it might go off by accident." Mr. Kirkpatrick laughed, and gave him the weapon. Hall examined it carefully and said, "We've got better than that. We'll leave it for you at Louden's, at Grubbenbong, so that you may get it when you pass." Mrs. Robinson and the cook were released and ordered to get a "first-class dinner for the gentlemen, and we'll pay for it." The prisoners were well treated. Food was brought in at intervals, and bottles of brandy were placed on the table for all to help themselves as they pleased. Several boxes of cigars were ordered, and these were opened and the cigars thrown along the table. Robinson had promised not to "try any hanky panky," and was allowed to go to the bar. Everything ordered was paid for without delay or dispute. Gilbert walked to the lock-up, called out the solitary policeman who was stationed in the town, and made him march down to the hotel. Here he was given his musket, and ordered to pace up and down before the verandah as if on sentry duty. When they grew tired of showing their contempt for "the force" in this manner the gun was tak-

Chapter XVIII

en away and the policeman conducted into the dining-room and placed with the other prisoners to "enjoy himself like the rest." The robbers drank very little themselves. Occasionally they ordered a bottle of English beer, and drew the cork themselves after having examined it carefully to make sure that it had not been tampered with.

On the Wednesday morning Mr. Hibberson begged hard to be allowed to go. He said that he and his friends had enjoyed themselves very much, and would have been willing to stay longer to oblige, but the river was beginning to rise, and if it came down as usual at that time of the year they might not be able to cross for a month. This would interfere seriously with their business. The bushrangers listened to this plea, and then withdrew. After a consultation which lasted several minutes, Hall came back, and said they thought it was "a fair thing." They were very much obliged to the gentlemen for their contributions towards the general amusement, and they graciously gave them permission to fetch their horses from the stable and start. An hour or so later the other persons in the dining-room were told that they might go. This spree must have been an expensive one. The bushrangers only took a few pounds to start with, while they paid for everything that was consumed by the crowd between 1.30 a.m. on Monday and noon on Wednesday. At first there had been a feeling of restraint, caused, perhaps, by fear or uncertainty, but this soon wore off, and the party ended by being a very merry one. Several games were started. Songs were sung, and one of the bullock-drivers had a concertina and played dance music; several of the members of the party danced. The women and children were allowed to go to bed, but the men had to sleep with their heads on the table. The bushrangers only slept for short naps in turn. On leaving Canowindra the bushrangers rode straight to Mr. Grant's place, at Balubula, called him out, and accused him of having given information to the police as to their movements. As a punishment they burned his house, stacks, and standing crop.

A week later, on October 24th, Hall, Gilbert, O'Meally, Vane, and Burke rode up to Assistant Gold Commissioner Keightley's house, at Dunn's Plains, near Rockley, and called on him to come out. Mr. Keightley had been standing on the verandah, and on seeing them coming had rushed in and slammed the door. As he did not obey, the bushrangers fired some shots at the windows. Keightley returned the fire, and Burke fell, crying out "I'm done for." There was very little ammunition in the house and when this was expended Keightley surrendered. He asked only that the women should not be molested. Vane swore he would avenge Burke by shooting Keightley. Mrs. Baldock, wife of the camp-keeper, who was acting as general servant at the time, rushed between the men and pushed Vane back, crying at the time, "Oh! don't shoot him! Recollect his wife and her little baby." Dr. Peechy, who was present, also interfered, but was knocked down with the butt of a revolver. Mrs. Baldock again pushed Vane away, saying, "Don't hurt the doctor. He never did you any harm." Vane was much excited and swore a great deal, but he did not even push the woman away.

Presently Hall, who had been some distance away, came up and told Vane to keep cool. He added that it was impossible to say in the mêlée who shot Burke. "Why," he exclaimed, "I might have done it myself." After a short time order was restored, and the doctor then said that Burke was not dead. He offered to go to Rockley for his instruments and to return immediately. Hall said "What's the good? Better shoot him and put him out of his misery." A discussion followed, and at length permission was given to the doctor to go to his house for his instruments, after he had solemnly promised "not to bring the traps" on them. After the doctor's departure O'Meally declared his intention of taking Keightley down the paddock and shooting him. He told the Gold Commissioner "to come on," but Mrs. Keightley rushed between them and said he should shoot her before he took her husband away. Hall again interfered and order was restored. When the doctor returned he found that Burke was dead.

A lengthy discussion took place as to what should be done with Keightley. O'Meally and Vane wished to shoot him. Hall and Gilbert were in favour of holding him to ransom, and Mrs. Keightley undertook to pay them £500 if they would spare his life. Finally an agreement was arrived at. Mrs. Keightley was to ride to Bathurst and bring back the money by two p.m. the next day (Sunday). If she failed to return at that time, or brought any one back with her, her husband and Doctor Peechy were to be shot. The distance from Rockley to Bathurst was twenty-five miles, but Mrs. Keightley started without misgiving. The bushrangers refused to stop

Chapter XVIII

in the house during the night in case of surprise. They took their prisoners and camped with them on a knoll, some distance away, from the top of which they had a good view of the Bathurst Road for several miles. This they declared would give them time to shoot their hostages and ride away if treachery was attempted. Mrs. Keightley obtained the necessary amount of money from her father, Mr. Bolton, M.L.A., and returned home an hour before the stipulated time. She handed the money to Ben Hall, who complimented her on her endurance and pluck. Then Mr. Keightley and Dr. Peechy were told that they were free, and the bushrangers mounted and rode off. When this outrage was reported, the rewards offered for the capture, dead or alive, of Hall, Gilbert, O'Meally, and Vane, were increased to £1000, while £100 was offered for the capture of any other of their accomplices.

A bullock-driver left Burrangong, after having disposed of his load of produce, and camped near the Burrangong Creek, a few miles from the diggings, when three men with blackened faces, and further disguised with spectacles, called on him. They demanded the £45 which he had received in payment for his load, proving that they had somehow established a very effective system of espionage in the diggings. He admitted that that was the sum for which he had sold his load, but denied having the money, asserting that he had paid it away. They disbelieved him, and searched him and his dray, shaking out his blankets and tarpaulin. They found about £3 in notes and silver, and went off with it. The bullock-driver had been too wide awake for them. He had heard them coming along the road, and knowing how the district was infested with robbers, had hastily thrust his roll of notes under a log near his camp fire.

Peter Toohey was driving the mail coach on the road between Burrangong and Cowra, when he was ordered to bail up by three armed men. Instead of obeying he lashed his horses into a gallop, and did not pull up until he reached Mr. Allen's station at Wattamundera. The bushrangers followed for a mile or more and snapped their revolvers at him, but they were either not loaded or missed fire. In recording this event the Burrangong Courier remarked that this was probably the fastest three miles on record for a "Cobb's coach." This, however, is very doubtful. The Courier does not give the time, but some very tail tales of coach-racing have been given in the Victorian newspapers of the races run by opposition coaches on the roads from Melbourne to Bendigo and from Geelong to Ballarat in early diggings days.

The same paper reported that Constable Clark chased and captured two supposed bushrangers near Marengo on August 30th. When they reached the lock-up they were identified as Kate Meally and Elizabeth Mayhew. They were detained, but the next morning Sergeant Monaghan asked the magistrate to discharge the prisoners, as he had ascertained from enquiries that the girls only went out "for a bit of a spree in their brothers' clothes."

Mr. David Henry Campbell was sitting in his house on the Goimbla sheep station on the evening of November 19th when he heard footsteps on the verandah. Being suspicious as to the character of the visitors, he seized his gun and retreated to an inner room, while his brother William retired by another door. Mrs. Campbell was in the bedroom. The bushrangers came to the front door, and fired into the room. Mr. Campbell returned the fire, and the bushrangers retreated. They went to the stackyard, and fired the barn and haystack. They then returned to the house, which was illuminated by the blazing of the barn and stack. Mrs. Campbell came out of the bedroom, and spoke a few words to her husband. Then she crossed the front parlour in full view of the bushrangers, took a second gun and a powder flask from the corner, and returned to her husband. The bushrangers fired at her, but missed, and they then retreated along the verandah to where the shadow cast by the blazing stack concealed them. After waiting a few minutes Mrs. Campbell, thinking, as she could hear no sound except the roaring of the flames, that the bushrangers had gone away, stealthily crossed the front room and peeped out of the window. She saw three men standing near the stackyard, and went back to inform her husband. Mr. Campbell immediately left the house by the back door, crept gently along the fence, taking care to keep in the shadow, and approached the men as closely as possible without giving them the alarm. He recognised the man nearest to him as O'Meally, and fired. O'neally fell. Almost at the same moment the police, having seen the reflection of the fire miles away, and had ridden over to ascertain its cause, came galloping up. Hall and Gilbert, the two other bushrangers, hastily mounted their horses and went off under cover of the darkness. O'Meally's body was conveyed to Bathurst,

CHAPTER XVIII

where an inquest was held, and a verdict of justifiable homicide was returned. The Bathurst Times reported that locks of O'Meally's hair were being shown about and sold in the town, and protested against it. The paper said that the authorities had no right to allow this desecration of the body, even of a bushranger and murderer. "The police," it added, "would not have dared to touch his hair had he been alive. Probably Pottinger and the army of troopers that swarmed round Goimbla when the danger was passed each took a lock of his hair in memoriam when their enemy lay prostrate and dead." A public meeting was held in Sydney on March 3rd to consider what means should be adopted to recognise the bravery of Mr. Campbell in daring to resist the bushrangers and shooting O'Meally. A number of prominent men gave addresses, and it was resolved that a public subscription should be taken up to recoup him for the loss of his barn and stacks. The amount collected at the meeting and during a few days after totalled £1100. Mr. Campbell was also awarded a gold medal by the Government.

The violent deaths of Lowry, Burke, and O'Meally, in so short a time, seemed to have very little effect on the gang, which continued its depredations. Neither did these deaths prevent other young men from adopting the "profession of bushranger." In fact the deaths of a few bushrangers appear to have had less effect in deterring the criminally disposed from taking to the roads than the immunity enjoyed by the leaders offered encouragement. Bushranging was increasing instead of diminishing, although for a, few months very little was heard of the Hall and Gilbert Gang.

There was also some comedy mingled with the prevailing tragedy. For instance, a blackfellow met Alexander Sinclair, near Killoshiel, and enquired how far it was to Bathurst? Sinclair told him, and was immediately ordered to "get off that horse." The rider hesitated, but the darkey pushed him off the saddle, sprang into it himself, and galloped away threatening to shoot Sinclair if he followed, although it is very doubtful whether he had any arms on him. The same blackfellow took possession of another horse in a similar manner a few hours later some miles along the road. He rode both horses until they knocked up, and then abandoned them. They were afterwards found feeding in the bush with their saddles and bridles still on. It was supposed that the blackfellow was just pining for a gallop and adopted this means of gratifying himself. He was not traced.

Sergeant Donohoe captured William Dunne after an exciting chase through the ranges, and as the sergeant did not know his way back to the high road, he compelled his prisoner to lie down and waited patiently until some other policemen went out in search of him. Neither the sergeant nor his prisoner had any food for forty-eight hours. The police also captured George Bermingham. This man was a printer, born in Sydney, and was twenty-one years of age. When taken he was full of braggadocio, boasted loudly of the number of people he had stuck up, and talked familiarly of Vane and Johnny Gilbert. He laughed at the idea of Ben Hall having been shot as had been rumoured, and said, "Wait till he's spent the five hundred quid he got from Keightley, and you'll soon hear of him again." Sergeant Donohoe said he had followed Dunne because he recognised the. magnificent chestnut horse he was riding as one ridden by the robbers of the Cooma mail. Dunne and Bermingham were sent to gaol for ten years for having been concerned in this robbery.

In the last week of November, Hall and Gilbert stuck up the Burrowa mail. Hall expressed his disgust at the number of cheques found in the letters, and requested some of the passengers to cash them. As no one volunteered to oblige him he continued—"If I thought it would injure them (the people who posted cheques presumably) I'd burn the —— lot." The two bushrangers sat down to open the letters, leaving the passengers perfectly free. Gilbert took up one letter which had a black border and laid it aside unopened, with the remark "We must respect death." In one of the letters a piece of wedding cake was found, and Gilbert proposed that they should eat it, but Hall objected, saying "It may be a trap." This caution was common to all the bushrangers. They were in constant dread of being poisoned, and were therefore very cautious as to what they ate or drank. One of the passengers, Mr. Robert Handley, described the two bushrangers as being well-dressed, healthy looking, and very civil.

The following morning Hall and Gilbert went to Coffey's Inn, near Burrowa, and ordered breakfast. When they had finished their meal they walked out on to the road and stopped every one who passed, compelling them to go into the bar after handing over their money. Mr. Campbell, however, refused to stand when challenged. He struck spurs to his horse and galloped away. Hall fired at him and then rushed to the verandah and

Chapter XVIII

mounted his horse. He galloped only a short distance and then returned, Campbell having too good a start. The bushrangers "shouted" for their prisoners in the bar several times "for the good of the house," and paid for what they ordered. It was said that they spent nearly as much as they had obtained from the persons robbed.

On December 16th Mr. Henry Morgan, one of the proprietors of the Burrangang Star, was driving, with his newly-married wife, between Bowning and Binalong, when he was ordered to bail up by Hall and Gilbert. Gilbert was in high spirits. He exchanged hats with Morgan, and put his poncho on Mrs. Morgan, declaring that she would make "a first-rate bushranger." The newspaper man and his wife were taken into the bush, and detained from eight a.m. till six p.m. During this time Mr. George Franklin and his wife and four bullock drays were stuck up. One of the bullock-drivers named Sheedy had four bottles of gin on his dray, and these were opened and the liquor served round. The robbers asked Mrs. Franklin to cook breakfast "for the crowd," taking the necessary provisions from the loading on the drays. During the afternoon a number of other persons were brought into "the camp." All except one man were allowed to move about freely. This one man was tied, and was spoken to very roughly and uncivilly. The man was supposed to be "a telegram," and this show of harshness "a stall." At six o'clock the camp was broken up, and the prisoners permitted to resume their journeys.

This performance was repeated the next and the two following days, near the same spot, and although the individual losses were generally small, the aggregate amount of money collected must have been considerable. Only in one instance was any violence used. A bullock-driver named Lake refused to turn out his pockets. Gilbert pressed the muzzle of his revolver against Lake's face and said: "If you don't do what you're told I'll shove this down your —— mouth." Hall felt Lake's pockets and took out £5 in notes and some silver. At night, when released, Lake asked for some of his money back to pay expenses along the road. Gilbert replied: "If you're a —— carrier your name's good for what you want. If you hadn't been so —— jolly you'd have got something. We always divide with them that behave themselves."

In the week ending December 23rd, the Molong, the Cooma, the Tuena, and the Hartley mails were stuck up and robbed, proving that either the gang was divided or that more than one party was at work in the district.

A party including Messrs. Sheedy, Bass, Hutchinson, and other residents of the district, with several ladies, when returning home from one of the numerous race parties held during the Christmas holidays, were ordered to "bail up." A lad was leading the racer Black Diamond, owned by Mr. Sheedy, and let him go. Ben Hall was furious. He galloped after the racer, swearing, and tried to head him, but failed. He came back and threatened the boy and Mr. Sheedy, but soon grew cool. The ladies were treated very civilly, but the robbers took watches and other valuables and all the money they could find from the gentlemen. Black Diamond was found safe in his stable when Mr. Sheedy reached home.

Nineteen

A Heavy Sessions at Goulburn; Ben Hall Hard Pushed; An Amateur Mail Robber; Discovery of Frank Gardiner; His Trial and Sentence; The Old Man; A Brush with the Police; The Chinkies Show Fight; Messrs. Hall & Co. Take a Lease of the Main Southern Road; Capture of Mount and Dunleavy; Johnny Dunn; A Desperate Duel and Death of Sergeant Parry; A Country Ball and its Sequel.

Bushranging by no means died out with the close of 1863. During the holidays the activity of the robbers continued, and the disease spread to other districts. It will, however, perhaps be better to continue the history of this gang, and return later on to the actions of other gangs elsewhere. On February 7th, 1864, Inspector Brennan and Constables Lovett and Roche went to a sly-grog shanty, as the places where strong drinks were sold without a licence were called, and captured George Lynam and Michael Seary. The horses of the two bushrangers were so exhausted with hard riding that although they mounted and rode away when the police came, they were soon caught, in spite of their long start. They were charged and convicted of having robbed a number of persons at William Sidwell's, Governor's Arms Hotel, Towrang, two miles from Goulburn, in company with James Crookwell and Daniel Matthews. Lynam also, in company with John Southgate, stuck up and robbed Thomas Cummins, Robert Sherwood, and others at Mr. Cornelius O'Brien's Station, near Binalong. They also stuck up Mr. Dwyer's place at Pudman's Creek, and after having made a bundle of all that was worth taking away, compelled Mrs. Ann Dwyer to cook thirty-four eggs and a quantity of bacon for them. They tied Dwyer, struck Mrs. Dwyer, and threatened to burn the place down unless they were told where the money was hidden. Jane Dwyer, daughter of Ann Dwyer, said that when they went in to search the bedroom, Lynam exclaimed, pointing to the crucifix, "There's Jesus Christ. He ought to be burned, and I've a good mind to do it." They smashed the furniture and broke open boxes and cupboards in their search for money. Lynam was sent to gaol for fifteen years, while Seary, Matthews, Crookwell, and

Southgate were sentenced to ten years each for some offences, and to fifteen years for others, but as the sentences were all made concurrent all the prisoners were practically sentenced to fifteen years' imprisonment.

At the same sessions Charles Jones, alias William Herbert, and Frank Stanley, alias Wright, were sentenced to twelve years for various acts of highway robbery. Some of these young men were said to have assisted in some of the robberies effected by the Hall and Gilbert gang, and were suspected of being on their way to join that gang. James Hill and James Jones went to William Duguid's house at Mils, Twofold Bay, on March 13th, and stuck up all hands. It was early in the morning when they arrived, and they sent everybody about the place into the kitchen and then searched the house. Jones remained on guard while Hill went with the stockman to fetch up the horses. Mr. Duguid warned Jones that he expected the police and advised him to go before they came to avoid bloodshed. Jones laughed, and ostentatiously loaded the double-barrelled gun which he had just taken from Duguid's bedroom. Hill returned with the horses, and while the bushrangers were selecting the ones they liked the police arrived.

Sub-Inspector John Garder Hussey challenged the bushrangers and called on them to surrender. For a minute or two the shooting was very brisk, but it did not last long. Jones and Hussey fell wounded almost simultaneously, and Hill ran away. He was followed by Constable Zollner and captured, while Sergeant Chandler secured Jones. The wounds were not very serious, but the bushrangers were sent to gaol for fifteen years. Ah Ling and ten other Chinese were living together in a hut on the Abercrombie Goldfield. On May and John Taylor and Thomas Webb drove the Chinamen into the kitchen and called them up one by one to be robbed. The first victim was Ah Wee. When asked for his gold he replied "No savee." He afterwards said he had none. Webb got a rope, tied it round the Chinaman's neck, and hauled him up to a sapling beam which ran across the building. After hanging for several minutes Ah Wee was let down and asked whether he "saveed now?" He handed out his gold and explained at the trial that it made him "welly sick." Ah Yong, Ah See, and two or three others were served in the same way, and the others gave up their gold without further compulsion. The prisoners were sent to gaol for two years. The session was a remarkably heavy one, and the majority of the cases tried were for robbery under arms.

Chapter XIX

While the police had been very successful in bringing a number of outsiders to justice, the better known members of the gang continued to keep the district alive. The Yass Courier reported that nearly every one in the district had turned out to hunt Ben Hall, who was reported to have paid them a visit. The bushranger had been so hard pressed that he was forced to abandon Willy the Weasel, owned by Mr. Garry. The horse was completely knocked up, otherwise the bushranger would not have let him go, as he was a favourite. The stock-riders of the district had expressed great contempt for the police, their opinions being summed up as follows: "They can't catch him. They don't know how to ride down a hill." Many of the "hills" in the district would be elsewhere considered almost as precipices.

The Young (Burrangong) Daily Tribune the same week reported that a day or two ago Ben Hall walked alone into the stables at Groggan station, Bland Plains, said "Good morning, boys," and then proceeded coolly to tie up the three men and a boy. Having secured these to his entire satisfaction, he walked to the house and asked to see Mr. Chisholm. On that gentleman coming to the door Hall said, "Good morning, Mr. Chisholm. I've come for Troubadour."

"You've left him so long you might do without him now," returned Mr. Chisholm. "Oh," exclaimed Hall, "you're getting too flash. If you consort with traps you'll have to be taught manners." They walked to the stables, where Hall put saddles and bridles on Troubadour and Union Jack. The last-named had won the Champion Plate at the Wagga Wagga races on New Year's Day, and had only been brought home under police escort a day or two before. Hall also selected two other horses, which he said he "liked the look of," and put bridles on them. He then made Mr. Chisholm fill two three-bushel bags with clothing from the store, and these he packed on the spare horses. Then he mounted Troubadour, and leading the others started away. He had scarcely moved, however, before he pulled up again, and said to Mr. Chisholm, "That's a good looking watch of yours. I want it. Hand it over." Mr. Chisholm did so, and the bushranger then rode off. It may be explained that the reason why no opposition was attempted was because it was believed that Hall had plenty of support if he had required it. He never walked unless he was compelled, and it was thought that his mates with the horses were not far off. It was also suggested that Hall had a bad mount after he lost Willy the Weasel and that he did not wish to let Mr. Chisholm see him riding an inferior horse.

The mail coach from Wagga Wagga having failed to arrive at Cootamundra at the usual time, on May 12th, the contractor, Mr. Burke, supposed that it had been stuck up somewhere along the road and rode out to make enquiries. At about three miles from Cootamundra he found a number of letters lying scattered about the road. He gathered them up and continued his search. At length he found the mail-man drunk in a public-house near Murrumburrah. The fellow had robbed the mail himself, no doubt with the intention of laying the blame on the bushrangers. He was convicted and sentenced to seven years' penal servitude.

The mail was stuck up at Mumble Flat, between Orange and Wellington, on March 1st. A portion of the loading consisted of carbines and revolvers for the police, "all of which," said the Orange Guardian, "were borne off to be used against them."

The Bathurst-Sydney coach was stuck up at Lapstone Hill by three armed men. The passengers were Michael Duffy, Constable McKay, in charge of a female lunatic, and three Chinamen. After having collected the money from the passengers and searched the letters, the robbers extinguished the coach lamps, took the horses out, and drove them up the hill. The driver waited for half an hour, as he had been ordered to do, and then started to catch his horses. This he managed to do with some difficulty, and on his return he drove on to Penrith. From thence the passengers and the broken mail-bags were taken to Sydney by train. John Forster was arrested in a house at Strawberry Hills, Sydney, and charged with having, with others, stuck up and robbed the mail coach between Penrith and Hartley at two a.m. Ah Lung, one of the passengers on the coach, recognised a sash which the prisoner wore round his waist as his property, and said he carried his money in it. Forster was sent to gaol for ten years.

About this time great excitement was caused throughout New South Wales by the report that Frank Gardiner had been discovered and arrested by Detective McGlone on March 3rd, at Apis Creek, on the road from Rockhampton to the Peak Downs diggings, Queensland. Gardiner was keeping a shanty, or roadside store, with Mrs. Brown, who passed as his

Chapter XIX

wife. Gardiner was brought to Sydney and duly committed for trial. In connection with this case Mr. (afterwards Sir) E. Deas Thompson laid a return on the table of the Legislative Assembly showing that the amount stolen by Gardiner previous to his disappearance was about £21,000. Of this total, £13,694 had been stolen in the robbery of the Lachlan Escort, and £5,335 had been recovered by the police under Sir Frederick Pottinger.

No murders were charged against Gardiner, but he was convicted on three counts for highway robbery. On each of these counts he was sentenced, on the first to twelve years and on the other two to ten years each. The first three years in irons in each case. The sentences were made cumulative, and aggregated thirty-two years. It will be remembered that Captain Melville, the bushranger, was sentenced to a similar term of imprisonment in Victoria about twelve years before, and there were many people in New South Wales who thought that Gardiner had been too harshly dealt with. Such a sentence, they said, deprived a man of all hope, and rendered him desperate, and they would not be surprised if Gardiner rebelled against it as Melville had done. Those who held this view were, however, in the minority. The majority said bushranging must be stamped out at any cost, and until this was effected the sentences could not be too severe.

On the 10th of May Ben Hall, Gilbert, and a new recruit known as "the Old Man," rode up to McGregor's Inn at Bong Bong, where a number of men were on the verandah. The bushrangers ordered these men to "throw your arms up," enforcing the order with revolvers. There were some twenty visitors on the verandah and in the bar, and these were ranged along the wall in the dining room, with Hall on guard. Gilbert and "the Old Man" walked down the yard to the stables, where several racehorses were in the stalls under the charge of Constables Scott and Macnamara, who were escorting them to Burrangong for the races on Queen's birthday. Gilbert called to the constables to "leave those horses." The constables drew their revolvers, and fired by way of reply. The bushrangers fired, and Hall left the dining-room to take part in the scrimmage. For some minutes the shooting was very brisk, but no one appeared to be hurt. The police were on foot and under cover of the stables, but the bushrangers were mounted and in the open yard. Suddenly the firing ceased as if by mutual consent, and Gilbert shouted that they would be back presently. The bushrangers then rode away. As Hall went out of the gate his cabbage tree hat fell off, and a cry was raised that he had been hit. He rode off, however, without showing any symptoms of injury. Believing that the bushrangers had gone for reinforcements the two constables barricaded the stables, and sent a messenger to the nearest police depôt for assistance. About midnight Sir Frederick Pottinger arrived with four troopers, but the bushrangers did not return.

On the following afternoon the mail coach was stuck up at Emu Flat, between Burrangong and Yass. A passenger named Michael Curran saved his gold watch and chain by dropping them among the straw in the bottom of the coach, but a valuable gold ring and £21 in notes were taken from him. Ben Hall also exchanged an old poncho for a valuable rug, and an old clay pipe for a very fine meerschaum. Some distance away Mr. Barnes met the coach, and the driver, J. Roberts, who knew him, warned Barnes that the bushrangers were on the road. Barnes laughed and went on. He was stopped and robbed, and as he did not hand out his money very readily when ordered to do so, he was very roughly treated and was threatened with death. Several teams were also robbed. The bushrangers were riding the racers Teddington, Harkaway, and Troubadour.

During this "reign of terror," the Press, especially of the country districts, continued to urge the necessity for suppressing the "bush telegraphs" and other sympathisers of the bushrangers, and said that while so many who aided them either by giving them information of the movements of the police or providing them with hiding places when they were hard pressed were at large the police had little chance of making headway against the evil doers. The Yass Courier, for instance, spoke of "the wealthy relations—of the bushrangers—with whom the police are afraid to interfere, but whose places never have and never will be stuck up." The paper "perforce refrains from publishing the names of these people on account of the state of the libel law," but it charges them with "comforting and assisting the bushrangers." It seems difficult to understand what the police were expected to do, or to see what action could be taken against a settler because his place was not raided, and who had some more or less distant relative "on the roads." But this serves to show how closely the Press enquired into the antecedents and relationships of the bushrangers.

CHAPTER XIX

A man, believed to be Johnny Gilbert, accompanied by a lad named Ryan, stopped to dinner at the Korowatha Inn. They talked freely of bushranging, and laughed at the report that Hall had been hit at McGregor's, as the newspapers had reported. They affirmed that "the traps could not fire straight enough to hit a haystack."

On the 22nd of June, the Bathurst Times said: "After an immunity from bushranging crimes in this district for some months, the gang has appeared once more and commenced operations. On the 18th, the mail coach for Orange and the Lachlan started an hour late from this town in consequence of the heavy mail. There were on board James Naime and seven passengers. About eighteen miles out, near the turn-off road to Guyong, three men jumped out of the bush and ordered the mail-man to 'bail up.' The coach was taken off the road, where the passengers were robbed and the letters torn open. The driver and passengers were then told that they would be detained until the down mail came. While they were waiting, a little boy was stopped and one pound of tea and 1s. 6d. in money were taken from him. The boy's father, a farmer living near, came out to look for his son, and was run in among the crowd. After some dispute, the tea and the 1s. 6d. were given back, but the father and son were compelled to remain until the other coach came by. The down mail, driven by John Fagan, arrived about midnight and was stopped. Fagan was asked what made him so late, and replied that the roads were bad with the rains. The letters were opened, except those in the registered bag, which the robbers missed. About two a.m. the robbers told their prisoners that they might go, and walked away." It was said that this was not the Gilbert and Hall gang, as the robbers had no horses. The police started in pursuit from Bathurst and Orange as soon as news of the robbery reached these towns.

Ben Hall and his gang stuck up and robbed Pearce and Hillier's store at Canowindra, and held the town for the day as on a previous occasion. The following afternoon, June 23rd, they called at Mr. Rothsay's station, took four horses from the stables, and set fire to a stack containing about 14 tons of hay as a "caution to traitors."

Ben Hall, Johnny Gilbert, John Dunleavy, and James Mount (hitherto known as "the Old Man") stuck up the Carcour and Cowra coaches. They then rode on to the Half-Way House Hotel and compelled the landlord to hand over £76. They held the road for several hours, robbing all who passed, and bringing them to the hotel, where they "shouted for all hands" several times. This time the bushrangers drank port wine. They took several well-bred horses from the stables. One of these got loose and galloped along the road. He was followed by Dunleavy, who failed to head him. The horse was caught next day and sent to Bathurst for safety.

Two armed men endeavoured to stick up the Chinese Camp at Gilmandyke Creek, near Rockley. The Chinese fought bravely, returning the bushrangers' fire in a spirited manner with shot guns. A bushranger named Clayton was wounded and captured, when the other man rode away.

The Chinese were highly commended for their pluck, and several of the newspapers said that they had set a good example for white men to follow.

Hall and Mount went to Mr. Jamieson's station on the Bland River, and informed the proprietor that they intended to stop for the night. They called the men up, asked their names and how much money each one had. Having obtained this information they announced that they did not intend to take anything from any one. Possibly this decision may have been due to the fact that the total amount acknowledged to be in the possession of those present was small. Whether this was so or not, however, matters little. They ordered supper to be served, and made all present sit down to the table in the dining-room. When the meal was over and the table cleared, Mr. Jamieson was asked to bring out some rum from the store. A pint pot, filled with hot water with plenty of salt in it, was placed on the table, and Hall announced that if any one present refused to sing or to contribute in some other way to the general amusement, he would be compelled to swallow the contents of this pannikin. Then they made a night of it. In the morning half the men were lying on the ground in a drunken sleep, but the bushrangers were quite sober, having drunk very little. They spent half-an-hour in the stable cleaning their horses, had breakfast, and rode away, declaring that they had enjoyed themselves immensely, and thanking Mr. Jamieson for the entertainment he had afforded them.

They called at the next station and took the racehorse "Plover" out of the stable. Mount ordered the stock-man to fetch the horses out of the paddock, as he wanted to select one or two of the best stock-horses. While

Chapter XIX

they were talking, the stock-man moved round from Mount's right hand side to the left. The bushranger immediately shifted his revolver from the right hand to the left, remarking quietly: "I can shoot just as straight left-handed as right." Hall said he had enjoyed many a good laugh at the newspaper yarns about himself. He added that Brown's men were "jolly good fellows." In the evening they stuck up the Gundagai mail near Jugiong. When opening the letters Hall found a bulky roll of bank notes.

"Ah!" he said, "This is what I like." He took a number of newspapers away with him, "just to see what they say about me." From thence they rode straight to the Chinese camp at Wombat, "to give the Chinkies a lesson." The Chinese were very slow in producing their gold, and the bushrangers fired in among them, killing one and wounding another. The next day, Sunday, they stuck up a number of Chinamen on the road and took their gold, but did not ill-treat them. In the afternoon they went to Mr. McCarthy's store in Jugiong and compelled him to open the door. They selected a quantity of clothing and drapery, which they placed on a spare pack horse they had with them. In the evening they stuck up the Gundagai mail within a mile of the place where they had stuck it up a few days before. Hall took out a roll of half notes from one packet. "This is a green trick, this is," he said, holding them up. "It's little trouble to us to match half notes." This series of outrages, following so closely one on the other, naturally stirred the police up to increased activity, and the bushrangers were so closely followed that a brush took place between them and the police in the last week of October. In this fight, which lasted only a very short time, Dunleavy was severely wounded and surrendered, while Mount was captured.

James Mount was an escaped convict, out on a ticket-of-leave. He was forty-five years of age, but had been called "The Old Man" before his name was known, to distinguish him from the young men and boys who formed the body of this gang. Mount was tried and convicted of highway robbery in Bathurst, and was sentenced to ten years' imprisonment.

In commenting upon the capture of Mount and Dunleavy the Goulburn Herald announced that their loss to the gang had been to some extent compensated for by the accession of Johnny Dunn, who was born in

Murrum Hurrah. Earlier in the year 1864 Dunn had won the principal prize at the Yass race meeting with the Binalong horse, Ringleader. He was an excellent rider, and would no doubt give the police some trouble.

"Messrs. Hall, Gilbert, and Dunn seem to have obtained a lease of the Main Southern road," said the Yass Courier of November 19th. They robbed the up and down mails from Gundagai two consecutive weeks. On the last of these four robberies the coach was bailed up at Deep Creek, near Jugiong, at about four p.m. Messrs. Bradley and Sheahan, passengers, had alighted to walk up the steep hill, and were some hundred yards or so ahead of the coach, when three men suddenly appeared from behind the scrub and ordered them to "bail up." "All right," replied Mr. Sheahan, holding his hands above his head. Hall said, "That'll do. We've got a little township of our own up there. Come on." He pointed up the hill as he spoke. They followed him until they came to a small, clear spot, surrounded with high trees and scrub. Here they saw twelve bullock drays and a number of men. Several horses were hitched to the trees round the clearing, and the men who owned them, as well as the bullock-drivers and some footmen, were seated on the ground. When asked for his money Sheahan replied, "Got none. Search if you like."

"Oh, you're not a bad sort," said Hall, "we'll take your word for it." Bradley took out a cheque for £1, saying, "That's all I've got. I brought it to pay my way on the trip." Hall put his hand into Bradley's pocket, and finding nothing there told him to keep the cheque. A cask of port wine, which was found on one of the bullock drays, was tapped, and the wine was handed round to all present in a quart pot in which tea had been made, as was evident by its colour. When the letters had been searched, the bushrangers told the company that they might go.

Expecting that the return mail would be robbed again next day Mr. Ross, police magistrate, and Constable Roche in private clothes went as passengers, while Inspector O'Neil and Sergeant Edmund Parry rode beside the coach on horseback. At Black Springs, near Jugiong, the bushrangers appeared as had been anticipated, and on emerging from the bush one of them shouted out, "Hullo, here's the bobbies." Hall said, "There's only two. Rush the ———." The three bushrangers then rode forward shouting

Chapter XIX

"Come on, you ——, fight like men." Sergeant Parry rode forward and encountered Gilbert, and a desperate duel on horseback with revolvers took place until Parry fell. In the meantime Inspector O'Neil had kept under cover of the coach and managed to keep the other two bushrangers at bay until Parry fell, when he surrendered. Mr. Ross fired several shots, but what became of Constable Roche is not known. He was not captured or wounded. He simply disappeared in the scrub. When all was quiet Gilbert dismounted, turned over Parry's body, and remarked coolly "He got it in the cobbera. It's all over with him. Well, I'm sorry for it. He's the bravest trap I've met yet." The coach was taken off the road to where several bullock teams, two horse carts with their Chinese owners, a buggy with Mr. and Mrs. Hayes, and several footmen and horsemen—among whom was Constable McLaughlin, who had fired away his ammunition before he surrendered—were collected together. The robbers searched the letters as usual, took all the police horses and arms, collected the money, watches, and other valuables from the crowd and rode away saying "We'll rob the mail to-morrow if all the traps in the colony are here." Whether this threat was mere braggadocio, or whether the bushrangers intended to draw the police here so that they might operate in safety elsewhere, has been frequently argued without any definite result. The police were on the road, and the bushrangers did not put in an appearance. That is what is known. The day following, however, the gang stuck up the Binalong mail, and after searching the letters, burned letters and papers to "put a stop to the English correspondence."

A day or two later, "Messrs. Hall & Co." took possession of the road between the Fourteen Mile and the Fifeen Mile rushes at Burrangong and bailed up about thirty men, women, and boys. A bridle took the fancy of one of the gang, and he insisted on taking it and giving his own in return. With this exception, and the taking of a quantity of bread and butter found on the drays bailed up, nothing was stolen. The bushrangers explained that they expected some gold buyers along the road, and when they came the camp would be broken up. In the meantime they wanted every one to enjoy the picnic. The women were set to work to cut up and serve out the bread and butter. Fires were lighted and tea made. Then races and other sports were organised for the boys. One of the bailed-up men was a newsvendor, and the bushrangers "borrowed" his papers and took it in turn to lie down and read the news. At last one of the boys contrived to sneak away unseen, and as soon as his escape was discovered the camp was broken up and the robbers rode away.

On December 19th, the Hon. William Macleay, M.L.C., was driving in a buggy from Towrang to Shelly's Flat, when he noticed a large crowd a little way ahead. He sent his coachman on with the buggy and got down to make enquiries. As he drew near he saw that a number of people were standing round two bullock drays, while one or two men were breaking open the boxes on the drays. Mr. Macleay asked a man what was the matter, and the man motioned to him to keep quiet. Mr. Macleay conjectured that it was the bushrangers robbing the drays, and withdrew as quietly as he had joined the crowd. He walked on to Plum's Inn, where he found a wedding party enjoying themselves. He told the landlord what he had seen and his suspicions, and advised those present to take precautions to avoid being robbed. Some time later the bushrangers came up, and seeing a number of men on the verandah with guns and revolvers in their hands, fired. Mr. Macleay immediately returned the fire. The bushrangers drew together some distance away, and held a consultation. They apparently decided that the risk was too great, as they went off along the road. For beating off the bushrangers, and proving that a show of resistance might prevent robberies, Mr. Macleay was awarded a gold medal by the New South Wales Government. As a per contra, the fact that the bushrangers robbed the drays openly in the main road in this instance, instead of taking them into the bush, was cited as evidence that they were growing bolder and more careless of the police.

Hall, Gilbert, and Dunn rode up to a store at Binda, owned by an ex-policeman named Morris, on December 21st, and took about £100 from his cashbox. They informed Morris that a ball was being held at the Flag Hotel, and insisted on himself and Mrs. Morris dressing themselves, and accompanying the bushrangers to the ball. Morris at first objected, but finally gave way. When they reached the Flag Hotel the bushrangers mixed freely with the crowd, dancing and otherwise enjoying themselves. Presently some "bush telegraph" informed the bushrangers that Morris had been sounding several of the men present as to the probability of effect-

Chapter XIX

ing a capture. Gilbert and Dunn drew their revolvers and started to look for Morris, who, having been informed of what had transpired, jumped through an open window, and ran towards where the bushrangers' horses were tied to trees. His intention was to take one and ride for the police. The bushrangers, however, caught sight of him, and divining his intention ran and fired at Morris. This compelled him to turn aside and take refuge behind a tree. The bushrangers made no attempt to follow him. They removed their horses to a safer place, then walked to the store, piled a quantity of brushwood on the verandah, and set fire to it. Then they mounted their horses, and sat and watched the blaze until the house was well alight, when they rode off. There were more than a hundred persons at the ball, but no attempt was made to prevent the bushrangers from burning down the store. In connection with this "act of vengeance" Christina McKinnon and Ellen and Margaret Monks were arrested and charged with having aided and abetted in burning down Morris's store. The girls had been dancing with the bushrangers, and had accompanied them when they went to the store. The police said that they were well known as "bush telegraphs," and cited instances in which it was supposed that they had given notice to the bushrangers of the approach of the police. Margaret Monks was discharged, but the other two were sent to gaol, the evidence showing that they had assisted the bushrangers in piling wood on the verandah of the store.

Mr. D. Davis, auctioneer, of Yass, had been conducting a sale at Murrumburrah, and was returning home on December 10th when he was stuck up. He had on him £109 1s. 5d., the proceeds of the sale, principally in cheques. When these were handed out Ben Hall was in a furious rage, and threatened to burn them. Gilbert proposed that he should gallop on and "change them before they're stopped." There was £1 5s. 6d. in cash, and of this they kept £1, returning the silver. They then rode rapidly away. Nothing more was heard of the cheques, the only thing known of them being that they were never cashed.

Twenty

Meeting the Gold Escort; Murder of Constable Nelson; A Brush with the Police; Attempt to Stick Up the Araluen Gold Escort; Death of Constable Kelly and Pluck of Constable Burns; Sir Frederick Pottinger Resigns; Death of Ben Hall; Sketch of his Life; Death of Johnny Gilbert; Record of John Dunn and the Gang; Capture and Trial of Johnny Dunn; His Execution; Fate of the Chief Members of the Gardiner Gang.

Like many other young men I spent a few years on the diggings in hopes of making "my pile," and early in 1865 I, in company with two mates, left the King's Plains, where we had just finished working out a hole, and started for Apple Tree Flat, near Mudgee, where a rush had recently taken place. We were well mounted, and had a pack-horse which "belonged to the firm." One of my mates was a keen sportsman, and his horse had won several prizes at those country meetings known as "Publican's Races," from the fact that they were organised by a publican and held near his house for obvious business reasons. We were travelling steadily along the road leading from Blaney to Bathurst, near Back Creek, when we saw the Government Gold Escort in the distance. The police authorities of New South Wales had learned a lesson from the Great Escort Robbery of 1862, and no longer mounted all the police on the coach or drag in which the gold was conveyed to Sydney. At the place we had arrived at the road, a chain and a half wide (99 feet), had been cleared through a stretch of heavy forest timber. It ran as straight as possible as far as the eye could reach, and was bordered on either side by a dense growth of timber and scrub rising to a height of from 200 to 300 feet like a wall of greenery. In the centre of the roadway was a metalled or gravelled road about fifteen feet wide.

The remainder on either side was graded to near the timber line, where a small cutting to carry off surface water was made. We rode on the soft grassy side slopes and left the metalled or gravelled road for vehicles. It was in the centre of this gorge in the forest that we first sighted the escort. First rode a single trooper; at fifty yards distance came two more; then, at about the same distance, came the escort cart, drawn by four horses, the driver and another policeman sitting on the front seat, while a third trooper sat behind. A mounted trooper also rode one on each side of the cart. Fifty yards further back were two more troopers, while the rear was brought up by another single trooper. The troopers had their carbines ready in their hands, the butts resting on their thighs. When the leading trooper came within hail of us, he cried "Halt," and raised his rifle. We halted. The two troopers behind him came forward at a rapid pace until they were near enough to support him, if necessary. The cart stopped, and the other troopers gathered round it ready to defend it. The sergeant in charge inquired what our names were, where we were going, and what was our business. We told him. He said our horses were superior to those usually ridden by diggers. We replied that we didn't care about riding old screws. He asked whether the two guns we carried were loaded. We informed him that one was loaded with shot in case we came across a duck or a pigeon.

He told us to sit up straight and follow him. Then he motioned to the two troopers just behind him. He led the way while the troopers followed behind us. We all kept to the side of the road; the cart having been drawn up on the other side. The other troopers sat on their horses, carbine in hand, as we passed. It was a most impressive show of force out there in the bush. The sergeant and two troopers conducted us for about a hundred yards past the cart and then pulled up. The sergeant said it was difficult to tell what men were by their appearance. He advised us to be very careful, and asked if we had any gold or money with us. We told him that we had been at Lambing Flat, and knew what the state of the country was. We did not feel disposed to carry gold or very much money with us while there were banks in every town. He said we were right and wished us good day after telling us to ride straight on and not attempt to turn back. We laughed and said we were travelling in the opposite direction and had no desire to turn back.

In talking the matter over in our camp that night we decided that great as the improvement in the escort service had been it would not be impossible to rob the escort again. If, for instance, we had been part of a gang of bushrangers, sent to draw the attention of the police to us, while another portion of the gang had been hidden in the scrub, opposite where the cart stood, the troopers might have been shot down almost without a chance of defending themselves. However, the escort protection seems to have been sufficient, as it was not robbed again, although one or two attempts were made in other districts.

During the first week or two of 1865 very little was heard of Messrs. Hall & Co., but on January 26th the three principal members of the firm (Hall, Gilbert, and Dunn), stuck up Mr. Kimberley's store in Main Street, Collector. Dunn was stationed on guard on the verandah while Hall and Gilbert went inside to select such articles as they required or fancied. Constable Nelson, the only policeman stationed in the little town, was at the lock-up, and on being informed of what was going on he loaded his carbine and walked down the street towards the store. Dunn saw him coming and withdrew out of sight behind the fence at the corner of the verandah, and when the constable was only a few yards distant the robber fired at him. The constable fell, and Dunn, coming out of his hiding-place, walked to where he was lying, put his revolver close to the constable's head, and fired again. Hearing the shots, Hall and Gilbert came out, and on seeing what had been done, held a whispered consultation, and then mounted their horses and rode away. They went straight to Alfred Cramp's farm at Binda, and ordered dinner. While they were still at table a party of police galloped up, dismounted, and rushed into the front door of the house as the bushrangers went out of the back door. A few shots were fired, but the bushrangers mounted and escaped, owing to the superiority of their horses. The news of Constable Nelson's death had been conveyed to the police at once, and they had followed close on the tracks of the bushrangers.

In February a number of persons were stuck up near Illalong, on the road between Yass and Burrangong. The robbers were said to have no connection with the firm of Hall & Co., as they robbed their victims of their coats and vests. The Hall gang never did this. If they saw a man with a coat or vest, or any other article of clothing to which they took a fancy, they would exchange with him, but they only stole clothes from the stores. However, while the police were out in search of these plebeian bushrangers, they happened to come across Hall and Gilbert at Lodge's

Chapter XX

Inn, Breadalbane Plains, and captured their horses. It was supposed that the two robbers had been sleeping in the barn. They rushed out when the police came, and went across a cleared paddock, both parties firing their revolvers. Constable Wiles was wounded, and Ben Hall was supposed to have been wounded, as he fell. He was up again in a moment, however, and succeeded in reaching the timber, the ground being too rough and heavily-timbered for the police horses to make their way through it.

A daring attempt was made by Hall and three others to stick up the Araluen escort on March 16th. The bushrangers fired from behind trees as the escort cart was going up Major's Creek Mount, at the same place where a similar attempt had been made about two and a half years previously. Constable Kelly fell wounded, and died a few days later. Constable Burns, who was driving, jumped off the cart, put a stone behind the wheel, and then fired, shouting "Come on." Mr. Blatchford, J.P., who had been riding beside the driver, remained on his seat until a voice from behind the trees cried out, "Shoot the —— on the cart." He then jumped down quickly, but was wounded in the leg. He fell, but got up again immediately and ran down the hill to Neonan's Hotel for assistance. Constable Stapleton and his companion forced their horses up the steep cutting which bordered the road, and disappeared among the trees. Burns, thus left alone with the cart, sheltered himself behind it as well as he could, and kept blazing away coolly from his cover. Suddenly, Constable Stapleton and his companion attacked the robbers in the rear. Gilbert turned sharply, and said, "You're a good shot, take that," and shot the constable's horse. The two policemen, however, kept up the firing, and the bushrangers mounted their horses and rode away. Mr. Blatchford presented Constable Burns with a cheque for £50, as a reward for the pluck he had shown in defending his charge.

It was at about this time that Sir Frederick Pottinger, who was in command of the police in this district, was charged with having neglected his duty. Sir Frederick had ridden in a gentleman's race on the Wowingragong course. It was rumoured that the bushrangers, for whom he was supposed to be looking, had been on the course too, and had not been recognised. Sir Frederick was called to Sydney to attend an inquiry, and resigned his position in the force. About a month later he died from the effects of a wound from a pistol, accidently fired by himself.

The gang yarded a mob of horses at a station near Murrumburrah and picked out several of the finest horses, which they took away, leaving their own knocked-up horses in their place. They rode to Wombat, where they stuck up a mob of Chinamen, one of whom was shot to make the others "shell out" their gold more quickly. Then the bushrangers travelled to Forbes, and on the following day robbed Mr. Jones's store of £81 in cash and a quantity of clothing and drapery. Information was given to the police in the town as soon as the robbers left the store, and a party of police with two black trackers followed them.

On the following evening, May 5th, they came on two hobbled horses feeding near the Billabong Creek. These were recognised as horses which had been ridden by the bushrangers, and the police watched them carefully without allowing themselves to be seen. This was not difficult, as there were thick patches of scrub about the flat. Half-an-hour later a man came out of one of these patches of scrub, unhobbled the horses, and led them away for about two hundred yards to where there was better grass. It was at that time too dark to distinguish him. He rehobbled the horses and retired into the scrub once more. The police drew up closer to this patch with great caution and watched till morning. At daybreak the man appeared again and looked round to ascertain whether the horses were in sight, and Inspector Davidson immediately recognised him as Ben Hall and called on him to stand. Hall turned to go back into the patch of scrub, and the inspector fired at him. Sergeant Condell and the four policemen also fired, and Hall stopped and leaned on a sapling for support. Then Constable Hopkiss took steady aim and fired again, and Hall let his revolver fall from his hand. The police went forward and Hall said "I'm hit. Shoot me dead." He relaxed his hold on the sapling, staggered forward and fell. The police rushed up, but he died before any attempt could be made to staunch the blood.

On the body being examined one rifle and six revolver bullet wounds were found, any one of which should have proved fatal. The bushrangers' horses were soon caught, the body was strapped on one of them, and the party returned to Forbes. The police were much surprised to find Hall alone, but conjectured that Gilbert and Dunn had gone down the Lachlan River to some of the great stations to procure horses, all the racehorses about Burrangong having been pretty well exhausted. The two captured with Hall were in very poor condition, and had evidently been ridden hard. It was supposed that they had knocked up, and that Hall had stayed behind while his companions sought fresh mounts. He thought he was quite safe in the scrub, so far sway from his usual haunts.

Benjamin Hall was about twenty-eight years of age. His father had come to the Wedden Mountains district in about 1840, when little Ben was about three years old. The elder Hall had worked for Mr. Ranken for some years, and had always borne a good character. When Ben was old enough he had engaged as stockman with Mr. Hamilton, of Tomanbil. He saved money, and took up a small station for himself at the Pinnacle, about fifteen miles from Forbes. He married a daughter of another settler. He had no sympathy with the bushrangers when the outbreak under Gardiner occurred, and the police frequently stopped for a night at his house when looking for the bushrangers near his station. His wife was of a flighty disposition, and was seduced, it was said, by a police official, and Hall joined the gang "to meet the man who ruined my happiness." Such was the story currently believed in the neighbourhood, and Ben was the only one of the bushrangers for whom the general public, apart from those who were related to or interested in them, felt any sympathy. Before "he took to the bush," he was known as a steady, industrious, kind-hearted young man, and numbers could scarcely believe that it was the same Ben Hall, the noted bushranger, of whom everybody was talking.

The death of Ben Hall no doubt had a depressing effect on the bushrangers generally, but it by no means put an end to their depredations. On the 11th May, a horse was stolen from Murrumburrah, and on the following day the horses at Mr. Furlonge's station were rounded up and a racehorse taken away, the Murrumburrah horse being left instead of it. Information was immediately sent to the police, and a party, with the aid of a black tracker, followed the tracks towards Binalong. The place being near the house where Johnny Dunn's parents lived, the police camped near and watched the little township all night, but saw nothing to excite their suspicions. In the morning a lad named Thomas Kelly, brother of one or two convicted bushrangers, was asked whether any one was staying at his grandfather's house, and replied, "No." Constables Hales and King, however, walked up to old Kelly's place, and pushed the door open. Gilbert and Dunn were in the front room, and immediately fired at the police, who retreated. A few minutes passed, during which the police were looking to their revolvers, and then the two bushrangers were seen to emerge by the back door and walk steadily down the paddock. The police followed, and some shots were exchanged. Near the fence the bushrangers made a stand, and there was a pause for a second or so. Then Constables Hales and Bright fired together, and Gilbert fell. Dunn jumped over the fence and dashed in among the trees. Some of the police followed, but he soon disappeared. On examination it was found that a bullet had entered Gilbert's breast and passed out below the left shoulder-blade, having travelled through the left ventricle of the heart. He was then about twenty-five years of age. Old Kelly was arrested and charged with having harboured bushrangers, and was sent to gaol.

John Dunn, the last of this notorious trio, did not long survive his two mates. His record as given in the Yass Courier is very instructive. He joined Hall and Gilbert a few days after the capture of Mount and the wounding of Dunleavy, and on the 24th of October robbed Mr. Chisholm on the highway near Goulburn. On the 28th he stuck up Mr. Macansh's station. On the 28th robbed the Albury mail near Jugiong. On November the 8th robbed Mr. Rossi's station, near Goulburn. On the 9th robbed the Southern mail six miles from Goulburn. On the 11th robbed the Yass mail on Breadalbane Plains. On the 25th robbed the Gundagai mail near Jugiong, and had a desperate fight with the police, Sergeant Parry being shot by Gilbert. On the 19th robbed Mr. Clarke's station at Bolero. On December 29th stuck up the Goulburn mail near Towrang. On the 27th stuck up Mr. Morris's store at Binda, forced Mr. and Mrs. Morris to go to a ball, and finally burned his store and dwelling-house. On the 30th stuck up Mr. Davidson and others on the Murrumburrah Plains. On January 19th, 1865, stuck up Mr. James Christie's store. On the 25th stuck up Mr. Ross and others on the Gap Road. On the 27th stuck up a number of carriers and the hotel at Collector, and shot Constable Nelson. On February 6th stuck up the Goulburn mail twelve miles from Goulburn. On the 18th stole race-horses from Messrs. McAlister's and Bowne's. On the 23rd had a desperate fight with the police on Bradalbane Plains, when several were wounded and the robbers lost their horses. On March 13th stuck up the Gundaroo

Chapter XX

mail near Geary's Gap. On the 14th attempted to rob the Araluen escort at Major's Creek, when one policeman was mortally wounded, two others put to flight, while the fourth beat off the bushrangers and saved the gold. On the 22nd seen at Gardiner's old haunt near the Pinnacle. On the 24th went to Mr. Atkin's place, near the Billabong Creek, had a good dinner and enjoyed themselves, besides feeding the horses they had stolen from Mr. Morton the day before. Left on the 25th, taking clothes for winter wear and about £90 in cash from Mr. Jones's store, Forbes. On April 1st stuck up Mr. Sutton's station at Boramble. On the 10th robbed Mr. Watt's Inn at Newra. On the 11th robbed Mr. Gallimore's store and the White Horse Inn at Black Rock. On the 18th bailed up the Newbiggen Inn, organised a *soirée dansante*, and compelled all hands and the cook to take part in it. Afterwards robbed Mr. Lee's station at Larras Lake. On the 25th robbed Mr. Cropper's station on the Lachlan. On May 8th robbed two travellers on the Cowra Road, eighteen miles from Marengo. On the 11th robbed Mr. Furlonge's station. On the 14th four policemen attacked the bushrangers near Binalong, when Gilbert was shot and Dunn wounded. On the 15th Dunn alone stuck up Julian's station, and took a racehorse, a saddle and bridle, and some food. He was not heard of again until December 18th, when he was recognised by the police near Mr. McPhail's station, Walgett, and pursued. He escaped, but two days later a man in whom he had confided gave information to the police as to his whereabouts, and a desperate struggle took place, Dunn being wounded in three places and Constable McHale also severely wounded; Dunn, however, was captured.

This record of the achievements of the gang during the time that Dunn was a member—namely, from October 24th, 1864, to May 15th, 1865, or rather less than seven months—although not quite complete, serves to give a very vivid idea of the terrible scourge which the bushrangers were to the country. The gang was not more active during the time covered by this record than it had been before, or since it was first organised by Frank Gardiner in 1861, while some of the most extensive robberies committed by the gang belong to the earlier period. However, with the capture of Johnny Dunn this gang ceased to exist, and we have only to finish the story of his life before turning back to take notice of the proceedings of other gangs of bushrangers in other parts of the colony.

Constable McHale and John Dunn were conveyed as carefully as possible, and by slow stages, from Walgett to the lock-up at Dubbo, to be nursed back to health. After some weeks, Dunn appeared to be growing strong, and as his character was well known, it was deemed expedient to put him in irons. He resented this treatment, very naturally perhaps, and refused to eat. He groaned so continuously that he prevented McHale, who was in bed in the same room in the watch-house, from sleeping. The police were taken in by this shamming, and thought that Dunn was dying. They therefore took off his irons. The watch-house was an ordinary four-roomed weatherboard cottage with a verandah. It had been built as a residence for the local policeman. Behind, was a stronger building divided into two or three cells for the safe-keeping of the few evildoers likely to be arrested in this settlement on the borders of civilisation. The sick men were in bed in the cottage, the window of which was only a couple of feet above the level of the plain on which the town of Dubbo stands. Dunn was not altogether shamming. He was very weak, but he was strong enough when his irons were removed to watch for an opportunity to escape. He placed his pillow length-ways in the bed, covered it with the sheet, which was the only covering required in that district at that time of the year, and placed a red silk handkerchief where his head was supposed to rest, as if to keep the flies or mosquitoes off his face. This was no doubt done to induce McHale, and any one else who came into the room, to believe that he was still sleeping. However, when daylight came, McHale saw that the thing in the other bed was not Dunn and pounded on the floor with a boot, being too weak to shout. At the time the police on duty in the next room were laughing and joking about something, and it was some minutes before McHale could make them hear. At length one of them came in, and on being told that Dunn was gone, gave the alarm. The tracks in the dust outside showed that the robber had simply stepped out of the window, which was kept open on account of the heat, and had made for the bush. It was Sunday morning, January 11th, 1866, and very few people were about in the little town. The tracks were lost among the number of tracks in the roadway and there was no one to give the police any information as to the direction in which the bushranger had gone. Search parties were organised and sent out in all directions.

Chapter XX

About two miles away a brickmaker was watching his kiln and gathering brushwood for his fire, although it was Sunday morning, when a man crawled out from behind a log and begged for a "drink of water, for God's sake." It was Dunn. He told the brickmaker who he was and begged him to lend him a horse to get away. "Only save me from hanging and I'll make it up to you," he cried, but the brickmaker refused. He went and caught his horse and rode into Dubbo to inform the police, who returned with him and recaptured the runaway. Dunn was forwarded to Bathurst without delay and was lodged in the gaol, while Smith, the brickmaker, was rewarded for the assistance he had rendered in effecting the recapture of the noted bushranger.

By the latter end of February Dunn was sufficiently recovered from the effects of his wound to be placed on trial. He was charged with the murder of Constable Nelson. The evidence shows that a number of persons had been stuck up on the road between Taradale and Collector. They were marched to Kimberley's Hotel and taken inside by Hall and Gilbert, while Dunn remained outside in charge of the horses. Dunn called a boy, who was standing in the street and who chanced to be the son of Constable Nelson, and told him to hold the horses and not let them go unless he wanted his brains blown out. The party in the hotel were singing and dancing, and the constable hearing the noise walked from the watch-house to where his son was and asked him what was going on. The boy told him the bushrangers were there and the constable returned to his house for his gun. When he came back he did not see Dunn, who was hiding behind the fence, and walked towards the front door of the hotel, when he was shot as already related. Gilbert came to the door immediately and Dunn cried out "I've shot the trap." Gilbert walked to where the body was lying, turned it over, and took off the belt, saying "This is just what I wanted. I've lost mine." At that moment Hall came up and the three bushrangers took their horses and went off. Dunn was found guilty and sentenced to death. He was hung on March 19th, 1866. He was of slight build and only twenty-two years old when he died.

Of the chief members of this gang Gardiner was sentenced to thirty-two years' penal servitude; Vane surrendered owing to the influence of Father McCarthy and was sent to gaol for fifteen years; Bow and Fordyce were sentenced to death, but their sentences were commuted to fifteen years' imprisonment; Manns, Peisley, and Dunn were hanged; Lowry, Ben Hall, and Gilbert were shot by the police, and Burke and O'Meally by civilians; Mount or "the Old Man" was sent to gaol for ten years.

There were others who either claimed or were supposed to be members of this gang, but it is difficult to say with certainty how far these claims were justified. Some of these have already been referred to, and others will be mentioned further on. Probably some who intended to join the gang were captured before they had an opportunity to do so. Others merely said they had been out with Ben Hall or Johnny Gilbert on account of the kudos they gained among their fellows. However this may be, the majority of the members of this gang were quite young men, many of them little more than boys. Several were under twenty years of age, and all with the exception of Mount, sometime known as "the Old Man," under thirty. Their lives may have been exciting, but they were short, and none of them, with the exception of Gardiner perhaps, made any money by their robberies. They all died poor.

Twenty-one

Bloodthirsty Morgan; Morgan's Opinion of the Police; Murder of Sergeant McGinnerty; Murder at the Round Hill Station; A Pseudo Morgan; Morgan Threatens to Brand all Hands; He Shoots Sergeant Smyth; Challenged to Visit Victoria; He Accepts the Challenge; His Death at Peechelba.

Daniel Morgan began his career as a bushranger shortly after the Great Escort Robbery, by sticking up travellers on the roads about Wagga Wagga. His headquarters generally were said to be in the huge patch of scrub, which stretched away southward, from the Murrumbidgee River across the low ranges between Wagga Wagga and Narrandera. He was credited with being the most bloodthirsty of the New South Wales bushrangers after Willmore. We have seen that some of the members of the chief gang of this era held human life very cheaply, but it was the general opinion that, except in the case of a few Chinamen, these bushrangers murdered only when on the warpath. In many cases they met the police boldly, and fought with some degree of fairness; while Morgan, on more than one occasion, fired on unarmed, and in some cases sleeping men. For some months he pursued his career without much interference from the police, and it was said that some of the members of the Hall and Gilbert gang had made a raid to the Southern district. When it became apparent that he had no connection with that gang and continued his depredations alone, a party of police was detailed to hunt him down about the middle of 1863.

In August of that year, this party of police tracked him for several days, and came on his camp on the 22nd. A desperate fight took place, in which Morgan's mate was severely wounded and crawled into the bush to die. This man was known as "German Bill." On the other side, Mr. Bayliss, J.P., a volunteer who accompanied the police, was severely wounded. He recovered, however, and was awarded a gold medal by the New South Wales Government for bravery in opposing bushrangers. Morgan made his escape in the scrub. Later on the same day a shepherd was shot dead on Brookong station, and it was supposed that the murderer was in league with Morgan. About Christmas Morgan with three companions watched the road, near Narrandera, with the intention of sticking-up several wealthy squatters who were in the habit of travelling to Melbourne at about that time of the year. Fortunately for themselves, they that year took a cross track, and thus escaped the meeting. While waiting Morgan took about 2lb. of cheese from a bullock driver named John Cole. There were several cheeses in the dray, and when Morgan said he should "like a bit" Cole offered him one, and told him to "take the lot." Morgan replied that "the —— traps would risk their necks climbing over the area railings for a leg of mutton. I don't know what they'd do for a whole cheese, but this lump's enough for me." He afterwards remarked that the police generally were "a sour milk lot."

During the next few months robberies occurred in various parts of the extensive tract of country between Wagga Wagga and Deniliquin, and were, of course, all attributed to the Morgan gang. On April 16th, 1864, Mr. George Elliott, of Burrangong, with a stockman named Donnelly reached Deniliquin, with a mob of horses for sale. In consequence of some rumours which spread through the town, Mr. Elliott was closely questioned by the sergeant of police, and after some hesitation admitted that he had been stuck up by Morgan and robbed of £127 17s. and a bay horse with saddle and bridle, on the road between Narrandera and Jerilderie. He said that when he got rid of his horses he would have to return home by the same route, and thought it prudent to hold his tongue, "the least said the soonest mended," as there was no saying whom he might meet on the road.

In June, Sergeant McGinnerty and Constable Churchley were riding along the road to Tumberumba, when they overtook a horseman near Copabella. McGinnerty civilly said "Good-day" as they passed, in the usual Australian fashion. The man looked at him and replied, "Oh, you're one of the —— wretches looking for bushrangers, are you?" and hastily drew a revolver and shot McGinnerty through the breast. The sergeant's horse bolted, and the bushranger galloped after him into the bush. Constable Churchley rode back to Copabella for assistance, and on his return with a party and fresh horses found McGinnerty's hat lying in the road, and opposite to it, at some distance away, the body. It was supposed that the

Chapter XXI

bushranger had placed the hat on the road to indicate where the body was, and to facilitate its discovery. The robber must have ridden straight from the scene of this cold-blooded murder to the Round Hill station, where he mustered all the men and drove them into the carpenter's shop. He then went to the house, called out the proprietor, Mr. Watson, and led him to the door of the carpenter's shop. He enquired whether the men had sufficient rations. "If they haven't," said Mr. Watson, "they've only got to say so and they'll get more." "Well, I'm Dan Morgan, I just wanted to know, and you'd better give them a nobbler," replied the bushranger. Mr. Watson said he'd no objection to the men having a nobbler, and sent to the house. The messenger returned with four bottles of spirits, and each man was given a nobbler in a pannikin. The men laughed and took it as a good joke. One of them asked the bushranger whether he had "stolen his stirrup irons from Mr. Johnstone?" Morgan with a curse immediately drew his pistol, and fired into the room. The men ran out. Morgan followed them, shouting, "You —— wretches, do you want to give me away?" He fired several times, until John McLean fell wounded. By this time the men had sheltered themselves behind trees. Seeing no one to shoot at Morgan dismounted, lifted McLean carefully on to his horse, and led the animal to the house. Mr. Watson and some of the women took McLean in, and Morgan mounted and rode away. Then it was discovered that another man, John Heriot, was lying wounded in the carpenter's shop. Heriot's injury consisted of a broken leg, and he was placed in a buggy and conveyed with as little delay as possible to the hospital at Albury. But McLean's wound was too serious to admit of his removal, and he died after lingering in pain for two or three days.

At the inquest held on the body, Edward Smith, stockman at the Round Hill station, deposed that Morgan had called at the station two days after the attack to enquire how McLean was, and had sat at the bedside for several hours. At that time there were numerous parties of police and civilians searching the country round in all directions in hopes of finding him. A verdict of wilful murder was returned against Daniel Morgan on June 23rd, and a few days later a proclamation was issued by which the reward offered for his capture dead or alive was increased from £500 to £1000.

A man walked into the bar of the Five Mile Creek Inn, near Bogolong, and called for a nobbler of brandy, which was supplied him. He then demanded another, which the barman refused to give him until he had paid for the one he had drank. "Be careful what you do," exclaimed the customer, "I'm Dan Morgan." He drew out a pistol, and the barman rushed from behind the counter, jumped through a window, and ran. The customer followed him to the window, but the barman could not say how much further. The barman, however, ran right round the house. When he returned to the window through which he had made his escape, he saw the bushranger's pistol lying on the sill. He grasped it, and having recovered from his momentary panic, walked into the bar in time to see the pseudo Morgan helping himself out of a bottle. The barman at once grappled with him, and the cook, the only other man in the house at the time, hearing the scuffling, came in. The man was soon secured, and in due time was handed over to the custody of the police. He was identified as a fiddler, who travelled about the country playing for a living. He was sent to gaol for a few months as a caution not to obtain grog again under false pretences by personating a bushranger.

Morgan, with three mates, visited Yarribee station, stuck up Mr. Mate, the overseer, with two bushmen and the bullock-driver, and tied their hands behind them. He demanded the key of the store, which was given to him. He opened the door and selected a quantity of articles which he packed on a horse. He served out tobacco, gin, and porter to the men whom he had made prisoners, having added several, who had arrived at the station after he began operations, to their number. The liquor had its effect, and some of the men became uproarious. Morgan swore at them and ordered them to be quiet, and as they did not obey he brought out the station brand—P.T—put it in the fire, and swore he would brand every one of them on the cheek. Whether the threat frightened the men into quietness, or whether the bushranger thought better of his purpose, is not known. Morgan, however, rode away with his plunder without using the branding-iron.

Under the heading "Comforting Bushrangers," the Deniliquin Chronicle of the 18th December said:—"Mr. —— we hear has given orders that whenever Morgan calls at his station he is to be given everything he wants, and when he does not call food is to be taken into the bush and left for

Chapter XXI

him." The paper goes on to accuse the unnamed squatter with "holding a candle to the devil." But it is difficult to see where the blame comes in. The stations were from twenty-five to fifty miles apart, and except at lambing and shearing times had few men employed on them. The police in the district were not very numerous, and even if they had been very much stronger than they were they could not have prevented a daring, reckless man like Morgan from setting fire to the grass. It was so easy at that time for even an offended bushman to have revenge, for any real or supposed slight or injury, by starting a blaze which would destroy the grass over hundreds of square miles before it could be stopped, and this might go very far towards ruining a squatter. In face of this danger a few clothes or a quantity of food was a trifling loss. Certainly Morgan never did fire the grass, because, perhaps, there was no profit in it for himself, but there can be no doubt that he would have done it had he desired to have revenge on any particular run holder.

One of the many stories told about the brutality of Morgan was that he went to a cattle station near Jerilderie, and asked to see the overseer. The overseer's wife informed him that her husband was away at a back station mustering and branding, and that she and the children were the only persons at home at the head station. Morgan replied that he was sorry for it. He'd travelled to the station specially for the purpose of shooting the overseer, who was too friendly with the police, He then demanded a sum of money which he said he knew the overseer had recently received. The woman declared that her husband had no money at the station, or if he had that she was not aware where he kept it. Morgan refused to believe her. He made her boil him a number of eggs, declaring that he would eat nothing else, as there was too much strychnine and arsenic about these stations. When these were ready he examined them carefully, rejecting all which had cracks in the shells and eating the sound ones only. He then made up the fire until there was a big blaze, when he once more asked her for the money, and as she persisted in declaring that she had none he seized her by the shoulders, forced her back until she was seated on the blazing logs, and held her there until her clothes were on fire. Then he allowed her to get up, and seizing a bucket of water standing near he dashed it over her to put the fire out. Nothwithstanding this she was severely burned. When he mounted and rode away he said he would soon be round again and hoped then to find the overseer at home.

Sergeant Smyth and Constables Cannon, Baxter, and Reed, who were out seeking for the bushranger Morgan, camped one night in September near Kyamba. They had put up a tent and were seated inside. They had a candle and this threw their shadows on the canvas and afforded a magnificent mark, which the bushranger could not resist firing at. The shot wounded Sergeant Smyth, but he and the constables rushed out of the tent and blazed away, but without seeing their assailant. It was supposed that this attack was made by Morgan, but nothing was seen of the bushranger. Sergeant Smyth fired twice after being wounded and then he fainted. He was taken without delay to Doodal Cooma station and a doctor was found, but he never rallied and died a fortnight later.

It was said that Morgan was on the Wagga Wagga race course at the Christmas races, and that he had lunch at the booth where the magistrates, the police inspectors, and the leading merchants and shopkeepers of the town went, and that afterwards he rode into the town itself without being recognised by the police.

On March 18th, 1865, he stuck up Mr. Rand's station at Mohanga, collected all the men in one room, and ordered Mr. Rand to fetch some grog from the store. This having been done, Morgan asked one of the men whether he could play the concertina, and being answered in the affirmative, told him to get his instrument and "amuse the company." When all was ready the bushranger said to Mr. Rand: "I understand you are a good dancer. Will you favour the company with a reel?" Mr. Rand said he should be only too pleased, and began at once. Morgan watched him critically and applauded every now and then, but when Mr. Rand stopped, he raised his pistol and said: "Once more, please, you dance very nicely," and thus he kept the squatter jigging till midnight, when he was allowed to retire. In the morning Morgan took from the store a quantity of clothing and some other articles, including a gun. He then asked for a horse, saddle, and bridle, to pack his plunder on, and got them.

At Jerilderie, when engaged in one of his usual robberies, he spoke in the most contemptuous terms of the police. He said that the Victorian police

Chapter XXI

had been blowing that they would soon catch him if he crossed the border, and declared that he would soon show them that they were no smarter than the New South Wales police, who were "frightened to go near any place where they thought they might find him."

A Beechworth paper, commenting on this report, challenged Morgan to cross the Murray, and prophesied that if he dared to do so he would be either dead or in gaol within forty-eight hours. This challenge, it was said, gave great umbrage to the bushranger, who had apparently, owing, perhaps, to his long immunity from arrest, developed the belief that he was invincible. He was reported to have referred to it frequently, and to have asserted his intention to cross the Murray River and "take the flashness out of the Victorian people and police." Accordingly, early in April, he made a raid south of the Murray. Mounted on Mr. Bowler's racing mare, Victoria, Morgan stuck up Mr. McKinnon's station on the Little River. He crossed the King River, and set fire to Mr. Evans's barns and granary for "having shot my fingers off," an event which had taken place some time previously, in one of his many encounters on the "other side." Morgan then stuck up and robbed a number of carriers on the road between Wangaratta and Benalla.

He also stuck up Mr. Warby's station, and on the evening of April 8th arrived at Peechelba station, owned by Messrs. Macpherson and Rutherford. Morgan rode up and knocked at the door of Mr. Macpherson's house. It was opened by Mr. Macpherson's son. Morgan, pistol in hand, ordered him to bail up. Then everybody in the house were called in and compelled to range themselves in line along the wall of the dining-room. A housemaid named Alice Macdonald, thinking he was joking, refused to stand up against the wall "like a child." Morgan her by the arm to force her into line, when she smacked his face. Raising his pistol he said, "My young lady, I must take the flashness out of you. Do you know who I am?" "No," replied the girl. "Well, I'm Morgan. Will you take your place?" The girl pouted but did as she was told. Morgan placed two revolvers on the table and sat down. He said he had had no sleep for three nights, but he hoped to return to New South Wales next day and have a good sleep. He asked a servant to make him some tea and allowed her to leave the room. Then he said that he had heard music as he approached the house, and he asked

245

which of the ladies played? On being told "Miss Macpherson," he asked her to favour him with a tune. She replied "Certainly, Mr. Morgan." "Call me Morgan," he said, "I hate to be Mistered." Mr. Macpherson asked him what had induced him to lead such a life? "I was forced to it," he replied. "I was tried at Castlemaine for a crime of which I was innocent and received a heavy sentence. Well, I escaped from the stockade and there you are. What else could I do?"

The party sat all night, and Morgan chatted freely, but his vigilance relaxed so that Alice Macdonald contrived to slip out without being seen and went to Mr. Rutherford's house, about a quarter of a mile away, and informed Mr. Rutherford of what had taken place. She went back again immediately in case the bushranger should miss her. Morgan informed the company that he was born at Appin, in New South Wales, and that his parents were still living. In the meantime Mr. Rutherford mustered all the men on the station and despatched a messenger to the police at Wangaratta. He posted sentinels all round Mr. Macpherson's house, hiding them behind bushes or any other cover. In the morning Morgan ate a hearty breakfast and then walked out on the verandah. Mr. Macpherson invited him to take a glass of whisky and poured out some for himself. Morgan replied that he rarely drank. He was almost a teetotaller. However, not wishing to appear churlish, he accepted half a glass. He went into a bedroom to wash his hands and face and comb his hair, and Alice Keenan, one of the servants, took advantage of the opportunity to carry a can of coffee to the watchers outside. When Morgan had washed he stepped out on the verandah again and reminded Mr. Macpherson that he had promised to let him have a fresh horse. Mr. Macpherson replied that he had not forgotten it. He called to his son and they walked together towards the paddock to catch the horse, while Morgan waited on the verandah. They had not gone far, however, when Morgan started to follow them, and John Quinlan shot him from behind a bush. The bushranger fell, crying "Why didn't you challenge me?" He was carried indoors, and every attention possible was paid to him, but he died at about half-past one, or, as nearly as could be ascertained, forty-eight hours after he crossed the Victorian border.

The £1,000 reward was divided as follows:—John Quinlan £300; Alice Macdonald 250; James Frazer, who rode into Wangaratta and back—

forty-two miles—in three hours and a-half, £200; Donald Clarke, who fetched guns from the school house, cleaned and loaded them, £100; Alice Keenan, who communicated between the parties inside and outside the house, £50. The remaining £100 were given to Mr. Rutherford and Inspector Singleton (£50 each) to be divided among the civilians and the police who took part in the capture, according to the merits of their performances.

The news of the death of Morgan was received generally throughout Australia with satisfaction. There were a few people whose love of fair play impelled them to express the opinion that he should have been challenged, but the majority held that he was little better than a wild beast, and should be treated accordingly. He had given no notice to Sergeants McGinnerty and Smyth, nor to the unarmed men among whom he had fired at the Round Hill Station, and it is doubtful whether those who declared that he should have been accorded "fair play" would, knowing the character of the man, have risked their lives by challenging him in circumstances similar to those in which he was captured. There was a tendency among a portion of the people of Victoria to glorify that colony at the expense of the mother colony over the capture of Morgan. It was said that bushrangers would never receive the public sympathy and support in Victoria which they did in New South Wales, and attributed this to the fact that Victoria had never had a penal settlement within its borders.

There has always been an absurd jealousy between the people of Melbourne and those of Sydney, and there can be no doubt that it has been somewhat of a disadvantage to the colonies generally. In this case there is no ground for believing that the character of the people of New South Wales, which was a penal colony, differs in any essential degree from that of the people of any other portion of Australia. As a matter of fact, the Australias are so intimately connected together,—it is so easy for the residents of one colony to make their way into any other colony, and the people as a body are more prone to moving about than those of any other civilised country,—that any claim of superiority either in extraction, morals, or in any other particular, by the residents of any one colony over those of any other colony is absurd. It is true that there was no English penal settlement within the present bounds of the colony of Victoria, but in former times that colony was a portion of the penal colony of New South Wales, while the founders of Melbourne came from another penal colony, namely, Van Diemen's Land. Many of the early settlers were emancipated convicts from either one or the other of these penal settlements. But even if this had not been the case, the whole population of Australia was so thoroughly intermixed during the great rushes to the Victorian diggings that there is absolutely no excuse for any pretence of superiority on this account in this the smallest of the colonies on the main land. I do not say this out of any ill-feeling towards Victoria, or with the desire to glorify any other colony, at her expense, but simply to point out the folly of such petty and absurd jealousies as have tended to keep the colonies apart hitherto. As a plain matter of fact South Australia is the only one of the seven colonies which can claim not to have had a convict origin. That colony was founded directly from England by a syndicate. All the other colonies were either portions of or were founded from New South Wales, about the convict origin of which colony there can be no doubt. But even South Australia, wedged in as it is between what have been two convict colonies, could not escape the contagion. But, judging from the statistics, Australia as a whole does not appear to have suffered much, now that the bushrangers have been disposed of. The percentage of crime in each of the colonies is lower than in most other civilised communities, and the "convict colonies," as they were called, do not show a higher percentage of crime than the "free colonies." I have already pointed out that the condition of Victoria, during the years 1853-55, was worse than that of any of the so-called convict colonies at any time, so far as the number and ferocity of the bushrangers were concerned, and we shall soon see that Victoria can produce native-born bushrangers as well as New South Wales. Only a few months after the peans of self-glorification had been sung by the Victorian press over the death of Morgan in that colony, the same papers lamented the fact that while bushranging appeared to have been stamped out in the mother colony, it still flourished in Victoria.

Twenty-two

The Brothers Clarke; The Raid at Nerigundah; Deaths of William Fletcher and Constable O'Grady; Murder of Four Special Constables at Jinden; Annie Clarke at Goulburn; Capture of Thomas and John Clarke; A Terrible Record; A Plucky Woman; An Attempt to Escape Custody; "Shoot Away, I Can't Stop You"; Some Daring Robberies; Murder and Cremation of the Brothers Pohlmann; Blue Cap.

The brothers Clarke, of Manaro, although they did not belong to the Gardiner gang, were more or less closely connected with it. There were three of them, Thomas, James, and John, and their education was on similar lines to that which I have described as prevalent in the Western Ranges. They were cattle duffers and horse planters until the police began to enquire too closely into their mode of life, when they "took to the bush." James was probably saved from the more elevated fate of his elder and younger brothers by being arrested on suspicion of having been concerned with Ben Hall, Johnny Gilbert, and others in the robbery of the Cowra mail, but as the evidence of his presence on that occasion was inconclusive he was acquitted, and charged with having received stolen property, a number of the banknotes stolen from the mail having been found in his possession. He was convicted, and was sentenced to seven years' penal servitude on January 12, 1865. He was probably kept out of mischief during the troublous times by this imprisonment.

Thomas and John, the eldest and youngest of this interesting family, operated over the district in which the redoubtable Jackey Jackey first earned his notoriety as a bushranger, but they did not confine their operations within any strictly defined limits, and therefore they, as it may be said, overlapped with the Hall and Gilbert gang. The elder brother Thomas was arrested in October, 1864, on a charge of highway robbery, but contrived, to effect his escape from the Braidwood gaol. He stole several racehorses from residents in the neighbourhood of Jembaicumbene and Mericumbene, stuck up the Araluen mail, robbed the Post Office at Michelago, besides sticking-up and robbing numbers of travellers on the roads about

Braidwood and Moruya. On January 12th, the very day on which his brother James was being tried, he stuck up Mr. George Summer's store at Jembaicumbene, and on the following day he bailed up John Frazer and Kenneth Matheson, on Major's Creek Mount, and robbed them of £36 10s. in money, and a bank draft for a large amount. In these enterprises he was assisted by several young men and lads residing in the district. In April, Thomas Clarke, Patrick Connell, Tom Connell, William Fletcher, and two or three other young men were returning home from the racecourse at Bega, where races had been held, when Clarke stuck up a Chinaman, who was travelling from the Gulph Diggings, and took his gold and money. A little farther along the road the party met the mail boy, and Clarke compelled him to exchange his horse, saddle, and bridle for those stolen from the Chinaman. Some miles from the scene of this outrage the party met Mr. John Emmott, and ordered him to bail up; but he, having a considerable amount of gold and money about him, wheeled his horse and started to gallop away. By this time others of the party had become excited, and several of them chased Emmott, and fired their revolvers at him. Emmott fell wounded and his horse was killed. About £100 in money and a parcel of gold dust was taken from him, and the party went on, leaving Mr. Emmott to make his way to where he could obtain surgical aid as best he could.

On the following day they arrived at the Gulph Diggings, stuck up Mr. Pollock's store, and stole between two hundred and three hundred ounces of gold, besides all the money that they could find. On leaving the store they met Charles Nash in the street, and Clarke greeted him with "Hullo, Charlie, back from the Bega races?" "Yes," replied Nash. "Then fork out," cried Clarke, bringing out his revolver. Nash at first thought this was a joke, and began to laugh, but on the remainder of the gang crowding round and presenting their revolvers in a threatening manner he put his hand in his pocket, took out about thirty shillings, and handed it over with the remark, "That's all I've got." He was then permitted to pass on. Fletcher then led the way to the butcher's shop owned by R. Drew, and, putting his revolver to the butcher's head, told him to "shell out." Drew put his hands behind him and made no reply. Then the rest of the gang crowded in and called for a light, declaring their intention to search the place. Drew

Chapter XXII

told them to "clear out." They refused, and threatened to shoot him. The dispute grew so loud that it reached the ears of Constable Miles O'Grady, the only policeman stationed on the little diggings, who was ill in bed. O'Grady got up and dressed, and went to the butcher's shop. He enquired what the row was about, and ordered the crowd to leave the shop. Fletcher turned round and fired at the constable, but missed. O'Grady immediately returned the fire, and Fletcher fell dead. One of Fletcher's mates then shot O'Grady, who died a few days later. The bushrangers rushed to their horses, mounted, and galloped away out of the township.

The Moruya Examiner said that William Fletcher was little more than a boy, and was born in the district. He had ridden in the St. Patrick's Day races on March 17th at Mullenderee only a few weeks before. His father was a farmer in the district, and had always borne a good character. The boy had been digging for gold at Araluen, Nerrigundah, The Gulph, and other diggings in that neighbourhood. It was his first essay at bushranging. His mind had probably been inflamed by the stories told of Gardiner, Ben Hall, and Johnny Gilbert, and he had been induced to endeavour to emulate their actions by the boastings of Thomas Clarke. Several young men who had taken part in this fray returned home afterwards, and were arrested by the police. Some of them were acquitted on account of their previous good character, and because there was no evidence to prove that they had done more than accompany the robbers. Thomas Clarke, his uncle Patrick Connell, his cousin Tom Connell, with Bill Scott and one or two others, who escaped to the ranges, continued to commit depredations similar to those described in the previous chapter.

In September, 1866, John Carrol, Patrick Kennagh, Eneas McDonnell, and John Phegan were sent by the police authorities to the Braidwood district, to assist the police in the capture of the Clarke gang. Phegan had been mining in the district and was well acquainted with the ranges. He paid a visit to Mrs. Clarke, and was received with some suspicion as a stranger. On his second visit Mrs. Clarke and her two daughters became quite friendly, and asked Phegan to write out a petition in favour of her second son James, who was a prisoner on Cockatoo Island. The party camped as if engaged in surveying, and Phegan said that Kennagh knew more about writing out petitions than he did. He therefore took Kennagh to the place and introduced him to Mrs. Clarke. They wrote out the petition and left. During the next few days they saw the girls frequently. In the absence of their brothers these girls looked after the cattle, and were riding about the ranges every day. They passed the camp several times and spoke in a friendly manner.

On the 4th of October, the party had been pretending to survey a flat, and under this pretence had searched a gunyah[1] hidden among the timber. This gunyah was believed to be one of the rendezvous of the bushrangers, and was closely watched in the hopes that the bushrangers might visit it. On the day named, the special constables had finished their work and were standing round the camp fire, when a gun was fired, and the bullet passed between the men and struck the tree against which the fire was built. The party had their guns ready and returned the fire, although they could not see what they were shooting at. In the morning a flask half full of powder was picked up, but this gave no indication as to who had attacked the party. After this no pretence of friendship was made, and Carrol and the party under his charge openly took up the pursuit of the bushrangers, penetrating the mountains and searching everywhere where they thought it probable that the bushrangers might camp.

In January, 1867, the bodies of the four men were found near their camp on the Jinden station in the Jingera ranges, in the Braidwood district. How or when they were shot is not known, but it is supposed that they were somehow drawn into an ambush and shot down. Carrol's body was lying on its back, and a handkerchief thrown across it with a one pound note pinned to it. The bodies of Carrol and Kennagh were close together, while the other two were half a mile away. Three revolvers were lying beside Phegan. One of the men had £14 on him, and another £19. The bodies were found by Mr. Edward Smith's stockman when riding through the ranges after cattle, on the 9th January, and as they were in an advanced state of decomposition, they must have been there for several days. The Governor, Sir John Young, immediately issued a proclamation, calling upon magistrates, freeholders, and all other of Her Majesty's subjects, resident in the police districts of Braidwood, Browlee, Qeanbeyan, Eden, Bega, and Cooma to assist the police in the capture of the "notorious outlaw, Thomas Clarke, whose life is forfeit to the laws of his country." The Colonial Secretary, (Mr.

[1] *an Aboriginal bush hut, typically made of sheets of bark and branches*

CHAPTER XXII

afterwards Sir) Henry Parkes, offered a reward of £5,000 for the capture of the persons guilty of murdering the four special constables. A free pardon was also offered to any accomplice, not being the actual murderer. Carrol, Kennagh, and Phegan had been warders in Darlinghurst gaol, and had volunteered to attempt the capture of the bushranger Clarke, and McDonnell was an ex-policeman who had accumulated a considerable sum of money in business, and was about to visit Ireland, his native country, but who volunteered to join this party before going home. The firing had been heard at Jinden station, three miles from the camp, but no notice had been taken, as it was attributed to opossum hunters. According to the medical evidence, the men were killed with rifle bullets fired at close range—not more than twenty yards. Phegan and McDonnell were first shot, McDonnell only having one wound, which was fatal. Phegan was shot in the right side, and appears to have turned over after falling, and to have been then shot on the other side to finish him. Carrot and Kennagh appear to have been kneeling when shot, and had perhaps surrendered. The ostentatious disregard of the money on the bodies shows, said the Sydney Morning Herald, that revenge and not plunder was the object of the murderers.

No certain knowledge as to how these men came to their death has since been arrived at. According to rumour three of them were shot by Thomas Clarke and the fourth by Bill Scott, who was afterwards wounded in a brush with the police, and as is believed killed by Clarke, as the bushranger known as German Bill had been killed by Morgan, to prevent him from falling into the hands of the authorities and being induced to give evidence against his former companions. In both cases, however, the end of the missing bushranger is uncertain.

At the Criminal Sessions, held in Goulburn in April, 1867, Thomas Cunningham, Charles Hugh Gough, alias Wyndham, alias Bennett, James Baldwin, and Harry Brown were each sentenced to fifteen years' imprisonment for various acts of bushranging in various parts of the district. William Johnson for robbing and shooting at a man received a sentence of only two years. Several of these bushrangers came from the neighbourhood of Braidwood, and the Yass Courier reported that Annie Clarke, one of the sisters of the bushrangers, stayed in Goulburn during the time that the sessions lasted, her visit doubtless being one of sympathy with some of the prisoners. She was about twenty years of age, with a fine figure and good features. She was observed to change her costume four times in one day. In the morning she was very quietly dressed. Later she came out in a second costume, also very quiet and neat. But in the afternoon she walked about the streets in blood red silk, with red hat and feathers to match, and later towards evening she came out in a bright blue silk dress, white shawl, and a hat with white feathers.

At Wellington, in the same month, John Kelly was sentenced to fourteen years' hard labour, the first two in irons, for highway robbery.

At this time the reward offered for the capture of Thomas Clarke was raised to £1,000, while £500 was offered for his brother John, who had just "turned out." A similar sum was offered for the capture of Bill Scott, whose death had not then been ascertained, or for any other member of the gang.

On April 26th, Senior Constable Wright, and Constables James Wright, Lenehan, Walsh, and Egan, with the assistance of a black tracker known as Sir Watkin Wynne, tracked the bushrangers to a hut not far from where the four special constables had been murdered. The hut or cottage stood in a small cultivation paddock in which there was a small haystack. The constables watched the hut from behind this haystack until morning. At daybreak two racehorses were seen feeding behind the hut, and Constable Walsh, making a détour round the hut so as not to be heard by the occupants, walked down and caught these horses. He was leading them towards the haystack when the door opened and the two brothers Clarke came out of the house and fired at him. The other troopers immediately rushed forward from behind the stack and summoned the Clarkes to surrender. They made no reply, but went inside and shut the door. The police then took up positions, Constable Lenehan with Sir Watkin stopping at the stack with the horses at about two hundred yards from the hut and nearly facing it. The Senior Constable and Constable Wright went to a fallen tree about fifty yards to the right of the hut, while Constables Egan and Walsh went to about the same distance to the left, where there was no cover. The paddock in which the house stood had been recently ploughed, and the heavy rains which had fallen made the ground difficult to travel over.

Chapter XXII

The hut was built of slabs, and these had shrunk away from each other, leaving interstices through which the bushrangers could point their guns and revolvers. The bushrangers kept up an irregular fire until Constable Walsh was wounded in the thigh and Sir Watkin in the shoulder, when the other four troopers made a rush, forced open the door, and entered. The bushrangers surrendered. They had two revolvers, two double-barrelled guns, two revolving rifles, one single-barrelled gun, and a horse pistol. The tracker's wound was so severe that he had to have his arm amputated, and he bore the operation with the stoical indifference of his race. He walked downstairs from the upper ward of the Braidwood Hospital to the dissecting room, and after his arm had been cut off and the stump bound up he walked up again as coolly "as if he had merely had his finger punctured," said the Braidwood Dispatch. He was supposed to be about fifty years of age, and was well-built and "handsome for a blackfellow." He was promoted to the rank of sergeant-major, and had two stripes placed on his arm, of which he was very proud. Senior Constable William Wright was made sub-inspector, and the other constables engaged were promoted and rewarded.

Thomas and John Clarke were placed on trial charged with having wounded Constable Walsh and Black Tracker Sir Watkin, while in the execution of their duty. In two years Thomas Clarke had committed nine mail robberies. and had stuck up and robbed thirty-six individuals, some of whom had been wounded. He was also suspected of having caused the deaths of at least two persons. John Clarke had taken part in twenty-six of these robberies. They were found guilty, and the Chief Justice—the late Sir Alfred Stephen—in his address said:—"I never knew a bushranger (except one who is now suffering sentences aggregating thirty-two years) who made any money by it...I will read you a list of bushrangers...many of them young men, capable of better things, but who died violent deaths. Peisley executed; Davis sentenced to death; Gardiner sentenced to thirty-two years' hard labour; Gilbert shot dead; Hall shot dead; Bow and Fordyce sentenced to death, but their sentences commuted to imprisonment for life; Manns executed; O'Meally shot dead; Burke shot dead; Gordon sentenced to death; Dunleavy sentenced to death; Dunn executed; Lowry shot dead; Vane a long sentence; Foley a long sentence; Morgan shot dead; yourselves, Thomas and John Clarke, about to be sentenced to death; Fletcher shot dead; Patrick Connell shot dead; Tom Connell sentenced to death, but sentence commuted to imprisonment for life; Bill Scott, a companion of your own, believed to have been murdered by you…The list shows six shot dead and ten wounded…Unfortunately there were seven constables shot dead and sixteen wounded in three years…since 1863… The murders believed to have been committed by you bushrangers are appalling to think of. How many wives have been made widows, how many children orphans, what loss of property, what sorrow you have caused!…and yet, these bushrangers, the scum of the earth, the lowest of the low, the most wicked of the wicked, are occasionally held up for our admiration! But better days are coming. It is the old leaven of convictism not yet worked out, but brighter days are coming. You will not live to see them, but others will."

Sentence was then passed in the usual form, and the brothers were hung on June 25th, 1867.

Meanwhile robberies were frequent in other districts. Mrs. Colonel Pitt, with her daughter and Mrs. Colonel Campbell, were driving along the Mechanics' Bay Road, near the Domain, Forbes, when a servant who was leading the horses at the time was knocked down by an armed man. Another robber tried to seize the reins, but Mrs. Pitt stood up in the buggy and raised them out of his reach. She brought the butt of the whip so heavily down on the bushranger's head that he fell. Mrs. Pitt shouted and whipped the horses, and they galloped up the hill and did not stop until they reached Parnell, where the police were informed of what had occurred. A couple of troopers immediately started down the road, and found the servant lying where the outrage was said to have been perpetrated. He had been severely beaten, but was still alive. He was taken without any unnecessary delay to the hospital at Forbes, where he subsequently recovered. The robbers were tracked and followed and were captured next day, March 5th, 1865. They were Richard Middleton, alias Ruggy Dick, John Wilson, and Thomas Tracey. They were tried, convicted, and sent to gaol for long periods.

On the 20th a man went into Richardson's Inn, Evans' Plains, and ordered those in the bar to "bail up." He obtained about £5. He had been travelling on foot, but when he left the bar he mounted a horse, belonging to one of the men he had robbed, and which was hitched to a verandah post, and rode straight into Bathurst, where he was captured while spending the money he had stolen in the bar of a public house.

On the 19th, two armed men rode up to Mr. Ryan's house, on the Burrowa River, and ordered Mrs. Ryan to hand out her money. She refused, and one of the ruffians struck her with the butt of his revolver. An old man named Billy Dunn, who worked on the farm, jumped up from the table where he was at dinner to protect his mistress, when the other bushranger ordered him to sit down again, adding, "I'll shoot you if you interfere." The leader again demanded the money, and Mrs. Ryan struck him in the face, when he fired and wounded her on the knee. As she fell he struck her again with the pistol. They ransacked the house, and at length found a roll containing £94 in bank notes, which the old couple had just received by the Sydney mail. They also took a nugget of gold and several rings, brooches, and other articles of jewellery. The robbers were supposed to live in the neighbourhood and to have known that the money had been received from Sydney. They kept their faces covered, however, and the police could not obtain a description which would enable them to identify any persons as the robbers.

The Bathurst mail was stuck up and robbed on February 2nd, 1866, near Pulpit Hill, by two young men named Seymour and John Ford, who were followed and captured next day.

On the 14th of April, 1866, Sergeant John Healey, with Constables William Raymond, Edward William Mitchell, and Andrew Kilpatrick, left Berrima in charge of eleven prisoners, whom they were to take to the gaol in Sydney. The prisoners were seated in the body of the coach, and were connected together by "a marching chain," to which their handcuffs and leg irons were attached. The police were armed each with a short carbine and a revolver. The three constables sat in the body of the coach with the prisoners, while the sergeant sat on the box seat with the driver and a passenger named Whatmore. The coach stopped for change of horses at Bargo Brush, and the prisoners were taken out of the coach into the public-house yard. One of them, Thomas Berryman, produced keys with which to unlock the handcuffs from his pocket, and asked Webster, another prisoner, whether he would be one to "rush the police." Webster said "No," as he had only twelve months to serve, and was then threatened with vengeance if he informed the police, and was called "a —— hound," and a coward. Webster therefore promised to say nothing as to what the other prisoners proposed to do. After the halt the prisoners were again placed in the coach, and when they had travelled about three miles they made a sudden and combined rush on the constables.

The prisoners who engaged in this mutiny were James Crookwell, William Lee, Thomas Berryman, John Owens, and Michael Slattery. Five others, Webster, Bland, Foster, Hindmarsh, and Smith, sat still and helped neither party. They had refused to join in the attempt at escape, but had promised not to give warning to the police. Crookwell snatched a revolver from Constable Raymond's belt and shouted, "Shoot the ——." Raymond had been seized by two of the prisoners, but he shook himself free and jumped out of the coach. Sergeant Healey was also seized by some of the prisoners, who attempted to drag him backwards into the coach. He also got free and jumped down: he ran to the side of the coach and called to the prisoners to surrender, and as they did not do so, he pulled the trigger, but the rifle missed fire. Crookwell had got a revolver in his hand, and was struggling with Constable Kilpatrick, and Healey made a blow at the convict with the gun but struck an iron bar in the coach and smashed the stock. Healey then threw away his rifle and drew his revolver. He fired and wounded Slattery, but at the same time Constable Raymond fell. Bland and Slattery were also wounded, and then the prisoners gave in. The passenger, Mr. Robert Whatmore, a publican at Bargo Brush, had got on to the coach when it left his place to go to Picton. He had his coat torn in the struggle. When it was over he borrowed a horse and rode to Picton for a doctor. The body of Constable Raymond and the wounded prisoners were put into the coach, and the sergeant and constables walked until they were met by the police from Picton. When tried, the prisoners denied having shot Constable Raymond, and said that he had been killed by the fire from the police guns. This, however, was denied by all the witnesses in the case. The six prisoners named were found guilty of murder, and were all sentenced to death.

Chapter XXII

Sergeant Grainger and Constable Carroll chased a young man on the Carcour Road on suspicion that he was a bushranger. When asked by the sergeant where he was going, he replied, "Looking for work." The sergeant made him unstrap a coat which was fastened across the pommel of his saddle, and a small revolver was found in it. "What do you carry that for?" inquired the sergeant. "For protection," was the reply. The sergeant then snatched away the coat and saw that the man had a large revolver in his hand. He was told that if he attempted to raise this weapon he would be shot at once, and seeing that escape was impossible he surrendered and allowed the police to handcuff him. Then the sergeant opened his vest to ascertain what caused a protuberance there, and found a pair of false whiskers and moustaches. He was identified as John Miles, who had raided the Chinese Camp at Mookerawa, besides committing several highway robberies on Evans' Plains and in the neighbourhood of Orange. He was sent to gaol for ten years, the Judge saying that the prisoner had used less violence than was usual with bushrangers, and had not ill-treated the Chinamen further than by taking their gold.

Henry Evans, a settler at Little Plains, near Burrowa, was stuck up by two armed men on January 7th, 1867. When asked to give up his money he said that he had none. He never had more than a few shillings in the house. This was disbelieved, and the bushrangers threatened to take him out and shoot him. "Shoot away," he replied coolly, "I can't stop you." They tied him up and ransacked the place, breaking the furniture and even stamping on Mrs. Evans's best bonnet. Being unable to find any money they made a bundle of some clothing and strapped it on a pack-horse. Evans complained that the rope with which his hands were bound was cutting his wrists. "Serve you right," exclaimed the bushranger, "you deserve no better."

Mr. Kelly's store on the One Mile Creek, Emu Creek Goldfield, was stuck up by John Kerr, alias Maher, and John Shepherd. Kelly, with his wife and children, and a man named Gibbons were locked up in a back room while the robbers were making a bundle of clothing, drapery, and other articles in the store. Gibbons, however, succeeded in forcing open a back window, without being heard by the robbers, and making his escape. He ran to the police station and gave information, but the robbers discovered his escape before the arrival of the police, and decamped without their booty. This, however, did not save them. They were followed and captured by Sergeant O'Donnell and Constable McGlone. They were convicted of more than one robbery on the Cowra Road.

On Saturday night, June 8th, Cummings, while awaiting his trial for highway robbery, made an attempt to escape from the Bathurst Gaol. He filed a link of the chain of his leg-irons with a small pocket knife, which he had somehow procured, tore up two boards from the floor of his cell, crawled under the joists and scraped away the mortar so as to loosen several bricks in the gaol wall. The opening was only about ten inches square, but he contrived to squeeze through. Of course, when his cell was found empty on the Sunday morning, the excitement in the gaol was very great, but Mr. Forbes, the head gaoler, soon found the prisoner seated in the summer house in his private garden. "Here I am," cried the bushranger; "I did my best, but could not succeed." The prisoner had found some pieces of scantling in the outer yard, but they were not long enough to enable him to reach the top of the wall which encloses the gaol yard. An examination into the state of the gaol showed that the boards were quite rotten, and that the walls themselves were not very strong, the bricks being quite soft and rotten.

Several bullock-drivers were stuck up by John Egan and Patrick Ryan on the Orange Road, in August, 1867. On the 16th Robert and John Tait, father and son, and Edward Barrell were camped together when the bushrangers rode up and ordered them to "fork out." The robbers took all their money and some articles from the drays. On the 19th they repeated the operation on some other bullock-drivers. They were followed by Sergeant Rush and Constable Lawrence and arrested about forty-five miles from where the robberies were committed. At the Bathurst Assizes the prisoners called seven witnesses to prove an alibi, but they contradicted each other under cross-examination, and on the prisoners being found guilty his Honour, Judge Hargrave, directed that they should be prosecuted for perjury. The prisoners were sentenced to fifteen years' imprisonment. Another bushranger, John Foran, who was convicted on three charges, was also sentenced to fifteen years.

CHAPTER XXII

Patrick Fitzgerald, alias Paddy Wandong, was charged at Wellington on October 21st, 1867, with having on the 21st December bailed up Thomas Goodall, a free selector, on the Castlereagh River. The prisoner rushed into the house in the night and ran into the bed-room. Mr. Goodall was sitting in another room and heard his wife scream and cry "Don't kill me." The prisoner, who was a half-caste, seized her by the throat and pulled her out of bed. The other man, Ted Kelly, stuck up Mr. Goodall. The prisoner said he was at Curbin, five miles away, but as he was positively identified and was well-known in the district he was convicted and sentenced to fifteen years' hard labour. The judge said that Kelly had been tried for his share in the crime and had been sentenced nearly twelve months since. Circumstances connected with bushranging had greatly altered since then, and this would naturally induce him to be less severe; yet, having passed a sentence on one man, he could not now pass a lighter sentence on an accomplice who was no less guilty.

On the 24th of November, 1867, a party of forty or fifty shearers and others had assembled at Mr. William Whittaker's store on the Willandra Billabong, about a mile and a half from Mossgiel station, for the purpose of holding a race meeting, when they were bailed up by John Williams, William Brookman, Edward Kelly, and John Payne, and robbed of a considerable amount. Afterwards Michael McNamara, a constable stationed at Booligal, about sixty miles from Mossgiel, but who was at Mossgiel on duty at the time, was talking to Mr. Dobbins on the verandah of the store, when Williams and Brookman came up, and asked Dobbins if he was Constable McNamara. Dobbins replied "No." Brookman then turned to the constable and asked him the same question. The bushrangers each had a revolver in his hand, and so the constable also said "No," and made a rush at Brookman. In the struggle they got inside the store, and Brookman's pistol exploded, the bullet shattering McNamara's wrist. Brookman was shouting for help, and another shot was fired, wounding Constable McNamara in the back of the head. Mr. Peerman, overseer of the Mossgiel sheep station, and Mr. Edward Crombie rushed up and secured Williams and Brookman, who were placed in a hut and watched by Messrs. F. G. Desailly, Robertson, and others. The two bushrangers had five revolvers all loaded, except two barrels which had recently been fired. Williams had

£82 1s. 10d. and Brookman £34 8s. 8d., making in all £116 10s. 6d. The two bushrangers were charged on January 14th, 1868, at Deniliquin, with having wounded with intent to kill Michael McNamara, a constable in the execution of his duty. Williams, it was said, was a bullock driver, who had recently sold his team for the purpose of turning bushranger. Brookman was under seventeen years of age, and very boyish in appearance. Mr. George Milner Stephen, who appeared for the prisoners, pleaded hard for a light sentence on Brookman on account of his youth, and also because his family were respectable people. The Chief Justice said that in a recent case of a bushranger who put a pistol to the head of an advancing constable, the jury had found that there was no intent to kill, for what reason no one could tell. In the present case the arresting constable had not been killed, and the jury must decide as to the intent. With regard to the youth of one of the prisoners, it was an ascertained fact that lads when they became bushrangers were more bloodthirsty, brutal, cruel, and fiendish than grown men. The prisoners were sentenced to death, and the boy when he heard the sentence said "Thank you." His sentence was afterwards commuted to imprisonment for life.

Edward Kelly and John Payne pleaded guilty to the robberies at Whittaker's, and to two other charges of bushranging. They had been followed by the police, and Payne was captured while Kelly got away, but not without a wound. Subsequently Payne led the police to the camp, and thus assisted them to capture his wounded mate. For this act of humanity, the judge sentenced him to ten years' imprisonment on two charges, the sentences to be concurrent; while Kelly was sentenced to two terms of fifteen years each, or thirty years in all.

Walter Maher, another bushranger, also pleaded guilty to a charge of highway robbery, and was sentenced to ten years' imprisonment.

Charley Johnson and Miller, alias Slater, who had been arrested and lodged in the lock-up at Denison Town, on April 3rd, 1868, made a rush on the watch-house keeper when he entered their cell, knocked him down and took his revolver. They fired two shots at him and walked away. They called at the blacksmith's shop and made the blacksmith take off their irons. Then they left the town, to resume their bushranging career. On the

Chapter XXII

following morning they stuck up and robbed Mr. Ashton of about £10. On the 6th they stuck up the Green Swamp Inn, kept by Mr. McNaughton. In the evening they walked into Mr. Tuckerman's Hotel, in Mudgee, and called for drinks. When these had been served they ordered all in the bar to bail up, and began collecting the money. When they had obtained all they could they walked away, no attempt being made to detain them. They went into Langbridge's hotel, and collected the money in the same way. Then they returned, mounted their horses, and left the town by the Green Swamp Road. They stopped for supper at Landell's Hotel, about a mile from the town.

In the meantime a party under Constable Campbell, composed principally of those who had been robbed, started in pursuit. They rode rapidly, and as they came up to the front of Landell's Hotel the bushrangers left by the back door, the horses they had ridden being captured, as they were hitched to the verandah. On the following morning Mr. Farrar was returning from Gulgong to Mudgee when he saw three mounted men, whom he took to be bushrangers. He started to gallop away, when he recognised Constable Webb's voice, and pulled up. He informed the police that he had stayed at Matthew Homer's Inn on the previous night, and had been suddenly wakened by a blow on the head from the butt of a revolver. He was ordered to keep quiet and to get up. He did so, and was compelled to lead the way to the stable, saddle and bridle his horse, and give the animal to the bushrangers. He had no idea who they were, and had been too much confused by the blow on his head to notice their appearance. They afterwards roused up Mr. Homer and compelled him to supply them with horses, giving Farrar his horse back again. On obtaining this information the party in pursuit rode on to Homer's Inn to make further enquiries, while at the same time the bushrangers must have been riding through the bush to Mudgee, and so passed their pursuers. They called at Tuckerman's Hotel, and had breakfast. As soon as their presence in the town was known, another party was made up to capture them. When the bushrangers left the town they were again followed, and were overtaken near Bambera Hill, where a fight took place, but when the pursuers had expended all their ammunition they returned to Mudgee, while the bushrangers proceeded to stick up and rob the Barragon mail. They were captured subsequently, and sent to gaol.

The murder of the brothers Pohlmann, hawkers, was reported in the Wagga Wagga Express of April 11th, 1868. The hawker's waggon had been found standing a little off the road which runs along the bank of the Yanco Creek from Narrandera to Jerilderie. A few yards away was a gunyah of boughs and bushes, supposed to have been constructed by the brothers to shelter their camp fire from the wind. Not far away were the ashes of a large fire, and on this being carefully examined some metal buttons and remains of charred bones furnished incontrovertible evidence that some human being had been cremated there. The drawers and lockers with which the waggon was provided were open and had evidently been ransacked. The clothes and drapery were disarranged and scattered about the waggon, while of the large stock of jewellery which the brothers were known to carry with them nothing could be found. When the report was first published a rumour spread around that one of the brothers had murdered the other and had made off with the more valuable articles. A sister, who resided in Sydney, wrote to the Press stating her opinion that this was not true. Her brothers were too fond of each other to quarrel, and as they had been very successful there was no motive for the robbery. She added that there was a secret receptacle in the axle bed of the waggon known only to herself and her brothers, and it was their custom to carry their money and the most valuable articles of jewellery in this cache. She felt certain that if the police searched they would find this secret hiding place with its contents intact. The police did search, and found £73, some gold watches, and other valuables hidden as Miss Pohlmann declared they would be. This effectually disproved the rumour about one brother having murdered the other, and made it evident that both had been murdered. A number of suspicious characters were arrested and discharged, and it was thought, as time passed away, that this murder would have to be included among the many undiscoverable crimes. Two years had elapsed, and the murder was almost forgotten, when a man named Robert Campbell was arrested and charged with the crime. One witness said he had been camped on the sand hill near the Yanco Creek, on March 13th, 1868. This sand hill was a favourite camping ground, because there was plenty of scrub on it, and there was no timber for firewood for miles on either side. He had just finished his supper when Campbell came up and asked him to take some tea to his

Chapter XXII

mate who was lying ill about a quarter of a mile away. Witness told him he could take the tea himself, but he refused. The reason why witness would not take the tea was because Campbell bore a bad character. Campbell went away, and witness removed his camp some distance away, as he believed that Campbell was "up to some mischief." The following morning, soon after he resumed his journey, he met the Pohlmanns going towards the camping ground. No one could be found who had seen the Pohlmanns after this, and the evidence as to the time when they left Gillenbah tallied with the time when they were seen by this witness. The police succeeded in tracing some of the jewellery which had belonged to the Pohlmanns, and which Campbell had sold. He was convicted of murder, and was hung on October 5th, 1870, but as he made no confession the manner in which he carried out his crime can never be known.

On April 20th, 1868, Robert Cotterall, alias Blue Cap, was tried at Wagga Wagga for having stuck up and robbed Carl Seeman at Rock Station, Reedy Creek, in June, 1867; and William Marshall, Jeremiah Lehane, and several others at various places, between July 15th and October 24th. The prisoner had made a hard struggle when run down by the police, and had been wounded. He was still very ill when brought to trial. He was deathly pale, and wore a green shade over his eyes. He looked very little like the popular ideal of a bold bushranger. He was convicted and sent to gaol for ten years.

Twenty-three

Bushranging in the Northern District of New South Wales; Captain Thunderbolt Robs the Toll Bar; A Chinaman Bushranger; A Long Chase; A Fight with the Police; "Next, Please"; The Bushranger Rutherford; Captain Thunderbolt and the German Band; Desperate Duel between Captain Thunderbolt and Constable Walker; Thunderbolt's Death.

It must not be supposed that while the Southern and Western districts of New South Wales were harried by bushrangers, that the great Northern district escaped from this scourge. As a fact, although bushranging began rather later than in the Western district, the Northern district was in no degree behind the others in interest at this time.

In April, 1864, Peter, James, and Acton Clarke, three brothers, with John Conroy and a boy of twelve, named Samuel Carter, were riding together towards Culgoa, near Warland's Range. The boy had cantered some distance ahead, when he was ordered to "bail up" by a mounted man, who suddenly came out from behind a clump of trees. The boy took no notice and the man fired at him and missed. The boy galloped away and the man started to follow him, when he caught sight of the other travellers, who had just appeared round a bend in the road. The bushranger stopped his horse, turned to meet them, and ordered them to dismount. They did so. The bushranger also dismounted and came towards them. He demanded their money, and they felt in their pockets to get it out. Just then Peter Clarke made a rush, threw his arms round the bushranger, and tried to throw him. There was a short struggle, and a pistol went off. Peter Clarke fell dead, and the bushranger broke away from him. The other travellers had come forward and endeavoured to assist Peter, but had been unable to grasp hold of the bushranger, as the wrestlers shifted so rapidly.

Now, however, they caught him as he was trying to reach his horse. In the struggle both James Clarke and Conroy were wounded, but the bushranger was overpowered and disarmed. They tied his arms and took him along with them. About two miles along the road they came upon two men tied to trees, who said that they had been stuck up and robbed by the prisoner about two hours before. The prisoner was handed over to the police, and was identified as Harry Wilson, twenty years of age. He was taken to Maitland and charged with wilful murder. He was convicted, and hung on October 4th. A public meeting was held at Murrurundi and a committee was appointed to raise a subscription for the purpose of erecting a monument to Peter Clarke, who had "sacrificed his life in the cause of order and justice." This project was duly carried out.

Mr. Samuel Turner, travelling from Bingera Goldfield to Newcastle in a buggy, put up for the night at Britten's Hotel, Willowtree. Next morning (Sunday, October 19th) he started early, intending to breakfast at Wallabadah. He had gone barely ten miles, however, when he was stuck up by a man riding a fine-looking horse. The robber took him off the road, tied him to one tree and hitched his horse to another. He robbed Mr. Turner of about £12, a gold watch and chain, and a bunch of keys, and rode away. Mr. Turner struggled desperately and succeeded in getting loose. He was leading his horse through the scrub towards the road when the robber returned, tied him up more securely than before, and cautioned him not to "try that dodge again." This time Mr. Turner remained quiet, and about an hour later the bushranger returned again, directing Mr. McShane where to drive his mail coach. When the coach had been placed in a satisfactory position the robber tied McShane and a passenger back to back, with a sapling between them, and laid them on the ground. The bushranger then sat down to go through the letters. McShane said, "You'd better leave them alone, you'll get nothing out of them." "Won't I," replied the bushranger. "What do you call this? It's a hundred and forty quid anyway." He held up a roll of bank notes as he spoke. Having finished the letters he told them to remain quiet until he "got the other mail," and went away again towards the road. It was fully two hours later when he again returned, directing Smith, the driver of the other mail, where to drive. Smith said his horses were young ones and would not stand. "All right," replied the bushranger, "stand at their heads, but, mind, no hanky panky." The only passenger was Mrs. O'Dell. She was politely requested to take a seat on a log and was not interfered with or asked for her money. By a strange coincidence her husband had been a passenger on the coach a week before and had been robbed at the same place, presumably by the same bushranger. By the present transaction the Bank of New South Wales lost £274, and it was doubtful whether this included the "hundred and forty quid" or not.

J. Lowe's mail coach, plying between Mudgee and Sofala, was stuck up by an armed bushranger about two miles from Peel. It was not known whether this highwayman came from the Northern or the Western district, the place where the robbery took place lying between the two and being raided occasionally from either side.

On December 16th a toll-keeper named Delany was "sitting at the receipt of custom" in the toll-house on the road between Maitland and Rutherford, when a man pushed the door open, presented a pistol at his head, and cried out "Give me your money." Delany was of course considerably startled by the suddenness of this attack, but he replied "I've got none." "No —— nonsense!" cried the bushranger. "Give it here!" "I tell you," exclaimed Delany, "there's no money here. My mate's just taken it to Maitland." The bushranger stepped into the house, pushed Delany aside, opened the cupboard, and took out the cash box, saying at the same time, "I'm Captain Thunderbolt." Delany made no attempt to resist this violence, and the bushranger put the box under his arm and walked away up the road to where he had hitched his horse to the fence. He mounted and rode away, and a few minutes afterwards O'Brien, the lessee of the toll-bar, returned from the town. Delany told him what had occurred, and leaving O'Brien in charge walked towards the Spread Eagle Inn at the Rutherford Racecourse. Near the inn he came upon the bushranger, who exclaimed, "Hulloa, come after me?" "No," replied Delany, "I'm going to the pub." "Has your mate gone for the crushers?" asked the bushranger. "No," was the reply, "he's minding the bar." Captain Thunderbolt kept silence for a moment, as if thinking, then he said, "I was told that young Fogarty, the flash fighting man, was keeping the bar, and I wanted to take it out of him. I didn't want to hurt you. You'll find your cash box behind that clump of trees and here's your money." He handed Delany about four shillings, mostly in coppers, and Delany walked away, picked up the cash box, which was uninjured, and went back to the toll-house.

The bushranger walked into the bar of the inn and asked if he could have

Chapter XXIII

something to eat. Mrs. Byrne, the landlady, replied "Certainly," and went out to cut him some bread and meat. He sat down and waited, and on her return ate the bread and meat as if he was very hungry. When he had finished he asked "How much?" "Oh nothing," replied Mrs. Byrne, "we never charge for a little thing like that." "Well," said the robber, "I came here to stick you up, but as you're so —— hospitable, I won't." He then asked for a bottle of rum, paid for it, and went away. About half-a-mile away he met Godfrey Parsons, who was taking his sick wife to Maitland, to see the doctor. Thunderbolt ordered him to "bail up and hand out." Parsons replied, "We've only two pounds, and we want that for the doctor." The bushranger asked what was the matter with Mrs. Parsons and how long she had been ill. Parsons told him. "Well," said the robber, "I'm a bushranger, but I don't rob sick women; pass on." Mrs. Parsons had £30 in her pocket and was crying at the prospect of losing it.

Further along the road Thunderbolt met a man and four women, and stopped to joke with them. He said he thought it —— unfair that one man should have four women, while he could not get one. As they were laughing a trooper rode up, and the bushranger immediately challenged him to fight; the trooper, however, said he had no ammunition with him. "I've been chased by you traps near —— Armidale," exclaimed Thunderbolt, "but they pulled up at the Black Rock. They were afraid of getting bogged in the Green Swamp if they followed me."

He stopped a number of other people during the afternoon, robbing some and letting others go, and in the evening went back to the Spread Eagle to tea. He chatted for some time with Mrs. Byrne, telling her of his exploits. Just after his departure four troopers rode up. Information as to the proceedings of the bushranger had reached Maitland, and these troopers had been sent out to catch him if possible. They made some enquiries, and then followed in the direction in which Thunderbolt had gone, overtaking him as he was talking quietly to a man on the road. The foremost trooper presented his pistol at the bushranger's head, and said "You're my prisoner." "Am I?" cried Thunderbolt with a laugh, as he put spurs to his horse and galloped away. After a long chase, and the expenditure of a large quantity of Government ammunition, the bushranger escaped in the dark, the troopers' horses being almost too tired to return to Maitland. In its comments on this escapade of the new bushranger the Maitland Mercury enquires: "Is this hitherto quiet district to be disturbed as the Western district has been for so long a time?" and events proved that it was.

Within a few days the Northern mail was stuck up by two armed men. One of the robbers was said to be in a state of trepidation the whole time. Perhaps this may account for the bushrangers missing two registered letters, one containing £60 and the other £30, and a small bag of gold-dust in a package. A gentleman who was accompanying the mail cart on horseback was allowed to continue his journey because he said he was on a visit to a sick friend. He was required to promise, "as a gentleman," not to give any information to the police, and he kept his word, but on his arrival in Tamworth he made a bet that the mail coach would not arrive by three p.m. The mail was delayed less than half an hour, however, and the driver nearly made up the lost time by fast driving. The gentleman therefore lost his bet in spite of the special knowledge he had acquired. The robbers were followed at once, and on January 6th, 1865, William Mackie and Robert Johnstone were committed for trial for this robbery. Mackie was identified as a bushranger who had been previously convicted at Bathurst for robbery under arms, but had made his escape while being conveyed to Sydney to be sent to Cockatoo Island. The prisoners were taken from Bathurst to Penrith by coach. From thence they went to Sydney by train. They were handcuffed in the guard's van, the door being open, as the day was very hot. When running along the embankment near Fairfield, between Liverpool and Parramatta, Mackie, ironed as he was, jumped out. The train was travelling at a fast rate, and it ran some distance before notice could be conveyed to the driver and the train stopped. It was expected that the prisoner would be found dead at the foot of the embankment, but nothing could be seen of him. It was then believed that he had crawled somewhere into the scrub to die, but although diligent search was made no body could be discovered. He was now sent to Cockatoo to undergo his original sentence, and Johnstone was sent to keep him company. It was said that they intended to join Captain Thunderbolt.

An attempt was made to stick up the Northern mail about twelve miles north of Singleton, on January 7th. A shot was fired from behind a culvert on the road, as the coach was passing, 2nd a voice called out "Bail up." The

Chapter XXIII

driver, however, instead of obeying, lashed his horses, took his foot off the brake, and the coach plunged down the hill at a tremendous rate, and at the imminent risk of a capsize. Two robbers came out from behind the culvert and fired. The passengers declared that they heard the whizz of the bullets, but no one was hurt, and the coach reached the level ground safely.

On the same day the branch mail from Bendemeer was stuck up and robbed near Stringy Barks, proving that more than one party was raiding on the Great North Road. There were no passengers, but a number of half notes were taken. The robbers handed the driver several cheques to "take care of," one being for £1,000. No violence was used.

The Northern mail was robbed again on January 30th, at Black Hill, about two miles from Muswellbrook, by four armed men. There were three male and one female passengers. The amount stolen was estimated at between £700 and £800. These and several minor robberies on the road were all credited to Captain Thunderbolt, or to men who were trying to join him, and it was said that the immunity enjoyed by him encouraged other evil-disposed persons to take to the road.

In one case at least a Chinaman turned bushranger. Constable Ward was returning to his station at Coonanbarabran from Mudgee, on February 21st, when he was informed that a Chinaman had recently stuck up and robbed a number of persons in the neighbourhood. The constable followed him into the bush, found his camp, and called on the Asiatic to come out and surrender. Instead of obeying the Chinaman exclaimed, "You —— policeeman, me shootee you!" and did so. The constable, though wounded, returned to the nearest farm, from whence news of the occurrence was sent to the police-station. A party was organised and the Chinaman was soon hunted down. He was convicted of attempting to murder a constable while in the execution of his duty, and was hung. Constable Ward recovered from his wound.

On April 6th, Mr. Hughes, of Bourke & Hughes, squatters, informed the police at Dubbo, that the hotel at the Fisheries had been stuck up and robbed, and volunteered to assist in the capture of the bushrangers. They tracked the robbers to Canonbar, about a hundred and twenty miles, when Mr. Hughes's horse knocked up. There they were informed that the bushrangers had passed three days before, and had stolen fresh horses from Mr. Baird's station, Bellerengar, leaving their knocked-up ones in exchange. The black trackers were thrown off the trail by this manoeuvre, as they followed the tracks of the abandoned horses for several miles before they discovered their error. They soon, however, picked up the new tracks, although the bushrangers had kept off the road as much as possible, as if aware that they were being followed. They rode through the scrub and across arid or rocky patches wherever they could find them, but the black boys followed them with unerring skill and with but little delay. The bushrangers stuck up and robbed several people on the road and took fresh horses, provisions, and other necessaries from the stations as they went along. At Martell's Inn the police were informed that the bushrangers were only twelve hours ahead. We will now leave the pursuers and see what the pursued were doing.

They stuck up Mr. Strahan's station and then went on to Gordon's Inn, where they called for drinks like ordinary travellers, shouting for all those in the bar. Then the leader, Daniel Sullivan, produced his pistol, while his two mates went to the door to prevent any of the men inside from running away. They collected about £4 from the landlord and those in the bar, then they put their pistols in their pockets and began "shouting" again. When the £4 was expended, they again produced their pistols, compelled the landlord to hand over the cash, and proceeded to spend it as before. The money had been expended some three or four times, when Sullivan left his mates, Clarke and Donnelly, to "keep the game alive," mounted his horse and rode into the bush. Mr. Gordon was compelled to remain in the bar to serve out the liquors called for, but Mrs. Gordon went on to the verandah to ascertain whether she could find any one to send to Molong to give the alarm. Presently she saw three dusty, weather-stained travellers walking towards the inn, and thought that they were more bushrangers. Fortunately she did not go into the bar to tell her husband, and when Sergeant Cleary, with Constables Brown and Johnston, came up they speedily told her who they were, and were informed in their turn that the men they had ridden so far to arrest were inside. The police entered the bar, and covering the two bushrangers with their revolvers called on them to surrender. Instead of obeying, Clarke put his hand to his belt and was immediately shot.

Chapter XXIII

Donnelly made a rush towards the corner of the bar, where their guns were standing against the wall, and he also was shot just before he reached them. A moment later Sullivan rode up to the front of the hotel, unconscious of the change which had taken place during his absence, and when he found himself covered by the police weapons he was so dumbfounded that he permitted himself to be pulled from his horse and handcuffed without resistance. The police had left their horses some distance away in charge of the black tracker. Now they went for their horses and fed them as well as themselves. Later on a cart was procured, and the body of Donnelly was disposed in the bottom. Beside it, wrapped in a blanket, was the wounded man, Clarke, while Sullivan, being uninjured, was mounted on horseback, and the whole party proceeded to Molong, where an inquest was held on Donnelly's body. Sullivan, and Clarke, who recovered from his wound, were subsequently tried and convicted.

On April 29th, the Tamworth Examiner said:—"A week ago we reported that Frederick Ward, alias Captain Thunderbolt, had stuck up the Warialda mail. He afterwards went to Mr. Lloyd's Manilla station and took two first-class horses. Then he stuck up Cheeseborough's and Lethbridge's stations. From the 10th to the 24th nothing was heard of him, but on the last-mentioned date he and another stuck up Munro's Inn, at Boggy Creek. Mr. Munro challenged them to fight singly, either with fists or pistols, but they laughed at him and shot a valuable dog. They drank a large quantity of spirits, and collected between £70 and £80. They went on to Walford's Inn at Millie, sticking up Mr. Baldwin on the road. Mr. Watford, having been informed of their approach, had hidden away everything of value, so that they got very little, except more grog. The police also had been informed, and three troopers, with a black tracker, soon arrived on the scene. As they approached, the bushranger on guard outside whistled, and the other man came out and mounted, Thunderbolt waving a revolver and pointing to a field behind the house as a challenge. He led his men to the clearing and made a stand. The police followed, and a number of shots were fired on both sides. The police closed up, and Constable Dalton shot one of the bushrangers, a mere lad, and he fell. Dalton shouted to Constable Morris to 'look after him,' and turned towards Thunderbolt, when the boy raised himself on his elbow and fired. Constable Lynch shot the boy in the neck, probably in time to save Dalton's life. Ward made a dash forward, perhaps with a view to driving the police away from the boy and carrying him off, but the police fire was too brisk, and after a few more rounds the robber turned and rode into the bush. The police followed, but as their horses had travelled fifty miles that morning, they were obliged to give up the chase. The robber who was killed, was identified as John Thompson, aged sixteen."

The Namoi mail was robbed by one white man and two blacks, near Tamworth, and on September 17th the mail from Walgett to Singleton was stuck up at Brigalow Creek. The passengers and driver were conducted some distance off the road, to where a fire had been kindled, and were told to "make some tea and enjoy yourselves while we look after the bags." James Boyd, alias McGrath, and Charles Stanmore were arrested after a smart chase, and were convicted of having robbed the Walgett mail. A number of similiar robberies occurred from time to time in various parts of this extensive district, and the police were kept constantly busy.

In December 1865, Ward, riding Mr. Duff's racer Eucalyptus, stuck up Cook's Inn at Quirindi on the 18th; J. M. Davis's Inn at Currabubula on the 10th, and Griffin's Inn at Carroll on the 23rd. At this last-named place he pulled up, and said to his mate in a loud voice, "Let's have a glass of brandy. We want it this wet evening." They dismounted, and stepped on to the verandah. As he entered the door Thunderbolt raised the corner of his mackintosh to display his pistols, and said, "I'll trouble you, ladies and gentlemen, to bail up." The women began to scream, and Ward said, "Don't be afraid. We shan't hurt any one. We only want a little money." A traveller who had entered some time before drew away from the bar, and joined the bushrangers. The other men present were ranged in single row along the wall, and when all were in position each man was called up in turn to be searched. The proceedings were very suggestive of the "next, please," in a barber's shop. While this was going on several people entered, and were compelled to take their places at the end of the queue. The bushrangers held the bar from five to nine p.m., pausing in their work every now and then to order drinks for all hands. Shortly after nine o'clock two men rode up to the verandah, and shouted "Landlord." The robbers looked out, and recognising the horsemen, retreated into the back room.

Chapter XXIII

Mr. Griffin went to the door, and said in a low tone to Constable Lang, "We're all stuck up here." "Which are the bushrangers?" asked the constable, and on being told that they were in the back room he rode to the door and fired. The shot was returned, and the shooting continued until the constable was wounded in the arm and his horse in the neck. The bushrangers went out through the back door, and escaped in the darkness into the bush, but they left their horses behind.

Early in 1866 Ward and his gang made a raid across the Queensland border, robbing stations, hotels, and travellers in the Curriwillinghi district, but he soon returned to his own district, and in March the Tamworth and Wee Waa mail was stuck up near Bullingall by two armed men supposed to be Ward and another. The driver of the Northern mail was also ordered to bail up near Murrurundi, and as he did not obey with due alacrity he was speedily brought to a standstill by one of his horses being shot dead. After going through the letters the bushrangers rode into the town and took a quantity of clothes, some money, and some jewellery and other valuables from Barton's and Johnstone's stores and Humphries' Hotel.

The Northern mail was robbed by three armed men at the Red Post Hill, near Falbrook. It was just before dawn when the driver was ordered to bail up. The robbers were on foot and had a number of pieces of rope ready to tie up the passengers. Mr. Moore, of Abingdon, attempted to run away, but was followed and knocked down with the butt of a pistol. The six passengers and the driver were tightly bound either to the fence or to trees, and their money and watches taken away from them. The robbers then mounted the coach and drove away along the road. As soon as it was out of sight the bound men began to struggle for liberty. Mr. Moore was the first to succeed in breaking loose and he untied Mr. Dines and the others. They followed the coach along the road towards Singleton, but had not gone very far when they were overtaken by Mr. Wyndham on horseback. They informed him of their circumstances and he rode rapidly away to give notice to the police in Singleton. He found the coach standing on the road within a mile of the town but did not stay to examine it. The police started out immediately and arrived at the coach almost as soon as the driver and passengers. Only one of the bags had been cut open, and no damage was done to anything else on the coach. The police spent the whole day in searching, but failed to find any tracks or to ascertain in which direction the robbers had gone.

James Booth, William Willis, alias Dunkley, and Thomas Hampton were arrested in a public house at the corner of Goulburn and Pitt Streets, Sydney, by Detectives Camphin and Finigan on April 17th, 1866, and charged with having robbed the Singleton mail on the previous day. The coach had arrived at the Red Post Hill, between Muswellbrook and Singleton, when the men sprang out from behind the trees bordering the road and sang out, "Bail up, stand and deliver, throw up your arms." Mr. Moore, one of the passengers, jumped out of the back of the coach, and Hampton chased him and brought him back. Mr. Button, a Government railway guard, also tried to get down, but Willis told him that he would blow his "—— brains out" if he didn't sit still. The passengers were all tied up and robbed. One of them, George Beved, said that Willis was the man who threatened to "Blow the roof of his —— skull off" when Moore was wrestling with Hampton. The prisoners were also charged with having bailed up and robbed the mail near Campbelltown, on April 10th. The proceedings were of the usual character. The prisoners were convicted on both charges and were sentenced, Willis to ten years' and Booth and Hampton each to eight years' imprisonment.

The April Sessions at Bathurst were unusually heavy. John Weekes was sentenced to death for the murder of Mr. Scheffts at Grenfell, and John Connors for attempted murder in another bushranging exploit. Besides these, Patrick Foran and James Kelly were sent to gaol for ten years for sticking up the Half-Way House on the Carcoar Road, and other acts of bushranging; James Kennedy, alias Southgate, to fifteen years for sticking up John Edwards, William Woodley, and Henry Rodwell, at Murdering Swamp on January 1st—Kennedy also pleaded guilty to robbing John Fawcett and John Eaton; Charles Rutherford, who had been engaged in several robberies in company with William Mackie, who, as already related, had jumped out of the train while being conveyed to Sydney, and was afterwards captured in the Northern district, was sentenced to seven years' penal servitude; Smith and Moran sentenced to seventeen years each, and Kerr to ten years. These, with some prisoners, sentenced for minor offences, were being conveyed to Sydney to gaol on April 25th, 1867. There were fifteen prisoners in all, guarded by eight troopers. Sergeant Casey, in

Chapter XXIII

charge, was seated on the box seat of the Cobb's coach. The prisoners were inside chained together in two gangs of seven and eight respectively. Constables Madden and Kennedy were seated, unarmed, with the prisoners, while the other five troopers rode beside the coach fully armed. At Pulpit Hill the prisoners, notwithstanding the heavy force opposed to them, made a desperate attempt to escape, and in the melee Constable Holmes was killed, while Rutherford and another prisoner got away in the bush. Rutherford immediately returned to his old haunts and recommenced his depredations. In December, 1867, he was captured by Sergeant Cleary, of Bourke, and was conveyed to the lock-up, but he again contrived to escape. In January, 1868, he stuck up the Boggy Creek and Galathera Inns, and robbed numbers of people on the road. He then went to Mr. Beauvais' inn at Cannonbar and called on the landlord to bail up. Mr. Beauvais, however, had a pistol in the till and knew how to use it. On pretence of taking out the money, to hand over as commanded, he got out his revolver and shot the bushranger. He was awarded a silver medal by the Government for this act.

The districts raided by Rutherford and Thunderbolt overlapped, so that it is difficult to decide which of these two bushrangers were responsible for many of the outrages. Ward, however, was not idle. In company with a boy named Mason, he stuck up and robbed the Northern, the Walcha, and several other mails in the district. He was frequently chased by the police, but being a magnificent rider, with an intimate knowledge of every gully, ravine or hill in the extensive district over which he ranged, he always contrived to escape. Sometimes he was very hard pressed, as, for instance, when he was compelled to abandon Talleyrand, a racehorse for the recovery of which Mr. Wyndham had offered a reward of £100, in April, 1869. His companions were captured one after the other. They were generally boys of from sixteen to twenty, but Thunderbolt continued his career unchecked. No doubt he owed many of his hairbreadth escapes to the superiority of his horses. He would travel two hundred miles to steal a noted racehorse. Thus he stole Mr. Samuel Clift's horse, John Brown, from Breeza. The horse had run on the Maitland and Sydney courses.

One of the stories told about Ward was that he stuck up a German band at Goonoo Goonoo Gap, and made the Teutons play for him, besides giving him their money. The Germans pleaded hard. They said they were only poor men, and that their wives and children would suffer if they were robbed. Thunderbolt told them that he must have money. He was waiting for the principal winner at the Tamworth Races, he added, and he promised that if he caught him he would return the Germans their money. He took down their names and addresses. Notwithstanding this the Germans departed very sorrowful. They never expected to see their money again. Nevertheless, on their arrival at their home in Warwick, Queensland, they found a Post Office Order for £20 awaiting them. It was surmised, therefore, that Thunderbolt had captured the winner.

On May 25, 1870, Ward met Mr. Blanche, innkeeper, near Uralla, returning home with his wife from a drive, and called on him to bail up. Blanche laughed, but took no further notice of the order. Ward exclaimed, "No humbugging. You wouldn't let me have a bottle of rum the other night, though I offered £5 for it." Blanche replied that he never served any one after hours. He then took four shillings and sixpence from his pocket and said, "This is all the money I've got. You can have that." The robber said, "The missus has more than that." "No," cried Mrs. Blanche, "I've no money. We only came for a drive." Ward seemed to consider for a moment, and then told Mr. Blanche to drive on. Several men came up the by-road from Carlisle Gully, and Ward stopped and robbed them. An old man named Williamson, and an Italian dealer named Giovanni Cappisote, were also stopped, but after handing over a gold watch and chain, a small nugget of gold, and £3 13s. 6d. in money, the dealer was allowed to depart. The other men were taken to Blanche's Inn, where Williamson was ordered to shout. He did so, and then Ward shouted. They danced, and sang, and enjoyed themselves. Becoming quieter, Ward asked Blanche whether he remembered a fight between a bushranger and the police at the Rocks, about three hundred yards away, seven years before. Blanche said he remembered it well. "Well," cried Ward, "I'm the man; I was shot in the leg." Ward went on to relate more of his exploits, the narrative being interspersed with songs and dances.

In the meantime, Cappisote drove on to a selector's farm about a mile and a half along the road. Here he told Mrs. Dorrington what had happened. He borrowed a saddle and bridle, took his horse from the cart,

Chapter XXIII

and rode to Uralla; making a wide détour round Blanche's house. He told the police where the bushranger was, and Constables Mulhall and Walker armed and mounted at once. Mulhall had the faster horse and he reached Blanche's first. As he rode up he saw Ward and a young man, both mounted on gray horses, riding along the road. He followed them, and as he approached Ward turned round in his saddle and fired. Mulhall returned the fire but his horse bolted. The trooper soon pulled him up. He wheeled and, seeing one of the men on the grays gallop away, followed shouting to Walker to "look after the other fellow."

The "other fellow" was Thunderbolt, and he turned off the road and rode down the steep hill towards the Rocky River, followed by Constable Walker. Both men fired a shot occasionally when an opportunity offered but neither spoke. On reaching the bank of the river, Ward plunged in, intending to cross and escape up the opposite range, but Walker shot his horse. Ward fell into the river, which was shallow there, and he rose immediately. Walker galloped along the bank past a deep hole and crossed. Then he returned to where Ward was standing in the water and called on him to surrender. "Who the fuck are you?" enquired Ward roughly. "Never mind who I am," replied Walker, "put your hands up." "Are you a trooper?" asked Ward. "Yes," replied Walker. "Married?" continued Ward. "Yes," said Walker. "Well, remember your family," said Ward. "Oh, that's all right," returned the trooper. "Will you come out and surrender?" "No," cried Ward, "I'll die first." "Then it's you and me for it," said Walker. The trooper urged his horse into the river. The animal objected at first and then entered with a rush into deep water. Walker raised his revolver above his head to keep it dry. Ward fired several shots, none of which took effect. When the horse steadied Walker fired again and Ward fell. He rose again immediately and tried to scramble up the bank. Walker struck him with the butt of his revolver and the bushranger fell back into the deep hole and sank. The trooper slipped from his horse, and reaching down grabbed Ward's shirt and pulled him up. He dragged the bushranger out of the hole, up the steep bank, and laid him out on the grass, believing him to be dead. Then he remounted and rode to Blanche's Hotel for assistance to bring the body in. Several of the men about there volunteered to help, but on their reaching the river they found that the bushranger had disappeared. A search was made, but it was too dark to look for tracks. The next morning at daybreak the police and several civilians went to the spot and found a trail of blood. They followed it, and found Ward hidden under some bushes. He was placed in a cart and taken to Uralla, but he died before night. The young man chased by Constable Mulhall said he had gone after Ward to try and get back a horse which the bushranger had stolen from him, and as nothing detrimental to his character was known he was discharged at the police court.

Constable Walker was highly complimented for the pluck and determination he had shown in this desperate encounter with the noted bushranger in a deep water hole in a mountain stream with no one looking on. Of the many brave actions recorded of the police this was perhaps the bravest and the most tragical. The constable was promoted and paid his well-earned reward.

In referring to this duel the Melbourne Argus spoke of Ward as the last of the "professional bushrangers" of New South Wales, and said: "With a much more compact territory than New South Wales, and with a population which can entertain no ancestral or traditional sympathies with burglars or highwaymen, we are nevertheless amenable to the same reproaches as those with which the neighbouring colony was assailed a few years ago."

I have already dealt with this mild pharisaical glorification of Victoria as compared with New South Wales, and have no intention of enlarging upon it here. I refer to it merely to remind the reader that bushrangers were at work elsewhere than in New South Wales at this time.

Twenty-four

BUSHRANGING IN THE WILD PAROO; A RAID INTO SOUTH AUSTRALIA; A RELIC OF THE BUSHRANGING ERA; AGITATION FOR THE RELEASE OF GARDINER; OFFICIAL REPORTS AS TO TWENTY-FOUR BUSHRANGERS STILL IN GAOL; THE CASES OF GARDINER AND WILLIAM BROOKMAN; GARDINER AND THE OTHER BUSHRANGERS RELEASED; GARDINER LEAVES THE COUNTRY.

Bushranging in New South Wales practically ceased with the death of Frederick Ward, alias Captain Thunderbolt. Previously to his tragical death in the New England River, the few stragglers from the big gangs had been captured, and any new men who attempted to revive the "reign of terror" were speedily dealt with by the police. There were some few robberies besides those already related which may be mentioned here. They were distributed over a wide range of country, one party even crossing the border into South Australia, where the bushranger had hitherto been known only by hearsay. But these later bushrangers did not inspire the terror which those who had passed away had done. They were very small fry as compared with Gardiner, Gilbert, Hall, Dunn, Morgan, Thunderbolt, and their companions. Three bushrangers stuck up Mr. Wearne's station at Crookwell on January 6th, 1869 and stole £80 worth of property. The Carcoar mail was bailed up on the mountains, near the Bathurst Road, by two bushrangers, when £15 were taken from the passengers and the bags were searched. A desperate attempt was made to stick up the Joint Stock Bank at Braidwood, but the robbers were beaten off. The Southern mail was robbed on May 10th between Goulburn and Marulan. An attempt was made to stick up the Yass mail on the 24th. Mr. Longfield, a passenger, was wounded, but the robber was forced to retire without having effected his purpose.

In December, a number of people were bailed up and robbed in the Paroo and Warrego districts. The "Wild Paroo" had not been very long reclaimed from its original desert state, but this did not prevent an enterprising bushranger from finding his way there, though he did not continue his career for any very lengthened period. He stuck up Messrs. Lyons

& Martin's station, and made the men sit on the top rail of the stock-yard fence while he rolled up a parcel of goods which he selected from the store. Messrs. Browne, Zouch, and Bradley drove up in a buggy while he was thus engaged, and were ordered to dismount and take their places on the fence with the station hands. The robber escorted them, pistol in hand, from where the buggy stood to the stock-yard. While walking across this intervening space, the bushranger inadvertently, or carelessly perhaps, stepped rather too near to Mr. Browne, who stood six feet five inches in his socks, and was proportionately strong. With a whoop Mr. Browne pounced on to him and held him as in a vice. This turned the tables completely. The men on the fence got off, and the bushranger was in his turn securely tied to the fence and kept there until the police could be brought from the nearest town, Bourke, about a hundred and fifty miles away, to conduct him to prison. After this, bushranging does not appear to have been popular in this district.

On the 9th May, 1869, Mr. Henry Kidder Gillham, manager of the Australian Joint Stock Bank at Braidwood, returned home at eight p.m., and entered by the side gate, when a man sprang out from the shadow and called on him to stand. The bushranger presented a revolver, which Mr. Gillham pushed aside, when another man struck him with a life preserver and knocked him down. Two shots were fired from revolvers. Michael Collins, a gardener living on the bank premises, was in the kitchen when the two bushrangers entered. One of them called out: "Not a word, or it will be the worse for you." The tall man had a "Northumberland voice— that is, he could not pronounce the letter *r*." They tied Collins, and went out of the kitchen. In the meantime the firing had been heard, and Mr. Finnigan, a teacher, with Sergeant Duffy and Constable Luke Dacy, ran to the bank. When they got there two men ran out of the garden, and after a chase, during which several shots were fired, Joseph Horne was captured. He had no boots on. The other man, John Bollard, escaped at the time, but was tracked and captured subsequently. The Chief Justice, Sir Alfred Stephen, said that Home had been sentenced to seven years' hard labour at Maitland. He was afterwards convicted in Melbourne and had escaped from Pentridge stockade, having been shot in the shoulder. Home said that punishment had made him what he was, and pleaded hard for Bollard,

Chapter XXIV

who was young and had been enticed from the right path by him. Home was sentenced to fifteen years' imprisonment and Bollard to ten years.

John Baker and William Bertram divided their attentions between New South Wales and South Australia. In May, 1869, warrants were issued for their arrest for horse stealing from the Mount Murchison station. They took to the road and stuck up a number of people. In October they bailed up a hawker named Charles Young, who resisted and was shot dead. This occurred at the Barrier Ranges, not a great way from where the Broken Hill silver-lead lode was afterwards discovered. Bertram was followed and captured, and was subsequently tried, convicted, and hung at Bathurst. Baker escaped for the time and made his way to Koringa. Said the South Australian Register, "He showed a remarkable want of caution in returning to a district where he had passed his hobble-de-hoy years and was consequently well known." He had been employed as a horse-breaker at the Cross Roads Grounds, Burra Burra, about seven years previously and had afterwards worked for Messrs. Macdonald & Hockin, mail coach proprietors, on the Great Northern Road. On his arrival at Koringa he went into a barber's shop and asked to have his hair cut and dyed. The hairdresser refused to dye it. Baker swore at him, but could not change his determination. The bushranger also grumbled at the time spent in cutting his hair, and continually urged the barber to "hurry up." When the job was completed Baker walked to Redruth, and sat down in the main street opposite the Court House, where the police sessions were being held at the time.

There were a number of people about, but Baker sat and cut his tobacco with all the nonchalance of innocence. He filled and lighted his pipe, and was smoking comfortably, when Corporal Smith and Constable Walker came up and said "You're our prisoner." "What for?" asked Baker. "Bushranging," was the short reply. Baker sprang up from his seat, and raced away at a great rate along the road. He was speedily followed by the police on horseback and brought back. He struggled furiously, slipping his hands from the handcuffs with the greatest ease. The police, however, carried him into the lock-up, and put him into a cell. When questioned, he said he had brought a mob of horses down country for sale, and carried a revolver for his own protection. In the same cell was a man named Dobson arrested for horse stealing, who had been quiet until Baker came. But the door was barely closed and locked when the gaoler heard a suspicious noise in the cell. On opening the door he found that Baker and Dobson were trying to make a hole in the roof with a heavy board seat which they had wrenched from its mortice, and were now using as a battering-ram. Baker was placed in another cell and ironed. He was a small wiry man, very active, and a daring rider. In company with Bertram he had stuck up the Mount Murchison station; stuck up Mr. Cobham's station two hundred miles from Wilcannia, and taken money, a revolver, and several horses; stolen the horse he was riding from Mr. O'Leary, of Poolamacca; robbed and murdered a hawker at the Barrier ranges, and stuck up and robbed a number of people on the roads about Tiers, Gummeracha, and other places near the Murray River, on both sides of the New South Wales-South Australian border. When Bertram was captured, Baker endeavoured to induce a young man whom he met to join him, telling him that they could easily raise £200 to £300, but the young fellow replied that he "didn't want to be hung yet." Baker was extradited to New South Wales, and was tried and hung at Bathurst early in 1871.

On May 20th, 1870, The Queanbeyan Age reported the finding of a mail bag near the Big Hill. The bag was still locked and the seal intact, but the bottom had been ripped open. It had evidently, from its appearance, been lying in the bush for a long time, probably several years. It was referred to as "a relic of the bygone bushranging era in the district."

The Muswellbrook and Cassilis coach was stuck up at Wappinguey, on November 1st, 1870, by two armed men. When ordered to bail up, E. Cummins, the driver, enquired "What for?" "You'll soon see. Drive into that bit of scrub," was the reply. Cummins did as he was ordered, and when the coach was out of sight of the road he was made to get down and hold his horses while the robbers went through the letter bags. When they had finished, they told him to gather up the letters and go.

On the 3rd, Mr. Bellamy was lying under his cart asleep, about three miles from Forbes, on the Currajong Road, when he was awakened by some one calling "Come out o' that." He asked what was the matter, and was told to come out unless he wanted his "brains blown out." He crawled from under the tarpaulin which covered his cart, and handed the bushrangers

Chapter XXIV

three £1 notes. "Where's the rest? We know what you got for your load at Forbes," said one of the bushrangers. "I paid it away to a man I owed it to," replied Bellamy. "That won't do. You never stopped anywhere; we were watching you. Where is it?" As Bellamy still persisted in saying that he had paid away the money, he was compelled to stand with his face to the wheel and was tied there. A handkerchief was also tied round his head, with the knot thrust into his mouth, as a gag. They shook out Bellamy's blankets, searched the feed-bag of his horses, and hunted everywhere, until at length they discovered thirteen £1 notes tucked under the tilt of the cart. Having secured their booty they cautioned Bellamy not to move for an hour under pain of being shot, and went away. Two of them jumped over the track in what was called the road, to avoid leaving footmarks in the dust, but the third appeared to be stiff and walked across into the bush. After they had been out of sight for a time, Bellamy began to struggle. He capsized the spring cart before he succeeded in breaking the rope, but as soon as he got loose he walked back to Forbes and informed the police of the robbery. The robbers were followed and found in a public-house drinking, a day or two after the robbery.

One day, about this time, a man walked into the branch bank at Cassilis, pointed a pistol at the head of the cashier, and ordered him to "bail up, or I'll blow your brains out." "Will you, by God?" cried the cashier, as he placed his hands on the counter and vaulted over. The would-be robber was so startled by this unexpected action on the part of the cashier that he dropped his weapon and ran. The cashier immediately gave chase along Main Street, and soon captured and brought back the pseudo bushranger. The news spread rapidly, and in a few minutes the whole population of the little township was in the Main Street. It was soon learned that the only policeman stationed in the town had gone to Mudgee "on a case," the would-be robber was therefore treated to a good cuffing and some threats, and turned adrift. The revolver was found to be old, rusty, and useless, but for some time it hung in the bank chamber as a caution to bushrangers. It may be there yet for all I know. This attempted bank robbery appears to have been conducive to thirst, as the bars of the two "hotels" were crowded for the rest of the day by a laughing and jeering mob of citizens.

This little comedy furnishes a very appropriate finish to the story of the many tragedies which were enacted during this the most serious outbreak of bushranging which has occurred in New South Wales. During the following two or three years the people were gradually becoming convinced that the crime of bushranging had been thoroughly stamped out, and a sort of reaction set in. Letters appeared in the newspapers, in which the writers urged that some clemency might safely be shown to some of the young men who were still in gaol. In spite of the brutal indifference which many of the bushrangers had shown for human life, it was almost impossible to help admiring the reckless courage exhibited by them. One thought was frequently expressed in various ways. It was that these bushrangers would have made magnificent soldiers if they had been properly trained and made amenable to discipline. There was in fact a disposition to regard them much as the philosopher regards diet, as "matter in the wrong place."

Although no record of the movement can be found in the newspapers and other publications of the period, there can be no doubt that the growth of the spirit of humanitarianism, now so prominent a characteristic of the Anglo-Saxon in all parts of the world, had an immense influence. The convict system, which was regarded as the basis of bushranging, had long since passed away. The convicts themselves had almost died out, and had ceased to be a prominent class in the community. Here and there one of the old fellows lingered and told stories of the barbarous times which had once existed in the colonies. But they were generally incapacitated by age from doing much harm. There had been a time when horror and detestation of the convicts was very general, but even these feelings had gone now, and there was a prevalent opinion that the convicts had been made worse by the brutal discipline to which they had been subjected. The very papers which were most strenuous in their exhortations to the Government of the day to stamp out bushranging at any cost, and which urged the police and all orderly citizens to slay and kill any person who interfered with the mails or who molested travellers on the high roads, now admitted that the bushrangers had been harshly dealt with. Those who had been convicted of murder, or of attempts to murder, had been hung or shot, while the lesser criminals had been sentenced to penal servitude for life or for very long periods. The juries all over the country had shown no leanings towards mercy or clemency, and the judges had treated the bushrangers with

Chapter XXIV

great severity. The people generally, it was asserted, had given ample proof that they would not tolerate a reign of terror such as the bushrangers had striven so hard to establish, and if there should ever be another outbreak, which was not considered probable, it would be crushed out long before it could possibly assume such vast proportions as it had gained during the past era. If there were evil-disposed persons in the colony they would be aware that public opinion was opposed to them and would hesitate before they decided to adopt bushranging as a profession. It is worthy of note that although the brutalities exercised under the old convict system were said to have tended towards the demoralisation of the community, and were largely responsible for the prevalence of bushranging and other crimes, the practice of flogging for serious offences is still the law in many of the colonies.

The general public, however, is seldom logical, and therefore even the Australians still strive to abolish brutal crimes by punishments no less brutal, although the history of the colonies affords such ample evidence of the futility of these means. But the spirit of mercy was abroad. Public meetings were held in all centres of population, petitions were sent to the Governor and the Legislature, and the Press was full of letters praying that mercy might be shown to the evil-doers. The prisoner most frequently mentioned was Frank Gardiner. It is true that he had organised the first gang, and had given a vent to the evil passions of a class. But for him this terrible bushranging era might never have been inaugurated. But he had never committed murder, and had retired from the country and endeavoured to lead a lawful life after only a few months on the road. It had been said that he was engaged in sly grog selling, even when he was ostensibly keeping a store on the road to the diggings in Queensland, but if so it was for the Queensland authorities, not those of New South Wales, to punish him for this offence against the licensing laws. The Queensland authorities had, however, never made any charge against him, and the report might not be true. At length the Chief Justice (the late Sir Alfred Stephen) wrote to the Sydney newspapers. His letter appeared on June 23rd, 1874. Sir Alfred said that the end and aim of all punishment are, first, the preventing of individuals, and secondly, the deterring of other individuals, from the committing of similar crimes…Sentences aggregating thirty-two years had been passed in a time of great excitement, and the punishment seemed to have been measured more in view of the crimes he was supposed to have committed than with reference solely to those which were proved against him...He could not say whether the reported reformation was sincere, but he thought that the prisoner had been sufficiently punished and, therefore, recommended a conditional pardon.

Emanating from such a source, this opinion carried great weight, and almost coincident with its publication, the Governor, Sir Hercules Robinson, afterwards Lord Rosmead, laid before the Executive Council six petitions signed by a number of well known and responsible persons in various parts of the colony praying for the release of the convict Gardiner. He said it was true that no hope of an absolute remission of his sentence had ever been held out to him, but in the Governor's minute of December 5th, 1872, it had been implied that if the prisoner continued to conduct himself well he might hope for remission at the end of ten years.

Official returns were laid on the table showing the number of prisoners still in penal servitude for highway robbery. The prisoner whose case attracted most attention next to Gardiner was William Brookman. His parents were said to be respectable. He was only seventeen years of age when he was charged on January 16th, 1868, with wounding with intent to murder. He was convicted and sentenced to death, but his sentence was commuted to fifteen years' penal servitude. It was said to have been his first and only attempt at highway robbery, and he had never previously been arrested or charged with any offence against the law. At the time of this enquiry he had served six and a-half years of his sentence.

The other bushrangers in gaol were:—Samuel Clarke, sentenced April 8th, 1866. Served five years, one month. No previous conviction.

Daniel Shea, sentenced November 6th, 1865. Served eight years, six months. Previously sentenced for two years for horse stealing.

William Willis, alias Dunkley, sentenced May 16th, 1866. Served eight years. Three previous convictions for horse stealing, of nine months, eighteen months, and six months respectively.

Alexander Fordyce, sentenced February 23rd, 1863. Served eleven years, nine months. No previous conviction.

John Payne, sentenced January 14th, 1868. Served six years, six months. No previous conviction.

James Jones, sentenced March 31st, 1864. Served ten years, one month. No previous conviction.

Robert Cotterall, alias Blue Cap, sentenced April 29th, 1868. Served six years, one month. No previous conviction.

James Boyd, alias McGrath, sentenced February 24th, 1864. Served nine years, three months. Previously sent to gaol for five years for horse stealing.

Thomas Cunningham, alias Smith, sentenced April 9th, 1867. Served seven years, one month. No previous conviction.

Charles Hugh Gough, alias Wyndham, alias Bennett, sentenced April 9th, 1867, served seven years, one month. Previously sentenced to three years for assault with intent to rob.

Thomas Dargue, sentenced March 28th, 1867. Served seven years, two months. No previous conviction.

Henry Dargue, sentenced March 28th, 1867. Served seven years, two months. No previous conviction.

John Kelly, sentenced March 11th, 1867. Served seven years, two months. Previously sentenced to two years for embezzlement.

Edward Kelly, sentenced January 14th, 1867. Served six years, seven months. No previous conviction.

James Smith, sentenced April 15th, 1866. Served seven years, one month. Previously sentenced to three years for horse stealing.

John Foran, sentenced October 18th, 1867. Served six years, seven months. No previous conviction.

John Williams, sentenced to death January 14th, 1868. Sentence commuted to fifteen years' penal servitude. Served six years, four months. No previous conviction.

William H. Simmons, sentenced April 6th, 1868. Served six years, one month. Previously sentenced to ten years on two charges of larceny.

William Taverner, sentenced April 5th, 1867. Served five years, one month. No previous conviction.

Daniel Taylor, sentenced October 24th, 1865. Served eight years, one month. No previous conviction.

John Bow, sentenced February 26th, 1863. Sentence death, commuted to imprisonment for life. Served eleven years, six months. No previous conviction.

John Bollard, sentenced October 19th, 1869. Served four years, seven months. No previous conviction.

All these prisoners were very young men, little more than boys, when they were convicted; and, of the twenty-three, sixteen had had no charges brought against them previously to their arrest for highway robbery. The four others who had been previously convicted of horse stealing were cattle duffers and horse planters, which had been, a few years before, scarcely considered to be crimes by the residents of the districts in which these young men were born; although the law, when it came to be enforced in these districts, called these acts criminal. It was said that if Gardiner was to be released these young men, who had been led away principally by his example, should also have their sentences remitted.

The reports with such comments as had been made on them by the Executive Council were placed before the Legislative Assembly, and on July 3rd a debate began relative to the cases of Gardiner and Brookman, it being understood that the decision in the case of Brookman should apply to the other twenty-two named in the reports. On a division being taken the vote stood twenty-six for and twenty-six against a remission of the sentences. The Speaker gave his casting vote with the ayes, and it was consequently resolved that the two prisoners should be released on July 8th, 1874.

The Governor extended the prerogative of mercy to the others named above, and they were all released at the same time. In the case of Gardiner the pardon was coupled with the condition that he should leave the colony forthwith, consequently a short time after his release he sailed to California, and was reported to have died there about nine years later. Mrs. Brown, his paramour, had died in New Zealand during his incarceration.

The release of the bushrangers was not carried without opposition, however. A monster meeting of diggers was held at Grenfell to protest against any mercy being shown them. Large meetings were held elsewhere, and it

Chapter XXIV

was said that remitting the sentences of the bushrangers was tantamount to encouraging other evil-disposed persons to rebel against the laws. The speakers deplored the action of the Governor, the Executive, and the Legislature, and prophesied a new outbreak of lawlessness. But the spirit of the opposition was less active than that of the persons in favour of mercy, while the majority of the population were more or less indifferent. And so ended the great outbreak of bushranging in New South Wales.

Twenty-Five

Bushranging in Victoria; Robert Bourke; Harry Power: He Escapes from Pentridge Gaol and Sticks Up the Mail; An Amateur Bushranger; The Police Hunt Power Down and Capture him Asleep; A Peacock as "Watch Dog"; The Power Procession at Beechworth; The Trial of Power; His Sentence; Engaged to Lecture on Board the Success; His Death.

While New South Wales was the chief centre of bushranging during this epoch, the neighbouring colonies were not entirely free from the disease. In those cases in which the epidemic flowed, as it were, over the borders of the mother colony—as when Morgan, Thunderbolt, and Bertram crossed into Victoria, Queensland, and South Australia respectively—the inroads have been dealt with in connection with the careers of these particular bushrangers in order not to break the continuity of their stories. Having described the rise and fall of bushranging in the older colony, it is now necessary to return to Victoria and continue the narrative there. Bushranging in this colony during this epoch was rather a survival from the past than a new development, and, with one notable exception, the police dealt promptly with the lawbreakers. The exception will be noticed in due course.

On September 5th, 1862, Mr. Ryan, the landlord of the Travellers' Rest Hotel at Yalla-y-poora, was at breakfast with his family and a visitor named Reid, when two armed men entered the room. One stood at the door, while the other, pistol in hand, stepped forward and cried "Bail up." They tied Messrs. Ryan and Reid, and took ten shillings from the till and ten one pound notes from under the mattress of the bed, where it had been hidden. They did not search the women, but they broke some of the furniture in the bedroom while hunting for the money. One of the robbers pulled the boots off Mr. Reid's feet and put them on his own, leaving a very much worn and damaged pair in their place. They also took Reid's horse, saddle, and bridle from the stable. Mr. Reid told them that he was only a poor man, and that the loss of his horse would ruin him. The robber replied, "Well, he ain't the sort we want. I'll leave him for you at Macpherson's as soon as I get a better one." When they had left Mrs. Ryan untied her husband and their guest, and Ryan mounted his horse and rode to Ararat to give information to the police. Constables Lawler and Griffen followed the bushrangers, and tracked them to a hut near Mount Sturgeon, in the Grampian Ranges. The police expected a fight, but they rushed the hut and captured the robbers without a shot being fired, although one of them named Regent had a loaded revolver in his hand. They were taken to the gaol at Ararat, and were convicted and sentenced in due course.

In July, 1864, a sensation was caused in the Kilmore district by a report which gained currency, that Gardiner and his gang had stuck up a number of people near Yea. A party of volunteers was speedily organised to assist the police in hunting down the bushrangers. The pursuers were divided into small parties, and on the evening of the 20th one of these, composed of Mr. Grant and Constable Buck, came upon three suspicious-looking characters camped on Pack Bullock Flat with a mob of horses. Constable Buck asked where they were going, when one replied "To Melbourne," and another "To the Jordan." Buck called on them to surrender, when one man sprang forward and clutched him by the throat. Another rushed at Grant, who was unarmed. Grant turned and ran to where they had left their horses, calling on Buck to come away, and Buck broke loose and joined him. Buck however lost his revolver in the struggle. They rode away to find help, and returned with Mr. Grant's brother, George Grant, and Mr. Walker. Grant shot one bushranger dead, Walker stunned a second with a blow on the head with the butt of his gun, while Buck captured the third after a smart run. The captured men were convicted of robbery by violence, and it was said that the horses they had with them had been stolen from various stations.

Robert Bourke was employed as cook at Mr. Broughton's, Humewood Station, on the Murrumbidgee River, New South Wales, and appears to have been suddenly affected with the bushranging mania. He ferried himself across the river, and with the assistance of a young lad named Quinn stuck up and robbed several people in the neighbourhood. He was said to "know every bulga from Barren Jack to Manaro," but did not stop long in that district, perhaps because it had already been "worked out" by the Brothers Clarke and other bushrangers. In September, 1868, he crossed the Murray River, and stuck up and robbed travellers on the road near Wodonga and Wangaratta, gradually working southwards. On October 4th he appeared at Mr. Hurst's station, Diamond Creek, about fifteen miles from Melbourne, where a daring attempt was made to capture him. The story is that Bourke called at William Horner's on the 2nd, and asked for a bed. He was told that there was none to spare, when he drew a revolver and cried "Bail up." Homer slammed the door in his face. Bourke fired, and the bullet passed through the door panel, but did no great injury. He tried to push the door open, but, failing in this, he began to "parley." He said he was hungry, and would go away quietly if he was given something to eat. Homer then opened the door and gave him a pannikin of tea and some bread and cold meat. He sat down on a log and made a good meal. When he had finished he asked for some "tucker for the road" and a horse, saddle, and bridle. Horner said that the horses were all down the paddock, and he did not intend to run them in until next morning, but he could have some "tucker." He then gave him a large piece of bread and some meat. They talked together very amicably. Bourke said, "I'm a bushranger from New South Wales, and I've come here to see if your police are as clever as you blow about them. They'll never take me alive." He went away, and, it is supposed, slept in the bush. On the morning of the 4th he went to Hurst's place and asked for some breakfast. Thinking he was an ordinary tramp, Miss Hurst gave him some bread and meat in the kitchen, but, as he sat at table, she noticed that he carried pistols in his belt. She went into another room and informed her brother Henry, who loaded a double-barrelled gun to be ready for any emergency. He walked into the kitchen, carrying the gun behind him, to have a look at their suspicious guest, and asked him where he came from and where he was going? "From Cape Schank to Kilmore," was the reply. "Then you're not travelling in the right direction," remarked young Hurst. Bourke jumped up from the table, as if in a passion, and cried "Do you doubt my word? Do you want to insult me?" He drew his revolver and Hurst brought his gun round and fired. He missed, and Bourke immediately shot him in the chest. Although he was severely wounded young Hurst rushed forward and grappled with

Chapter XXV

the bushranger, while Mr. Abbott and two or three other men ran in to ascertain what the shooting was about. They secured the bushranger and carried young Hurst to bed, but, although every attention was paid to him, he died in a few hours. Bourke was identified by the police as a man who had been sentenced to three years' imprisonment for horsestealing at Ararat. When he had served his term he was of course discharged and, as was surmised, went to New South Wales and obtained work on a station. He lived quietly for about eighteen months, when he started bushranging as related. He was twenty-five years of age at the date of his conviction for the murder of Henry Hurst.

The central figure in Victoria of this era was undoubtedly Harry Power. This notorious bushranger arrived in Victoria from Ireland shortly before the proclamation of the discovery of gold at Ballarat, and went to the diggings. In March, 1855, he was seen near Daisy Hill, in the Maryborough district, riding a valuable horse, the description of which tallied with that of a horse which had been stolen and for which the police were seeking. He was stopped and challenged to show his receipt for the horse. Instead of producing it or saying where it was deposited, Power disputed the right of the police to stop him on the highway and drew a revolver. The police, very naturally perhaps, took this as a tacit admission that he could not show any right to the horse, and sought to apprehend him. Several shots were fired and at last one of the troopers fell wounded. Power put spurs to his horse and galloped away. A warrant was immediately issued for his arrest and he was followed and captured. He was convicted of "wounding with intent to do grievous bodily harm," and was sentenced to fourteen years' penal servitude. A short time before the expiration of his term he was employed in drawing refuse from the Pentridge Gaol to the rubbish heap in a go-cart. A number of other prisoners were similarly employed. While the cart he was helping to draw was being tipped Power contrived to secrete himself under a corner of the heap. He was not missed until evening, when the prisoners employed at this work were mustered. The prisoners at work with him must of course have been aware of his evasion, but professed ignorance in accordance with convict etiquette. A search was made and his hiding place was discovered, but Power was gone. He stole some clothes from a farm not far from Pentridge, and the blade of an old pair of sheep shears to defend himself, with, as he declared that he would not be captured alive. Shortly after his escape, on May 7th, 1869, he stuck up the mail coach near Porepunkah and continued to rob in the Ovens and Beechworth districts for several months, when he made a raid into New South Wales, going as far as Adelong. He returned about the end of September to his old district and stayed there for the remainder of his career.

Commenting on his actions, the Ovens and Murray Advertiser said— "Possessed of a thorough knowledge of the country, this scoundrel has made periodical descents to the settled districts, and afterwards, like a hunted dog, betaken himself to the ranges. From a certain portion of the population he—or whoever else has been masquerading in his name—has received succour and information, while the police have been misled and deceived." The article from which this extract was made was copied and italicised in the Melbourne Argus, and made the subject of a leading article, in which it was contended that if bushranging was to be stamped out the sympathisers and "bush telegraphs" must be restrained from aiding the bushranger with food and information. The Government was urged to pass a special Act to enable the police to contend with the difficulty. It was said on the other hand that the Outlawry Act, if strictly applied, would meet the case.

William Moore, of Buffalo, was returning from a trip to Eldorado, where he had sold his load of farm produce, when a young man rode up and asked him "Where have you been?"

"What's that to you?" returned Moore. The young fellow said "I only asked a civil question." "Well," said Moore, "I've been to Eldorado, and I'm going home. Will that satisfy you?" The young man nodded, and cantered on. As he passed, Moore noticed that he had pistols in his belt, and hastily took a roll of notes, worth £35, from his pocket, and thrust it into an empty flour sack in the dray. The young man only rode forward about fifty yards, and then wheeled round, revolver in hand, and cried "Bail up." Moore stopped, and willingly turned out his pockets, displaying a half-crown, which he handed to the robber, who rode away. In reporting this robbery Mr. Moore said that he believed that this was the young man's first attempt at highway robbery, as he trembled violently and seemed glad

CHAPTER XXV

when it was over. The Ovens and Murray Advertiser of May 7, 1870, in commenting on this case, said: "It shows the necessity of more determined efforts to capture Harry Power, who has for more than a year robbed rich and poor alike in this neighbourhood, and it is the immunity which he has for so long enjoyed that encourages young lads to imitate him."

Shortly before, in April, Patrick Stanton, otherwise known as Jack Muck, was captured after a smart run. He was convicted of having stuck up and robbed a coloured man, a well-known splitter and timber cutter, on the Black Dog Creek. The splitter had been to town to be paid for a number of posts and rails, and was returning home along the Rutherglen Road when he was bailed up.

The Kilmore Free Press reported that Power had been seen in Mr. Dunlop's paddock at Mount William. He was firing at a mark on a tree. No one interfered with him.

On May 2nd, Edward Kelly was arrested at Greta and was charged with having assisted Power in some of his robberies. He was not identified by the witnesses, and was therefore discharged.

On the 27th Superintendents Nicholson and Hare, Sergeant Montford, and Black-tracker Donald left Wangaratta and made a journey into the ranges near the head of the King River. It was believed that they had received special information from a friend of the bushranger. At the head of the glen, near where Power's camp was, a family named Quinn resided, and it was said that Power would never be caught while they were there. The Quinns owned several dogs and a peacock, which it was believed would never allow any person to pass up the ravine without giving notice. The peacock was reported to be the "best watch dog of the lot." His screams could be heard far away whenever a stranger approached the hut, and he generally gave the first signal, and thus roused the dogs. On this occasion, however, the police passed without either the peacock or the dogs giving a sign. They came to a hollow tree with holes in the stem. This tree had been mentioned as "Power's look-out," and it was reported that he frequently went into it to survey the country round, through the holes, without exposing himself. There was plenty of room inside for more than one man, and the natural holes formed by the decay of the tree had been added to by augur holes bored at a convenient height for spying through. They examined it, but it was empty. All round was a dense growth of cherry and wattle scrub, which they cautiously pushed their way through, and peeped into a small clearing. A gunyah of bark stood in the middle of this space, and before it was a fire burning. Creeping cautiously up, the police saw a man's leg sticking out from under the gunyah. One of them seized it, and drew the man out on his back. It was Harry Power. He had been lying asleep under the impression that he was perfectly safe. He gave a loud howl on being thus rudely awakened, and then asked, "Who are you?" "The police," was the reply. "No fear," said Power; "you couldn't have got past Quinn's; the dogs and the peacock would not have let you." "We did," replied Inspector Nicholson; "the dogs and the peacock never saw us, but there were several men there and Quinn himself—they saw us." "You've given us a great deal of trouble, Power," said Inspector Hare, "but we've got you at last." "I'm very sorry I didn't hear you," remarked Power; "I'd have dropped some of you if I had."

In the gunyah were a Government revolver, stolen from the police, loaded and capped; a double-barrelled gun, hanging from the ridge pole, loaded ready for use; and a loaded pistol lying close beside the sleeping bushranger. There were also a box of slugs, a powder flask, two boxes of caps not quite full, a carpet-bag full of clothes, and a saddle and bridle. The bed was a very comfortable one, with a good supply of blankets.

The police informed Power that they had been out in the ranges for more than a week and were starving. They had not had a mouthful of food for more than twenty-four hours, and were anxious to get back to town. "There's plenty of tucker here," said Power. "Where?" asked the police. "In that tree," replied Power. They went to the tree and saw a bag hung up among the branches, as is common in the bush. In this "bush safe" they found part of a large home-baked loaf, some potatoes, tea and sugar, and a piece of fresh beef. "Golly, what a feed we'll have," cried Donald, the black, when he saw the food. The police cut the beef into steaks and fried them and had a good meal. In their search they found £15 4s. 6d. in bank notes and money.

They mounted Power on the horse ridden by the black tracker, while

Chapter XXV

Donald mounted behind Sergeant Montford, and left the camp. They reached Wangaratta at seven p.m. on Sunday, June 5th, 1870, eleven days after the death of Captain Thunderbolt in New South Wales. The news of the capture had already been noised abroad in the district, and numbers of people, who were out for their Sunday evening ramble, crowded the streets of Wangaratta to see the noted bushranger. Power waved his hand in response to their cheers, and cried "They've caught poor Harry Power, but they caught him asleep."

On Tuesday, the 7th, Power was removed to Beechworth gaol, and a number of men and women in carriages, buggies, spring carts, and other vehicles, or on horseback, went along the road to meet him and escort him into the town. The procession as it passed over Newtown Bridge was quite an imposing one, and there were collected the majority of the residents who had neither horse nor vehicle. Power was sitting in a police cart, and bowing right and left to the crowd as if he had been some high potentate. He wished the people "Good morning," and continually repeated his formula about having been captured asleep. On his arrival at the gaol he greeted Mr. Stewart as an old friend, and hoped they would never fall out. He made a short speech, in which he publicly thanked the police for the kind and considerate manner in which he had been treated since his arrest.

The Ovens Spectator at this time said: "Henry Power, alias Johnson, is a hale, hearty-looking man, although past the meridian of life, with grisly hair and beard, and certainly not of such an appearance as one would expect a bushranger to have."

On October 2nd Henry Power was tried on four charges of highway robbery. On May 7th, 1869, he bailed up Arthur Woodside, a squatter at Happy Valley, as he was riding towards Bright. The robber took a horse, saddle, bridle, and spurs, giving in exchange a knocked-up horse, a broken saddle, a bridle tied up with string, and one rusty spur. While Mr. Woodside was giving his evidence Power exclaimed, "Speak up, young man. You spoke different to that when I met you on the road." The mail coach from Beechworth was bailed up at the same time. Power asked the driver, Edward Coady, to throw out the gold. Coady replied, "There is none." "I was told there was," exclaimed Power. "Any parcels?" Coady threw down two, which Power opened. There was only one passenger, a Chinaman, and Power asked him for the key of his carpet bag. At first the Chinaman said "No savvy," but, on the revolver being pointed at his head, he handed over the key. Power searched the bag, but took nothing out. This was the first case.

On August 28th, the same mail was bailed up. At that time there were three passengers—Mr. Hazleton, Ellen Hart (a servant), and Mrs. Li Goon. A boy also got on to the coach at Boyd's for a ride down the hill. The coach had just passed the gap when the driver had to put the the break on and pull up, because the roadway was blocked with logs and saplings. Mr. Hazleton exclaimed "Who did this?" when Power stepped out from behind a tree and replied "I did. Put up your hands." The passengers were made to alight and turn out their pockets. Hazleton made a step forward to hand his watch and chain to the robber, but Power cried out "Stand back," and raised his revolver. He then told Hazleton to put the watch on the ground and retire, and when this had been done Power went forward and picked it up. Mrs. Li Goon said she had no money, but when Power threatened to shoot her she gave him fourteen shillings. "It's all I've got and I'll want a cup of coffee," she said. "All right," returned the bushranger, "take this," and he gave her back one shilling. The robber took £2 13s. 6d. out of Coady's pocket-book. There was also a threepenny-piece in it, and Power told the coachman to give it to the boy. Mrs. Boyd came down the hill on horseback, and was bailed up. She said she had no money. "I don't see how ladies can go riding round with handsome dresses and fine saddles and bridles without money," cried Power. "Here, give me your horse." Mrs. Boyd said if he would allow her to ride home she would bring him some money, but he refused to trust to her promise, and took the horse. He stuck up several Chinamen and a white man, and took their money from them. He said to them "It's a cold day, but I've got a nice fire down there, go and sit by it;" and he pointed down the hill. He was in a good temper and gave the boy a shilling. The little fellow immediately offered to give him the shilling and the threepenny-piece for his sister's horse. Power laughed and gave the horse to the boy to lead to where his sister was sitting. This was the second case.

The third charge was the robbing of John Whorouly. Power said "I don't

Chapter XXV

like robbing a poor man, but I must have money." The fourth charge was the sticking up of Thomas Oliver Thomas, on the Buckland Road. When called on to bail up, Thomas wheeled his horse round, and Power shouted "If you run away I'll fire. My gun will carry three hundred yards." Power asked for his money, and Thomas replied "I've got none." "That's a lie," cried Power, "turn it out." Power repeatedly threatened Thomas with his revolver.

Power was found guilty on each of the four counts, and was sentenced to fifteen years' penal servitude.

Power served out his full sentence. At about the time of his discharge the Victorian Government sold the hulk Success, the President and the other hulks purchased to supply the want of prison accommodation in "the roaring fifties" having been sold years before. The Success had been utilised as a training ship, and had been kept. In the case of the other hulks, it had been stipulated in the terms of sale that they were to be broken up, but this clause was omitted in the case of the Success. Consequently she was purchased by some speculators, and fitted up as a representative convict hulk for exhibition purposes, and Harry Power was engaged to add interest to the show. The ship was exhibited in Melbourne, and was then taken round to Sydney. She was visited by a number of people during the two or three weeks when she was berthed at Circular Quay, and she was then taken down the harbour to be fitted for a voyage to London. Here she sank at her moorings. With the appliances in Sydney so small a vessel was soon raised, but her immersion had damaged the wax figures intended to represent the prisoners who had once been confined in her, and the other exhibits. While these were being replaced or cleaned, Harry Power was sent into the country districts for the benefit of his health. He was fishing in the Murray River near Swan Hill, on November 7th, 1891, when he fell in and was drowned. At the inquest held on his body, a verdict of accidental death was returned. The Success shortly after left Australia for England without any living representative of the bushranging times on board of her.

Twenty-six

Bushranging in New Zealand; Alleged fears of the Escort being robbed; The First Bushranger, Henry Beresford Garrett; The Maungapatau Murders; Arrest of Sullivan, Kelly, Burgess, and Levy in Nelson; Sullivan's Confession; The Discovery of the Bodies; Sullivan's Release.

The reports of extensive and rich discoveries of gold in the Otago Province, New Zealand, in 1861, naturally attracted the floating population of Australia to that quarter. In September the escort brought down to Dunedin for shipment a smaller amount of "the precious metal" than had been obtained in any previous month since the goldfield was first proclaimed. Several reasons were given to account for this falling off. One was that the weather had been abnormally cold, and the freezing of the rivers had for a time put a stop to sluicing. Another was that the gold buyers declined to pay more than £3 10s. per ounce, and the majority of the diggers, having come from Ballarat and Bendigo where £4 and £3 18s. 6d. per ounce were paid respectively, refused to send their gold down and were keeping it for an anticipated rise in the price. The Southern Cross, however, said that the principal reason why the diggers were not sending their gold forward was the fear of bushrangers. The guard sent with the escort was wholly inadequate in the mountains through which it had to pass, and therefore the diggers declined to entrust their earnings to its care. The Otago Witness pooh-poohed this assertion and declared that there had never yet been a case of bushranging in the colony, and that if a fair price was offered for it by the banks and other gold buyers the gold retained on the diggings would speedily be placed on the market. The bank authorities, on being questioned, said that the New Zealand gold contained a larger proportion of silver than either the Ballarat or Bendigo gold, and was therefore of less value than the gold won on those diggings.

The boast of the Otago Witness that there were no bushrangers in New Zealand did not hold good for very long. Henry Beresford Garrett, who was arrested in London on the charge of robbing the Bank of Victoria at Ballarat as already related, and who was convicted in August, 1855, and sentenced to ten years' hard labour, was liberated from the Pentridge Gaol, Melbourne, in August, 1861, on a ticketof-leave, after having served six years. Early in 1862 he made his appearance as the first bushranger on record in New Zealand. The scene he chose for his operations was the country between the Otago Goldfields and Dunedin. In one day he is reported to have stuck up and robbed no less than twenty-three persons near Gabriel's Gully, now known as the town of Lawrence. His career, however, was short if lively, for he was captured before the end of the year and sent to gaol for eight years.

In May, 1865, footpads were said to be becoming numerous about Auckland. The New Zealand Herald reported the story of a man being bailed up while walking along Beach Street towards Mechanic's Bay. A soldier, however, chanced to come along at the time and the robber bolted. These petty offenders, however, appear to have been speedily dealt with, and nothing more was heard about bushranging until the public was startled by the reports of "the horrible Maungapatau murders," as they were called.

It appears that Thomas Kelly, alias Noon, Richard H. Burgess, alias Miller, and Philip Levy went to the new rush known as the West Coast Diggings, early in 1866, and committed several robberies there. They were shortly afterwards joined by John Joseph Sullivan, a recent arrival from Victoria. On June 14th, Stephen Owens, landlord of the Mitre Hotel, Nelson, went to the wharf to meet the coastal steamer Wallaby, as she arrived from the west coast, and saw four men on board. They were very shabbily dressed, but he gave one of his cards to Levy and told him that he and his mates could obtain accommodation at the hotel. On the following day, Sullivan and Kelly came to the hotel in new clothes. Sullivan gave the landlord two bank notes for twenty pounds each, and one ten pound note, and asked him to take care of them for him. There was nothing remarkable in this. Diggers were frequently very shabby when they returned from the diggings, and until they had time to buy new clothes. Sullivan and Kelly appeared to have plenty of money with them, as they spent it freely. They each ordered a pair of trousers and a velvet vest from Charles Flood, tailor, paying £4 each for them. They also spent £3 17s. 6d. for clothing at

Merrington's draper's shop, and Kelly paid besides £3 5s. for a dress for a woman. He afterwards bought a bonnet, a mantle, and other articles of feminine wear.

Levy and Burgess went to lodge at an oyster shop kept by Francis Porcelli. They were covered with mud when they went there first, but bought new clothes at J. M. Richardson's and other places in the town.

On June 21st, the four men were arrested and charged with the murder of Felix Mathieu. They were remanded while the police made enquiries. Sullivan turned Queen's evidence, and the tale he told may be summarised as follows.

Sullivan landed at the Grey River from Victoria in 1865 with the intention of digging. He was unlucky, and, chancing to make the acquaintance of Kelly, Levy, and Burgess, who had been sticking up people on the roads about the diggings for several months, he joined them. One day they informed him that Mr. E. B. Fox, a gold buyer, of Maori Gully, was expected to pass along the road, and they intended to bail him up, as he was sure to have some gold or money on him. Kelly, Levy, and Burgess hid themselves in some bushes beside the road, while Sullivan was stationed on the road with a long-handled shovel, so that those who passed along might take him for a road repairer. Owing to this disguise he could keep watch without exciting suspicion. He had not been long on watch when a man named George Dobson came along, and asked how far it was to the coal pits. Sullivan replied "About half a mile," and the man thanked him and walked on. When he was opposite where the other bushrangers were hidden they fired and killed him under the belief that he was Fox. When they discovered their mistake they dragged the body off the road and buried it, and as it began to rain heavily they all went to their tent. A day or two later they went to the road again, and took up positions as before, Levy giving orders that not a man should be allowed to pass without being searched. Sullivan again appeared as a road-repairer, and was pretending to be at work when an old man named James Battle, commonly known in the district as "Old Jamie," came along with a sluicing shovel on his shoulder. Sullivan said "Good day, mate. Where are you bound for?" Old Jamie replied that he was going to "look for a ship," as the diggings were "played

Chapter XXVI

out." Sullivan went to the ambush and reported that the man was an old whaler and not worth robbing, but Levy said he must be brought back. Sullivan, therefore, followed him and brought him back without difficulty, as he had no suspicion. Kelly and Burgess seized him, tied his hands behind him, and led him away into the bush. When they returned they said he would not trouble them any more. They divided £3 15s., which they had taken from the old man. He had informed them that he had not done well at the diggings, and had, therefore, taken a job of cutting flax to earn sufficient money to enable him to get away.

Shortly after Old Jamie had been thus disposed of, Felix Mathieu, John Kempthorne, James Dudley, and James de Pontius, storekeepers and gold buyers from the Deep Creek Diggings, passed along the road on their way from Nelson to Canvas Town. Two of the bushrangers stepped out from their ambush and confronted them, calling upon them to stand. They wheeled their horses, intending to gallop away, but found the other two bushrangers facing them, revolvers in hand. The four travellers then surrendered and allowed their hands to be tied behind them. Levy, Burgess, and Kelly led them away into the bush, while Sullivan followed the pack horse which had been let go, and which galloped a short distance along the road and then stopped and began to feed. Sullivan very soon caught it, and led it off the road. He took the gold and other valuables out of the portmanteau, which was strapped on the saddle, and shot the horse. Then he went to the camp to meet his mates.

The four bodies were discovered by William Flett, when he was out looking for horses in the bush. They were lying less than half-a-mile from the roadway on the Nelson side of the third creek from Franklyn's Flat. Mathieu's body was lying in the loose ground broken up by the uprooting of a large tree by the wind. It was on its back, the hands tied behind, and the feet tied together at the ankles. It was sheltered and partially hidden by the upturned roots of the fallen tree. Dudley's body was about eighteen yards away with a handkerchief tied tightly round the throat. Kempthorne's body was some twenty yards further, lying on its back, untied. The body of De Pontius was lying some thirty yards further along with a number of stones piled loosely around it, suggesting the idea that they had been thrown at it from a short distance. Dr. Vickerman said that Kempthorne had been shot in the head behind the ear. The bullet and some paper were found in the wound, showing that the shot had been fired at close range. Mathieu had been shot in the stomach, and then stabbed. The wound was under the fifth rib, and had apparently been made with a large knife. De Pontius had a bullet-wound in the back of the head, and the right side of the face was smashed, as if from the blows of rocks or stones. It was supposed that the bullet had not killed him at once, and he was therefore stoned to death. Dudley had been strangled.

A revolver was found in the gorse hedge at Toitoi by Constable Peter Levy. A gun, identified by James Street as one which had been stolen from his place on the Kamieri River, near Hokitiki, in the January previous, was also found by the constable not far away.

Mrs. Mathieu identified Levy as a man who had frequently visited her husband's store at Deep Creek, and exclaimed when she saw him in the court, "Oh, Levy, Levy, how could you be such a villain?"

The police ascertained that Sullivan had sold to the banks in Nelson gold to the value of £106 7s. 6d. Kelly had sold gold to the value of £76 and a few shillings, and Levy had sold another lot. These, with three nuggets which were sold together for £5 3s. 4d., made a total of about £230 disposed of by the robbers since the murders had been committed. It was, of course, impossible to say what proportion had been stolen from each of the four victims, or whether the whole of it had been taken from them.

George Jervis, a publican at Canvas Town, said that he gave the prisoners permission to camp in an unoccupied hut not far from his hotel. When they were leaving Burgess said "Good-bye, old boy; we're going away from this —— country. There's nothing to be done here." The publican had no suspicion as to the characters of the men, but thought that they had not been very lucky recently.

Old Jamie left the diggings a short time before, and crossed the river. The old man was well-known in the district. His body was discovered by George James Baker, of Nelson, one of the volunteers who accompanied Sergeant Major Shallcross and the police who started out to search for the missing men when the murders were first reported. There was some freshly-turned up earth near a fern root which attracted Mr. Baker's attention.

Chapter XXVI

A log had been rolled across the place, and on this being rolled aside and the earth scraped away, a portion of the clothing was seen. The body was buried in a shallow hole, lying on its back, and only just covered with loose earth. The trousers had been torn off, but the other clothing remained.

The trial lasted for three days, Kelly, Levy, and Burgess being found guilty and sentenced to death on September 17th, 1866. Sullivan was tried separately on the 19th for the murder of Old Jamie, and a verdict of guilty was recorded against him. He, however, received a pardon in accordance with the terms of the Governor's proclamation.

Felix Mathieu was well-known in Australia. He was a native of Marseilles, about forty years of age at the time of his death, and had been in the colonies about twelve years. On his first arrival he was employed as barman at the Union Hotel, Beechworth, after which he opened a baker's shop at Spring Creek. When the rush took place to the Snowy River in New South Wales he went there and opened a store, and later on he kept a store at the Lambing Flat (Burrangong) and another at the Lachlan (Forbes).

From there he went to the west coast, New Zealand, where he met his death as recorded.

Levy had been tried at Castlemaine, Victoria, about six years before, on the charge of murdering a woman with whom he was living, but was acquitted for want of confirmatory evidence.

Sullivan had been transported to Van Diemen's Land, from whence he went to Victoria in 1853. He opened a butcher's shop at Ironbark Gully, Bendigo, where he was well known. He removed and opened the Halfway Inn on the road between Bendigo and Inglewood. At the time that he sailed to New Zealand he left his wife in charge of a store at Mount Korong and sold an allotment of land at Wedderburn to raise money to pay for his trip. He was certainly not driven to crime through want or poverty, and if, as he said, he was unlucky on the New Zealand diggings, he could without much difficulty or delay have obtained remittances from Victoria which would at least have been sufficient to, enable him to return home.

After his companions in crime had been executed, Sullivan was kept in gaol for some months, popular feeling being so strong that it was deemed inexpedient to release him at once. It was during this time that he made some further revelations about his late companions. Soon after he joined Burgess, Kelly, and Levy, he said he saw a young man sitting propped up against the butt of a tree. He was dead. Sullivan asked whether the body was to be buried?' Kelly replied "No, better leave it where it is. It will make people think he died from exhaustion. I've put many a man away like that." It was supposed that he referred to the wild times immediately following the discovery of gold in Victoria. The young man in question had been strangled, and the robbers had taken from his body a silver watch, a gold chain, a compass, a few shillings in money, and a deposit receipt for £32, which they burned, to prevent it from turning up in evidence against them.

Soon after his release he returned to Victoria, but was recognised at Bendigo and other places and boycotted. People refused to sell him food or to have any dealings with him whatever. The Government was urged to put the Criminals' Influx Prevention Act (18 Vict., No. 3) in force against him, but his case did not come under the provisions of that Act, as he had not been sentenced to penal servitude since his departure from Victoria. He drifted from town to town, and finally made his way to Sydney, from whence, it was said, he went to South America and was lost to sight.

The story of bushranging in New Zealand further illustrates the intimate relationship between the colonies to which I have already referred. Garrett, the first New Zealand bushranger, was an old Victorian criminal, and the Maungapatau murderers, with whom the record terminates, also went to the islands from the same colony, some of them, if not all, having been previously transported from Great Britain to Van Diemen's Land.

It may be advisable here, perhaps, to say a few words with regard to Sullivan's evidence. The point in it to which I wish to draw the attention of the reader is the partial exculpation of himself. Substantially, the confession was no doubt correct, but we have only Sullivan's own word to prove that the murders were committed by his companions and that he himself only shot a horse. We notice a similar effort on the part of Daniel Charters and others who have turned Queen's evidence to minimise the share they took in the outrages with which they were charged. Charters, indeed, went rather further than the majority of informers and stated that he was sent away to take care of the horses while the escort was robbed, because he was too frightened to "risk his —— skin." He thus openly admitted his cowardice in order apparently to justify himself, to himself, for turning informer. Of course, his evidence may have been true in this particular, but the constancy of this principle in informers generally of claiming that they merely took a very secondary share in the crimes which they are the means of bringing home to their fellows, tends to raise a suspicion that they do, as a rule, consciously or unconsciously, endeavour to excuse themselves to the public, and perhaps also to themselves, as a sort of relief perhaps to their own conscience, for turning informer. Their action in this respect contrasts strongly with that of men like Pierce, the cannibal, or John Lynch, in making confessions after they have been convicted. In these and other cases which might be cited the condemned man appears to be anxious to let the public know how very bad their actions have been. I do not say that they exaggerate their crimes, but merely that they are particular that even the smallest facts shall be made public. At the same time, they endeavour to satisfy their own consciences in some way or other for what they have done. Pierce, for instance, excused himself by saying that he must either have killed and eaten his companions or starved, although this is not borne out by the facts as far as they are known of his last act of cannibalism. Lynch, on the other hand, endeavoured to prove that he was the instrument of divine vengeance, that he had a mission. But, whatever the excuse put forward may be, the fact remains that they take care that their crimes shall be known to the very smallest particulars. This point is I think worthy of the investigation of the criminologist.

Twenty-seven

Bushranging in Queensland; Some Bushrangers from Over the Southern Border; A Bogus Ben Halt; The Wild Scotchman: Queensland's Only Bushranger; A Man of Many Aliases; He goes to Fight a Duel with Sir Frederick Pottinger; He Escapes from the Steamer; Recaptured and Tried.

There was still another of the Australian colonies which was affected by the evil influence of the bushranging mania inaugurated by Frank Gardiner. This colony was Queensland. In May, 1864, Harry, the mailman, was travelling along the road between Bodumba and Leyburn, when he was stopped by an old man and a boy, one of whom asked him, civilly enough, which was the road to Warwick. Harry, very obligingly, pulled up to tell them where to turn off, when the old man drew a pistol and ordered him to dismount. Harry protested against this outrage, and said he was a Government employee, but this only produced a reiteration of the order with a threat to blow out his brains if he did not obey. He then dismounted, and was tied very tightly, the robbers paying no attention whatever to his complaints that the rope was cutting his wrists. The robbers went through the bags, which they left on the ground, and, when they had finished, the old man mounted Harry's horse, while the boy climbed on to the pack-horse, and rode away. Harry, who was left lying on the ground, rolled himself over and over to where there were some jagged rocks by the side of the road. Selecting the one with the sharpest edge, he wriggled about until he got the rope across it, and then moved his body backwards and forwards until the strands of the rope which bound his hands together behind his back parted. Having freed his hands, he soon untied the rope round his legs and walked to Goondiwindi, where he reported the robbery to the police. The Brisbane Courier in reporting this robbery said it was the first case of bushranging that had taken place in Queensland, and hoped that that colony was not about to have its peace disturbed as that of the southern colonies had recently been by bushrangers. The Courier, of course, did not consider the convicts who escaped into the bush when Moreton Bay was a penal settlement as bushrangers in the modern acceptation of the term. Some of the more notorious of these have already been dealt with in Chapter xv, but if we accept the new meaning of the term "bushranger," the Courier was, no doubt, correct in its assertion that this was the first case that had occurred in the colony. Of course a rumour was raised that the perpetrator was Gilbert and some of his gang, but the description given of the robbers shows that this rumour was absurd.

About a month later a bushranger named Wright stuck up and robbed a number of people in the Rockhampton district. He was speedily followed by the police and some black trackers, and was shot, early in July, at Wipend, on the Mackenzie River, a few miles off of the Peak Downs Road. He was riding a racehorse which he had stolen from Mr. Cranston, a squatter of that district.

In September a man entered the bar of the Shearers' Arms Inn at Knebsworth, and cried out "Bail up! I'm Ben Hall!" The proprietor, Mr. Philip Hardy, took a revolver out of a drawer under the counter. The bushranger, seeing him do this, fired, and missed. Mr. Hardy returned the fire, and wounded the bushranger. The landlord ran round from behind the bar, collared his assailant, and after a struggle thrust him into a back room. Having locked the door and made his prisoner secure, as he thought, Mr. Hardy ran to the police station to report. He returned in a few minutes accompanied by a constable, but the bird had flown. The window of the room in which he had been shut was wide open, so that the bushranger had merely to step out and walk away. It is probable therefore that he was making his way to the bush at the back of the house almost as soon as the door was locked. He lost his horse, however, as the animal was hitched to the verandah post in front, and was taken away by the constable.

One or two other cases occurred, but they were all of a paltry character, until the Celtic blood of Alpin Macpherson, alias John Bruce, alias Mar, alias Kerr, alias Scotia or Scotchie, generally known as the Wild Scotchman, was stirred to emulate the heroic deeds of Hall, Gilbert and Co. Macpherson was born in Scotland and was taken to Queensland when very young by his father. The elder Macpherson worked for Mr. McConnell at Cressbrook and was generally respected by those who knew him. His son Alpin was sent to school in the town and was a favourite with his teachers on account of his diligence. When old enough he was apprenticed to Mr. Petrie, a stonemason in Brisbane, and was again well-liked by his master and the members of his family. Alpin was a diligent reader and a fluent speaker. He became a prominent member of the Debating Class in the Brisbane Mechanics' School of Arts. When Mr. Lilley, afterwards Attorney-General, was attacked at a political meeting at the Valley, with mud, over-ripe tomatoes, and other missiles, on account of his Militia Bill, which was strongly opposed, young Macpherson defended him bravely, receiving some bruises. Soon afterwards, without any apparent reason, he ran away from his apprenticeship and took to the roads. He began his bushranging career by sticking up Wills's Hotel on the Houghton River, after the manner popular with the Hall and Gilbert gang. From thence he went to New South Wales to "fight a duel with Sir Frederick Pottinger," the head of the police force in that colony. This determination he announced himself. The records of this portion of his career are somewhat obscure. It is known that he did exchange shots with Sir Frederick Pottinger and some troopers, and that he received a slight wound, but it is doubtful whether he ever-joined Hall and Gilbert, and committed robberies in their company, as he said he did. However, he did not remain in New South Wales very long. He returned to Queensland and robbed the mails, stuck up travellers, stole racehorses, and otherwise endeavoured to work up to the standard ideal of the real Australian bushranger.

He had been thus employed for some months when Mr. W. Nott, manager of the Manduran station, saw him in a paddock belonging to the station, and recognised him. Believing that he was there with the intention of stealing some of the horses, Mr. Nott hastily collected a party and started in pursuit. The party consisted of Messrs. Nott, Curry, Gadsden, and J. Walsh. They came in sight of their quarry about five miles away, as he was travelling along the Port Curtis Road. He was riding slowly when first seen, but, on observing the pursuers closing upon him, Macpherson let go his packhorse, wheeled off the road, and galloped down the side of a steep range. His pursuers followed. When he reached the level ground at

Chapter XXVII

the foot of the range, the Wild Scotchman pulled up, and began to unstrap the double-barrelled gun which he carried across the pommel of his saddle. Before he could succeed, however, Mr. Nott came close up and cried "Put up your hands or I'll fire." The rifle barrel was only a few feet away, and as the other men came up at once with arms ready for use, the Wild Scotchman yielded. "All right," he said, "I give up." "I knew you were not policemen," he said later, "by the way you came down that ridge, but you wouldn't have caught me if my horse had not been done up." They took away his arms, and then returned to the station, two of the captors riding with the bushranger between them, while the other two rode close behind. In the pack on the horse which he abandoned was found a beautifully-fitted case of surgical instruments, with lint and other necessaries for treating wounds. He also carried a pocket compass, an American axe, and some other useful articles. The axe was required for cutting fences or for making temporary stockyards to catch horses in.

A warrant had been issued for his arrest for his attack on Sir Frederick Pottinger and the police in New South Wales, and the Wild Scotchman was therefore extradited to stand his trial in New South Wales on a charge of shooting with intent to do grievous bodily harm. His arrival in Sydney was coincident with the resignation of that officer as already related. Sir Frederick, however, was summoned to appear against him, and it was on his journey to Sydney for this purpose that the accident happened which put an end to Sir Frederick's life and the prosecution against the Wild Scotchman at the same time.

The Wild Scotchman was returned to Queensland in charge of the police. He was sent from Brisbane to Port Denison, and was there committed for trial and remanded to Rockhampton, the nearest assize town, for that purpose. He was shipped on board the steamer Diamantina in charge of Constable Maher. He was accommodated with leg irons, his hands being so small that he could easily slip them through any ordinary handcuffs. In fact he boasted freely that the handcuffs to hold him "had not yet been made." When the steamer reached Mackay he was seated reading near the galley, but he had behaved so quietly all through the earlier part of the passage that the constable did not think it necessary to disturb him by taking him below. There was, of course, the usual bustle while the steamer was at the wharf, and Constable Maher appears to have lost sight of his prisoner, and did not miss him until the vessel had been an hour at sea. Then a search was instituted, but no Wild Scotchman could be found, and as the Maryborough Chronicle remarked, "Constable Maher reached Rockhampton minus his prisoner."

How he got ashore and removed his leg-irons was a mystery which was not solved for some time. However, his escape did not profit him much. He went to a paddock on the Kolongo station with the intention of stealing a horse to enable him to stick up the mail coach, and "make a rise." But a party was organised by Mr. Hall, and he was recaptured without attaining his purpose. This time greater care was exercised by the police to whom he was handed over, and he reached Rockhampton, where he was tried on several charges of highway robbery and sentenced to twenty years' penal servitude.

There can be no doubt that young Macpherson, like many other high-spirited young men, was led away by the glamour which gathered round the bushrangers Hall, Gilbert, and their young associates; and which appears to have appealed so strongly to the youth of certain temperaments as to blind them to the enormity of the crimes committed by these bushrangers. The quiet bush life in Australia afforded them no escape valve by which their desire for excitement might be worked off. They did not pause to realise that their fight against society was hopeless from the beginning, and that in taking to the bush they were setting themselves, almost single handed, against the whole force of public opinion in the colony. Had they lived in Europe they might, perhaps, have enlisted in the army and thus been able to do something to satisfy their cravings for notoriety and adventure in a legitimate way. In Australia, however, there was no standing army, and even if there had been there was nothing for it to do in the colonies, and no chance of its ever being employed outside, where hard blows were to be struck and glory won. It may be true that even soldiers do not always find congenial work for them to do, and that many of them have lived very humdrum lives, but there is always the hope that they may be called on to defend their country, or to fight for its aggrandisement, and this hope

CHAPTER XXVII

is sufficient to induce them to enlist, when they are brought under the control of the disciplinarian and kept out of mischief until their boyish enthusiasm subsides and they are old enough to enter into the business of life. However, Queensland's "only bushranger," the Wild Scotchman, was captured after a brief but exciting career of about eighteen months, and the colony has not been troubled by bushrangers since.

Twenty-eight

Captain Moonlite; The "Reverend Gentleman" Robs the Bank, and Nearly Makes his Escape; He Breaks out of Ballarat Gaol; He Becomes a Reformed Character; He Sticks Up Wantabadgery Station; A Desperate Battle with the Police; Moonlite is Captured; His Young Companions in Crime; Sentenced to Death; The Wild Horse Hunters Turn Bushrangers; An Abortive Attempt to Rob a Bank.

From about June, 1872, to April, 1878, or nearly six years, Australia was free from bushrangers. With the exception of the two or three robberies in the far west of New South Wales, so far west as to be almost out of the colony, the roads were safe; travellers journeyed in all directions without fear of molestation; and the public, as well as the authorities, began to congratulate themselves once more on having at length definitely stamped out the scourge of bushranging. Since the shooting of Thunderbolt and the capture of Power, there had been no sign of a recrudescence of the crime, and bushranging was beginning to be referred to as belonging to a past age. But this peaceful condition of the country was not always to continue. The old leaven of convictism so frequently referred to, had not as yet been so completely eliminated as the public and the authorities hoped and believed. Reports began to spread about in 1878 that robberies had been committed in the neighbourhood where Power had so long set the police at defiance, and shortly afterwards the name of Ned Kelly began to be associated with them. Ned Kelly is still spoken of as the last of the bushrangers, and as his death closes the story, it may be as well to deal with some other bushrangers who finished their careers before "the gentleman of the Strathbogie Ranges."

The most remarkable of these was George Scott, alias Captain Moonlite. His story belongs partly to the former era, but I have reserved it in order to make it more complete than would have been possible had it been divided. Scott was born in the North of Ireland, and emigrated to Victoria. He went to the diggings at a time when agents from New Zealand were endeavouring to raise a corps in Victoria for service against the Maoris.

He enlisted and fought through the war in 1861-65, being wounded in the leg. On his return to Victoria he showed a strong desire to join the Church, and as he was well educated and a good speaker he was appointed lay reader at Bacchus Marsh, with a view to his being ordained a minister of the Church of England, when the Bishop of Melbourne should consider him worthy of the charge. His duties as lay reader were to travel round the settlement, to read prayers and conduct services, his head quarters being in the town at Mount Egerton. His chief friends here were the manager of the Union Bank and the schoolmaster. He soon came to be respected and liked in the district. One night, however, a masked man walked into the living apartments connected with the bank and ordered the manager, who was alone, to bail up. The manager recognised the voice and asked him whether he thought this a suitable practical joke for a clergyman. Scott replied that he would soon find it was no joke. He threatened to shoot the manager unless he surrendered and did as he was ordered. He then gagged the manager, took him across the street to the school-house, and compelled him to sign the following statement:—"Captain Moonlite has stuck me up and robbed the bank."

There was no one at the school-house, Scott having apparently timed his visit when he knew the school would be empty. Leaving the paper on the desk in the school-house, Scott took the manager back to the bank, tied him hand and foot, and then took about £1000 worth in notes and coin from the safe. The schoolmaster found the paper lying on the desk when he went to open the school next morning, and at first did not know what to make of it. He handed it to the police, who, on going to the bank, found the manager gagged and tied. Having heard his story the police considered it absurd, and arrested the manager and schoolmaster as having been jointly concerned in the crime. The idea of charging the minister, as Scott was generally called, appeared to be preposterous, the more especially as Scott was very active in trying to find incriminating evidence against his quondam friends. Being intimately acquainted with the lives led by the two men, he was able to supply the police with several facts, true or false, which were considered strong circumstantial proofs of their guilt. They were committed for trial, Scott being bound over as a witness against them. He did not wait for the trial, however, but went to Sydney, where he put up at one of the leading hotels and spent money lavishly. He represented himself as a wealthy visitor to the colonies travelling for pleasure, and spoke of his intention to visit some of the South Sea Islands. For this purpose he purchased a yacht, for which he paid partly in cash and partly by a cheque for £150. This cheque was returned by the bank on which it was drawn as valueless, and the man who had sold him the yacht immediately communicated with the police. Scott had already set sail, but the police followed him in a steam launch and caught him just outside the Heads. He was brought back and tried for fraud and was sent to gaol for eighteen months.

Even the flight of Scott from Mount Egerton did not at first convince the police and others of his guilt in connection with the bank robbery, but without his evidence the case against the bank manager and the schoolmaster was so weak that it broke down, and they were discharged. Later on a warrant was issued for the arrest of Scott, alias Captain Moonlite, but he was then in gaol in New South Wales. On his release he was rearrested, and extradited to Victoria to be tried for the bank robbery. He was taken to Ballarat, and lodged in the newly-built gaol, a most substantial structure of blue stone (basalt). The building stands in a large courtyard, surrounded by a wall twenty-five feet high, also constructed of basalt. Looked at from the outside it appears to be one of the most hopeless places for a prisoner to escape from imaginable, but Scott had been educated as an engineer, and therefore what might have been impossible for another man was not so for him. There was a wooden partition which divided one cell into two. Scott was imprisoned awaiting trial in one portion of the cell, and a man named Dermoodie in the other portion. Scott cut through this partition, and with the aid of Dermoodie contrived to take the lock off the door. The two men walked into the corridor and hid in a dark corner until the warder came round, when Scott sprang on him, grasped him by the throat, and with the assistance of Dermoodie gagged and tied him. Scott then took the keys, and having shut the warder into the cell, with the door closed, so that any other warder in passing it would not notice that it had been opened, walked down the passage. With the keys he opened four more cells and liberated the prisoners in them. He made them take the

Chapter XXVIII

blankets from their beds and follow him, after carefully closing the doors again. He opened the door leading into the great yard and went to a dark corner under the wall where he tore the blankets into strips and tied them together to form a rope. Scott then stood up against the wall. One of the other men climbed up and stood on his shoulders, another climbed up and stood on his, and so on until the last, Dermoodie, was able to take the rope and sit on the wall. With the aid of the rope each man was enabled to go up in turn to where Dermoodie was, and was then lowered down on the other side. Here they stood on each others' shoulders as before, to enable Dermoodie to climb down, then the others followed in turn, and they were free. The south-eastern corner of the gaol wall stands near the edge of the hill where the ground slopes sharply down to Golden Gully. The six men went down the slope to a safe distance, and then Scott said they must part, as they would have a better chance of getting away separately than if they all kept together. The four men liberated by Scott to help him over the wall were speedily caught, some in Ballarat and the others not far away, but as they were not bushrangers we have nothing further to do with them. Scott and Dermoodie went away together and slept in the bush. Scott said they must have money, and proposed to rob a bank, which he said could be easily done, but Dermoodie said he had only been arrested for a small offence, and he had made his case bad enough by escaping. He did not wish to make it worse. Scott called him a coward, a contemptible cur, and said he should never leave that spot alive. He gave him five minutes to say his prayers. He was in a terrible rage, but before the five minutes were over he said that Dermoodie was not worth killing, gave him a few kicks and blows, and ordered him out of his sight, an order which was quickly obeyed. Dermoodie went back to Ballarat and was recaptured a day or two after his escape, while Scott was found about a week later in a hut near Bendigo. He was tried, and was sentenced to ten years' imprisonment for the bank robbery, and to one years' imprisonment in irons for breaking gaol.

Scott behaved in the most exemplary manner while he was in Pentridge, and contrived to convince both the chaplain and the gaol authorities that he intended to live "on the square" for the future. He was allowed all the remission possible under the rules for good conduct, and was released in

March, 1879. He was a forcible and fluent speaker, and he made a living by open-air lecturing in Melbourne on prison discipline and other subjects. About this time the Kelly gang was at the zenith of its career, when suddenly Scott disappeared from his usual haunts in Melbourne. Probably his imagination was stirred by the reports current about the Kellys; perhaps he was prompted by jealousy of their doings; or, perhaps, by a sudden desire for notoriety. However this may be, he was gone.

On Saturday, November 15th, 1879, at about three p.m., six armed men rode up to Mr. C. F. J. Macdonald's station at Wantabadgery, on the Murrumbidgee River, New South Wales, and bailed up all the men at work there. Nineteen men were collected from various places about the station and marched into the dining-room of Mr. Macdonald's house. Mr. Miles was then ordered to unlock the door of the store, and the robbers selected a quantity of clothing and other goods which they required or fancied. They were engaged in packing these on some spare horses when Mr. Weir, of Eurongilly, and a schoolmaster rode up, and were called on to bail up. The schoolmaster refused, and one of the bushrangers loudly declared that he would shoot him. Hearing the altercation, the leader of the gang came out of the store, seized the schoolmaster by the leg, and dragged him from the horse, saying at the same time, "You —— old fool, get down and do as you're told. I'm Moonlite." He pushed the schoolmaster along, and forced him to go into the dining-room where the other men were sitting.

Towards evening Mr. Baynes, the manager of the station, returned from a back station, and was bailed up and conducted to the dining-room. The women had been told that they would not be interfered with, and were ordered to cook dinner. When it was ready it was served in the dining-room, where all partook of the food, the bushrangers sitting down in turn, while two remained on guard. After the meal some grog, obtained from the station store, was served round, and Mr. Macdonald was permitted to retire to bed. The others remained at the table all night, the bushrangers taking it in turn to sleep like the others with their heads on the table.

Breakfast on the following (Sunday) morning was taken as supper had been on the previous evening. During the meal Mr. Baynes said to one of the young bushrangers who was seated near him, "This is bad work."

Chapter XXVIII

Moonlite, who was sitting on the other side of the large table, heard him and jumped up. He charged Mr. Baynes with trying to tamper with his men, and swore that he would shoot him. He seemed to be in a paroxysm of rage, and flourished his revolver about in a dangerous manner. The women, however, clustered round, assuring him that Mr. Baynes did not mean any harm, and begging him to spare him. In a few minutes Scott's rage had evaporated, and he sat down again and went on with his meal apparently oblivious of Mr. Baynes's presence. During the morning several men came to the station, and were bailed up and marched into the dining-room. One of these men was leading a young filly which had only recently been broken in. Scott admired her very much and said, "She'll just suit me." He led her round and then tried to mount her, but she was very skittish and would not let him. This threw him into a passion and he became violent, thus frightening the filly and making her more ungovernable. At length he swore that if she did not stand still he would shoot her, and as she continued to rear and try to get away he drew his revolver and sent a bullet through her head. When his fit of passion had passed off, Moonlite said he was sorry he had killed the mare, but she should have stood still when he told her. He then ordered Lindon, the groom, to put the horses into the buggy, and, taking Mr. Alexander Macdonald as a hostage, drove to the house of the superintendent of the station, Mr. Reid. Here he obtained a Whitworth rifle and some ammunition. He then forced Mr. and Mrs. Reid to mount the buggy, and drove away to Paterson's Australian Arms Hotel, which he stuck up, taking two shot guns and a revolver. He ordered Mr. and Mrs. Paterson to walk to the station, and, to ensure obedience, put their two little children into the buggy and drove away. On the return journey to the station he stuck up seven more men, and compelled them to march in front of the buggy to the station, and go into the dining-room.

As Moonlite jumped down from the buggy he caught sight of Mr. Baynes standing on the verandah. He rushed across to him, and charged him with attempting to corrupt his men. He ordered Mr. Baynes to be pinioned with a fishing line, and had him lifted into the buggy, saying "I'll drive under that tree and you can tie the rope to the limb, and we'll leave this gentlemen hanging there." A rope was tied round Mr. Baynes's neck ready, but the women, seeing these preparations for a tragedy, again gathered round Moonlite and begged him to let Mr. Baynes go. At first he refused, saying "The gentleman does not deserve it," but gradually he became less violent, and finally ordered Baynes to be untied. Then he called a muster of all the men in the dining-room and counted thirty-five.

After having given orders as to the custody of his prisoners, Moonlite mounted a horse and rode round, going for some distance along the road on each side of the homestead. He met a man coming from the adjoining station, Eurongilly, where he worked. "Hulloa," cried Moonlite, "where are you going with that pistol?" "To fight the bushrangers," replied the man. "By G——," exclaimed Scott, "you've found them, here we are. Hand over that revolver and we'll try you for unlawfully carrying firearms." The man was compelled to obey, and was taken into the dining-room. Moonlite took his seat as judge, having appointed two of his mates and two of the station hands as jury, and the trial was carried out as nearly in the orthodox manner as circumstances would permit. The charge was read by the clerk, witnesses were heard and cross-examined; the judge summed up, and the verdict returned was "Not guilty." Scott turned to the prisoner and said, "You may think yourself —— lucky. If the jury had found you guilty, I'd have given you five minutes to live." He then ordered the prisoner to be discharged, and said it was dinner time.

In the afternoon the vigilance of the bushrangers relaxed so far that Alexander Macdonald contrived to make his escape. He got a horse and rode to Wagga Wagga, twenty-five miles away. He informed the police of what had taken place, and Constables Howe, Hedley, Williamson, and Johns saddled their horses and started back with him to Wantabadgery, where they arrived at four a.m. on Monday morning. The robbers were still in possession, and the police hoped to find them unprepared, but this was not the case, and the police retreated to Mr. James Beveridge's station, Tarrandera Park, where they obtained fresh horses. By this time five more troopers had arrived from Gundagai, sixty-five miles away, and the police decided that they were strong enough to begin the attack. The people who had been detained in the dining-room speedily made their escape and collected on a ridge a short distance from the scene of battle, other persons, attracted by the sound of the firing, rode up from the stations round until

Chapter XXVIII

some three hundred spectators of the fight were collected on the ridge, but they left the police to do the fighting unaided. Constable Bowen, who had already shot a bushranger in the Thunderbolt rising, was the first to make any impression, and a great cheer went up as one of Moonlite's men was seen to fall. The bushrangers went into the house, and the police took shelter in a hut some distance away. They advanced very cautiously, and Constable Bowen shot a second man, falling wounded himself almost at the same time. Some time afterwards Constable Carroll, who had crept close up to the verandah, in spite of the heavy fusilade which was kept up, shot a third bushranger, and soon after the other three came out and surrendered. Moonlite asked Mr. Wise to go for a doctor to attend to Nesbit, saying "Poor fellow! He was shot trying to save me."

James Nesbit, alias Lyons, who was shot dead, was born in Melbourne and was twenty-three years of age. Augustus or Gus Wernicke (also from Melbourne), aged nineteen, died a few days after the battle. Graham Bennett, also born in Victoria, was twenty years of age. He was wounded in the arm and recovered. Thomas Williams, alias Jones, nineteen years old, was born in Ballarat, Victoria. Thomas Rogan was born at Hay, New South Wales, but had been living for some years in Melbourne, where he became acquainted with Scott. Scott, the leader, was thirty-seven years of age.

Constable Bowen died of his wound on the Sunday following the fight, and the prisoners were tried on the charge of murdering him. The trial took place at Darlinghurst Court House, Sydney, and lasted for four days. A verdict of guilty was returned, but the jury recommended Rogan, Bennett, and Williams to mercy on account of their youth and the belief that they had been led into crime by Scott. In consequence of this the sentences on Bennett and Williams were commuted to imprisonment for life, but although some pressure was brought to bear on the Governor, Lord Augustus Loftus, the executive declined to extend mercy to Rogan. He and Scott were therefore hung in Darlinghurst gaol.

One of the witnesses at the trial, named Ah Goon, said that he had been robbed of a gold watch and chain valued at £25. When taking these and some money from him, Scott said he was "a —— Chinaman who took the bread out of the mouths of honest workers." It is worthy of note also that on the second day of the trial of the prisoners at Darlinghurst, the Melbourne Argus reported that James P. Nesbitt, father of the recently killed bushranger, was charged at the City Police Court, Melbourne, with having thrashed and abused his wife, the mother of the bushranger. He was ordered to be bound over to keep the peace for six months under a penalty of £25, and as the money was not forthcoming, he was sent to gaol.

The gallantry of the police in breaking up this gang of bushrangers at so early a stage in its career was duly recognised. The police authorities voted a reward of £100 to Constable Carroll, £75 to Constable Curran, and £50 each to the other constables engaged in the fight. A public monument was erected to Constable Bowen, and a pension was settled on his wife, while the Government undertook the care and education of his children. The police were paraded in Sydney; the Inspector General, Mr. E. Fosbery, read a letter from the Colonial Secretary (the late Sir Henry Parkes) publicly thanking the police constables for their services. After this ceremony, the purses containing the rewards were presented and acknowledged.

It is impossible to divide the bushranging of this epoch so as to keep the story of the different colonies concerned separate as I have in the previous epochs, because both the Moonlite and the Kelly gang operated in both Victoria and New South Wales. The small number of bushrangers who worked separately from these gangs are not worth dividing and may be dealt with here.

In February, 1879, three young men who had been engaged in running in and capturing warrigal horses on the lower Murrumbidgee, thought, perhaps, that that employment was less profitable than bushranging, and took to the roads. Their names were Thomas Gorman (twenty-one), Charles Jones (twenty), and William Kaye (nineteen). They bailed up a few travellers on the road between Balranald and Ivanhoe, and were then joined by William Hobbs, otherwise known as Hoppy Bill, because he had a crooked leg and arm. Hobbs had been employed as cook at the Hatfield sheep station, and was about thirty years of age. On the 21st they stuck up Mr. Grainger's store at Hatfield, about sixty miles north of Balranald, and stole £50 worth of clothing and other goods, two horses, with saddles and bridles. On the following day they stopped a hawker, saying "Bail up.

Chapter XXVIII

We're the Kellys," and took £40 worth of goods and jewellery from his waggon. On the 23rd they arrived at Till Till station, and bailed up twenty-five persons there. Mrs. Crombie, wife of the manager, was very much frightened at first, but they soothed her by telling her that they "wouldn't hurt any one." They took six horses, a quantity of ammunition, and some other articles from the store. When they left they said that they intended to stick up Woolpagerie station.

In the meantime Mr. John Thomas Day, storeman at Grainger's, travelled as fast as his horse could go to Moulamein, and informed the police of the sticking up of the store. He was sworn in as a special constable, and accompanied by troopers Beresford and Powers and a black tracker, started in pursuit. They rode one hundred and eighty miles between nine a.m. on Sunday and seven p.m. on Monday, changing horses at Clare, where they came on the tracks of the bushrangers. On their arrival at Kilferra Mr. Casey supplied them with remounts, and joined in the chase. The tracks led down to the Four Mile Dam, where the pursuers came on the bushrangers in camp preparing their supper. As they went forward the bushrangers came to meet them, crying out, "Bail up." The police replied, "Surrender in the Queen's name." Both parties fired, and Constable Powers fell wounded in the shoulder. The bushrangers then threw down their arms and surrendered. They were tried on April 19th for shooting with intent to murder, and were found guilty. When asked if they had anything to urge why sentence of death should not be passed on them, Hobbs was the only one who spoke, and he said, "God forgive me if I have to die." Sentences of death were pronounced, but these were subsequently commuted to imprisonment for life.

On Wednesday, November 5th, 1879, an attempt was made to stick up the Bank of Australasia at Moe in the Gippsland district of Victoria. At first it was supposed that the Kellys had paid a visit to this part of the colony. The bank was a wooden building, situated about fifty yards from the Moe railway station, and nearly opposite the Selector's Arms Hotel. The bank closed at the usual time and nothing occurred until about nine o'clock p.m. At that time Mr. Hector Munro, the manager, was sitting in his parlour behind the bank chamber reading. He was alone in the house, his wife having gone up the main street to the grocer's shop. There was a knock at the door, and on Mr. Munro opening it, a man with a white cap over his head, with holes to look through cut in it, tried to force his way in. Munro endeavoured to slam the door to, but the white cap individual had got his foot inside and managed to push his way in. "Who are you? What do you want?" cried Munro, but no answer was returned. Munro still held the man and endeavoured to drag him out of the house. The white cap drew a pistol, but Munro clutched him by the arm, and in the struggle the pistol went off without doing any damage, except to the wall. Then another white-capped man appeared and struck Munro on the head. At the same time several people rushed over from the hotel to ascertain what the shooting was about, and the two would-be robbers bolted. Sergeant Irwin and two constables, with Dr. Archibald Macdonald and several other civilians, followed the bushrangers. They picked up two felt hats and a serge mask in the yard, not far from the back door of the bank. It was, however, too dark to do anything further that night, but at daylight the tracks were carefully followed, and shortly before six a.m. Constable Beck and Dr. Macdonald found two men sitting on the Trafalgar railway platform. The doctor covered them with his rifle while the constable handcuffed them. The men said that the constable was making a great mistake, as they were unacquainted with each other, having arrived there by different routes. They were waiting for the train from Melbourne to go further up country to look for work. Constable Beck replied, "Oh, that's all right; I'll stand the racket. What's your names?" As they hesitated, he continued, "Now, no humbug; I know you. You don't live far away, and if you give false names you'll soon be bowled out." They then admitted that they were brothers, and that their names were Robert and James Shanks. Their ages were twenty-three and twenty-one years respectively. Two revolvers were found in their carpet bags, and the white caps were picked up not far from the platform. They were convicted of having attempted to rob the bank, and assaulted the manager.

Twenty-nine

The Kelly Gang; Horse-stealing, a Great Industry of the District; Faking the Brands; Assault on Constable Fitzpatrick; The Bush Telegraphs; Murder of Sergeant Kennedy and Constables Scanlan and Lonergan; Sticking up of the Faithfull Creek Station Robbery of the National Bank at Euroa; A Big Haul.

In the early years of Australian settlement bushranging was one of the normal conditions in the colonies, and therefore attracted little notice. Even the exploits of such heroes of the roads as Mike Howe, Brady, the Jewboy, and Jackey Jackey are very briefly related in the Press, and, with the exception of the first-named, about whom Mr. James Bonwick has written a romance, very little has been heard of them since the age in which they lived. In the next epoch the doings of the bushrangers were dwarfed in the public estimation by the sensational reports of the gold finds, and although in consequence of the growth of population and the great increase in the number of newspapers their actions received a wider publicity than those of their predecessors the accounts of them are still meagre. The sensational inauguration of the next era by the Gardiner gang—the sticking up and robbing of the Government Gold Escort—attracted wider notice to the bushrangers of that epoch, and some notice of them appears even in the English Press. But the notoriety of even the most celebrated of the bushrangers of that epoch was nothing as compared with that of the Kelly gang, about whom more columns of newspaper matter have been printed than of all the bushrangers together in the earlier epochs. Several histories of the Kelly gang have also been published, the best known, perhaps, being those of Mr. Superintendent Hare, who was for a time in charge of the police who were trying to capture the bushrangers, and Mr. John McWhirter, the reporter of the Melbourne Age, who accompanied the police in their final and successful effort to suppress the gang. Mr. McWhirter's "History" is largely compiled from the reports which had appeared in the Age, and Mr. Hare is also largely indebted to the same source. The Kellys have also inspired more than one drama, although the subject is not a favourite one with moralists, and the representation of bushranging dramas has not met with favour from a large section of the community. In this connection we may note the influence of modern science. The stage of the performances of the earlier bushrangers was confined to their own locality. They were rarely heard of outside the colony in which they appeared. In the next stage the telegraph carried news of their performances all over Australia, and occasionally a stray newspaper paragraph was quoted in England. With the Kellys, however, it was different. Notices of their exploits were even sent across the ocean by cable, and the British public naturally desired to hear more of these daring robbers, and therefore extracts from the newspapers of Australia appeared more frequently in the English Press than at any former epoch. The consequence is that we can reconstruct the history of the Kellys more easily than that of any other bushranging family. The father of Ned Kelly was transported from Ireland. The maiden name of his wife was Ellen Quinn. The eldest son, Ned, was born at Wallan Wallan in 1854. Jim was born in 1856, and Dan in 1861. There were besides four daughters — namely, Mrs. Gunn, Mrs. Skillian, and Kate and Grace Kelly. In 1871, the second son, James, then about fifteen years of age, was sentenced to five years' imprisonment on two charges of horse-stealing. On his discharge in 1876 he went to New South Wales and stuck up a number of people. He was captured almost immediately, and sent to gaol for ten years. Edward, commonly known as Ned Kelly, was arrested in 1870 and charged with having assisted Power in one of his numerous bushranging exploits, but was acquitted, as none of the witnesses could swear to his identity. It is said that on more than one occasion he took care of Power's horses while that worthy was engaged in robbing. In 1871 he was sent to gaol for three years for horse-stealing.

Horse-stealing appears to have been the principal industry of the district, as cattle-duffing had been of the Wedden Mountain district, and of Manaro, and the Kellys, the Harts, the Byrnes, and others in this district, were quite as adept in "faking" brands as the Lowrys, the O'Meallys, or the Clarkes had been. But science had made advances even in these mountains since the era of the Gardiner gang. In earlier times the brands of horses and cattle were "faked"—i.e., altered so as to represent something different from what they were intended to do—by branding over them and adding

Chapter XXIX

to them. There were some expert blacksmiths among the cattle-duffers, and these would make a brand to fit over an old brand and completely change its character. For instance, a simple A brand might have a circle burned round it thus—(A), or it might have another letter conjoined to it thus—A-B. The manner in which brands might be "faked" was endless, and when it was impossible to "fake" a brand it was "blotched," or burned over, so that the original design could not be recognised. The Kellys and their companions in the Warby and Strathbogie ranges, however, did not go to the trouble of making special brands to "fake" other brands. They obtained the same results by the use of iodine, which burned such marks into the skins of the stolen animals as were desired. The plan adopted was to make raids into distant parts, collect a mob of horses, drive them into an inaccessible ravine in the mountains, "fake" their brands and keep them until the sores had healed and the brands looked old. Then the animals, having got fat in the meantime, were driven to market and sold without fear of detection. Horses stolen in the north—some even from across the New South Wales border—were driven south to Melbourne, Ballarat, Geelong, or some other large town, and sold openly in the public sale yards; while those stolen in the south were driven to some northern market, sometimes being taken as far as Sydney.

In 1876, Daniel, the youngest of the Kelly boys, was sent to gaol for three months for having taken part in a house-breaking robbery in conjunction with the Lloyds, who were connected by marriage with the Kellys. In the following year, 1887, warrants were issued for his arrest on six charges of horse-stealing, but he could not be found. On April 15th, 1878, Constable Alexander Fitzpatrick, having learned that Dan Kelly was at home, went to the Kellys' hut at Greta, to arrest him. "This hut," said the Benalla Standard, "was a well-known trysting-place for the bushranger Power." The constable rode up, and seeing Dan standing at the door said to him, "You're my prisoner." "All right," replied Dan nonchalantly. The constable dismounted and hitched his horse to a sapling, when Dan said that he had been riding all day and had had nothing to eat. After some conversation the constable agreed to wait while Dan had some food, before taking him to Benalla, and Dan went in and sat down. As he did so Mrs. Kelly said to Fitzpatrick, "You won't take Dan out o' this to-night."

"Shut up, mother," exclaimed Dan, "it's all right." The old woman continued to grumble in an undertone, while she placed bread and meat and tea on the table. Presently she asked the constable, "Have you got a warrant?" "I've got a telegram, and that's as good," replied Fitzpatrick. The constable was standing at the door, and Dan, who took his arrest coolly, as if it was a mere matter of course, told his mother not to make a row about it, as it did not matter, and then invited the constable to take some food. Fitzpatrick accepted the invitation, and went in. As he seated himself Mrs. Kelly remarked, "If my son Ned was here, he'd throw you out of the window." Dan was looking out of the window at the time, and he exclaimed "Here he is." Fitzpatrick very naturally turned to look, and Dan pounced on to him. Mrs. Kelly seized a heavy garden spade which had been used as a fire shovel and was much damaged, and struck Fitzpatrick a furious blow on the head, making a dint in his helmet. Fitzpatrick fell down, and several people hearing the noise rushed in. Among them were Ned Kelly, William Skillian (husband of one of the Kelly girls), and William Williams, alias Bricky. Ned Kelly held a revolver in his hand which was still smoking, and Fitzpatrick was wounded in the arm. Ned said, "I'm sorry I fired. You're the civilest —— trap I've seen." He offered to cut the bullet out and bind up the wound, but Fitzpatrick refused to let him touch it. Then Ned said that the constable could not be allowed to go away until the bullet was cut out and he had promised not to tell how he got wounded. "You can say your pistol went off by accident," he said. "Tell him if he does tell he won't live long after," cried Mrs. Kelly. The old woman was again told to "shut up." Fitzpatrick, knowing the men he had to deal with, promised not to say who had wounded him, and took his knife from his pocket. He cut a small gash, over where the bullet was, and squeezed it out. Then he twisted his handkerchief round the wound and said it was "all right." Ned Kelly picked up the bullet and put it away on a shelf, and a few minutes later the constable was allowed to mount his horse and go. On the following day a party of troopers went to the Eleven Mile Creek and arrested Mrs. Ellen Kelly, William Skillian, and William Williams. A search was made for Ned and Dan Kelly, but they could not be found. Skillian and Williams, when brought up for trial for their share in this assault, declared that they only came in after the shot was fired, and had taken no part whatever in

CHAPTER XXIX

the scrimmage. They were, however, sentenced to six years' imprisonment, while Mrs. Kelly was sent to gaol for three years.

It was generally understood that Ned and Dan Kelly were in hiding somewhere in the neighbourhood, and some twenty-five troopers with black trackers were told off to search for them. Fourteen men, residents in the neighbour hood, were arrested under the Outlawry Act, on suspicion that they had harboured or aided and abetted the bushrangers, and were remanded from week to week for sonic three months, while the police were seeking for evidence against them. Mr. Zincke, who appeared at the police court on behalf of the prisoners, protested against this arbitrary act of the police, and urged that it was illegal to detain as prisoners persons against whom no specific charge had been made. "If the Kellys were caught," he said, "these men would be told to go about their business." He stated his belief that the Outlawry Act would not warrant these proceedings and that the law was being strained in a dangerous manner. The magistrates on the bench generally listened to his pleadings with exemplary patience and then granted the remand asked for by the police. There can be very little doubt that Mr. Zincke was perfectly justified in saying that these proceedings were illegal, but the magistrates of Beechworth and other parts of the disturbed district had learned by experience that, as long as the sympathisers and "bush telegraphs" were at liberty, the police had very little chance of capturing the bushrangers, and so, during the whole time that the Kelly gang was in existence, a number of people were kept locked up because they were suspected of giving food or assistance to the outlaws and, more important than all, of giving the bushrangers information as to the movements of the police. The number of persons thus held under restraint varied from month to month. Sometimes a few were discharged while others took their places. The largest number in the police cells at any one time was thirty-five. But the authorities after all acted in a half-hearted and inefficient manner. They arrested only men and boys, while the women and girls were left free to assist the bushrangers as they pleased, and the women were quite as active and quite as efficient in affording assistance and information to the bushrangers as the men could have possibly been.

On October 26th one of the parties of police in search of the outlaws went into camp at Stringy Bark Creek, about eight miles on the King River side of the Wombat Range. Sergeant Kennedy was supposed to have received information from a friend of the Kellys as to their whereabouts, and thus to have penetrated nearly to their hiding place. The friend who had informed the police, however, also told the Kellys of their appproach. The country is densely covered with stringy bark trees and scrub, and is almost impenetrable. Sergeant Kennedy and Constable Scanlan had gone into the scrub to endeavour to ascertain the whereabouts of the two Kellys, while Constables Lonergan and McIntyre were left in charge of the camp. Lonergan was employed in making tea, ready for the two who were away, when four men on horseback came up and cried "Bail up! put up your hands." Lonergan made a jump to get behind a tree, putting his hand to his belt for a pistol at the same time, and was shot. He cried out "O Christ, I'm shot," and fell dead. Constable McIntyre was sitting down. He jumped up, but having no weapon upon him at the time he surrendered. Ned Kelly walked to Lonergan's body and examined it. Then he rose, and said, "What a pity! Why didn't the —— fool surrender?" He afterwards said that it was all Constable Fitzpatrick's fault. "He'd no right to lag my mother and brother-in-law for nothing." Ned Kelly ordered Constable McIntyre to sit down as if nothing had happened, and warned him that he would be shot at once if he "gave the office" to the sergeant. The bushrangers then hid themselves behind the trees. Sergeant Kennedy and Constable Scanlan rode up some time later, unconscious that anything had happened. When they came close McIntyre said, "Sergeant, we're surrounded. You'd better surrender." Scanlan laughed, and put his hand to his belt, when Ned Kelly fired at him and missed. Scanlan jumped off his horse and made for a gum tree, but was shot dead before he reached it. Kennedy wheeled his horse round and started at a gallop, but had gone only a few yards when he was brought down with a rifle bullet. His horse, frightened at the noise and the fall of its rider, dashed through the camp, and as it passed Constable McIntyre threw himself across its back. He got into the saddle, and urged it forward, when it was brought down, shot by a rifle bullet through the heart. McIntyre fell clear, and crawled into a patch of scrub. He found a wombat hole near at hand. He crept into it, and lay there, while he could hear the bushrangers walking round searching for him in the scrub, and swearing that they would "do for" him when they caught him. When it

Chapter XXIX

was quite dark he crawled out of his hole and walked twenty miles to Mansfield to inform the police of what had taken place.

Inspector Pewtress, with a party of police, started from Melbourne on Sunday, the 27th, in a special train, and soon reached the camp in the ranges. The bodies of Lonergan and Scanlan were lying as they had fallen not far from where the fire had been lighted, but that of Sergeant Kennedy could not be seen from the camp. It was not found until the 31st, owing to the density of the scrub around the little cleared patch, where the camp had been pitched. Three bullet wounds were found in it, and a cloak had been thrown over the face to protect it from dingoes or the weather. It was said that Ned Kelly had ridden to his camp to fetch the cloak to cover Kennedy with, because he considered him to be the bravest man he had ever met.

Rewards of £100 each had been offered by the Victorian Government for the capture of Ned and Dan Kelly. Now the rewards were increased to £500, while similar rewards were offered for Steve Hart (twenty years of age) and Joe Byrnes (nineteen years of age).

It was reported that on October 31st the Kellys had stuck up and robbed Neil Christian and other persons at Bungowanah, near Baumgarten's, on the Murray River, but as the whole of that country was under water, in consequence of a flood in the river at that time, this was discredited. The police asserted that the Kellys were somewhere in the mountains, but they searched the "Rat's Castle" and other hiding places without success.

On the 8th December a rough-looking bushman called at Younghusband's station, on Faithfull's Creek, and asked if the manager, Mr. Macaulay, was about? An old man named Fitzgerald, employed on the station, replied that the manager was away and would not return till morning. He asked the man if he could do anything for him? The traveller replied "No, it's of no consequence." He walked to the house and said to Mrs. Fitzgerald, "I'm Ned Kelly. You needn't be frightened, we only want food for ourselves and our horses." Seeing the man talking to his wife, Fitzgerald went to them, and Mrs. Fitzgerald said to him "This is Mr. Kelly. He wants some refreshments." By this time Ned had his revolver in his hand. Fitzgerald grasped the situation and replied "Well, if the gentleman wants refreshments he'll have to have them." Ned gave a whistle and the other three bushrangers came forward and Dan took their horses to the stables. Joe Byrnes took care of the Fitzgeralds, while Ned and Steve Hart went round and collected all the men at work on the station and locked them up in the store room. Shortly afterwards a man named Gloster, who had a store in Seymour and who frequently travelled round with a spring cart loaded with goods for sale at the farms and stations, came to the station for a bucket of water to make tea with, and Ned ordered him to bail up. Knowing that Gloster was of a determined character Fitzgerald shouted to him to advise him to "give in." "What for?" asked Gloster. "I'm Ned Kelly," exclaimed that hero. "I don't care a —— who you are," returned Gloster. At this moment Dan Kelly came up and threatened to shoot Gloster, but Ned forbade him, and Fitzgerald persuaded Gloster that resistance was useless and prevailed on him to surrender.

When Macaulay, the manager, came home he was also bailed up. "What's the good of your sticking up the station?" he asked, "you've better horses than we have and anything else you require you can have without all this nonsense." Ned said he had a purpose. After some conversation, during which Macaulay said he had no intention of interfering with them, Macaulay was permitted to remain free, but was closely watched to prevent him from sending for the police. The bushrangers then searched Gloster's cart, selected suits of clothes for themselves, and made very free with the bottles of scent and other small articles.

On the following day, the 11th December, 1878, Messrs. McDougal, Dudley, and Casement, in a spring cart, were about to pass through the gate over the level crossing of the railway, close to the station. Mr. Jennant, who was riding, dismounted to open the gate for the cart to pass through, when Ned Kelly, on horseback, cried "Surrender, or you will be shot." Another bushranger, Joe Byrnes, walked down quickly from the station to assist his mate if necessary. Mr. McDougal, taking them for troopers as they carried handcuffs in their hands, asked what right they had to arrest them in this manner, when Ned replied, "Shut up. I'll shoot you if you give me any cheek." "You wouldn't shoot an old man unarmed," exclaimed McDougal. "Not if you surrender quietly," replied Ned. They said they surrendered, and Byrnes opened the gate and told them to drive

Chapter XXIX

to the homestead. As they came up a station hand who was standing at the store door said, "Gentlemen, allow me to introduce you to Mr. Edward Kelly." McDougal and his companions were not much surprised, as they had already begun to perceive that their captors were not troopers in plain clothes, as they had at first thought. The prisoners were taken into the store, the bushrangers telling them that the horses would be looked after.

The store-room was a long wooden building situated about twenty yards from the house. It had only one door and one window, both near together, so that it could easily be guarded. With so many men confined in it the air soon became foul, and the prisoners were allowed to come out in small batches to obtain some fresh air. Only the men were locked up, the women being left free and were not molested in any way.

At about three o'clock Ned Kelly asked Mr. Macaulay for a small cheque. Mr. Macaulay gave it to him. It was for £3. Then Joe Byrnes was left in charge of the station, while the others started away, Ned in Gloster's cart, Dan in McDougal's, and Hart on horseback. At about half-past four there was a knock at the door of the National Bank at Euroa, and when it was opened a man requested that a cheque might be cashed for him. The manager, Mr. Robert Scott, said it was after hours, and he could not open the bank again till morning. The man said it would inconvenience him greatly to have to call again, as he did not live in the town. He begged so hard that at length the manager consented to give him the money to oblige him. The manager opened the bank door, and as soon as they were inside the man said, "Put up your hands. I'm Ned Kelly." Taken by surprise, the manager was compelled to obey. The manager was forced to open the safe door and to hand over £1942 0s. 6d. in notes, gold, and silver, thirty-one ounces of smelted gold, five bags of cartridges, and two revolvers. There had been rumours that the Kellys intended to stick up a bank, and arms and ammunition had been sent from the head offices in Melbourne to most of the country branches. The National Bank at Euroa had been thus furnished, but in consequence of the cunning of the bushrangers the arms were useless. Mr. Scott had a loaded revolver on his table when Ned Kelly asked him to cash the cheque, but he was so unsuspicious of the character of his customer that he left it there when he went into the bank chamber. Having obtained all the money he could get Kelly turned to enter the private apartments, when Scott said, "If you go in there I'll strike you whatever the consequences may be."

Steve Hart put his revolver to Scott's face and said "Keep back." Kelly laughed, and walked through the door. He went along the passage, and looked out of the back door into the yard. Then he returned and told Scott to go and put his horse into the buggy. "That's the work of the groom," said Scott, "but he happens to be away just now." "I'll do it myself," returned Ned, and went into the yard. When the horse was harnessed, Kelly said he was going to take the family out for a drive. He made Scott get into Gloster's cart, and Mrs. Scott and the child into the buggy. Dan Kelly and Hart came on behind. When they had gone out of the little street Scott asked Ned where they were going. "To Younghusband's," was the reply. "I'll drive," said Scott, "I know the road." "All right," replied Ned, handing him the reins. "But if you try any pranks, look out." Ned Kelly treated Mrs. Scott with great politeness, so that she said that she could never believe he was the bloodthirsty villain he had been represented to be.

The telegraph wires had been cut on each side of the station soon after their arrival, and while the main body of the robbers was gone to Euroa a train stopped close to the station to set down a line repairer named Watts. As the railway station was some distance away it was thought that the train had brought the police, and Byrnes prepared to defend himself. He shut all the men in the store, and charged them to keep quiet. When Watts came to the station to enquire how the break in the line had occurred and to obtain assistance Byrnes bailed him up, and told him that he could repair the line later on. Nothing of importance occurred after this until the return of Ned and his mates with the bank manager and the money.

During their drive together Ned Kelly told Scott that he was —— sorry that Sergeant Kennedy had been shot. He was a brave man. "But," he added, "I couldn't help it. The police ought to surrender when they are called on." He showed Scott the presentation gold watch which had once belonged to Kennedy and which he had taken from the body "to remember him by."

Soon after their return to the station they all had tea, Ned Kelly telling his prisoners that he would not detain them much longer. The meal was

Chapter XXIX

barely over when a train drew up opposite the station and whistled. Ned Kelly shouted "Hullo boys, here's a special with the —— bobbies. We'll fight 'em. We're ready for 'em, however many there may be." The driver waited for a few minutes and then the train went out. It was soon ascertained that Watts, the line repairer, had arranged for the train to pick him up after he had had time to repair the break, but owing to his being shut up in the station store he had neither repaired the line nor been able to inform the engine driver of the reason of his non-success. At about half-past seven, the prisoners were mustered and told to remain in the store for three hours. Scott took out his watch and asked "Eleven?" "No," replied Ned, "half-past. If any one leaves before, I'll hear of it and make it —— hot for him. I'll track him down and shoot him dead. You can't escape me." Byrnes turned to Scott and said "That looks like a —— good watch. Let's see it." Scott handed him the watch and the robber put it in his pocket. This was a signal to the other bushrangers. One took Macaulay's watch, and another asked McDougal for his. McDougal took it from his pocket and said "I should be sorry to lose it. It is a keepsake from my dead mother." "Is it," said Kelly, "then we'll not take it." Ned Kelly warned Macaulay that he held him responsible for the men. "If you let them go before the time," he said, "I'll shoot you like a dingo the first time I see you." Shortly afterwards the bushrangers mounted their horses, which had been feeding in the stables during the time the station was held, and rode away. The men were released from the store but were kept at the station for about three hours. Mr. and Mrs. Scott returned to Euroa in their buggy and telegraphed the news of the robbery as soon as possible, which was not before the next morning. Gloster rode off to inform the police at the nearest town, and the information as to this daring outrage was spread about by others who had been robbed.

Thirty

The Kellys Stick up the Town of Jerilderie; Robbery of the Bank of New South Wales; A Symposium in the Royal Hotel; A Three-days' Spree; "Hurrah for the Good Old Times of Morgan and Ben Hall"; the Robbers Take a Rest for a Year; The Kelly Sympathisers Again; The Kellys Reappear; Murder of Aaron Sherritt.

After the bank robbery the "gentlemen of the Strathbogie Ranges" again retired to their mountain fastnesses. Occasionally a paragraph in one of the local newspapers recorded the movements of the police or furnished a story about the black trackers, but these notices were necessarily very meagre, as the police declined to furnish any information as to their proceedings or intentions, because this would be of more use to the bushrangers than to any one else. For more than a month nothing reliable had been heard of them. Even the reports of the arrest and detention of numbers of "bush telegraphs" failed to attract any attention, and the Kelly gang had almost ceased to be spoken of, when suddenly the whole country was roused by the news that the bushrangers had stuck up the town of Jerilderie, in New South Wales. Jerilderie is situated on the Yanko Creek, not far from its junction with the Billabong, and at that time contained about 300 inhabitants, a bank, four public-houses, a post and telegraph office, and several churches, schools, and other buildings. The local police station and lock-up was near the outside of the town, and there were two officers—Constables Devine and Richards—stationed there. At midnight of February 8th, 1879, a man roused Constable Devine from his bed, and informed him that a row had taken place at Davidson's Hotel and a man had been killed. He exhorted the constable to "come quick." Constable Devine woke Constable Richards and both dressed as hastily as possible. When they came out they were confronted by Ned Kelly, revolver in hand, and ordered to "bail up." Not having their arms on them, and being taken completely by surprise, the two constables surrendered at once and were locked up in the cells. The bushrangers then compelled Mrs. Devine, who had also partially dressed, to hand over all arms and ammunition, and took possession of the lock-up, remaining quietly there till morning, their horses being placed in the police stables at the rear. It was Sunday morning, and as the Catholic church had not yet been finished, the courthouse had been rented for religious purposes, and Mrs. Devine had been accustomed to clean up the place, set the temporary altar, and place the forms and chairs ready for mass. The bushrangers told her to perform her task as usual, after having extorted a promise from her that she would not mention their presence to any one, and to make certain of her keeping her word one of them, dressed as a constable, went with her to the court-house and stayed while she swept the floor and prepared the room. Then they returned to the lock-up, which was about one hundred yards from the courthouse, and remained there all day, the bushrangers, arrayed in the constables' uniforms, sitting quietly in the guard-room. No doubt numbers of people passed and saw them, but no one had any suspicion that the bushrangers were in charge instead of the police.

Early on Monday morning Byrnes took two horses to the blacksmith's shop to be shod, and the blacksmith, feeling some doubt as to the bonâ fides of the pseudo trooper, made a note of the brands on the horses. At about ten a.m. Ned and Dan Kelly, accompanied by Constable Richards, went to the Royal Hotel, the largest hotel in the town, where Richards formally introduced them to the proprietor, Mr. Cox. Ned informed Mr. Cox that he required the use of some rooms, as the gang intended sticking up the bank. He selected a large and a small room on the ground floor, near the bar, and conducted the few men about at the time into the large room, where they were ordered to remain until given permission to depart. Dan Kelly was placed on guard at the door to keep order and prevent anybody from escaping, and was instructed to shoot the first man who refused to do as he was told. On Mr. Cox passing his word, as a gentleman, not to mention their presence to any one who should come in, he was permitted to take charge of the bar as usual, and was given to understand that he would be held responsible for the discretion of the women and servants. Any one of them whom he could not trust was to be sent into the large room. The preliminaries were arranged so unostentatiously and quietly, that no rumour of the presence of the bushrangers had yet been heard, and as customers dropped into the hotel they were taken into the big room, and told to remain on penalty of death.

Having made these arrangements, Ned Kelly walked into the hotel yard to reconnoitre. There was a detached kitchen here, and the rear of the bank of New South Wales was only a few yards from the rear of this kitchen. The bank faced on another street, and there was no dividing fence between the yard at the back of the bank and the hotel yard. Hart was placed on watch near the kitchen, while Byrnes entered the back door of the bank. Mr. Living, the teller, was in the bank chamber. He was not surprised to hear a man enter by the back door, as Mr. Cox and other customers frequently came in that way, it being a short cut from the hotel. Suddenly, however, Byrnes came to the counter, pointed a revolver at Living's head, and cried out, "I'm Kelly, keep quiet." Living held his hands above his head. "Where's your pistols?" asked Byrnes. "I've got none," replied Living. Byrnes then ordered Living and the accountant Mackie to "Come over to the hotel." They came from behind the counter and did as they were told, Byrnes following them. When they reached the door of the large room Dan Kelly inquired, "Where's Tarleton?" "In his room," replied Living. "Then go and fetch him and no —— nonsense," said Dan. Living went back to the bank, but being unable to find the manager in his rooms began to fear that something might have happened to him. He was about to return to the hotel to inform the Kellys that he could not find the manager, when he heard a splashing. He went to the bathroom and knocked. Tarleton had been for a forty-mile ride that morning, and had just returned and was having a wash. When he opened the door and was informed that the town was in possession of the Kelly gang, and the bank was stuck up, he laughed heartily, believing it to be a huge joke. Living assured him that it was not a laughing matter, but he was still incredulous. However, he dressed and went to the hotel, where he soon discovered that what he had deemed impossible had come to pass. The three bank officials were placed in the large room. Tarleton, who took a seat next to Constable Richards, whispered, "I can knock Hart down, shall I?" "What's the good?" replied the constable, "Dan Kelly's there, and he'd shoot you down at once."

Ned Kelly had hitherto been walking round as a sort of inspector-general of the proceedings and giving orders. He now entered the room and

Chapter XXX

ordered drinks to be served all round. Then he made a speech in which he blamed Constable Fitzpatrick for all that had occurred. "I wasn't within a hundred miles of Greta when he was shot," said Ned, "and up to then I'd never killed a man in my life." He went on to say that he had stolen two hundred and eighty horses from Whitby's station, and had sold them at Baumgarten's. He took out a revolver and exclaimed: "This was Lonergan's! I took it from him. The gun I shot him with was a crooked, worn-out thing, not worth picking up. I shot him because he threatened my mother and my sister if they refused to tell where Ned Kelly was. The police are worse than the ―――― black trackers. I came here to shoot Devine and Richards, and I'm going to do it." The men at the table began to intercede for Richards, who was sitting quietly among them and who did not speak, but Kelly exclaimed dramatically, "He must die."

Ned got the key of the bank safe and took £1450 worth of notes and money from it. He also took £691 from the teller's drawers. While thus employed, Messrs. Gill, Hardie, and Rankin came in on business in the ordinary course and were ordered to bail up. They turned and ran. Ned Kelly followed and caught Rankin, but the others got away. Ned was furious at this escape. He said that news of their presence would be all over the place in a few minutes, and he swore he would shoot Rankin in revenge.

He took Rankin to the hotel, stood him up against the wall in the passage and flourished his revolver about. The men in the room pleaded that Rankin might be spared, and urged that he could not have prevented Gill and Hardie from running away. While this was going on Byrnes came in with Mr. Hardie and said that they could not find Gill, the proprietor of the local newspaper, as he had not returned to his office. Ned Kelly then let Rankin go and declared that he would burn the newspaper office. Mr. Gill it is said went out of the town and hid in a clump of trees by the side of the river till evening. Ned then walked down to McDougall's Hotel and shouted for about thirty men who were in or about the hotel at the time. On his return to the Royal Hotel he was informed that Hart had robbed the Rev. Mr. Gribble of a gold watch. He called Hart up and asked indignantly, "What right has a thing like you to rob a clergyman?" He swore a good deal and compelled Hart to give the watch back. Complaints were made that he had stolen a new saddle and bridle from a saddler's shop, and some other articles from other places. Ned called him a —— thief; and ordered him to return everything he had taken.

Ned Kelly paid more than one visit to the Post and Telegraph Office to "see how things were going on." The robbers had cut the wires on either side of the town before their entry and had chopped down seven telegraph posts in the main street near the office. They had given orders to Mr. Jefferson, the telegraph master, that no repairs should be attempted until permission was given, and Ned took care that these orders were obeyed. The robbers held the town for three days, in imitation of the manner in which the Hall and Gilbert gang had held Canowindra. Jerilderie was at this time slightly larger than Canowindra at the time when it had been stuck up and held, but there was less traffic through it, and consequently less connection between it and the outer world than with Canowindra. The road running through Jerilderie leads from Conargo to Narrandera. Jerilderie is about thirty miles from Conargo and sixty-five from Narrandera. All round are huge sheep and cattle stations, with only a few men employed on them except at shearing or mustering time. All through the remainder of the year the traffic is inconsiderable. There was in Jerilderie, however, a large wool-washing and fellmongery establishment which employed a fair number of workmen. Canowindra, on the other hand, was a wayside town on the main road from Bathurst to Forbes, the traffic being considerable all the year round. There were also several small diggings settlements not far away, and the residents of these frequently came to purchase articles from the stores at Canowindra. It was far easier, therefore, to isolate Jerilderie for three days than it had been Canowindra in the earlier days of bushranging. The Hall and Gilbert gang also robbed everybody except the landlord of the hotel they took possession of. The Kelly's, on the other hand, robbed no one outside of the bank. Jerilderie also was a much more compact town than Canowindra, the latter consisting of one long straggling street, with only a few houses outside this line, while Jerilderie had several cross streets, and at least two parallel with the river.

The robbers held the town from midnight on Saturday, until about four p.m. on the-Wednesday following. Shortly before the men were allowed to leave the Royal Hotel, Ned Kelly gave Living a paper which he said gave a history of his life, and the truth about what he had done. Living promised

Chapter XXX

that he would do his best to get it published, and handed it to Mr. Gill, who read it and forwarded it to the Government. It was a long rambling statement, in some parts quite incoherent, and much of it false. It was never published. At about four o'clock Byrnes left the town in the direction of the Murray River. He was riding his own horse, and had the money stolen from the bank packed on one of the police horses, which he was leading. A minute or two later Dan Kelly and Steve Hart mounted their horses, and galloped several times up and down the main street, flourishing their revolvers and shouting, "Hurrah for the good old times of Morgan and Ben Hall." Then they left the town along the main road. Ned Kelly, mounted on his gray mare and leading a second police horse, left some minutes later. Before going, he rode from the police station to the Royal Hotel, and told the men detained in the large room there that they were free.

The bushrangers had left the town by different routes, probably to prevent any information as to the road they had travelled from being furnished to the police, but no doubt they had arranged where they should meet outside at a safe distance. Late in the evening they rode up to Wannamurra station, about twenty-five miles from Jerilderie, when Ned Kelly asked Mr. A. Mackie whether his brother was at home yet? Mr. Mackie replied that he did not know. "I'm going to shoot him for giving horses to Living and Tarleton to ride to Deniliquin for the traps," said Ned. They all went to the station together, but evidence was soon brought forward to prove that the bank employees had not obtained horses from Mr. Mackie, and at length Ned exonerated that gentleman for what he called "his treachery," but forcibly expressed his intention of shooting Living. "I gave him back his life policy," he said, "and I only burned two or three of the bank books instead of the lot to oblige him. He asked for them, and I treated him as fair as I could, and now he takes advantage of my kindness to betray me." He walked up and down on the verandah of the house for several minutes swearing at Living, and more than once said he had a good mind to go back and "settle him" at once. His rage, however, soon subsided, and the gang proceeded on their way, no attempt being made to detain them.

Jerilderie lies about one hundred and fifty miles, as the crow flies, from where the bushrangers were supposed to have been hidden, in the Strathbogie Mountains, and when the news of the bank robbery at Jerilderie was telegraphed all over the country, wonder was everywhere expressed as to how the robbers had crossed this country, some of it thickly populated, without being perceived. The skill with which the robbery had been planned, the boldness and completeness of the arrangements, and the apparent ease with which it had been accomplished, made the Kelly gang the principal topic of conversation. The New South Wales Government issued a proclamation declaring Ned and Dan Kelly, Joe Byrnes, and Steve Hart outlaws, and offered a reward of £3000 for their capture, dead or alive. The associated banks of the colony supplemented this reward by another of £1000. The Victorian Government increased the rewards already offered to the same amount as was offered by the New South Wales Government, while the banks in that colony added another £1000; thus making the total reward offered for the capture of the four members of the gang £8000. Two thousand pounds per man was the highest reward ever offered for the capture of bushrangers in Australia.

For some time the police of New South Wales scoured the country round Jerilderie and the plains between that town and the Victorian border, while the Victorian police were quite as active on their side of the Murray River, until at length it was definitely ascertained that the bushrangers were safe back in their mountain fastnesses. The paragraphs published from time to time in the Beechworth, the Benalla, and the Wangaratta papers, and in local papers even further removed from the home of the Kellys, tend to show that although the black boys failed to follow a trail in the mountains with the certainty and skill displayed by them in leveller country, they still kept the outlaws in a continual state of fear of capture. Ned Kelly is reported to have called them "those six little black devils," and to have sworn to shoot them if ever he "got the chance."

"Those —— trackers," he cried, "I'd like to shoot 'em. They're no —— good in this country. They can't track in Victoria. I can track as well as they can out on the plains. I can run an emu's trail for miles as well as them. They may be good in Queensland or the plains, but they're no good in the mountains." Nevertheless they worried him, as his frequent complaints of their activity prove. The district was no doubt a difficult one to track in. None but a first-class horseman could ride through it with any degree of certainty, and no one but an aborigine or a white man born in the district

Chapter XXX

could cross the ravines and gullies without getting hopelessly "bushed," without a guide.

The arrests and detentions of Kelly's sympathisers continued with increased vigour. "Wild" Wright and his brother Tom, relatives of the Kellys, Frank Hart, brother of the bushranger, the Lloyds and others, passed a considerable portion of their time in the cells of the various lock-ups around the district. Robert Miller was arrested and detained because his daughter, a daring horsewoman, was observed to go into the mountains at night with what were supposed to be provisions for the bushrangers. She was followed more than once, but contrived to elude her pursuers by plunging up or down a steep mountain, or across an almost impassable gully. She never started twice in the same track, sometimes going up one spur or ravine, and next time choosing a different one, and leading even the black trackers astray. The newspapers frequently urged the folly of detaining the father while the daughter was left free to furnish the outlaws with food and news. The plain fact is, that when special laws have to be applied, there should be no exceptions; otherwise they are valueless. In this case the women were far more active and reliable partisans of the Kellys than the men, and, as there can be little doubt that the Outlawry Act was strained, to put it mildly, by the police and the local magistracy, with the connivance of the Government, another turn of the screw would not have made the actions of the authorities any more illegal, and might have made them efficient. However, determined as the authorities were to stamp out lawlessness, they did not carry their own illegal acts to this extreme point, and probably this postponed, though it did not prevent, the end which was inevitable, as it always must be when a few array themselves against an overwhelming majority.

It was about this time that the name of Aaron Sherritt was first heard of in conection with the bushrangers. Sherritt was the son of an ex-policeman. He was about twenty-four years of age and had settled in the district some time earlier. He selected one hundred and seven acres of ground on the Woolshed Creek, and the Kellys and Byrnes helped him to fence it in and clear part of it. He had, however, recently sold his farm to a Mr. Crawford, of Melbourne, and had built himself a hut at Sebastopol, about two miles away, until he could take up another selection. He was engaged to be married to a sister of Joe Byrnes. and was regarded as one of the family. He was suspected of having taken a share in some of the extensive horse-stealing raids in company with the Kellys and their friends, and had been in consequence an object of police suspicion and supervision. This was the man to whom the police made advances, and, by promising him the whole of the eight thousand pounds reward offered for the capture of the bushrangers, on condition that it should be through his aid and assistance that this capture was effected, they succeeded in winning him over to their side.

He led Superintendent Hare and a party of police into the innermost recesses of the mountains, and pointed out several camps where the bushrangers had been; but, in each case, the bushrangers appeared to have received warning and to have removed before the police came. Some thought that Sherritt was playing a double game, and that he contrived to let the bushrangers know when the police might be expected to arrive, but there appears to be no foundation for this opinion, as it delayed his chance of obtaining the reward. At first he was careful not to be seen in company with the police, but their association could not be kept secret for long, and Sherritt soon became suspected by the Kelly family. One day Mrs. Byrnes openly accused him of trying to betray her son. There was a row, and Sherritt was ordered from the house, his engagement with the daughter being broken off. After that Sherritt appeared more openly in company of the police, parties of whom were constantly watching the homes of the four bushrangers on the chance of capturing them should they visit their parents or other relatives. Sherritt married the daughter of another settler in the district, and all communications between him and the families of the bushrangers were broken off. Sherritt instead of being a friend was considered an enemy of the bushrangers.

During the latter half of 1879 and the first half of 1880 nothing of any importance was heard as to the movements of the bushrangers. More than once it was reported that they had left the country, sometimes it was said for New Zealand, and at other times for America, but these reports were invariably contradicted within a few days, and the Kellys were said to be still somewhere in the ranges. Sometimes it was said that the money stolen from the Jerilderie Bank must be all expended, and that the Kellys would be forced to leave their hiding-place shortly, but frequently, during the twelve months following that raid, nothing would be heard of the bushrangers for weeks, and the public almost forgot that there was such a gang in existence. Then suddenly came the news that the robbers had shot Aaron Sherritt on June 27th, 1880.

For some weeks a party of police had been secreted, as much as possible, in Sherritt's house, for the purpose of watching Byrne's mother's house, and four of them were quietly sitting in the inner room at the time of the murder. The particulars of the murder were as follows:—A German market-gardener named Antoine Weeks was living on the Woolshed Creek, not far from Sherritt's and Byrnes's houses. He was walking home on the evening of the day mentioned when he was met by Dan Kelly and Joe Byrnes. "Do you know who we are?" asked Dan. "No," replied Weeks. "Well, we're the Kellys," said Dan; "you do as we tell you and no harm will come to you." They handcuffed the German, and led him along the road to Sherritt's house. Here Dan told him to shout "Aaron." Weeks did so, and on Aaron Sherritt coming to the door to ascertain who wanted him, Byrnes shot him dead without a word.

The bushrangers took the handcuffs off of Weeks and told him to go home. Then they went to the door of the hut, called Mrs. Sherritt out, and told her that she had better send some of the —— traps in her house out to bury her husband, because "We've shot him for being a traitor." The Kellys were fully aware that the police were in the house, and called on them to come out and "fight like men."

If the constables had come out as invited they would have been courting almost certain death. A bright wood fire was burning in the hut and the front room was as bright as day, while all outside was as dark as possible. Had the police therefore left the shelter of the inner room and entered the front apartment they would have been shot down before they could have seen their enemies, whose whereabouts could only have been guessed at from their shots or from the flash of their revolvers. Going to the door under these conditions would have been almost tantamount to committing suicide. The bushrangers raged round the hut calling the police the most opprobious names and threatening and taunting them in hopes of inducing them to come into the light, but as the police kept quiet and made no reply whatever to their taunts the bushrangers swore that they would "burn 'em like rats in a trap." They fired through the windows and doors, but they appear to have been just as unwilling to enter the lighted room as the police were. In fact neither party would give the other a chance. The robbers remained round the hut at this labour of hate until two a.m., when they departed. At daybreak one of the troopers went to where the horses were kept, and rode to Benalla to give information of the reappearance of the Kellys, while the other three followed on the tracks of the outlaws.

Thirty-one

FIGHT BETWEEN THE POLICE AND THE BUSHRANGERS AT GLENROWAN; THE RAILWAY TORN UP; ATTEMPT TO WRECK THE POLICE TRAIN; THE GLENROWAN INN BESIEGED; NED KELLY IN ARMOUR; HIS CAPTURE; THE BURNING OF THE INN; DEATHS OF DAN KELLY, STEVE HART, AND JOE BYRNES; TRIAL AND CONVICTION OF NED KELLY; HIS DEATH; THE KELLY SHOW; DECREASE OF CRIME IN THE COLONIES.

As soon as the news of this fresh outrage was telegraphed to Melbourne, Sub-inspector O'Connor of Queensland, with his six black trackers, with Superintendent Hare, Inspector Pewtress, and several other officials of the Victorian police, a number of newspaper correspondents, and a few other favoured persons, started by special train for the scene of disorder. Eight troopers were picked up at Benalla, and at twenty-five minutes past three p.m. the train was stopped near the Glenrowan platform by Mr. Curnow, the local schoolmaster, who stood on the line waving a red scarf. He informed those on the train that the robbers had torn up the rails a short distance ahead, with a view to wrecking the train, and that they were waiting near to shoot the police or any one else who might be sent to capture them. A consultation was immediately held to decide as to the next step, and while this was going on, Constable Bracken, the local representative of the police force, arrived and reported that the bushrangers had taken possession of the Glenrowan Inn, not much more than a hundred yards distant, and that he had just made his escape from them.

The Glenrowan Inn was built on the Sydney Road, about half-way between Winton and Wangaratta, shortly after the discovery of gold at the Ovens River, in 1853. The glen was then a camping-place for teams travelling between Melbourne and the diggings. A second hotel was constructed later, and a small village, or what the Australians call a township, grew up on the little flat at the gap in the hills, locally known as the Futter's Range, a spur jutting out from the larger Strathbogie Range. For some years Glenrowan was quite a flourishing little town, the traffic to the diggings being large. But when the Great Northern Railway was opened in 1873 the village began to dwindle away. The railway carried the trade past it to the more conveniently situated and larger towns on either side, and consequently the population left for these towns. The two hotels remained, and there was also a store, a blacksmith's shop, and a few other houses, and these depended for their support on the fruit growers, market gardeners, and farmers who cultivated the rich alluvial flats with which the lower spurs of the mountains are interspersed. The railway platform had been constructed by the Government to accommodate the trade in fruit, vegetables, and other produce which formed the staple industry of the district in 1880.

The Glenrowan Inn was a long, low, weather-board building, with a wide verandah along the front. It stood some distance back from the road, with a large trough hewn from the stem of a tree in front for horses and bullocks to drink from. Near this was a sign-board with the names of the hotel and the proprietor on it thus:—

THE GLENROWAN INN

ANN JONES

BEST ACCOMMODATION

The robbers, it appears, did not go very far when they left Sherritt's hut. They were aware that, when the news of the murder reached Melbourne and other centres, an attempt would be made to follow them, and they seem to have made up their minds to a final effort to conquer the police force of the colony. They went to the camp of the line repairers and roused them up. James Reardon, on coming out of his hut, was ordered to get his tools, as the robbers were determined to rip up the line and wreck the train which they expected to arrive. Reardon at first refused, but on being threatened with death he gave in. He said that the tools were locked up and that he could not get them till morning, but he was told that the chest would soon be broken. His mate, Sullivan, was also secured, and at length they agreed to do as they were told. They went to a bend in the road, a short distance north of the platform, being under the impression that the train would arrive from Wangaratta or Beechworth. They ripped up a number of the rails and piled them across the track. Then they marched Reardon and his wife and child and Sullivan to the Glenrowan Inn, and took possession. They collected sixty-two people in the township, includ-

Chapter XXXI

ing Mr. John Stanistreet, the station-master, and escorted them to the hotel. Among the prisoners also was Constable Bracken. Ned Kelly walked about telling the people that the train would "soon be here" from Rushworth with the black trackers and "a lot of other —— and we're going to kill the lot." There was some confusion owing to the fears of the women and children, and while the bushrangers were engaged in restoring order, Constable Bracken contrived to get hold of the key of the front door. He watched for an opportunity, opened the door and ran out. He reported that three of the troopers who had been hidden in Sherritt's hut had followed the bushrangers, and had watched all their proceedings, but they had not ventured to attack them, as their ammunition was short, and they were not strong enough. Presently a man came out on to the verandah, and the police, recognising him as Ned Kelly, fired a volley. Ned laughed, and shouted "Shoot away, you —— you can't hurt us."

At this juncture Mr. Stanistreet came out of the house, and walked from the hotel to where the police were, at the imminent risk of being shot, as he was between the two firing parties. He escaped, however, and reported that Miss Jones, aged fourteen, and several other of the prisoners in the hotel had been wounded by the police fire, but none of the bushrangers had been hurt. Superintendent Hare had also been severely wounded by the bushrangers, the bullet having shattered the bones of his wrist. He was taken to the railway station-master's house and attended to. At about five p.m. Mrs. Jones, the landlady of the hotel, appeared on the verandah, wringing her hands and weeping. She called the police murderers, and said that her son had been killed and her daughter wounded. The police ceased firing, and the boy was brought out. He was still alive, and was sent off at once to the Wangaratta Hospital, where he died next day. An old man named Martin Cherry was also said to have been killed. Mrs. Jones and her children and servants, and the men and women who had been made prisoners by the bushrangers, left the hotel after dark during a truce, and firing was then kept up during the night.

About daybreak another party of troopers arrived from Benalla, Wangaratta, and Beechworth, making the attacking party about thirty strong. There was a lull in the firing for a time, while the newly-arrived men were being placed in positions, when suddenly a revolving rifle and a cap known to have belonged to Ned Kelly were found a hundred yards from the hotel at the rear of the attacking party. The rifle was stained with blood. The police were still discussing this find and speculating how the articles could have got there when they were fired at from behind a tree. The next moment an extraordinary figure marched across the space between two trees. The figure looked like a tall, stout man, with a nail can over his head. Sergeant Steel, Constable Kelly, and Railway-guard Dowsett fired at it simultaneously, but the bullets appeared to rebound from the body of the figure. Steel then fired at the legs, and at the second shot Ned Kelly, for he it was, fell, crying out "I'm done for." The police rushed forward, but Kelly raised himself on his elbow and fired, howling like a wild beast and declaring that they should never take him alive. He continued shooting, but the bullets "went wild," owing, perhaps, to his weakening through loss of blood, and he was soon grappled with and handcuffed. The armour worn by Ned is said to have been made from stolen plough-shares by a local blacksmith. It consisted of a helmet shaped like a nail can and coming down to the shoulders, with a slit in it to enable the wearer to see; and a breastplate, very long, with shoulder plates and back guard.

The steel averaged nearly a quarter of an inch in thickness, and the weight of the suit worn by Ned Kelly was ninety-seven pounds. The breastplate showed several dints where it had been struck by bullets, but it had not been pierced. Ned had, however, received two wounds in the groin, and one each in the left foot, right leg, right hand, and right arm. He was immediately removed to a safe distance, and placed under medical care. Notwithstanding the loss of one of their small number, the bushrangers kept up a brisk fire from the hotel. At one time a report was circulated that Joe Byrnes had been shot dead while drinking a glass of brandy in the bar, but as there was no apparent slackening in the fire this was discredited. At three p.m. Constable Charles Johnson, under cover of a volley from the besiegers, rushed up to the side of the hotel with a huge bundle of straw, which he placed in position and set fire to. The straw blazed up famously, but soon died out, and the spectators, of whom there was a goodly number, pronounced the attempt to fire the building a failure. It was at this time that Mrs. Skillian, a sister of the Kellys, rode up, dressed in a well-made black cloth riding habit and a Gainsborough hat. She advanced

Chapter XXXI

boldly towards the hotel, but was stopped by the police and warned of the danger she was courting. She replied that she was not afraid, but she desired to persuade her brother Dan to surrender. A consultation was held as to whether she should be permitted to try, but before a decision was arrived at the flames burst out of the roof of the building.

It may be as well to explain here that the wood of the district is principally stringy bark, and that the timber of these trees will not burn. It seems probable, therefore, that when the straw was ignited against the wall of the building, the calico sheeting, with which the rooms were lined and ceiled, caught fire and burned, while the stringy bark weather boards resisted the flames and only charred through slowly. However this may be, the furniture and other fittings burned fiercely, and the whole building was in a blaze. At this time the Rev. Father M. Gibney, a Roman Catholic priest from Perth, Western Australia, who was on a visit to the Benalla district at the time, walked up to the front door holding his crucifix in his hand. He was followed by a number of the police: When they entered the front door they saw the body of Joe Byrnes lying in the bar, in such a position as to make it probable that the report which had been spread as to his death had been true. The body was dragged out slightly scorched. Dan Kelly and Steve Hart were found dead in a small parlour off the bar. From the position in which they were lying it was conjectured that they had either committed suicide or that they had simultaneously shot each other. But there was no time to decide whether either or which of these conjectures were true.

As Father Gibney was about to stoop down to examine the bodies, a gust of wind swept the flames towards him and compelled him to retire. The building was thoroughly alight at last, and the priest and the police and others who had entered were forced out by the fierce heat. In a very short time afterwards the house collapsed, and nothing was left but a heap of ashes, the sign post and trough in front, and the detached kitchen at the rear. In this kitchen was found old Martin Cherry, severely wounded. He was carried out and placed under the doctor's care, but died before night. Close beside the kitchen was the body of a dog, which had been wounded by the attacking party and had crawled between the two buildings to die. Some time before the attempt to fire the building had been made, a telegram had been sent to Melbourne to ask for a small cannon to blow the house down with. Now a telegram was sent to say that it was not required. Consequently the 12-pounder Armstrong gun with the requisite number of men of the Garrison Artillery which had been sent off by special train were stopped at Seymour and sent back. When the fire had burned down sufficiently for an examination to be made, the two mounds of ashes which were all that remained of Dan Kelly and Steve Hart were given to Mrs. Skillian for burial, while the body of Joe Byrnes was reserved for an inquest to be held. Two other suits of armour, similar to that worn by Ned Kelly, were found, the lightest being ninety-two pounds. During the fight "Wild" Wright, Tom Wright, Frank Hart, Kate Kelly, several of the Lloyds and the Byrneses, and other relations and friends of the bushrangers, had been stationed on a ridge a short distance away to see the fun. There was also a large number of other and perhaps more disinterested spectators, some of them from Melbourne or Beechworth, or other even more distant localities. After the inquest the body of Joe Byrnes was given to his friends for burial.

Ned Kelly soon recovered from his wounds and was tried, convicted, and sentenced to death for the murder of Sergeant Kennedy. In conversations with Inspector Sadlier and other police officials before his trial, he said that the bushrangers had known of every movement of the police. They were aware that the police had been hiding in Sherritt's hut for more than a week, hoping to catch Joe if he visited his mother. The police had no right to stop a man from going to see his mother. When the special train arrived the intention of the bushrangers had been to rake it with shots as soon as it reached the place where the rails had been removed. "But," exclaimed Sadlier, "you would have killed all the people in the train." "Yes, of course, God help them," replied Ned, "they'd have got shot, but wouldn't they have shot me if they could?" He said that Steve Hart had visited his mother at Wangaratta, and "didn't we laugh when we saw it in the Wangaratta News afterwards. It was true, too, though the police didn't believe it." He also said that he had been told that after the sticking up of the banks at Euroa and Jerilderie, all the branch banks in Victoria sent their receipts to Melbourne almost daily. They were not going to stick up any more banks. It wasn't worth it. What they had intended to do was to stick up a railway

Chapter XXXI

train, and they'd have done it, "only those little black devils were always about."

On November the 5th, a mass meeting was held in the Hippodrome, in Stephen's Street, Melbourne, with Mr. Hamilton, President of the Society for the Abolition of Capital Punishment, in the chair. The principal speaker was Mr. David Gaunson, M.L.A., and a resolution was unanimously carried to the effect that the case of Edward Kelly was a fit one for the exercise of the Royal Prerogative of Mercy. The Melbourne Argos said that "those present belonged to the larrikin classes," but the attendance was estimated at 4000 persons (including 300 women) inside the building, and about 2000 outside who could not obtain admittance. Similar meetings were also held in Ballarat, Bendigo, Geelong, and other towns, but these efforts were of no avail, and Ned Kelly, "the last of the bushrangers," was hung in the Melbourne gaol, on November 11th, 1880.

Within a few days afterwards, a show was opened in Melbourne, with Kate Kelly, one of the sisters of the dead bushrangers, "mounted on Ned Kelly's celebrated grey mare." A suit of the armour used in the last great fight at Glenrowan, several guns, pistols, and revolvers alleged to have been used in the various raids committed by the bushrangers, some handcuffs and other articles which had belonged to, or were used by them, were exhibited, and some particulars of their careers were given in the form of a lecture, but the police authorities soon interfered and the show was closed. It was re-opened in Sydney, but was suppressed there as "tending towards immorality" almost immediately, and the Kellys returned to the obscurity of private life.

Thus ended the last act in the great tragedy which had supplied almost the only feature of romance to Australian history. Bushranging had been spoken of as "the national crime of Australia," but, as I have shown, there was very little bushranging outside the three colonies—New South Wales, Van Diemen's Land, and Victoria. It was rather an excrescence on, than a development of, Australian character. It has been estimated that the bushrangers in the colonies from the date of the great outbreak inaugurated by Frank Gardiner in 1861, to the death of Ned Kelly, with their more active partisans, never exceeded 300 persons, and the story of their exploits shows how even so small a party can disturb a whole country when the rebels are reckless and determined. It may be said in conclusion, that crime has steadily decreased in Australia from the cessation of transportation. At first, while the gold fever raged, the improvement was very slight, but from the date when the population settled down to steady work the criminal statistics, which are very complete in the colonies, show a steady diminution in crimes against the person or property. There was an increase in the years during which the Ben Hall and Gilbert gang, and their imitators in New South Wales, Victoria, and New Zealand, were most active, but even this did not materially affect the general result, and was speedily compensated for after the death of Thunderbolt and the capture of Power.

In this last epoch of bushranging the Moonlite and Kelly gangs arrested the movement to some degree, but far less sympathy was exhibited with them than in the earlier epoch, and their deeds did not inspire so many young men with the desire to go and do likewise, as those of Hall and Gilbert had done. In fact, bushranging had ceased to be popular, so that the retrogression was small in comparison. Since then numbers of gaols have been closed or converted to other uses. There was a time when every little town in New South Wales had its gaol. Now many of these gaols have been converted into factories or stores, or are used for municipal or other purposes. In Victoria the gaols were fewer but larger, and several of these have been closed, while others once full are now almost empty. A similar story might be told of each of the other colonies of the Australasian group, and Australia as a whole compares favourably with other civilised countries in criminal matters. What the Irishman calls "the bad drop" in the blood of the country has been purged away by the most drastic remedies, and it is extremely improbable that there will ever again be a Frank Gardiner or a Ned Kelly to incite the young and thoughtless to deeds of violence.

Ω

This is the document
given to me by Ned
Kelly when the Bank
at Jerilderie was stuck-up
in Feby 1879

Dear Sir I wish to acquaint you with some of the occurrences of the present past and future. In or about the spring of 1870 the ground was very soft a hawker named Mr Gould got his waggon bogged between Greta and my mother's house on the eleven mile creek, the ground was that rotten it would bog a duck in places so Mr. Gould had abandon his waggon for fear of loosing his horses in the spewy ground. he was stopping at my Mother's awaiting finer or dryer weather Mr. McCormack and his wife. hawkers also were camped in Greta the mosquitoes were very bad which they generally are in a wet spring and to help them

Mr. Johns had a horse called Ruita Cruta although a gelding was as clever as old Wombat or any other Stallion at running horses away and taking them on his beat which was from Greta swamp to the seven mile creek consequently he enticed McCormack's horse away from Greta. Mr. Gould was up early feeding his horses heard a bell and seen McCormack horses for he knew the horse well he sent his boy to take him back to Greta. When McCormack's got the horse they came straight out to Goold and accused him of working the horse; this was false, and Goold was amazed at the idea I could not help laughing to hear Mrs. McCormack accusing him of using the horse after him being so kind as to send his boy to take him from the Ruta Cruta and take him back to them. I pleaded Goulds innocence and Mrs McCormack turned on me and accused me of bringing the horse from Greta to Goolds waggon to pull him out of the bog I did not say much to the woman as my Mother was present but that same day me and my uncle was cutting calves Gould wrapped up a note and a pair of the calves testicles and gave them to me to give them to Mrs McCormack. I did not see her and I gave the parcel to a boy to give to her when she would come instead of giving it

to her he gave it to her husband consequently McCormack said he would summons me I told him neither me or Gould used their horse. he said I was a liar & he could welt me or any of my breed I was about 14 years of age but accepted the challenge and dismounting when Mrs McCormack struck my horse in the flank with a bullock's shin it jumped forward and my fist came in collision with McCormack's nose and caused him to loose his equillibrium and fall postrate I tied up my horse to finish the battle but McCormack got up and ran to the Police camp. Constable Hall asked me what the row was about I told him they

accused me and Gould of using their horse and I hit him and
I would do the same to him if he challenged me McCormack
pulled me and swore their lies against me I was sentenced to
three months for hitting him and three months for the parcel
and bound to keep the peace for 12 months. Mrs McCormack
gave good substantial evidence as she is well acquainted with
that place called Tasmania better known as the Dervon or
Vandiemans land and McCormack being a Police man over
the convicts and women being scarce released her from that
land of bondage and tyranny, and they came to

Victoria and are at present residents of Greta and on the 29th
of March I was released from prison and came home Wild
Wright came to the Eleven Mile to see Mr Gunn stopped
all night and lost his mare both him and me looked all day
for her and could not get her Wright who was a stranger to
me was in a hurry to get back to Mansfield and I gave him
another mare and he told me if I found his mare to keep her
until he brought mine back I was going to Wangaratta and
seen the mare and I caught her and took her with me all the
Police and Detective Berrill seen her as Martains girls used to
ride her about

the town during several days that I stopped at Petre Martains Star Hotel in Wangaratta. She was a chestnut mare white face docked tail very remarkable branded (M) as plain as the hands on a town clock. the property of a Telegraph Master in Mansfield he lost her on the 6th gazetted her on the 12th of March and I was a prisoner in Beechworth Gaol until the 29 of March therefore I could not have Stole the mare. I was riding the mare through Greta Constable Hall came to me and said he wanted me to sign some papers that I did not sign at Beechworth concerning my bail bonds I thought it was the truth he said the papers was at the Barracks and I had no idea he wanted to arrest me or I

would have quietly rode away instead of going to the Barracks. I was getting off when Hall caught hold of me and thought to throw me but made a mistake and came on the broad of his back himself in the dust the mare galloped away and instead of me putting my foot on Halls neck and taking his revolver and putting him in the lock up. I tried to catch the mare. Hall got up and snapped three or four caps at me and would have shot me but the colts patent refused. This is well known in Greta Hall never told me he wanted to arrest me until after he tried to shoot me when I heard the caps snapping I stood until Hall came close he had me covered and was shaking with fear and I knew he would pull the

trigger before he would be game to put his hand on me so I
duped, and jumped at him caught the revolver with one hand
and Hall by the collar with the other. I dare not strike him or
my sureties would loose the bond money I used to trip him
and let him take a mouth ful of dust now and again as he was
as helpless as a big guano after leaving a dead bullock or a
horse. I kept throwing him in the dust until I got him across
the street the very spot where Mrs 0'Briens Hotel stands now
the cellar was just dug then there was some brush fencing
where the post and rail was taking down and on this I threw
big cowardly Hall on his belly I straddled him and rooted
both spurs onto his thighs he roared like a big calf attacked
by dogs and shifted several yards of the fence I got his

hands at the back of his neck and trid to make him let the
revolver go but he stuck to it like grim death to a dead
volunteer he called for assistance to a man named Cohen
and Barnett, Lewis, Thompson, Jewitt two blacksmiths who
was looking on I dare not strike any of there as I was bound
to keep the peace or I could have spread those curs like dung
in a paddock they got ropes tied my hands and feet and Hall
beat me over the head with his six chambered colts revolver
nine stitches were put in some of the cuts by Dr Hastings
And when Wild Wright and my mother came they could
trace us across the street by the blood in the dust and which
spoiled the lustre of the paint on the gate-post of the Barracks
Hall sent for more Police and Doctor Hastings Next morning
I was handcuffed

The Jerilderie Letter

a rope tied from them to my legs and to the seat of the cart and taken to Wangaratta Hall was frightened I would throw him out of the cart so he tied me whilst Constable Arthur laughed at his cowardice for it was he who escorted me and Hall to Wangaratta. I was tried and committed as Hall swore I claimed the mare the Doctor died or he would have proved Hall a perjurer Hall has been tried several times for perjury but got clear as this is no crime in the Police force it is a credit to a Policeman to convict an innocent man but any muff can pot a guilty one Halls character is well known about El Dorado and Snowy Creek and Hall was considerably in debt to Mr L. O.Brien and he was going

to leave Greta Mr O.Brien seen no other chance of getting his money so there was a subscription collected for Hall and with the aid of this money he got James Murdock who was recently hung in Wagga Wagga to give false evidence against me but I was acquitted on the charge of horsestealing and on Halls and Murdocks evidence I was found guilty of receiving and got 3 years experience in Beechworth Pentridges dungeons. this is the only charge ever proved against me Therefore I can say I never was convicted of horse or cattle stealing My Brother Dan was never charged with assaulting a woman but he was sentenced to three months without the option of a fine and one month and two pounds fine for damaging property by Mr. Butler P.M. a sentence that there is no law to uphold therefore the Minister of Justice neglected his duty in that case, but there never was such a thing as Justice in the English laws but any amount of injustice to be had. Out of over thirty head of the very best horses the land could produce I could only find one when I got my liberty. Constable Flood stole and sold the most of them to the navvies on the railway line one bay cob he stole and sold four different times the line was completed and the men all gone when I came out and Flood was shifted to Oxley. he carried on the same game there all the stray horses that was any time without an owner and not in the Police Gazette Flood used to claim

He was doing a good trade at Oxley until Mr Brown of the Laceby Station got him shifted as he was always running his horses about. Flood is different to Sergeant Steel, Strachan, Hall and the most of Police a they have got to hire cads and if they fail the Police are quite helpless. But Flood can make a cheque single-handed he is the greatest horsestealer with the exception of myself and George King I know of. I never worked on a farm a horse and saddle was never traced to me after leaving employment since February 1873 I worked as a faller at Mr J. Saunders and R Rules sawmills then for Heach and Dockendorf I never worked for less than two pound ten a week since I left Pentridge

The Jerilderie Letter

and in 1875 or 1876 I was overseer for Saunders and Rule. Bourke's water--holes sawmills in Victoria since then I was on the King River, during my stay there I ran in a wild bull which I gave to Lydicher a farmer he sold him to Carr a Publican and Butcher who killed him for beef, sometime afterwards I was blamed for stealing this bull from James Whitty Boggy Creek I asked Whitty Oxley racecourse why he blamed me for stealing his bull he said he had found his bull and never blamed me but his son-in-law Farrell told him he heard I sold the bull to Carr not long afterwards I heard again I was blamed for stealing a mob of calves from Whitty and Farrell which I knew nothing about. I began to think they wanted

me to give them something to talk about. Therefore I started wholesale and retail horse and cattle dealing Whitty and Burns not being satisfied with all the picked land on the Boggy Creek and King River and the run of their stock on the certificate ground free and no one interfering with them paid heavy rent to the banks for all the open ground so as a poor man could keep no stock, and impounded every beast they could get, even off Government roads. If a poor man happened to leave his horse or bit of a poddy calf outside his paddock they would be impounded. I have known over 60 head of horses impounded in one day by Whitty and Burns all belonging to poor farmers they would have to leave their ploughing or harvest or other employment to go to Oxley. When they would get there perhaps not have money enough to release them and have to give a bill of sale or borrow the money which is no easy matter. And along with this sort of work, Farrell the Policeman stole a horse from George King and had him in Whitty and Farrells Paddocks until he left the force. And all this was the cause of me and my stepfather George King taking their horses and selling them to Baumgarten and Kennedy. the pick of them was taken to a good market and the culls were kept in Petersons paddock and their brands altered by me two was sold to Kennedy and the rest to Baumgarten who were strangers to me and I believe honest men.

They paid me full value for the horses and could not have known they were stolen. no person had anything to do with the stealing and selling of the horses but me and George King. William Cooke who was convicted for Whittys horses was innocent he was not in my company at Petersons. But it is not the place of the Police to convict guilty men as it is by them they get their living had the right parties been convicted it would have been a bad job for the Police as Berry would have sacked a great many of them only I came to their aid and kept them in their bilits and good employment and got them double pay and yet the ungrateful articles convicted my mother and an infant my brother-in-law and another man

The Jerilderie Letter

who was innocent and still annoy my brothers and sisters and the ignorant unicorns even threaten to shoot myself But as soon as I am dead they will be heels up in the muroo. there will be no more police required they will be sacked and supplanted by soldiers on low pay in the towns and special constables made of some of the farmers to make up for this double pay and expence. It will pay Government to give those people who are suffering innocence, justice and liberty. if not I will be compelled to show some colonial stratagem which will open the eyes of not only the Victoria Police and inhabitants but also the whole British army and now doubt they will acknowledge their hounds were barking at the

wrong stump. And that Fitzpatrick will be the cause of greater slaughter to the Union Jack than Saint Patrick was to the snakes and toads in Ireland. The Queen of England was as guilty as Baumgarten and Kennedy Williamson and Skillion of what they were convicted for When the horses were found on the Murray River I wrote a letter to Mr Swanhill of Lake Rowan to acquaint the Auctioneer and to advertize my horses for sale I brought some of them to that place but did not sell I sold some of them in Benalla Melbourne and other places and left the colony and became a rambling gambler soon after I left there was a warrant for me and the Police searched the place and watched night and day for two or three weeks and when they could not snare me they got a warrant against my brother Dan And on the 15 of April Fitzpatrick came to the Eleven Mile Creek to arrest him he had some conversation with a horse dealer whom he swore was William Skillion this man was not called in Beechworth, besides several other Witnesses, who alone could have proved Fitzpatricks falsehood after leaving this man he went to the house asked was Dan in Dan came out. I hear previous to this Fitzpatrick had some conversation with Williamson on the hill. he asked Dan to come to Greta with him as he had a warrant for him for stealing

Whitty's horses Dan said all right they both went inside Dan was having something to eat his mother asked Fitzpatrick what he wanted Dan for. the trooper said he had a warrant for him Dan then asked him to produce it he said it was only a telegram sent from Chiltren but Sergeant Whelan ordered him to releive Steel at Greta and call and arrest Dan and take him into Wangaratta next morning and get him remanded Dans mother said Dan need not go without a warrant unless he liked and that the trooper had no business on her premises without some Authority besides his own word The trooper pulled out his

The Jerilderie Letter

revolver and said he would blow her brains out if she interfered. in the arrest she told him it was a good job for him Ned was not there or he would ram the revolver down his throat Dan looked out and said Ned is coming now, the trooper being off his guard looked out and when Dan got his attention drawn he dropped the knife and fork which showed he had no murderous intent and slapped heenans hug on him took his revolver and kept him there until Skillion and Ryan came with horses which Dan sold that night. The trooper left and invented some scheme to say that he got shot which any man can see is false, he told Dan to

clear out that Sergeant Steel and Detective Brown and Strachan would be there before morning Strachan had been over the Murray trying to get up a case against him and they would convict him if they caught him as the stock society offored an enticement for witnesses to swear anything and the germans over the Murray would swear to the wrong man as well as the right. Next day Williamson and my mother was arrested and Skillion the day after who was not there at all at the time of the row which can be proved by 8 or 9 witnesses And the Police got great credit and praise in the papers for arresting the mother of 12 children one an infant on her breast and those two quiet hard working innocent men who would not know the difference a revolver and a saucepan handle and kept them six months awaiting trial and then convicted them on the evidence of the meanest article that ever the sun shone on it seems that the jury was well chosen by the Police as there was a discharged Sergeant amongst them which is contrary to law they thought it impossible for a Policeman to swear a lie but I can assure them it is by that means and hiring cads they get promoted I have heard from a trooper that he never knew Fitzpatrick to be one night sober and that he sold his sister to a chinaman but he looks a young strapping rather genteel more fit to be a

starcher to a laundress than a Policeman. For to a keen observer he has the wrong appearance or a manly heart the deceit and cowardice is too plain to be seen in the puny cabbage hearted looking face. I heard nothing of this transaction until very close on the trial I being then over 400 miles from Greta when I heard I was outlawed and a hundred pound reward for me for shooting at a trooper in Victoria and a hundred pound for any man that could prove a conviction of horse-stealing against me so I came back to Victoria knew I would get no justice if I gave myself up I enquired after my brother Dan and found him digging on Bullock Creek heard how the Police used to be blowing that they would not ask me to stand they would shoot me first and then cry surrender and how they used to rush into the house upset all the milk dishes break tins of eggs empty the flour out of the bags on to the ground and even the meat out of the cask and destroy all the provisions and shove the girls in front of them into the rooms like dogs so as if anyone was there they would shoot the girls first but they knew well I was not there or I would have scattered their blood and brains like rain I would manure the Eleven mile with their bloated carcasses and yet remember there is not one drop of murderous blood in my Veins

Superintendent Smith used to say to my sisters, see all the men I have out today I will have as many more tomorrow and we will blow him into pieces as small as paper that is in our guns Detective Ward and Constable Hayes took out their revolvers and threatened to shoot the girls and children in Mrs Skillions absence the greatest ruffians and murderers no matter how deprived would not be guilty of such a cowardly action, and this sort of cruelty and disgraceful and cowardly conduct to my brothers and sisters who had no protection coupled with the conviction of my mother and those men certainly made my blood boil as I dont think there is a man born could have

Ned Kelly

the patience to suffer it as long as I did or ever allow his blood to get cold while such insults as these were unavenged and yet in every paper that is printed I am called the blackest and coldest blooded murderer ever on record But if I hear any more of it I will not exactly show them what cold blooded murder is but wholesale and retail slaughter something different to shooting three troopers in self defence and robbing a bank. I would have been rather hot-blooded to throw down my rifle and let them shoot me and my innocent brother, they were not satisfied with frightening my sisters night and day and destroying their provisions and lagging my mother and infant

and those innocent men but should follow me and my brother into the wilds where he had been quietly digging neither molesting or inter-fering with anyone he was making good wages as the creek is very rich within half a mile from where I shot Kennedy. I was not there long and on the 25 of October I came on Police tracks between Table top and the bogs. I crossed them and returning in the evening I came on a dif-ferent lot of tracks making for the shingle hut I went to our camp and told my brother and his two mates me and my brother went and found their camp at the shingle hut about a mile from my brothers house saw they carried long

The Jerilderie Letter

firearms and we knew our doom was sealed if we could not beat those before the others would come As I knew the other party of Police would soon join them and if they came on us at our camp they would shoot us down like dogs at our work as we had only two guns. we thought it best to try and bail those up take their fire-arms and ammunition and horses and we could stand a chance with the rest We approached the spring as close as we could get to the camp as the intervening space being clear ground and no battery We saw two men at the logs they got up and one took a double barreled fowling-piece and fetched a horse down and hobbled him at the tent

we thought there were more men in the tent asleep those being on sentry we could have shot those two men without speaking but not wishing to take their lives we waited McIntyre laid the gun against a stump and Lonigan sat on the log I advanced, my brother Dan keepin McIntyre covered which he took to be constable Flood and had he not obeyed my orders, or at-tempted to reach for the gun or draw his revolver he would have been shot dead but when I called on them to throw up their hands McIntyre obeyed and Lonigan ran some six or seven yards to a battery of logs insted of dropping behind the one he was sitting on, he had just got to the logs and put his head up to take aim when I shot him that instant or he would have shot me as I took him to be Strachan the man who said he would not ask me to stand he would shoot me first like a dog. But it happened to be Lonigan the man who in company with Sergeant Whelan Fitzpatrick and King the Boot maker and constable O.Day that tried to put a pair of hand-cuffs on me in Benalla but could not and had to allow McInnis the miller to put them on, previous to Fitzpatrick swear-ing he was shot, I was fined two pounds for hitting Fitzpatrick and two pounds for not allowing five curs like Sergeant Whelan O.Day Fitz-patrick King and Lonigan who caught me by the privates

and would have sent me to Kingdom come only I was not ready and he is the man that blowed before he left Violet Town if Ned Kelly was to be shot he was the man would shoot him and no doubt he would shoot me even if I threw up my arms and laid down as he knew four of them could not arrest me single-handed not to talk of the rest of my mates, also either me or him would have to die, this he knew well therefore he had a right to keep out of my road, Fitzpatrick is the only one I hit out of the five in Benalla this shows my feeling towards him as he said we were good friends & even swore it but he was the biggest enemy I had in the country with the exception

The Jerilderie Letter

of Lonigan and he can be thankful I was not there when he took a revolver and threatened to shoot my mother in her own house it is not fire three shots and miss him at a yard and a half I dont think I would use a revolver to shoot a man like him when I was within a yard and a half of him or attempt to fire into a house where my mother brothers and sisters was. and according to Fitzpatricks statement all around him a man that is such a bad shot as to miss a man three times at a yard and a half would never attempt to fire into a house among a house full of women and children while I had a pairs of arms and bunch of fives on the end of them

that never failed to peg out anything they came in contact with and Fitzpatrick knew the weight of one of them only too well, as it run against him once in Benalla, and cost me two pound odd as he is very subject to fainting. As soon as I shot Lonigan he jumped up and staggered some distance from the logs with his hands raised and then fell he surrendered but too late I asked McIntyre who was in the tent he replied no one. I advanced and took possession of their two revolvers and fowling-piece which I loaded with bullets instead of shot. I asked McIntyre where his mates was he said they had gone down the creek, and he did not expect them that night he asked me was I going to shoot him and his mates. I told him no. I would shoot no man if he gave up his arms and leave the force he said the police all knew Fitzpatrick had wronged us. and he intended to leave the force, as he had bad health, and his life was insured, he told me he intended going home and that Kennedy and Scanlan were out looking for our camp and also about the other Police he told me the N.S.W Police had shot a man for shooting Sergeant Walling I told him if they did, they had shot the wrong man And I expect your gang came to do the same with me he said no they did not come to shoot me they came to apprehend me I asked him what they carried spenceir rifles and breech loading fowling pieces and so much ammunition for as the Police was

only supposed to carry one revolver and 6 cartridges in the revolver but they had eighteen rounds of revolver cartridges each three dozen for the fowling piece and twenty one spenceir-rifle cartridges and God knows how many they had away with the rifle this looked as if they meant not only to shoot me only to riddle me but I dont know either Kennedy Scanlan or him and had nothing against them, he said he would get them to give up their arms if I would not shoot them as I could not blame them, they had to do their duty I said I did not blame them for doing honest duty but I could not suffer them blowing me to pieces in my own native land and they knew Fitzpatrick wronged

THE JERILDERIE LETTER

us and why not make it public and convict him but no they would rather riddle poor unfortunate creoles. but they will rue the day ever Fitzpatrick got among them, Our two mates came over when they heard the shot fired but went back again for fear the Police might come to our camp while we were all away and manure bullock flat with us on our arrival. I stopped at the logs and Dan went back to the spring for fear the tropers would come in that way but I soon heard them coming up the creek. I told McIntyre to tell them to give up their arms, he spoke to Kennedy who was some distance in front of Scanlan he reached for his revolver and jumped off, on the off

side of his horse and got behind a tree when I called on them to throw up their arms and Scanlan who carried the rifle slewed his horse around to gallop away but the horse would not go and as quick as thought fired at me with the rifle without unslinging it and was in the act of firing again when I had to shoot him and he fell from his horse. I could have shot them without speaking but their lives was no good to me. McIntyre jumped on Kennedys horse and I allowed him to go as I did not like to shoot him after he surrendered or I would have shot him as he was between me and Kennedy therefore I could not shoot Kennedy without shooting him first. Kennedy kept firing from behind the tree my brother Dan advanced and Kennedy ran I followed him he stopped behind another tree and fired again. I shot him in the arm pit and he dropped his revolver and ran I fired again with the gun as he slewed around to surrender I did not know he had dropped his revolver. the bullet passed through the right side of his chest & he could not live or I would have let him go had they been my own brother I could not help shooting there or else let them shoot me which they would have done had their bullets been directed as they intended them. But as for handcuffing Kennedy to a tree or cutting his ear off or brutally treating any of them, is a falsehood, if Kennedys ear was cut off it was not done by me and none

of my mates was near him after he was shot I put his cloak over him and left him as well as I could and were they my own brothers I could not have been more sorry for them this cannot be called wilful murder for I was compelled to shoot them, or lie down and let them shoot me it would not be wilful murder if they packed our remains in, shattered into a mass of animated gore to Mansfield, they would have got great praise and credit as well as promotion but I am reconed a horrid brute because I had not been cowardly enough to lie down for them under such trying circumstances and insults to my people certainly their wives and children are to be pitied but they must remember those men came into the bush with the intention

The Jerilderie Letter

of scattering pieces of me and my brother all over the bush and yet they know and acknowledge I have been wronged and my mother and four or five men lagged innocent and is my brothers and sisters and my mother not to be pitied also who has no alternative only to put up with the brutal and cowardly conduct of a parcel of big ugly fat-necked wombat headed big bellied magpie legged narrow hipped splaw-footed sons of Irish Bailiffs or english landlords which is better known as Officers of Justice or Victorian Police who some calls honest gentlemen but I would like to know what business an honest man would have in the Police as it is an old saying It takes a rogue to catch a rogue and a

man that knows nothing about roguery would never enter the force an take an oath to arrest brother sister father or mother if required and to have a case and conviction if possible Any man knows it is possible to swear a lie and if a policeman looses a conviction for the sake of swearing a lie he has broke his oath therefore he is a perjurer either ways. A Policeman is a disgrace to his country, not alone to the mother that suckled him, in the first place he is a rogue in his heart but too cowardly to follow it up without having the force to disguise it. next he is traitor to his country ancestors and religion as they were all catholics before the Saxons and Cranmore yoke held sway since then they were perse cuted massacreed thrown into martrydom and tortured beyond the ideas of the present generation What would people say if they saw a strapping big lump of an Irishman shepherding sheep for fifteen bob a week or tailing turkeys in Tallarook ranges for a smile from Julia or even begging his tucker, they would say he ought to be ashamed of himself and tar-and--feather him But he would be a king to a policeman who for a lazy loafing cowardly bilit left the ash corner deserted the shamrock, the emblem of true wit and beauty to serve under a flag and nation that has destroyed massacreed and murdered their fore-fathers by the greatest of torture as rolling them down hill in spiked barrels

pulling their toe and finger nails and on the wheel. and every torture imaginable more was transported to Van Diemand's Land to pine their young lives away in starvation and misery among tyrants worse than the promised hell itself all of true blood bone and beauty, that was not murdered on their own soil, or had fled to America or other countries to bloom again another day, were doomed to Port Mcquarie Toweringabbie norfolk island and Emu plains and in those places of tyrany and condemnation many a blooming Irishman rather than subdue to the Saxon yoke Were flogged to death and bravely died in servile chains but true to the shamrock and a credit to Paddys land What would people say if I became a policeman and took an oath to arrest my brothers and sisters & relations and convict them by fair or foul means after the conviction of my mother and the persecutions and insults offered to myself and people Would they say I was a decent gentleman, and yet a police-man is still in worse and guilty of meaner actions than that The Queen must surely be proud of such herioc men as the Police and Irish soldiers as It takes eight or eleven of the biggest mud crushers in Melbourne to take one poor little half starved larrakin to a watch house. I have seen as many as eleven, big & ugly enough to lift Mount Macedon out of a crab hole more like the species of a baboon or Guerilla than a man.

actually come into a court house and swear they could not arrest one eight stone larrakin and them armed with battens and neddies without some civilians assistance and some of them going to the hospital from the affects of hits from the fists of the larrakin and the Magistrate would send the poor little Larrakin into a dungeon for being a better man than such a parcel of armed curs. What would England do if America declared war and hoisted a green flag as its all Irishmen that has got command of her armies forts and batteries even her very life guards and beef tasters are Irish would they not slew around and fight her with their own arms for the sake of the colour they dare not wear for years. and to reinstate it and rise old Erins isle once more, from the pressure and tyrannism of the English yoke, which has kept it in poverty and starvation, and caused them to wear the enemys coats. What else can England expect. Is there not big fat-necked Unicorns enough paid to torment and drive me to do thing which I dont wish to do, without the public assisting them I have never interefered with any person unless they deserved it, and yet there are civilians who take firearms against me, for what rea-son I do not know, unless they want me to turn on them and extermin-ate them without medicine. I shall be compelled to make an example of some of them if they cannot find no other employment

If I had robbed and plundered ravished and murdered everything I met young and old rich and poor. the public could not do any more than take firearms and Assisting the police as they have done, but by the light that shines pegged on an ant-bed with their bellies opened their fat taken out rendered and poured down their throat boiling hot will be fool to what pleasure I will give some of them and any person aiding or harbouring or assisting the Police in any way whatever or employing any person whom they know to be a detective or cad or those who would be so deprived as to take blood money will be outlawed and declared unfit to be allowed human buriel their property either consumed or confiscated and them theirs and all belonging to them exterminated off the face of the earth, the enemy I cannot catch myself I shall give a payable reward for, I would like to know who put that article that reminds me of a poodle dog half clipped in the lion fashion, called Brooke E. Smith Superin-tendent of Police he knows as much about commanding Police as Cap-tain Standish does about mustering mosquitoes and boiling them down for their fat on the back blocks of the Lachlan for he has a head like a turnip a stiff neck as big as his shoulders narrow hipped and pointed towards the feet like a vine stake and if there is any one to be called a murderer

regarding Kennedy, Scanlan and Lonigan it is that misplaced poodle he gets as much pay as a dozen good troopers, if there is any good in them, and what does he do for it he cannot look behind him without turning his whole frame it takes three or four police to keep sentry while he sleeps in Wangaratta, for fear of body snatchers do they think he is a superior animal to the men that has to guard him if so why not send the men that gets big pay and reconed superior to the common police after me and you shall soon save the country of high salaries to men that is fit for nothing else but getting better men than him self shot and sending orphan children to the industrial school to make prostitutes and cads of them for the Detectives and other evil dis-posed persons Send the high paid and men that received big salaries for years in a gang by themselves after me, As it makes no difference to them but it will give them a chance of showing whether they are worth more pay than a common trooper or not and I think the Public will soon find they are only in the road of good men and obtaining money under false pretences, I do not call McIntyre a coward for I reckon he is as game a man as wears the jacket as he had the presence of mind to know his position, directly as he was spoken to, and only foolishness to disobey, it was cowardice that made Lonigan and the others fight it is only

foolhardiness to disobey an outlaw as any Police-man or other man who do not throw up their arms directly as I call on them knows the consequence which is a speedy dispatch to Kingdom Come, I wish those men who joined the stock protection society to with-draw their money and give it and as much more to the widows and orphans and poor of Greta district wher I spent and will again spend many a happy day fearless free and bold as it only aids the police to procure false witnesses and go whacks with men to steal horses and lag innocent men it would suit them far better to subscribe a sum and give it to the poor of their district and there is no fear of anyone stealing their property for no man could steal their horses without the knowledge of the poor if any man was mean enough to steal their property the poor would rise out to a man and find them if they were on the face of the earth it will always pay a rich man to be liberal with the poor and make as little enemies as he can as he shall find if the poor is on his side he shall loose nothing by it, If they depend in the police they shall be drove to destruction, As they can not and will not protect them if duffing and bushranging were abolished the police would have to cadge for their living I speak from experience as I have sold horses and cattle innumerable and yet eight head of the culls is all ever was found I never was interfered with whilst I kept up this successful

trade. I give fair warning to all those who has reason to fear me to sell out and give £10 out of every hundred towards the widow and orphan fund and do not attempt to reside in Victoria but as short a time as possible after reading this notice, neglect this and abide by the consequences, which shall be worse than the rust in the wheat in Victoria or the druth of a dry season to the grasshoppers in New South Wales I do not wish to give the order full force without giving timely warning. but I am a widows son outlawed and my orders must be obeyed.

INDEX

12th Regiment 181
21st Fusiliers 102
40th Regiment 42
46th Regiment 19
48th Regiment 20
57th Regiment 28
63rd Regiment 24, 28
96th Regiment 101, 167

A

Aarons, Mr. 69
Abbott, Mr. 295
Abercrombie Goldfield 216
Abercrombie Mountains 183
Aborigine 43–44, 233, 272–274
   Black Devils 344
   Black Jack 22
   Black Mary 18
   Black Tracker 42, 185, 193, 197, 200, 233, 254–255, 272–273, 311, 325, 344, 349, 351
      Donald 297-301
      Johnny Bein Bar 193
      Tommy 193
      Wynne, Sir Watkin 254–255
   Bushranger 274
   Eumarrah 27
   Half Caste 261
   Jacky Bullfrog 184
   Musquito 22–23, 27
   The Black War 23–30
   Wandong, Paddy 261
Adelaide 88, 130
Adelong 296
Adelphi Hotel 157
Admiralty Court 98
Aitcheson, Mr. 136
Aitcheson, Mrs. 137
Aitchison, Elliott 131
Aitken's Gap 134
Albury 234, 241

Alger, Philip 165
Allardyce, Mr. 109
Allen, Mr. 209
Allerton, Benjamin 181
Allman, Mr. 87
Anderson, James 142
Anderson, John 98
Anderson, Wesley 135
Anlezack's Inn 86
Appin 83, 246
Apple Tree Flat 194, 228
Araluen 231, 235, 249, 251
Ararat 293, 295
Argyle 45
Armidale 269
Arthur, Lieutenant Governor 21, 26–28, 31, 39
Ashby 138
Ashton, Mr. 263
Atkin, Mr. 235
Atkins, Henry 105
Atkins, John 149
Atkins, William 152
Atterill, James (alias Thompson) 102
Australia 124
Australian Arms Hotel 321
Australian Joint Stock Bank 196, 282

B

Bacchus Marsh 150, 317
Back Creek 228
Bagdad 170
Bailey, Dr. 158
Baker, George James 306
Baker, John 283
Balcombe, Mr. 68
Baldwin, James 253
Baldwin, Mr. 273
Balfour, Colonel 40

History of Australian Bushrangers

Ballan 150
Ballarat 124, 126, 132, 150, 153–156, 178, 210, 295, 302, 318–319, 323, 329, 355
  Bakery Hill 155
  Lydiard Street 155
Ballarat Goldfields 128
Balmain 12, 71, 84
Balranald 324
Balubula 207
Bambera Hill 263
Bankes, Anthony 102
Bank of Australasia 325
Bank of Australia 46
Bank of New South Wales 47, 187, 268, 340
Bank of Victoria 155, 156, 302
Bannister, Captain 38
Bargo Brush 61, 69, 84, 85, 257
Barker, Constable 94
Barnes, Mr. 199, 220
Barnett, Terence 64
Barrabool Hills 134
Barrack Square 9
Barragon 263
Barrell, Edward 260
Barren Jack 293
Barrier Ranges 283, 284
Barrow, Mr. 118
Barry, Judge 133
Barton, Mr. 56
Barwon River 125
Bass, Lieutenant 95
Bass, Mr. 214
Bass's Straits 172
Batavia 3
Batesford 150
Bates, Thomas 105
Bathurst 14, 45, 74, 92, 124, 166, 183, 200, 205, 208, 210, 223, 228, 237, 257, 270, 276, 283–284, 342
  Howick Street 205
  Piper Street 205
  William Street 205
Bathurst Assizes 260
Bathurst Free Press 184
Bathurst Gaol 260
Bathurst Road 281
Bathurst-Sydney Road 195
Bathurst Times 211, 221
Batman, John 38, 42
Battle, James (old Jamie) 304
Battye, Captain 185
Bawten, Mr. 61
Baxter, Constable 244
Bayles, Mr. and Mrs. 171
Baylie, John 134
Bayliss, Mr. 239
Baynes, Mr. 320–322
Beale, Susan 57
Bear, Mr. 90
Beauvais, Mr. 277
Beavors, George (alias Berry) 100
Beck, Constable 326
Beechworth 245, 307, 331, 344, 350–354
Beechworth District 296
Beechworth Gaol 299
Bega 250, 252
Bell 25
Bellamy, Mr. 284
Bell, Dr. 93
Bell, Lieutenants 24
Bellpost Hill 138
Benalla 245, 329, 344, 348, 349–351
Benalla Standard 329
Ben Bullen 196
Bendemeer 271
Bendigo 126, 130, 132, 134, 150, 151, 210, 302, 307–308, 319, 355
Bendigo Creek 152
Bennett, Graham 323
Bent, Mr. Ellis 20
Benyon, Mrs. 182

Index

Benyon's Inn 182
Benyon, Stephen 182
Benyon, William 182, 183
Beresford, Constable 325
Bermingham, George 212
Berrima 56, 58, 62, 65, 73, 84, 257
Berry, James 73–74
Berryman, Thomas 258
Bertram, William 283–284
Bethune, Walter 38
Beved, George 276
Beveridge, John (alias Anderson) 98
Beveridge, Mr. James 322
Biddington, Mr. 76
Bigga 182–183
Bigge, Commissioner 46
Bigge, Mr. F. E. 86
Bigge, Mr. J. T. 20
Big Gravel Pits 155
Big Hill 195, 284
Big River 165
Big Wombat 197
Billabong 179, 181, 338
Billabong Creek 232, 235
Binalong 192, 213, 215, 235
Binda 226, 230, 234
Bingera Goldfield 267
Birkett, Moses 172
Black Bull Inn 139
Black Dog Creek 297
Black Forest 132, 134
Black Hill 271
Black Horse Inn 62, 71
Black Rock 235, 269
Black Springs 224
Blanche, Mr. 278
Blanche, Mrs. 278
Blanche's Hotel 279
Bland, Mr. 258
Bland Plains 217

Bland River 222
Blaney 204, 228
Blatchford, Captain 141–142
Blatchford, Mr. 231
Bloody Tyrant Price 144
Bloomfield, Chief Constable 148
Bloomfield, Constable 146
Blowfly 9
Blue Ash 23
Blue Mountains 14, 45, 50, 92
Blunt, Henry 106
Bodenham, Thomas 31
Bodumba 310
Boeswetter, R. Mr. 152
Boggy Creek 273, 277
Bogolong 186, 241
Boldrewood, Rolf 51
Bolero 234
Bollard, John 282, 290
Bolton, Mr. 209
Bond, Mr. 90
Bong Bong 219
Bonny, Mrs. 108
Bonwick, Mr. James 327
Booker, Francis 24
Booth, James 276
Booth, John 119
Boramble 235
Bordmore, Mr 160
Boro 68
Boro Creek 69, 178
Borthwick 23
Boswell, Mr. 90
Botany Bay 1, 38, 98, 164
Bothwell 24
Boulton, John 155
Bourke 282
Bourke, Governor 26, 50
Bourke & Hughes 271

391

History of Australian Bushrangers

Bourke, Robert 293, 295
Bourke, Sir Richard 7
Bowe, Charles 134
Bowen, Constable 323–324
Bowenfels 92, 195
Bow, John 187, 189, 237, 290
Bowler, Mr. 245
Bowne, Mr. 234
Bowning 213
Boyd 53
Boyd, James (alias McGrath) 274, 289
Boyd, Mrs. 300
Boyle, Captain 100
Brace, Emanuel 53
Bracken, Constable 349–351
Bradley, Mr. 224, 282
Brady, Mathew 38, 66, 76
Brady, Mr. 6
Braidwood 67, 93, 250–255, 281–282
Braidwood Dispatch 255
Braidwood Gaol 249
Braidwood Hospital 255
Brannagan, Francis 142
Breadalbane Plains 231, 234
Break-o'-day Road 106
Brennan 86
Brennan, Inspector 215
Brennan, Mr. 179
Brennan, Mrs. 179
Brennan, Stephen 115
Brewers' Shanty 185
Brigalow Creek 274
Brigham, Commissioner 119
Bright 299
  Buckland Road 301
Bright, Constable 234
Brisbane 161–162, 312–313
  Cleveland Road 162
Brisbane Courier 310
Brisbane Mechanics' School of Arts 312

Brisbane River 161
Brisbane Valley 196
British Government 121
Britten's Hotel 267
Britton, Frederick 191
Broad Marsh 109
Broadribb, Mr. 23
Brodribb, Mr. 108
Broken Hill 283
Brookman, William 261, 288
Broomfield, James 105
Broughton 38
Broughton, Mr. 293
Browlee 252
Brown, Constable 272
Brown, Corporal 45
Browne, Mr. 282
Browne, Rev. Dr. 167
Brown, Harry 253
Brown, James 31, 199
Brown, John 130
Brown (J.P.), A. Mr. 193
Brown, Judge 120, 122
Brownlow, John 191
Brown Mountain 102
Brown, Mrs 201
Brown, Mrs. 218, 290
Brown's River 121
Brown, William 142
Bruce's Creek 129
Bryan, Mary 106
Bryant, James 38, 81
Bryant, Richard 142, 146
Bryan, William 154
Buck, Constable 293
Buckley, Mr. 155
Budge 78
Buffalo 296
Bullingall 275

Index

Bull, Servant 53
Bungendore 68, 74
Bungowanah 333
Buninyong 130–132, 135, 154
Burgess, Richard H. (alias Miller) 303–304, 307
Burke, Mr. 205, 208, 218, 238
Burns, Constable 231
Burns, John 38
Burnt Bridge 153
Burra Burra 283
Burragorang 50
Burrangang Star 213
Burrangong 178–180, 185, 192, 197, 200–201, 205, 209, 220, 225, 230, 233, 240, 307
Burrangong Creek 209
Burrangong Goldfield 184
Burrell, Mr. 24
Burridge, Mr. 183
Burrowa 176, 202, 212, 259
Burrowa River 257
Burrow, Arthur 153
Burton, Judge 13
Bushrangers' Act 80–87
Bushranging Act 12, 79
Bushy Plains 25
Button, Mr. 276
Byrne, Mrs. 269
Byrnes, Joe 333–334, 339–340, 346–347, 352–354
Byrnes, Mrs. 346
Byrnes, The 328, 354

C

Cadell, Master Willie 194, 195
California 128, 201, 290
Callan Park Lunatic Asylum 53
Caloola 190
Camden 85
Campbell, Constable 263
Campbell, Mr. 86

Campbell, Mr. Charles 68
Campbell, Mr. David Henry 210–212
Campbell, Mrs. 210
Campbell, Mrs. Colonel 256
Campbell, Robert 264
Campbell's River 200–201
Campbell's Station 188
Campbelltown 52, 61, 83, 106, 110, 168, 171, 276
Camphin, Detective 203, 276
Canada 190
Cannibalism 31–37
Cannon, Constable 244
Canonbar 271, 277
Canowindra 206–207, 221, 342
Canton 97
Canvas Town 147–148
Cape Schank 294
Cappisote, Giovanni 278
Captain Melville 136–145, 146, 157, 219
Captain Moonlite 316–322. *See also* Scott, George
Captain Norton 196
Captain Smith 40
Captain Thunderbolt 268–271, 299, 316, 356
Carcoar 204, 221, 281
Carcoar Road 259
Carew, Lieutenant 96, 99
Carew, Mrs. 99
Carlisle Gully 278
Carrol, John 251–252
Carroll, Constable 259, 323–324
Carrots (convict) 27
Carter, Samuel 266
Cartwright, Rev. Mr. 68
Casement, Mr. 334
Casey, Mr. 325
Casey, Sergeant 276
Cash and Kavanagh Gang 167
Cashan, Mr. (alias Nowlan) 92

393

Cash, Martin 109, 111, 119
Cassilis 193, 284–285
Castle Forbes 6, 48
Castlemaine 128, 246, 307
Castlereagh River 261
Caswell, Lieutenant 77
Cattle Duffing 328
Chain of Ponds 180
Chalker, Mr. John 57
Chalmers, Captain 171
Chamberlain, Mr. 91
Chandler, Sergeant 216
Chapman, Chief Constable 57
Charters, Daniel 187, 308
Cherry, Martin 351–353
Cherry Tree Hill 193
Chesley, John 142
Chief Police Magistrate of Sydney 11
Childs, Major Joseph 116
Chilwell 155
China 97, 98
Chinese 178, 216–218, 222–225, 232, 239, 250, 259, 271, 300
  Bushranger 271
  Goon, Ah 323
  Goon, Mrs. Li 300
  Ling, Ah 216
  Lung, Ah 218
  Wee, Ah 216
  Yong, Ah 216
Chinese Camp 259
Chisholm, Mr. 217, 234
Chitty, Robert 81
Chiver, Mr. 80
Christian, Neil 333
Christie, Lieutenant 69, 77
Christie, Mr. James 234
Christy, Captain 84
Churchley, Constable 240
Church of England 317

Circular Head Shipping Company 99
Cirkel, Mr. 197
City of Ballarat 155
City Police Court 324
Clare 325
Clarendon 105
Clark, Captain 24
Clark, Constable 210
Clarke, Acton 266
Clarke, Annie 253
Clarke, Donald 247
Clarke, James 249–251, 266
Clarke, John 249, 254–255
Clarke, Marcus 144
Clarke, Mr. 234
Clarke, Mr. John 109
Clarke, Mrs. 251
Clarke, Peter 266
Clarke, Samuel 288
Clarkes, The 328
Clarke, Thomas 249–255
Clarke, William 184
Clark, Mr. 25
Clayton, Bushranger 222
Clayton, Thomas 160
Cleary, Sergeant 193, 272, 277
Clegg, David 147
Clegg, James 160
Cleveland Point 161
Clifford, Mr. James 168
Clift, Mr. Samuel 277
Clifton Lodge 106
Clok, Henry 192
Clyde River 109
Coady, Edward 299
Cobham's, Mr. 284
Cockatoo Island 71–72, 92, 190, 251, 270
Cockburn, Private 103
Cocked Hat Hill 108

INDEX

Coffey's Inn 212
Cogan, Michael 168
Cohen, Convict 42
Colac 146
Cole, John 240
Collector 230, 234, 237
Collingwood 125
Collins, Michael 282
Collins Street 155, 157
Colonial Office 26, 125
Colonial Secretary 29, 324
Colony of Victoria 141
Commandant of Norfolk Island 115–116
Commercial Banking Company 187
Committee of Supercargoes 97
Commodore Inn 110
Conargo 342
Condell, Sergeant 188, 232
Connell, Constable Thomas 106
Connell, Morris 45
Connell, Mr. J. 23
Connell, Patrick 250–251
Connell, Tom 250–251
Connolly, Patrick 38
Connors, John 276
Conroy, John 266
Conway, John 106
Cook, Constable Samuel 48
Cook's River 52
Cook's Vale Creek 203
Cooma 212, 214, 252
Coombing 202
Coonamble 193
Coonanbarabran 271
Cooper, Patrick 160
Cootamundra 199, 218
Copabella 240
Cornelius, Bill 31
Cornish, Mr. 166
Cotham, Mr. 77

Cotterall, Robert (alias Blue Cap) 265, 289
Coulson, Mr. 168
Cowan, Convict 42
Cowey's Creek 139
Cowper, Mr. Thomas 60
Cowper, Sir Charles 204
Cowra 181, 209, 221, 235, 249
Cowra Road 260
Coxen's Tom 86
Cox, Mr. 89, 339–340
Cox, Mr. James 105
Cox, Thomas 35
Craddige, Constable 49
Craddige, Daniel 49
Cramp, Alfred 230
Cranston, Mr. 311
Crawford, James 38, 43
Crawford, Mr. 345
Creer, Captain 171
Cressbrook 312
Criminal Court 100
Criminals' Influx Prevention Act 130, 308
Crisp's Inn 64, 85
Crombie, Mr. Edward 261
Crookwell 281
Crookwell, James 215, 258
Cropper, Mr. 235
Cross Keys Hotel 149
Cross Roads Grounds 283
Crown Hotel 135
Crown Prosecutor 142
Crowther Station 184
Culgoa 266
Cummings, Mr. Kieran 206
Cummins, Larry 203
Cummins, Mr. E. 284
Cummins, Thomas 215
Cumsden, George 113
Cunliffe, Charles 110

395

Cunningham, Mr. 74
Cunningham, Mrs. 24
Cunningham, Thomas (alias Smith) 253, 289
Cupid 25
Curnow, Mr. 349
Curramore 105
Curran, Constable 324
Curran, Michael 220
Curran, Paddy 66, 72
Currawang 55, 202
Curry, Mr. 312
Custom House 12
Cuthertson, Lieutenant 35
Cutts, William 93

D

Dacy, Constable Luke 282
Daisy Hill 295
Daley, Constable 168
Dalton, Alexander 31
Dalton, Bushranger 171
Dalton, Constable 273
Dalton, James 111
Daly, Malachi 165
Daly, Patrick 197
Dandenong 89
Danger, Mr. 80
Daniels, Mary 23
Dargue, Henry 289
Dargue, Thomas 289
Darlinghurst Court House 323
Darlinghurst Gaol 55, 71, 253, 323
Darling, Mr. 89
Davey, Colonel 20
Davey, Lieutenant Governor 17–18
Davidson, Inspector 232
Davidson, Mr. 234
Davidson's Hotel 338
Davis, Bill 34

Davis, District Constable 169
Davis, Edward 76, 81
Davis, George James (alias Huntley) 98
Davis, John 190
Davis, Joseph 160
Davis, Michael Henry 181, 185
Davis, Mr. 131
Davis, Mr. D. 227
Davis, S. B. Mr. 152
Davis, William 102
Dawson, Mr. 25
Day, Mr. Edward Denny 81
Day, Mr. John Thomas 325
Deake, Mr. 78
Dean, Alexander 193
De Clouett, Mr. 205
Deep Creek 224
Dee River 109
Delany, Mr. 268
Deloraine 108
Denholme, Mr. 109
Deniliquin 240, 262, 343
Deniliquin Chronicle 242
Denison, Sir W. T. 120
Denison Town 262
Dennie, Mr. 146
Denovan, Mr. E. 23
Dermoodie, Mr. 318–319
Derwent river 8
Derwent River 28, 114
Desailly, Mr. 261
Devine, Constable 338
Devine, Mrs. 338
Diamond Creek 294
Dines, Mr. 275
District Constable of Avoca 171
Dixon, Constable 118
Dobbins, Mr. 261
Dobson, George 304

INDEX

Dobson, Mr. 283
Donaldson, Captain 28
Donnelly, Mr. 240
Donohoe, Johnny 52
Donohoe, Sergeant 212
Donovan, Daniel 142
Donovan, John 134
Doodal Cooma Station 244
Doran, Constable 170
Dorrington, Mrs. 278
Doughboy Hollow 78, 81
Douglas, Major 28
Douglass, John 154
Dowling, Sir James 57, 101
Downes, John 38
Downey, James 184
Downie, Daniel 105
Dowsett, Railway-Guard 352
Doyle, Michael 58
Draper, Mr. 131
Drew, Mr. 20
Drew, Mr. R. 250
Driscoll, William (Timothy, alias Dido) 168–170
Dubbo 236, 271
Dudley, James 305
Dudley, Mr. 334
Duffing (theft of stock) 176–177
Duffy, Michael 218
Duffy, Sergeant 282
Duffy, Thomas 161
Duguid, William 216
Duins, Sergeant 151
Duke of York Inn 40
Duncan, James 132
Duncan, Mr. W. A. 162
Duncan, William 119
Dunkley, Mr. 172
Dunleavy, John 57–58, 64, 221–222
Dunn, Aaron 106

Dunn, Billy 257
Dunne, William 212
Dunn, Johnny 223–224, 230, 233, 238
Dunn's Plains 207
Dunvegan Castle 59
Durgan, Billy 197–198
Duxbury, Mr. 171
Dwyer, Jane 215
Dwyer, Mr. 215
Dwyer, Mrs. Ann 215

E

Eaglehawk Gully 130
East Arm 24
Eaton, John 276
Eden 252
Edinburgh, Mr. 69
Edwards, John 276
Edwards, William 148
Effingham Banks 111
Egan, Constable 254
Egan, John 260
Ehrstein, Aaron von 181
Eldorado 296
Eleven Mile Creek 330
Ellerslie 106
Elliott, David 181
Elliott, Mr. George 240
Ellis, John 89
Ellison, George 149
Emerald Hill 147
Emmott, Mr. John 250
Emu Creek Goldfield 259
Emu Flat 220
Emu Plains 14
England 1, 97, 98, 144, 152, 175, 301
English Press 328
Esk River 24
Esk Valley 171

397

Eugowra 187
Eugowra Rocks 188, 190
Eumarrah 27
Eureka 153
Eureka Gang 134
Eureka Plateau 155
Euroa 335–337, 354
Eurongilly 320–322
Evans, Henry 259
Evans, Mr. 245
Evans' Plains 256, 259
Eve Creek 150
Everett, Arundell 191
Everett, John 81
Ewart, John 91
Executive Council 290

F

Fagan, Constable John 188
Fagan, John 221
Fairfield 270
Faithfull's Creek 333
Falbrook 275
Farrar, Mr. 263
Farrell, Christopher 129
Farrell, Mr. 148, 193
Farrer, Abraham 119
Fawcett, John 276
Ferguson, Mr. 99
Field, Mr. William 112
Field Police 102
Finegan, John 134
Finigan, Detective 276
Finnigan, Mr. 282
Fish River 191, 193, 196
Fitzgerald, Mr. 25
Fitzgerald, Patrick (alias Paddy Wandong) 261
Fitzpatrick, Constable 341
Fitzpatrick, Constable Alexander 329

Fitzpatrick, Patrick 55
Fitzroy, Sir Charles A. 163
Five Mile Creek Inn 241
Flag Hotel 226
Fleming, Mr. 90
Fletcher, John 108
Fletcher, William 250–251
Flett, William 305
Flinders Island 27, 30
Flogging
    4–12
Flood, Alexander 49
Flood, Charles 303
Flooks, Thomas 152
Flooks, T. Mr. 152
Flynn, Constable Patrick 105
Fogarty, Mr. 268
Fogarty, Young 89
Foley, Charles 191
Foley, Francis 201
Foley, John 196, 200
Foley, Mr. 74
Foley, Mrs. Margaret 74
Foley, Timothy 200
Foran, John 260, 289
Foran, Mr. 196
Foran, Patrick 276
Forbes 185, 187–188, 232–233, 235, 284–285, 307, 342
    Currajong Road 284
    Mechanics' Bay Road 256
Forbes, Judge 7
Forbes, Mr. 260
Ford, Henry 167
Ford, John 257
Ford, Seymour 257
Fordyce, Alexander 187, 189, 237, 288
Formosa 97
Forster, John 218
Forth River 99

INDEX

Fosbery, Mr. E. (Inspector General) 324
Foster, Mr. 258
Four Mile Dam 325
Fowler, Mr. H 90, 92
Fox, Mr. E. B. 304
France 95
Franklin, Mr. George 213
Franklin, Mrs. 213
Frank, Mr. 108, 200
Frazer, James 246
Frazer, John 250
Frazer, Mr. 83
Freere, Maurice 145
Freere, William 129
Freer, Sergeant 57
Frodsham, Mr. 172
Fryer's Creek 146
Fuller, Mr. 73
Furber, Mr. George 81
Furlonge, Mr. 235
Futter's Range 349
Fyan's Ford 137

G

Gadsden, Mr. 312
Gallimore, Mr. 235
Gammon Plains 94
Gap Road 234
Gardiner, Frank 178, 218, 235, 237–238, 287, 310, 355–356
Gardiner Gang 189, 201, 327–328
Gardiner, Mr. 197
Gardner, John 119
Garland, Mr. 204
Garrett, Dr. 39
Garrett, Henry Beresford 155, 302
Garroway, William 153
Garry, Mr. 217
Garvan, Rev. John Hill 81

Gatenby, Mr. Christopher 110
Gaugel, Mr. 24
Gaunson, Mr. David 355
Gawler 88
Geary's Gap 235
Geelong 124–125, 129, 134, 137, 146, 150–155, 178, 210, 329, 355
   Ballarat Road 137
   Corio Street 137–138
   Malop Street 138
   Moorabool Street 137, 159
   South Geelong 139
   Yarra Street 125
Geelong Court House 139
Geelong Gaol 124
Gellibrand, Mr. 109
George's River 61
German Bill 239, 253
Germans 278
Gibbons, Mr. 259
Gibney, Rev. Father M. 353
Gibson, Henry 201
Gibson, Mr. Thomas 129
Gidley 66
Gilbert, Johnny 249
Gilbert, Johnny (alias Roberts) 187, 190–201, 202, 205, 219, 221, 224, 230, 234, 237
Gilders, Mr. 24
Gillenbah 265
Gillham, Mr. Henry Kidder 282
Gilligan, Mr. James 106, 107
Gilligan, Mrs. 106
Gill, Mr. 341–343
Gilmandyke Creek 222
Gipps, Governor 67
Gippsland District 325
Glanvill, Richard 81
Glasgow 98
Glenorchy Probation Station 72, 121
Glen Rock 86

Glenrowan 349–355
   Sydney Road 349
Glenrowan Inn 349–350
Gloster, Mr. 334, 337
Goimbla 211
Golden Fleece Inn 94
Goldfields 124, 151–152, 160, 164
Goldman, Mr. 131
Goldsmith, District Constable 168
Gonzales, Ferdinand 161, 163
Goodall, Thomas 261
Goodison, Christopher 152
Goodwin, Sergeant 11
Goondiwindi 310
Goonoo Goonoo Gap 277
Gordon, Mr. 272
Gordon, Mrs. 272
Gordon, Richard 168
Gordon's Inn 272
Gorman, Thomas 324
Gough, Charles Hugh (alias Wyndham, alias Bennet) 253, 289
Goulburn 45, 66, 69, 84, 178, 180–181, 190, 203, 215, 234, 253, 281
Goulburn Chronicle 195
Goulburn Gaol 55
Goulburn Herald 223
Goulburn Plains 69
Gourlay, Mr. 90–92
Government Escort 151
Government Gold Escort 228, 327
Government House 118
Governor, Lieutenant 18
Governor of New South Wales 114, 123
Governor of Van Diemen's Land 114
Governor of Victoria 125
Governor's Arms Hotel 215
Grainger, Mr. 324
Grainger, Sergeant 259
Grampian Ranges 293

Grant, George 293
Grant, Mr. 207, 293
Gray, Major 24
Gray, Mr. 62, 84
Great Britain 1, 308
Great Dividing Range 176
Great Escort Robbery 228, 239
Great Northern Railway 349
Great Northern Road 76, 81, 283
Great North Road 180, 271
Great Sirius Cove 48
Green, Bushranger 88
Greenhill, Bob 31
Green Hills 77
Green, Lieutenant 39
Green Ponds 23, 122
Green Swamp 269
Green Swamp Inn 263
Greig, Mr. 186
Grenfell 276, 290
Greta 297, 341
Grey, Earl 163, 165
Gribble, Rev. Mr. 341
Griffen, Constable 293
Griffin, Daniel 108
Griffin, Mr. 275
Griffiths, Dennis 160
Griffiths, George 105
Griffiths, John 38
Grimes, Dr. 90
Grose's Farm 70
Grubbenbong 206
Gulgong 263
Gulph Diggings 250
Gummeracha 284
Gundagai 92, 223–224, 234, 322
Gundaroo 234
Gunn, John 105
Gunn, Mrs. 328

INDEX

Gunn, William 84
Guy, Mr. 138
Guyong 221
Gwynne, Colonel and Mrs. 84

H

Hales, Constable 233–234
Halfway House 171
Half-Way House 276
Half-Way House Hotel 221
Half-way Inn 307
Hall and Gilbert 312
Hall and Gilbert Gang 211, 216, 221, 342
Hall, Ben 201, 205–206, 209–214, 217,
    219–221, 224, 227, 230–232, 237–238,
    249, 311, 343, 356
Hall, Bushranger 55
Halliday's Inn 130
Hall, Mr. 314
Hamilton, Mr. 233, 355
Hammond, George 183
Hammond, James 148
Hammond, Mr. 202
Hampton, Thomas 276
Hancock, Mr. Allen 202
Handley, Mr. Robert 212
Hanlow, Mr. 199
Hanslip, George 157
Happy Valley 299
Hardie, Mr. 341
Hardy, Mr. Philip 311
Hare, Superintendent 297–298, 327, 346
Hargrave, Judge 260
Harper, Mr. James 57
Harper, William 100
Harris, Captain 95, 96
Harrison, Captain 90
Harrison, Mr. 86
Harrison, Samuel 105
Hart, Ellen 300

Hart, Frank 345, 354
Hartley 92, 191, 214
Hart, Steve 333–336, 340, 343, 353–354
Harts, The 328
Harvey, Constable 108
Harvey, Corporal 130
Hatfield 324
Haviland, Constable William 188
Hay 323
Hayes, Mr. and Mrs. 225
Hay, Mr. 109
Hazleton, Mr. 300
Healey, Sergeant John 257
Healy, John 192
Hearn, Mr. Charles 53
Hedley, Constable 322
Heffeman, Mr. 68
Henderson, Mr. Michael 77
Herbst, Constable 203
Heriot, John 241
Hewitt, Mr. Robert 184
Hexham 80
Hibberson, Mr. 206, 207
Hickson, Bushranger 172
Higgins, Mrs. Mary 58
Higginson, John 25
Hildebrand, Chief-Constable 85
Hill, James 216
Hindmarsh, Mr. 258
Hinton, Mr. 168
Hitchcock, Anthony 48
Hobart Town 10, 13, 17–19, 23, 27, 43, 95, 98,
    104, 108, 114, 119, 157, 168
  Brisbane Street 110
  Collins Street 10
  Elizabeth Street 10
  Harrington Street 109
Hobbs, William (aka Hoppy Bill) 324
Hobson's Bay 131, 133, 140, 152
Hockin, Mr. 283

401

Hogan, Bushranger 108–109
Holliston, Trooper 198
Holmes, Constable 277
Holyoak, William 22
Homer, Mr. 263
Homer's Inn 263
Hong Kong 3
Hooper, James 24
Hopkins, John 17
Hopkins, Jonas 105
Hopkins, Mr. 37
Hopkiss, Constable 232
Hoppy Jack 91
Horne, Joseph 282
Horner, William 294
Horse Bazaar 159
Horsington, Mr. 184
Horsley, Captain 80
Hosie, Constable 184
Houghton River 312
Houlihan, Michael 119
House of Commons 114
Howard's Inn 93
Howarth, Tom 85
Howe, Constable 322
Howell, Mr. 23
Howe, Michael 18
Howe, Mike 76, 327
Hughes, Mr. 25, 271
Hull Hill 81
Humbug Creek 187
Humewood Station 293
Humphrey, T. B. 60
Humphries' Hotel 275
Hunter, Alexander 90
Hunter, Mr. Campbell 90
Hunter River 48, 79, 80
Hunter's Hill 25
Huntley, Mr. 97
Hurn, Thomas 105

Hurst, Miss 294
Hurst, Mr. 294
Hussey, Sub-Inspector John Garder 216
Hutchinson, Mr. 214
Hutchinson, William 83
Hyde Park 83
Hyde Park Barracks 60, 86

I

Iceley, Mr. 202
Illalong 230
Inglewood 307
Inman, Mr. 88
Inspector General of Convicts 141, 144
Ireland 56, 295, 316
    Cavan 56
Ironbark Gully 307
Ironstone Bridge 56, 64
Irwin, Sergeant 326
Italians 278
Ivanhoe 324

J

Jackey Jackey 66, 68, 70, 76, 117–120, 178, 249, 327
Jackson, James 79
Jackson, Mr. 140
Jackson, Mr. J. 146
Jack the Kid 177
Jack the Rammer 53
Jacobsen, Samuel William 192
Jacques, Mr. 12
James, John (alias Johnston) 132
Jamieson, George 168
Jamieson, Mr. 222
Japan 97
Jay, Dr. 87
Jefferies, Mr. 37
Jefferson, Mr. 342

INDEX

Jeffs, Riley 106
Jembaicumbene 249–250
Jenkins, Henry (alias Billy from the Den) 168
Jenkins, John 53
Jennant, Mr. 334
Jepps, Mr. 89, 92
Jerilderie 240, 243–244, 264, 338–346, 354
   Bank 346
   Royal Hotel 339–342
Jerilderie Letter 342, 360–388
Jerusalem 102
Jervis, George 306
Jewboy Gang 76–78
Jewboy, The 66, 76, 81, 84, 327. See also Davis, Edward
Jingera Ranges 252
Johns, Constable 322
Johnson, Charley 262
Johnson, Constable Charles 352
Johnson, George 198
Johnson, Mr. 103
Johnson, William 253
Johnston, Constable 272
Johnstone, Mr. 241
Johnstone, Robert 270
Johnston, Henry 134
Joint Stock Bank 281
Joliffe, Mr. 79
Jones, Ann 350–351
Jones, Charles 324
Jones, Charles (alias William Herbert) 216
Jones, Convict John 170
Jones, David 48
Jones, Henry 147
Jones, James 216, 289
Jones, John (alias Jack the Lagger) 100
Jones, Miss 351
Jones, Mr. 232, 235
Jones, Richard 142
Jones, Thomas 109, 111–112
Jones, William 142
Joynes, John 167
Jugiong 223–224, 234
Julian, Mr. 67, 69
Junee 202
Junior, Mr. Amos 25

K

Kater, Mr. Henry Edward 195
Kavanagh, Lawrence 109, 111, 119–122
Kayes, Mr. 87
Kaye, William 324
Keenan, Alice 246–247
Keene, Henry 179, 181
Keightley, Assistant Gold Commissioner 207
Keightley, Mrs. 208
Keilor 135
Kelly, Bartley 100
Kelly, Bushranger 171
Kelly, Constable 231, 352
Kelly, Convict James 141
Kelly, Corporal 34
Kelly, Dan 328–337, 339–348, 353–357
Kelly, Edward 261–262, 289, 297
Kelly Gang 320, 324, 327–337
Kelly, Grace 328
Kelly, James 142, 276
Kelly, Jim 328
Kelly, John 254, 289
Kelly, Kate 328, 354, 355
Kelly, Mr. 259
Kelly, Mrs. Ellen 329–331
Kelly, Ned 316, 327–337, 338–348, 351–357
Kelly, Ted 261
Kelly, Thomas 233
Kelly, Thomas (alias Noon) 303–304, 307
Kelsey, George 172
Kemp, Mr. 25
Kempthorne, John 305

403

Kennagh, Patrick 251–252
Kennedy, Constable 277
Kennedy, Detective 184
Kennedy, James (alias Southgate) 276
Kennedy, Sergeant 332, 336, 354
Kerr, John (alias Maher) 259
Keys, Bushranger 54
Kildare 138, 154
Kilferra 325
Killoshiel 211
Kilmore 294
Kilmore District 293
Kilmore Free Press 297
Kilpatrick, Constable Andrew 257–258
Kimberley, Mr. 230
Kimberley's Hotel 237
King, Constable 233
King George's Sound 114
King, Mr. Phillip Gidley 66
King River 245, 297, 331
Kings Falls 83
King's Plains 164, 228
Kirby, Constable 109
Kirkpatrick, Mr. 206
Knebsworth 311
Koringa 283–284
Korowatha Inn 221
Kurraducbidgee 82
Kyamba 244
Kyneton 130, 151, 153

L

Lacey, George 38
Lachlan 185, 221, 235, 307
Lachlan Escort 219
Lachlan Goldfield 184
Lachlan Observer 197
Lachlan River 68, 187, 232
Ladrones Islands 97

Lady of the Lake Inn 146
Laggan 191
Lagge, Mr. 60
Lake Crescent 108, 172
Lake, Mr. 213
Lake River 23, 39
Lake Sorell 25
Lambeth, William 105
Lambing Flat 177, 184, 185, 200, 229, 307
Lamb's Valley 49
Landell's Hotel 263
Landregan, Kearns 56–59, 64
Landregan, Mary 57
Langbridge's Hotel 263
Lang, Constable 275
Langor, Mr. 90
La Perouse, Admiral 114
Lapstone Hill 218
Laragy, Constable 83
Larnack, Mr. John 48
Larnack, Mrs. 48
Larras Lake 235
Latrobe, Mr. Charles Joseph 125
Launceston 40, 99, 107, 108, 121, 170
  Westbury Road 170
Launceston Advertiser 11
Laurie, James 179
Lavendale, Isaac 180
Lawler, Constable 293
Lawler, Michael 179
Lawrence, Constable 260
Lawrence, Mr. 24
Layworth, William 148
Leake, Constable 170
Lee, Constable 200
Lee, Henry 108
Lee, Mr. 60, 235
Lee, William 258
Legislative Assembly 290
Legislative Council 130

Index

Lehane, Jeremiah 265
Lemon Springs 172
Lenehan, Constable 254
Leonard, Constable 180
Leverett, James 105
Levy, Constable Peter 306
Levy, Philip 303–304, 307
Lewis, Nicholas 100
Leyburn 310
Liardet, Mr. 132
Liardet's Beach 131, 133
Liberty Plains 52
Liddell, John 111
Lieutenant-Governor 120
Lilley, Mr. 312
Limerick Races Hotel 203
Lindon, Mr. 321
Little Plains 259
Little River 245
Little Wombat 184
Liverpool 14, 45, 52, 60, 85–86, 270
Liverpool Ranges 78
Living, Mr. 340–342
Lloyd, Lieutenant 167
Lloyds, The 329, 354
Lochinvar 180
Lockyer, Major 72
Loddon River 153
Lodge's Inn 230
Loftus, Lord Augustus 323
London 98, 131, 155, 156, 301, 302
   Oxford Street 156
London Chartered Bank 155
London Docks 97
Lonergan, Constable 332
Longbottom 84
Longfield, Mr. 281
Long, Mr. 39
Long, Mrs. N. 25
Long Ned 86
Long Swamp 74
Long Tom 86
Lord, Mr. 23
Lord, Mr. Frank 171
Lord, Mr. Simeon 171
Lottery Bill 47
Lovett, Constable 215
Lowe, Mr. J. 268
Lowe, Mr. Robert 193, 196
Lowry, Frederick 196, 203, 238
Lowrys, The 328
Lucas, Christopher 100
Lucette, Eugene 162
Lumley, Mr. Thomas 180
Lynam, George 215
Lynch, Constable 273
Lynch, John 56, 309
Lynch Law 128
Lynch, Patrick 115
Lynch, William 86
Lyndoch Valley 88
Lyons, Detective 184
Lyons, Mr. 281

M

Maberley, Bushranger 172
Macansh, Mr. 234
Macarthur, Mr. Francis 69
Macarthur, Mr. H. 45
Macarthur, Mr. James 14
Macarthur, Mr. John 47
Macaulay, Mr. 333
Macdonald, Alice 245–246
Macdonald, Dr. 109
Macdonald, Dr. Archibald 326
Macdonald, Mr. 283
Macdonald, Mr. Alexander 321–322
Macdonald, Mr. C. F. J. 320
Macdougall, Mr. 77

Mackay, Charles 192
Mackay, James 192
Mackay's Hotel 200
Mackenzie, Captain 102
Mackenzie, Mr 183
Mackenzie River 311
Mackie, Mr. A. 340–343
Mackie, William 180, 270, 276
Mack, William 146
Macleay M.L.C., Hon.William 226
Macnamara, Constable 219
Maconochie, Captain 114
Macpherson, Alpin (alias John Bruce, alias Mar, alias Kerr, alias Scotia or Scotchie 311
Macpherson, Miss 246
Macpherson, Mr. 245
Macquarie, Governor 19
Macquarie Harbour 31, 36, 43, 95, 98
Macquarie River 166
Macquarie Street 84
Madden, Constable 277
Madden, William 137
Maggleton, Trooper 52
Maguire, Thomas 78
Maher, Constable 313–314
Maher, Walter 262
Maitland 48, 49, 50, 76, 94, 180, 267–268, 282
Maitland Mercury 270
Major's Creek 235
Major's Creek Mount 231, 250
Malone, Owen 191
Malony, Thomas 142
Manaro 70, 164, 249, 293, 328
Mandagery Creek 188
Manduran Station 312
Manilla 97
Manns, Henry 187, 189, 238
Mansfield 333
Maoris 316
Marengo 192, 210, 235

Margate 98
Marine Station 168
Marnetti 25
Marquesas Estate 79
Marriott, Henry 155
Marsden, Constable George 105
Marsden, Rev. Samuel 45
Marseilles 307
Marshall, John 81
Marshall, Mr. 155
Marshall, William 265
Marsh, Mr. 90
Martell's Inn 272
Martin, Mr. 195, 282
Martin, Sir James 204
Marulan 281
Maryborough Chronicle 314
Maryborough District 295
Mason, James 130
Massey, Mr. 41
Massey, Mr. Thomas 106
Masson, Joseph 105–106
Mate, Mr. 242
Mathers, John 31
Matheson, Kenneth 250
Mathew, Father 57
Mathieu, Felix 304–305, 307
Mathieu, Mrs. 306
Matthew Homer's Inn 263
Matthews, Daniel 215
Maungapatau Murders 303, 308
Mayhew, Elizabeth 210
Maynard, Donald 55
Mayne, Bushranger 55
Mayne, Mr. Daniel 205
McAlister, Chief Constable 61
McAlister, Mr. 234
McCabe, James 38
McCall, John 112

Index

McCallum, alias Frank 140
McCallum, Frank (alias Captain Melville) 136–145
McCallum, James 105
McCann, John 86
McCarthy, Convict 170
McCarthy, Father 237
McCarthy, Mr. 46, 223
McCaskell, Mrs. 24
McConnell, Mr. 311
McCrae, Dr. 143
McCrae, Mr. 108
McDonald, Alexander 86
McDonald, Constable 200
McDonald, Dr. 57, 85
McDonald, Hector 20
McDonnell, Eneas 251
McDougall's Hotel 341
McDougal, Mr. 334, 337
McGinnerty, Sergeant 240, 247
McGlone, Constable 260
McGlone, Detective 218
McGrath, Rev. Mr. 68
McGregor's Inn 219
McGuire, Constable 73–74
McGuire, John 187, 189
McHale, Constable 235–236
McIntyre, Constable 332
McIntyre, Mr 92
McIvor 150–151
McIvor Goldfield 151
McKay, Captain 109
McKay, Constable 218
McKay, Mr. Alexander 199
McKenzie, Hugh 193
McKeon, Mr. 157
McKinnon, Christina 227
McKinnon, Mr. 245
McLachlan, Mr. Lachlan 126
McLaughlin, Constable 225

McLean, Alexander 154
McLean, John 241
McLean, Mr. 101
McLerie, Captain 190
McLerie, Mr. 158
McMahon, John (alias McManus) 180
McMahon's public-house 58
McMinn, Miss 205
McMinn's Hotel 205
McNamara, Constable Michael 261
McNaughton, Mr. 263
McPhail, Mr. 235
McPhillamy, Mr. 70
McShane, Mr. 267
McWhirter, Mr. John 327
Meadow Flat 93
Meally, Kate 210
Meander 28
Melbourne 38, 88, 90, 92, 124, 129, 132–134, 146–147, 153, 157, 173, 210, 240, 247–248, 282, 294, 303, 324, 329, 349, 354–355
   Collins Street 148
   Flagstaff Hill 135
   Flinders Street 133
   Little Collins Street 133
   Lonsdale Street 133
   Prince's Bridge 147–148
   Queen Street 88
   South Melbourne 131, 148
   Stephen's Street 355
Melbourne Age 327
Melbourne Argus 280, 296, 324, 355
Melbourne Club 90
Melbourne Gaol 125, 143, 355
Melville, Edward 131
Melville, George 152
Mericumbene 249
Merry & Co. 148
Messrs. Brasch & Sommerfeld 148
Messrs. C. Newton & Co. 157

Messrs. Hall & Co 230
Messrs. Jackson, Rae & Co 132
Messrs. Willis, Merry & Co 148
Mia-Mia Hotel 151
Michelago 249
Michel, Mr. 82
Micky Hunter 202
Middleton, Richard (alias Ruggy Dick) 256
Midgeley, Chief District Constable 167
Miles, John 259
Militia Bill 312
Miller 262
Miller, Mr. (alias Slater) 262
Miller, Robert 345
Millie 273
Mills, Peter 20
Mils 216
Mitchell, Constable Edward William 257
Mitchell, Robert 160
Mitchell, William Henry 153
Mitre Hotel 303
Modewarre 154
Moe 325
Mohanga 244
Molong 214, 273
Monks, Ellen 227
Monks, Margaret 227
Montagu, Judge 106, 111–112
Montefiore 165
Montford, Sergeant 297, 299
Mookerawa 259
Moonan, William 172
Moore, Mr. 275–276
Moore, William 296
Moran, Constable Henry 188
Moreton Bay 86, 160–163, 310
Morgan, Daniel 239–242
Morgan, Jacky 202
Morgan, James 132
Morgan, John 84

Morgan, Mr. Henry 213
Morgan, Mrs. 213
Morgan, William 146
Moriarty, Captain 28
Morris, Constable 117, 183, 273
Morris, Ensign Campbell 181
Morris, John 120, 123
Morris, Mr. 226
Morris, Mr. and Mrs. 234
Morris, Mrs. 226
Morton, J. Mr. 152
Morton, Mr. 235
Moruya 250
Moruya Examiner 251
Morven 105
Mosman's Bay 48
Mossgiel 261
Moulamein 325
Mount Alexander 132, 146, 151, 153
Mount Alexander Goldfield 128
Mount Barker 88
Mount Egerton 135, 317–318
Mount, James (the Old Man) 219–223, 238
Mount Korong 307
Mount Murchison 283–284
Mount Razorback 60
Mount Sturgeon 293
Mount Victoria 192
Mount William 297
Mr. Duxbury's Inn 171
Muddy Creek 154
Mudgee 92, 166, 193–195, 228, 263, 268, 271, 285
   Green Swamp Road 263
Mudie, Major 50
Mudie, Major James 6, 48
Mulhall, Constable 279–280
Mullenderee 251
Mulligan, John 64
Mulligan, Mrs. 62

INDEX

Mulligan's Farm 56, 62, 71
Mulrooney, Constable 170, 171
Mumble Flat 218
Munro, Mr. 273
Munro, Mr. Hector 325
Murderer's Flat 128
Murdering Swamp 276
Murphy 42
Murphy, Constable 183
Murphy, Jeremiah 152
Murphy, John 152
Murray, Mr. 67
Murray River 89, 130, 245, 284, 294, 301, 333, 344
Murrumbidgee 324
Murrumbidgee River 93, 239, 293, 320
Murrumburrah 218, 227, 232–233
Murrumburrah Plains 234
Murrum Hurrah 224
Murrurundi 77–78, 267, 275
Musquito 22–23, 27
Muswellbrook 80, 195, 271, 276, 284
Mutineers of the Bounty 123
Mutton Falls 200

N

Naime, Captain 19
Naime, James 221
Naisk, John 160
Namoi River 76–87
Napoleon the First 114
Napton, Benjamin 154
Narrandera 239–240, 264, 342
Nash, Charles 250
National Bank 335
Nattai 57
Nelson, Constable 230, 234, 237
Neonan's Hotel 231
Nerrigundah 251

Nesbit, James P. (alias Lyons) 323–324
Newbiggen Inn 235
New Caledonia 95
Newcastle 14, 267
New England Ranges 76
New England River 281
New Norfolk 24, 122
Newra 235
New South Wales 2, 15, 45, 55, 56, 76, 89, 92, 114, 124, 130, 144, 156, 163, 166, 176, 189, 194, 201, 218, 228, 239, 245, 247, 266, 280, 281–291, 292–295, 299, 312, 316–320, 328–329, 338, 355
  Wellington 165, 218, 254, 261
New South Wales Government 226, 344
New South Wales Legislative Assembly 204
Newtown Bridge 299
New Zealand 201, 290, 302, 307, 316, 346, 356
  Auckland 303
  Beach Street 303
  Mechanic's Bay 303
  Canvas Town 305, 306
  Deep Creek 306
  Deep Creek Diggings 305
  Dunedin 302
  Franklyn's Flat 305
  Gabriel's Gully 303
  Grey River 304
  Hokitiki 306
  Kamieri River 306
  Lawrence 303
  Maori Gully 304
  Nelson 303, 305–306
  Otago Goldfields 303
  Otago Province 302
  Otago Witness 302
  Toitoi 306
  West Coast Diggings 303
New Zealand Herald 303
Nicholas, Mr. 77
Nicholls, Constable 200
Nicholson, Inspector 298
Nicholson, Mr. 92

409

Nicholson, Superintendent 297
Nillenga 87
Noel, Chief Constable 57
Norfolk Island 7, 50, 68, 72, 86, 95, 100, 111, 113, 114, 119, 122, 160, 163
Norfolk Plains 24, 105
North Esk 24
North, Mr. 73
North Sydney 48
Norton, Captain 197–198
Nott, Mr. W. 312
Nugent, James 154

O

Oakden, Mr. Philip 167
Oakes, William 192
Oatland's Gaol 168
O'Brien, Daniel 191
O'Brien, Mr. 268
O'Brien, Mr. Cornelius 215
O'Brien, Mrs. 191
Ocean Child Inn 132
O'Connell, Sir Maurice 11
O'Connor, Sub-inspector 349
O'Connor, William 191
O'Dell, Mrs. 267
O'Donnell, James 86
O'Donnell, Sergeant 260
O'Farrell, Mr. 159
O'Grady, Constable Miles 251
O'Grady, Sergeant 181
Oldbury 60
O'Leary, Mr. 284
O'Meally, Mr. 197, 199, 205, 210, 238
O'Meallys, The 328
O'Neil, Inspector 224–225
One Mile Creek 259
Orange 124, 218, 221, 259
Orange Guardian 218

Orange Road 260
Oriental Bank 187
O'Sullivan, Jeremiah 160
Ouse River 24
Outlawry Act 296, 331, 345
Ovens 296
Ovens and Murray Advertiser 296–297
Ovens, Lieutenant 29
Ovens River 349
Ovens Spectator 299
Owens, Corporal Owen 140
Owens, John 258
Owens, Stephen 303

P

Pack Bullock Flat 293
Page River 81
Panton, Mr. 109
Parker, Mr. 25
Parkes, Sir Henry 253, 324
Paroo 281
Parramatta 61, 71, 77, 83, 86, 270
Parramatta River 71
Parrott, Samuel 48
Parry, Sergeant 234
Parry, Sergeant Edmund 224
Parsons, Godfrey 269
Parsons, Mrs. 269
Paterson, Mr. and Mrs. 321
Patrick Plains 25
Patrick's Plains 48, 76, 80
Patterson River 77
Payne, John 261–262, 289
Peachey, Mr. 98
Peacock, Constable 103
Peak Downs 218
Peak Downs Road 311
Peechy, Dr. 208–209
Peel 268

INDEX

Peerman, Mr. 261
Peet, Mr. 90
Peisley, John 181, 238
Penny, Mr. Joseph 104
Pennyweight Flat 153
Penrith 52, 218, 270
Pentonvillains 163
Pentonville 164
Pentridge Gaol 125, 178, 282, 295, 303, 319
Perdrotta, Mr. 205
Perfrement, Mr. 94
Perry, John 48
Perry, Matthew 106
Perry, Peter 172
Perth 98
Petrie, Mr. 312
Pewtress, Inspector 333
Phegan, John 251–252
Pickthorne, William 120, 123
Picton 258
Pierce, Alexander 31–37
Pike, Captain 80
Pilcock, Mr. 147
Pilot Island 162
Pinnacle 186, 233, 235
Piper's River 168
Piracy 95–101
Pirates' Bay 37
Pitcairn Islanders 123
Pitcairn, Mr. 23
Pitcher's Inn 170
Pitt, Mrs. Colonel 256
Plum's Inn 226
Pockett, Mr. 106
Pohlmann, Brothers 264
Pohlmann, Miss 264
Point Gellibrand 140
Police Magistrate 102
Pollock, Mr. 250
Pontius, James de 305

Ponto Island 166
Poolamacca 284
Poole, John 48
Popjoy 96–99
Porcelli, Francis 304
Porcupine 135
Porepunkah 296
Port Arthur 8, 36, 72, 95, 112, 121–122, 144
Port Curtis Road 312
Port Dalrymple 20
Port Denison 313
Port Essington 114
Portland 129
Portland Bay 89
Port Macquarie 84
Port Phillip 82, 88, 92, 129
Port Phillip District 124–125, 163
Port Sorell 25, 172
Post, Mr. 85
Post Office Stores 58
Potter, Mr. 79
Pottinger, Sir Frederick 186, 197–198, 211, 219–220, 231, 312–313
Poulston, Bushranger 172
Poulton, Mr. 159
Powell, Mr. 68
Powell, Mr. Frank 68
Power, Harry 295–301
Power, Mr. 172
Powers, Constable 325
Price, John 107, 118–119, 123
Price, Mr. John 141, 144, 163
Priest, Dr. 41
Pring, Mr. 184
Prosser's Forest 169
Pudman's Creek 215
Pugh, William 20
Pulpit Hill 257, 277
Purvis, Mr. 23

Q

Queanbeyan 69, 252
Queanbeyan Age 284
Queensland 152, 163, 218, 287, 292, 310, 349
   Curriwillinghi District 275
   Warwick 278
Quin, Edward 106
Quinlan, John 246
Quinn, Ellen 328
Quinn Family 297
Quinn, Mr. 293
Quinn, Thomas 154
Quirindi 78

R

Raby 52
Racehorse 202–203, 219, 228, 233–235, 249, 277, 311–312
   Black Diamond 214
   Chinaman 202
   Eucalyptus 274
   Harkaway 220
   Jacky Morgan 202
   John Brown 277
   Micky Hunter 202
   Old Cornus 202
   Plover 222
   Publican's Races 228
   Reign of Terror 202
   Retriever 205
   Ringleader 224
   Talleyrand 277
   Teddington 220
   Troubadour 217, 220
   Union Jack 217
   Victoria 245
   Willy the Weasel 217–218
Ralton, Mr. T 24
Rand, Mr. 244
Ranken, Mr. 233
Rankin, Mr. 341

Rankin, Mr. Arthur 68
Rat's Castle 333
Raymond, Constable William 257–258
Raynor, John 23
Ray's Hotel 154
Read, Mr. 88–89
Reardon, James 350
Red Bank 85
Red Post Hill 275–276
Redruth 283
Reed, Constable 244
Reedy Creek 193, 265
Ree, Mr. 103
Rees, Mr. 168
Regan, James 102
Regent, Mr. 293
Reid, Constable 25
Reid, Mr. 49, 292
Reid, Mr. and Mrs. 321
Renton, Thomas 41
Research Bay 96, 98
Resident Magistrate 125
Richards, Constable 338–340
Richardson, J. M. 304
Richardson's Inn 256
Rider, Charles 38
Rider, Mr. 90
Riley, James 48
Rio de Janeiro 97
River Dee 28
River Derwent 16
Roberts, Mr. 168, 188
Roberts, Mr. J. 202, 220
Roberts, Mrs. 152
Robertson, Mr. 23
Robertson, Mr. Gilbert 21–22, 28–29
Roberts, Thomas 107
Roberts, William 136, 153
Robinson, Mr. 172, 194, 206

INDEX

Robinson, Mr. G. A. 29
Robinson's Hotel 206
Robinson, Sir Hercules (Lord Rosmead) 288
Roche, Constable 215, 224–225
Rockhampton 218, 311–313
Rockley 207–208, 222
Rock Station 265
Rocky River 279
Rodwell, Henry 276
Rogan, Thomas 323
Roger, Mr. Joseph 55
Rogers, William 148
Roland, Mr 90
Romney, Mr. 104
Ross 104
Ross, Alexander 191
Ross, Charles 180, 191
Rossi, Mr. 234
Ross, Mr. 224
Round Hill 241
Royal Highlander Inn 88
Royal Prerogative of Mercy 355
Rumbold, Mr. 90
Rush, Sergeant 260
Rushworth 351
Russell, Mr. 37
Rutherford, Charles 268, 276
Rutherford, Mr. 245–247
Rutherglen Road 297
Rutledge, Richard 68
Ryan, Chief Constable 86
Ryan, James 48
Ryan, Jeremiah 38
Ryan, Master 221
Ryan, Mr. 257, 292
Ryan, Mrs. 257
Ryan, Patrick 260

S

Sadlier, Inspector 354
Sanderson, Sergeant 184
Sandwich Islands 97
Sandy Bay 172
Saunderson, Detective 203
Saunderson, Sergeant 187
Scanlan, Constable 332
Scheffts, Mr. 276
Schofield 86
Scone 84
Scotchy 68
Scotland 311
Scott, Bill 251–254
Scott, Constable 219
Scott, George 316–322
Scott, George (alias Captain Moonlite). *See also* Macpherson, Alpin (alias John Bruce, alias Mar, alias Kerr, alias Scotia or Scotchie
Scott, Messrs. Robert and Helenes 49
Scott, Mr. G. 24
Scott, Mr. Robert 49, 335–337
Scott, Mrs. 336–337
Scott, William 130
Scraggs, Mr. John 133
Scrimshaw, William 120, 123
Sealers' Cove 99
Sears, Henry 100
Seary, Michael 215
Sebastopol 345
Seeman, Carl 265
Select Committee 114
Selector's Arms Hotel 325
Serjeantson, Mr. 90
Shallcross, Sergeant Major 306
Shanklin, Mr. 112
Shanks, James 326
Shanks, Robert 326
Shannon, John 150
Sharland, Mr. 23

413

Shea, Daniel 288
Sheahan, Mr. 224
Shea, John 81
Shearers' Arms Inn 311
Sheedy, Mr. 213–214
Shelly's Flat 226
Shendon, Mr. 162
Shepherd, John 259
Shepherd, Mr. Charles Fisher 53
Shepherd, Mr. Israel 68
Sherritt, Aaron 345–347
Sherritt, Mrs. 347
Sherritt's Hut 350–354
Sherwin, Mr. 23, 90
Sherwood, Robert 215
Sidwell, William 215
Simmons, William H. 289
Simpeon, Mr. 77
Simpson, Charles 92
Simpson, Constable 183
Simpson, William 148
Sinclair, Alexander 211
Singapore 3
Singleton 270, 274–275
Singleton, Inspector 247
Skillian, Mrs. 328, 352, 354
Skillian, William 330
Skinner, Mr. and Mrs. 150
Slapdash 193
Slattery, Michael 258
Smart, Henry 167
Smith, Captain 40
Smith, Catherine 111
Smith, Corporal 283
Smith, Edward 241
Smith, Henry (alias Brennan) 142
Smith, James 289
Smith, Mr. 194, 258
Smith, Mr. Edward 252
Smith, Mr. Robert 69

Smith, Mrs. 196
Smith, Robert 181
Smith, Stephen 117
Smith, Thomas 25, 56
Smith, Thomas (alias Frank McCallum, alias Captain Melville) 140
Smyth, Sergeant 244, 247
Snail's Bay 48
Snell, Mr. Jonathan 180
Sneyd, Mr. 162
Snodgrass, Mr. P. 90
Snowy River 54, 307
Society for the Abolition of Capital Punishment 355
Sofala 268
Soldier Ant 17
Solomon, Mr. Myers 197–198
Sorell 24, 29, 39
Sorell, Lake 25
Sorell, Lieutenant Governor 19
South America 201, 308
South Australia 88, 248, 281–283, 292
South Australian Register 283
Southern Cross 302
South Esk 41
South Esk River 28, 106
Southgate, John 215
South, John 84
South Sea Islands 99, 318
Spence, Mr. 157
Spicer, William 178
Sportsman's Arms 154
Spread Eagle 269
Spring Bay 23
Spring Creek 307
Stacey, Mr. 172
Stag's Head Inn 53
Stallard, Alfred 152
Stanistreet, Mr. John 351
Stanley, Frank (alias Wright) 216

INDEX

Stanmore, Charles 274
Stanton, Patrick (alias Jack Muck) 297
Stapleton, Constable 231
Steel, Captain 74
Steele, Henry 81
Steel, Sergeant 352
Stephen, Mr. George Milner 262
Stephens, Henry 190
Stephen, Sir Alfred 82, 255, 282, 287
Stephenson, Mr. 105
Stephenson, Sergeant James 203
Stevenson, Alexander 98
Stevenson, Mr. 168
Stewart, Captain 24
Stewart, Mr. 299
St. Francis' Roman Catholic Church 133
Stipendiary Magistrate of the Island 118
Stocker, Mr. 25
Stokell, Mr. 103
Stonehouse, Robert 167
Stone Quarry 85
Stoney Creek 171
Stony Creek 197
Storm Bay 37
St. Patrick's Head 28, 168
St. Paul River 28
Stradbroke Island 160
Strahan, Mr. 272
Strathbogie Ranges 316, 338, 343, 349
Strawberry Hills 218
Streatham, Mr. 90
Street, James 306
Stringy Bark Creek 331
Stringy Barks 271
Stroud 77
Stroud, Thomas 148
Sturges 57
Suffolk, Owen 129
Sullivan, Daniel 272
Sullivan, John Joseph 303, 308

Sullivan, Mr. 350
Summerhill Creek 124
Summer, Mr. George 250
Sumner, Rev. Mr. 59
Sunderland 97
Supreme Court House 133
Sutherland, Mr. 23, 24
Sutton, Major 77
Sutton, Mr. 235
Swallow, Mr. 98
Swan Hill 301
Swan River 172
Sydney 9, 13, 16, 38, 45, 47, 52, 56, 61, 64, 68,
    76–87, 95, 100, 122, 124, 130, 157,
    162, 173, 190, 196, 212, 218, 228, 247,
    264, 270, 301, 308, 318, 329
  Circular Head 99
  Circular Quay 301
  Dog Trap Road 61, 86
  Five Dock 84
  George Street 47, 71, 83
  Goulburn Street 276
  Illawarra Road 61
  Liverpool Road 61
  Market Street 83
  Parramatta 38, 52
  Parramatta Road 52, 55, 70
  Petersham 52
  Pitt Street 157, 276
  Vaucluse 171
Sydney Gazette 64, 76–87
Sydney Morning Herald 253
Sydney University 70
Sykes, Mr. 171

T

Tait, John 260
Tait, Robert 260
Talbot, Mr. 181
Talbragar 193
Tamar River 24, 167, 168

415

Tamworth 78, 86, 87, 275
Tamworth Examiner 273
Tapsley 25
Taradale 237
Tarago 69, 178
Tarleton, Mr. 340
Tarrandera Park 322
Tasmania
  Georgetown 38
  Richmond 102
Tasmania (see also Van Diemen's Land) 172–173
  Brighton Road 167
  Georgetown 168
Tattersdale, Thomas 53
Taverner, William 289
Taylor, Daniel 290
Taylor, Edmund 153
Taylor, John 216
Taylor, Mr. 23
Telegraph Office 342
Telford, Alexander 98
Terrible Hollow 51
Thames Police Court 98
The Australian 52
The Black War 23
The Gulph 251
The Lachlan Miner 185
Thomas, Mr. B. B. 25
Thomas, Thomas Oliver 301
Thompson, James 105
Thompson, John 38, 274
Thompson, Sir E. Deas 219
Thomson, Mr. 23
Tierney, James 38
Tiers 102, 284
Till Till Station 325
Tinney, Mr. Hugh 56
Todd, Joseph 11
Tomanbil 233
Tomandra 165

Tomley, Mr. 102
Tompson, Alfred 92
Tompson, Edwin 92–93
Toogood's Inn 71
Toohey, Peter 209
Torpy, Mr. 186
Towrang 215, 226, 234
Towrang stockade 84
Tracey, Thomas 256
Trafalgar 326
Travellers' Rest Hotel 292
Travellers' Rest Inn 108
Travers, Mathew 31
Triffet, Mrs. 25
Triffet, Tom 34
Tuckerman's Hotel 263
Tuena 214
Tumberumba 240
Turner, Mr. 79
Turner, Mr. Samuel 267
Turon 124
Twaddell, Mr. 206
Twofold Bay 216

U

Underwood, Will 52
Union Bank 192, 317
Union Bank of Australia 148
Union Hotel 307
Upper Hunter 77
Uralla 278, 280

V

Vagrant Act 151
Valparaiso 97
Van Diemen's Land 2, 15, 16, 21, 23, 37, 38, 72, 89, 95, 98–99, 102, 113, 114, 123, 128, 130, 140, 144, 156, 163, 166, 170, 172, 248, 307, 355. *See also* Tasmania
Vane, Mr. 205, 208, 237

Index

Vardy, Mrs. 203
Vardy, Thomas 203
Vasco, Sarah 106
Vaut, Charles 81
Vickerman, Dr. 305
Victoria 124, 128, 139, 144, 160, 163, 178, 187, 190, 247, 292, 307, 318, 355
   Richmond 133
Victorian Government 301, 333, 344

W

Wagga Wagga 218, 239–240, 244, 265, 322
Wagga Wagga Express 264
Wagga Wagga Races 217
Wakool Hotel 181
Waldon, William 97
Walford's Inn 273
Walgett 235–236, 274
Walker, Abraham 41
Walker, Constable 279–280, 283
Walker, Isaac 38
Walker, Mr. 293
Walker, Mr. Commissary 41
Wallabadah 267
Wallan Wallan 328
Wallenbeen 199
Wallis' Creek 77
Walmsley, Bushranger 52
Walpole, Mr. 28
Walsh, Constable 254
Walsh, J. Mr. 312
Wangaratta 245–246, 294, 299, 344, 349–351
Wangaratta Hospital 351
Wangaratta News 354
Wannamurra Station 343
Wantabadgery 320, 322
Wappinguey 284
Warburton 20
Warby, Mr. 245
Ward, Constable 271

Ward, Constable William 106
Wardell, Dr. Robert 52
Ward, Frederick (alias Captain Thunderbolt) 273–280, 281
Ward, Mr. 109
Wardy Yallock 136
Warland's Range 266
Warner, Mr. 151
Warrego 281
Warwick 310
Waters 71
Watford, Mr. 273
Watson, Mr. 162, 241
Watson, William 179
Wattamundera 209
Watt's Inn 235
Watts, Mr. 20, 24
Watts, William (alias George Williams) 98
Waverley 190
Wearne, Mr. 281
Wearne, Thomas 137
Weasel Plain 23
Weatherboard Hut 92
Webb, Constable 263
Webb, Detective 156
Webber, Bushranger 52
Webb, Mrs. Anne 200
Webb, Mr. William 191
Webb, Thomas 216
Webster, Mr. 258
Wedden Mountain District 328
Wedden Mountains 192, 233
Wedderburn 307
Weekes, John 276
Weeks, Antoine 347
Wee Waa 275
Weir, Mr. 320
Wellington (NSW) 69
Welsh, Michael 55
Wentworth, Captain 28

417

Wernicke, Augustus (Gus) 323
Westbury 24
West, Dr. 189
Western Tiers 37
Westlick, Richard 18
West Maitland 77
Westwood, William 66
Westwood, William (alias Jackey Jackey) 117–123
Whampoa 97
Whatmore, Mr. Robert 257–258
Whelan, Thomas 100
Wheogo 187, 197
White Bay 48
White, Bushranger 74
White, Captain 40
Whitehead, Charles 100
Whitehead, Convict 17
White Horse Hotel 58
White Horse Inn 235
White, Mr. 150
Whiting, Henry 120, 123
Whittaker, Mr. William 261
Whitton 68
Whorouly, John 300
Wide Bay 162
Wight, Captain 24
Wightman, Mr. 76
Wilcannia 284
Wild Paroo 281
Wild Scotchman 311–315. *See also* Macpherson, Alpin (alias John Bruce, alias Mar, alias Kerr, alias Scotia or Scotchie
Wiles, Constable 231
Wilkinson, John 84
Willandra Billabong 261
William Cook 134
Williams, Charles 98
Williams, Constable 109
Williams, Dr. 96, 98

Williams, George 20, 192
Williams, Jack 89, 91
Williams, John 142, 261, 289
Williams, Lieutenant 42
Williams, Mr. 42
Williams, Mrs. 96, 99
Williamson, Constable 322
Williamson, Mr. 278
Williams, Thomas 142
Williams, Thomas (alias Jones) 323
Williamstown 132, 140–141
Williams, William (alias Bricky) 330
Willis, Judge 92
Willison, George 191
Willis, William (alias Dunkley) 276, 288
Willmore, Mr 239
Willmore, Thomas 164
Willowtree 267
Wills, Mr. 90
Wills's Hotel 312
Wilsmore 73
Wilsmore, Constable 73
Wilsmore, Mary 74
Wilson 86
Wilson, Bushranger 88, 168
Wilson, Colonel 11
Wilson, Dr. 69
Wilson, George 152
Wilson, Harry 202, 267
Wilson, James 97, 182
Wilson, John 256
Wilson, Mr. 136
Windeyer, Mr. 77
Windsor 14, 52
Windsor Court 46
Winstanley, Constable 110
Winter, Mr. 131, 172
Winter's Flat 131
Wintle, Mr. 143

INDEX

Wintle's Hotel 143
Winton 349
Wipend 311
Wise, Mr. 323
Wodonga 294
Wollombi 76–77
Wollombi Road 76–77
Wollongong 58
Wombat 58, 184, 223, 232
Wombat Brush 57
Wombat Flat 178
Wombat Range 332
Woodbury 80
Wood, Chief Constable George 82
Woodley, William 276
Wood, Mr. 23
Woodside, Arthur 299
Woodside Inn 191
Woodward, Mr. 192
Woolf, James (alias Mordecai) 100
Woolloomooloo Bay 11
Woolnorth 99
Woolpack Inn 57
Woolpagerie Station 325
Woolshed Creek 345, 347
Woore, Major 84
Woore, Mr. Thomas 84
Worrall, John 20
Wowingragong 231
Wright, Bushranger 311
Wright, Constable James 254
Wright, John 74
Wright, Senior Constable William 254–255
Wright, Stephen 106
Wright, Tom 345, 354
Wright, Wild 345, 354
Wrixon, Mr. 133
Wyndham, Mr. 275

Y

Yalla-y-poora 292
Yanko Creek 338
Yanky Bill 91
Yanky Jack 89
Yarra Yarra 147
Yarribee 242
Yass 55, 82, 93, 200, 220, 224, 230, 281
Yass Courier 192, 217, 220, 224, 234, 253
Yea 293
Young (Burrangong) Daily Tribune 217
Young, Charles 283
Younghusband's Station 333
Young, John (alias Lowe) 142
Young, Mr. 190
Young, Sir John 252
Young, William 148

Z

Zincke, Mr. 331
Zollner, Constable 216
Zouch, Ensign 50
Zouch, Mr. 282

419

www.ingramcontent.com/pod-product-compliance
Lightning Source LLC
Chambersburg PA
CBHW031324230426
43670CB00006B/230